FROM THE CAPTAIN
TO THE COLONEL

BOOKS BY ROBERT J. SERLING

Fiction

The Left Seat
The President's Plane Is Missing
She'll Never Get off the Ground
McDermott's Sky
Wings

Nonfiction

The Probable Cause
The Electra Story
Loud and Clear
Ceiling Unlimited
Maverick
Little Giant
The Only Way to Fly
This Is Yankee 200

FROM THE CAPTAIN

TO THE COLONEL

AN INFORMAL HISTORY OF EASTERN AIRLINES BY

ROBERT J. SERLING

THE DIAL PRESS
NEW YORK

For Aaron Priest, agent and friend

Published by
The Dial Press
1 Dag Hammarskjold Plaza
New York, New York 10017

All photographs unless otherwise noted courtesy Eastern Air Lines

Manufactured in the United States of America
First printing

Design by Francesca Belanger

Library of Congress Cataloging in Publication Data

Serling, Robert J
    From the captain to the colonel.

    1. Eastern Air Lines, Inc.—History.
2. Rickenbacker, Edward Vernon, 1890–1973.
3. Borman, Frank, 1928–   I. Title.
HE9803.E2S47   387.7′06′573   79–21535
ISBN 0–8037–4610–5

CONTENTS

FROM THE CAPTAIN
TO THE COLONEL

PROLOGUE

In a sense, this is an airline's biography as well as an airline's history.

For airlines tend to acquire a kind of image that approaches human personality—usually because such carriers reflect the character of the individuals who have ruled, guided, and nurtured them. It is a case of a company taking on the identity of its leader, becoming almost a mirror image.

In no other corporate field is this phenomenon as true as it is in the airline industry—or perhaps it is more accurate to use the past tense. It is not as true as it used to be; executive responsibility today is far more diffused and distributed by the very nature of the industry's greater complexity. The "one man" airline of the past has virtually disappeared.

Yet so commanding, so overwhelming were the personalities of these pioneering giants that at least some of their influence still exists in the carriers they once headed—the mirror image, in most cases, is just a little fuzzier.

Thus, American continues to reflect the policies of Cyrus Rowlett Smith—a businessman's airline with a reputation for efficiency and consistently good service that had been C.R.'s trademark since the days of the DC-3. Delta's emphasis on a rather informal, almost homespun brand of southern hospitality has carried over from the days when C. E. Woolman was the only airline chief executive who refused to have an unlisted phone number because he *wanted* passengers to call him. W. A. "Pat" Patterson made the word "United" synonymous with "integrity," and the giant carrier, the Free World's largest, is second to none in its sense of public responsibility.

There is Continental, an airline whose aggressiveness, flair for unique marketing, and competitive drive have to be equated with the personality and policies of the maverick who still runs

it: Robert F. Six. And while Donald Nyrop was a relative
Johnny-come-lately to the airline business, he is a throwback to
the rugged individualists of the past; up to December 31, 1978,
when Nyrop retired, Northwest Orient might as well have been
called Nyrop Airlines.

Some of the influence has faded, weakened, or deteriorated
—Juan Terry Trippe's Pan American is leaner, smaller, and with
far less political clout than in the glory days when Trippe's airline literally acted as an independent branch of the U.S. State
Department, writing what amounted to its own treaties when it
needed landing rights in other countries. Nor does TWA still
have the aura of Hollywoodish glamor that it possessed in the
forties and fifties under Howard Hughes, an era when even its
captains—invariably "Greek god" types—seemed to have been
selected by Central Casting.

But in almost every case there remains a residue from the
past, when airline chiefs were part pirate, part businessman, part
showman, and part gambler. Pan Am can still stage the spectacular in true Trippe style—a record-setting Fiftieth Anniversary
global flight and the first Pole-to-Pole commercial flight. TWA
can still do things à la Hughes: such as being the first airline to
illuminate its aircraft tails with spotlights. George Baker has
been dead for seventeen years, yet the National Airlines he
founded (reputedly with money earned flying illegal booze into
the U.S. from Canada) continues to have a rather flamboyant,
unconventional air, as if Baker's ghost were still calling a few
promotional shots. National's stewardesses, for example, rank
high in pulchritude, recalling the time Baker allegedly recruited
an entire stewardess class from a chorus line stranded in Pittsburgh when their show closed.

And then there is Eastern.

It would be easy to say that Eastern's image has done a 180-
degree turn from the years when it was known as "Captain
Eddie's airline." Easy, yes—but not entirely accurate. It is run
more efficiently and ranks respectably in consumer awareness, a
happy and very drastic achievement considering its former reputation for an almost arrogant indifference toward passengers.

Morale is vastly improved among officers and employees alike, in contrast with a tradition of high-level dissension and rank-and-file bitterness. Overall, it is not the old Eastern.

Yet in so many ways, some obvious and others subtle, Eastern is a fascinating example of an airline whose past is both a proud legacy and a burden that time has failed to erase completely. More than any other airline in the world, Eastern is a Jekyll-and-Hyde company, a kind of schizophrenic corporation whose history and the chief characters who wrote that history are a collection of paradoxes, contrasts, and contradictions.

There was Rickenbacker himself—an archconservative twenty-five miles to the right of Calvin Coolidge yet a true visionary when it came to aviation. Dictatorial, arbitrary, and stubborn to the point of blindness—but also capable of unselfish and generous kindness he tried to hide. Hated by many who worked for him and against him, but sincerely and deeply loved by just as many in both categories. Bitterly competitive, yet almost totally lacking in the instincts that made for effective competition. A man who worshipped at the shrine of technology—and simultaneously was afraid to take the lead in the greatest technological gamble of all: the pivotal step into the jet age.

And because Eastern for so many years *was* Rickenbacker, it, too, became an airline of inconsistency—an air carrier with a split personality. Its passenger relations were abysmal, so bad that EAL was the only airline in the world whose passengers actually formed an organization dedicated to its criticism and harassment. Yet it also provided the greatest single marketing innovation in the history of commercial aviation: the Air-Shuttle. It made money in years when most of the industry was foundering and faltering, and lost its proverbial shirt in years when other airlines were prospering. It was one of the major pioneers in U.S. civil aviation, but it ran dead last in converting to jet equipment. Throughout the Rickenbacker regime it at least enjoyed management stability—even though this stemmed largely from one-man rule—but then went in the opposite direction with management instability playing a major role in its misfortunes; Rickenbacker ran Eastern for twenty-five years, but over the succeeding eighteen years the airline's leadership changed hands six times. Only TWA played presidential musical chairs more often.

In many respects airline histories are carbon copies of one another. They all have Horatio Alger aspects—companies started on shoestrings, governed by imperious pioneers, and eventually growing into transportation giants. Every airline story is the saga of America's air transport industry and the telling of each is the telling of all. The humble, precarious beginnings . . . the tortuous, gallant fight to make civil flying safe, reliable, and respectable . . . the wheeling and dealing and vicious in-fighting of route development and mergers and executive blood-letting . . . the tragic steps backward that were fatal accidents and the incredible steps forward that were newer, faster, and safer aircraft.

This is the Eastern story, too, but only in a generalized way. Eastern's has the elements of a Greek tragedy, but the ending is happy. It is a carrier that was once the most profitable airline in the world and then came perilously close to extinction. It is a company that went from a closeknit family to corporate autonomy which made a shambles of morale and almost destroyed priceless loyalty. It is an airline whose leaders have included a benevolent despot, a figurehead who didn't want the job, a brilliant lawyer sabotaged by interference from above, a sensitive, articulate ex-pilot who saved Eastern from bankruptcy and then helplessly watched it slide right back into a financial morass, and a former astronaut with no airline background whatsoever who turned out to be the strongest chief since Rickenbacker himself.

A chasm of years, policies, philosophies, and personalities divides Captain Edward V. Rickenbacker from Colonel Frank Borman. Borman was born the year Eastern began operations under the name of Pitcairn Aviation. He was a seven-year-old schoolboy when Rickenbacker joined the airline as its general manager. But from the Captain to the Colonel came a legacy of personal leadership that is as much a part of Eastern today as its planes, its people, and its future plans.

The airline celebrated its fiftieth anniversary in 1978. And if it was a half century of trials and tribulations, of mistakes and mishaps, it also has been five decades of courage and come-backs, of achievements and advances.

This, then, is the story of Eastern Air Lines—a technologi-cal robot breathed into life by the men and women who have been its leaders and by their followers.

CHAPTER ONE

GENESIS

Harold Pitcairn was a tall, slender, soft-spoken young man who had been born with the proverbial silver spoon in his mouth and apparently didn't like the way it tasted.

Like most men with Scotch blood coursing through their veins, he was rather taciturn and cautious. In fact, to use a phrase unknown in his time, he also was considered by some to be a bit square. But like the airline he was to found, he was more complex and contradictory than people thought, possessing qualities not quite in keeping with his conservative, pragmatic ancestral background.

For one thing, Harold Pitcairn was something of a dreamer tinged with a streak of practicality. This was a status which normally would not have bothered his staid, well-heeled family except for the fact that his dreams centered around the horrifyingly dangerous airplane. It was bad enough to the Pitcairn clan that Harold had learned how to fly. It was even worse when he eventually announced his firm intentions of making a career and a business out of aviation.

This was heresy to a family concern that had erected a

viable and sizable empire. The Pitcairn Company was a holding company built out of judicious investments in a number of enterprises ranging from oil to the Pittsburgh Plate Glass Company. Harold's interest in commercial aviation was greeted with enthusiasm roughly akin to what the family would have displayed had he expressed a desire to start a chain of brothels.

One could hardly blame his parents. When Harold won his wings in 1916, the airplane was strictly a weapon of war and not a very efficient one at that. In the United States there were only six aircraft manufacturers of any stature and even these had primitive production facilities and only one major sales prospect: the U.S. Government, whose interest in the airplane was confined to limited military employment—primarily scouting and artillery observation. The year 1916 marked the first use of American-made aircraft in combat, when General Pershing assigned planes to reconnaissance duties in his Mexican campaign against Pancho Villa. But this was mere lip service to the Wright brothers' magnificent achievement and its potential. The airplane was the Army's unwanted stepchild, a technological Cinderella clothed in the rags of parsimonious funding and inadequate research. The total annual output of those six manufacturers— Curtiss, Burgess, Aeromarine, Thomas-Morse, Dayton-Wright, and Wright-Martin—wouldn't have filled a dirigible hangar.

Civil aviation was virtually nonexistent in this country. True, the first scheduled passenger service via airplane took place in the U.S. January 1, 1914—from St. Petersburg to Tampa, Florida, in a Benoist seaplane flown by Tony Jannus. Called the St. Petersburg–Tampa Airboat Line, the company lasted only four months and air transportation was in hibernation two years later when Pitcairn soloed—in a seaplane—and found that his Scotch corpuscles contained a disturbing percentage of high-octane fuel. He definitely was hooked, and he proudly showed his parents the precious pilot's certificate issued by the Fédération Aeronautique Internationale and signed by none other than Orville Wright, secretary of the Fédération's American affiliate, the National Aeronautic Association.

His parents, it must be reported, were not impressed and

did everything to discourage him—not only from flying but from his professed desire to start an aircraft-manufacturing company. If Harold Pitcairn was in love with flying, he was truly obsessed with the far more difficult facets of aircraft design. He was never really an exceptional pilot and there are some indications he was only about average. But from boyhood he had been fascinated by the technology of flight—among the models he had built was a delta-shaped dart four decades ahead of his time.

It was at this stage of his life that he met a young aeronautical engineer named Agnew Larsen who became not just a friend but a confidant and colleague. They shared their dreams, ambitions, and design theories; Larsen, too, had become intrigued with the Delta configuration and he was impressed with Pitcairn's scribbled drawings of an aircraft that could go straight up or straight down—ideas that someday would culminate in an American-made autogiro. They decided early in their close if informal association that both needed seasoning and experience, Pitcairn in the more prosaic business side of building airplanes and Larsen with the actual construction.

So Pitcairn enrolled in the University of Pennsylvania's Wharton School of Business Administration, ranked with Harvard's in this field, while Larsen went looking for an apprentice job with an airframe manufacturer. Pitcairn finished at Wharton in time to put his plans and hopes into mothballs and his lanky frame into uniform. In April 1917, he enlisted in the U.S. Army Signal Corps' Aviation Section as a flying cadet. Larsen got a job at the Thomas-Morse Aircraft Corporation in Ithaca, New York, where he gained some invaluable training in the nuts-and-bolts aspects of building airplanes.

The war's end found them far from their self-established goals. Pitcairn did have enough money to set Larsen up in a small workshed where the latter labored away at various designs that were mostly on paper or translated into models. But Pitcairn himself finally yielded to his father's insistence that he owed considerable responsibility to the family firm. He became treasurer of the Pitcairn Company and also president of a recently acquired sugar company—jobs that kept him busy but still failed to keep his mind from wandering frequently to Bryn Athyn, Pennsylvania, where Larsen plugged away, mostly on the design of a trim biplane they had dubbed the PA-1 (for Pitcairn Aviation).

In the summer of 1925 Harold Pitcairn finally won what amounted to emancipation—his father released him from his two corporate posts and agreed, albeit reluctantly, to bankroll Pitcairn Aviation as a subsidiary. The PA-1 became the center of the universe for both Pitcairn and Larsen. They hired one of the most highly regarded airmen in the U.S., James Ray, as their chief test pilot and built an airfield at Bryn Athyn adjacent to the small factory. The trim, fast little plane bore the name Fleetwing and the fuselage was black with gold wings; it flew as a racing plane late in the fall of 1925 and was rechristened the Fleet Aero for the occasion—Ray having talked them into entering what was actually a hybrid airplane in the Labor Day air races at Mitchell Field, New York. Larsen simply took the wings off another racing plane, attached them to the PA-1's fuselage, and replaced the Fleetwing's 90-HP OX-5 engine with a 200-HP Curtiss C-6.

The Fleet Aero finished a length ahead of Casey Jones's famed Oriole Special and was clocked at 140 miles per hour as it streaked across the finish line, not only carrying Ray to a surprise victory over his old teacher but establishing the name Pitcairn as a new force in aviation. But racing laurels were not on Harold Pitcairn's achievement agenda; even before that Labor Day race he had confided to Larsen that he had other plans for the PA-1—such as building a fleet of airplanes.

"A fleet?" Larsen asked. "Why on earth would you need a whole fleet?"

"So we can start an airline," said Harold Pitcairn.

Before Larsen went back to work on the more prosaic PA-1 prototype, minus the racing wings, he accompanied Pitcairn to Europe for a tour of aircraft plants and airline facilities. Harold was to comment later that the carrier which impressed him the most was Royal Dutch Airlines, more familiarly known as KLM; he particularly noted their decision to fly Fokker transports specifically designed for commercial air service, in contrast to other airlines operating military planes converted to civilian use.

Spain was on their itinerary, solely so they could meet Juan de la Cierva, creator of the world's first autogiro (de la Cierva called it an "auto-gyro"). Pitcairn, realizing the Spaniard was far ahead of his own still-on-paper theories, raised the possibilities of building an autogiro in the U.S. under a licensing agreement and de la Cierva expressed interest—years later the Pitcairn craft would become more famous than the man who actually invented it.

The two Americans saw much in European aviation that jolted their preconceived ideas of U.S. technical and operational supremacy. In truth, Europe was light-years ahead of American civil aviation. There was nothing on U.S. drawing boards to match the big Fokkers and the all-metal Junkers. Britain had been operating cross-channel flights in large transport planes since 1923, and the French airmail service surpassed our own in terms of route mileage, points served, and aircraft numbers. Most foreign governments subsidized their airlines—the French, for example, contributed one thousand francs a month to pilot salaries. Except for the federally-operated airmail service, U.S. civil aviation in the early 1920s consisted largely of barnstorming, stunt flying, and occasional charter trips; scheduled air service was virtually nonexistent.

All this changed on February 2, 1925, when a piece of legislation called the Contract Air Mail Act became law. More commonly known as the Kelly Act, after its chief sponsor, Representative Clarence Kelly of Pennsylvania, the bill turned the job of flying the mail over to private contractors; within weeks after passage more than five thousand applicants began bidding on the routes then being operated by the Post Office Department.

Among the handful of successful bidders was Pitcairn Aviation.

Harold Pitcairn, typically cautious, was not one of the earliest aspirants. His airline dreams were relatively modest for two reasons:

First, he had his eyes on a route that was not among the

first put up for bid—New York–Philadelphia–Washington–
Atlanta.

Second, he had no intention of plunging into an airline
operation, particularly a service geared primarily to mail and not
passengers, without planes designed expressly for that purpose;
what he had learned from inspecting KLM, the only European
airline making money at the time he toured the continent, was
very fresh in his mind.

So his first priority was not an airline but an airplane: the
PA-1. Ray had crashed the prototype on its first flight, due to the
embarrassing fact that the control cables had been installed the
wrong way, but fortunately Ray was only slightly injured. It was
back to the drawing board for Larsen, who built a second PA-1
carrying the designation Mark II and on March 18, 1926, the
handsome little Fleetwing successfully completed its maiden
flight.

Larsen continued to work on improved models, the most
significant decision being to make it purely a mail plane; the
original PA-1 had been designed to carry four passengers riding in
tandem in two open cockpits ahead of the pilot. Meanwhile Pitcairn expanded into what today would be called a fixed-base
operation. At nearby Willow Grove he established Pitcairn Field
and began doing a booming business in sightseeing and charter
trips, flying lessons, and any other aeronautical chores coming
under the general category of "have airplanes—will travel."
Under Jim Ray's supervision were eight full-time pilots. And
while Pitcairn Aviation thrived, its youthful president kept planning for its eventual entrance into the even more youthful airline
industry.

He had already dipped one toe tentatively into the chilly
waters of air carrier financing by buying stock in National Air
Transport, organized by a former editor at *The Wall Street
Journal*, Clement M. Keys. NAT had won Civil Air Mail Route
3 (CAM 3) between Chicago and Dallas; under the leadership
of Keys, a rather cold but extremely astute businessman, it was
the best-financed of all the new airlines. Its starting capital-

ization of ten million dollars, infinitesimal by today's standards, was staggering in 1926.

Meanwhile the Scotsman's obvious acumen had attracted the attention of another airline entrepreneur—former World War I ace Reed Chambers, whose Florida Airways was operating CAM 10 between Miami and Atlanta via Tampa and Jacksonville. Chambers had under-capitalized and was having his troubles—succinctly put, his debts were as large as his dreams.

He realized the chief reason his airline was stumbling—he had a dead-end route, incapable of making money with Atlanta as the terminus. In the fall of 1926 he called on Pitcairn with a proposition: The latter should bid for the still-open mail route between New York and Atlanta via Philadelphia and Washington, thus linking up with Florida Airways at the Georgia capital. Their discussions lasted three days, the third spent in Washington talking to postal officials. Included in Chambers's sales pitch was casual mention of a man who had invested modestly in Florida Airways.

"Captain Eddie Rickenbacker," Chambers said with the air of a practiced name-dropper—and Pitcairn *was* impressed. To this day some Eastern old-timers believe Rickenbacker, through his rather tenuous connection with Florida Airways, actually was in on the start of what was to become his own airline. In truth, there was no bond whatsoever between Florida Airways and Pitcairn, corporate or informal; all Chambers did was to convince Harold Pitcairn the time was ripe for him to get into the airmail business. By the time Pitcairn Aviation began operating an airmail route, Florida Airways had gone under and the Atlanta–Miami route was dormant.

The Post Office Department officially invited competitive bids for the New York–Atlanta route in 1926, but for reasons never explained there were no immediate takers. What prospects there were apparently retreated before the rising tide of red ink inundating the fledgling industry—Florida Airways wasn't the only carrier staggering and Keys's tightly run, well-managed NAT was one of the few making money. Not until September

1927 did Pitcairn bid for CAM 19, offering to carry the mail from New York to Atlanta via Philadelphia, Washington, Richmond, Greensboro (North Carolina), and Spartanburg (South Carolina).

Pitcairn's bid was $3.00 a pound, roughly the going rate for most carriers, although considerably over the $1.25 Keys had bid to get the New York–Chicago route (CAM 17) for NAT in that same year, adding this to his fast-growing conglomeration. Pitcairn's rate was sufficient for him to discard temporarily any ideas of running a combined mail-passenger service; he already had told Larsen to concentrate on improving the PA-1 into an efficient mail-plane.

Larsen did just that. Before the government awarded Pitcairn Aviation a contract on February 28, 1928, the shy, introverted designer (shyness was an attribute he shared with Pitcairn himself) had come up with the PA-5 Mailwing, a fast, sweet-flying little ship carrying only the pilot but with a six-hundred-pound mail capacity. Larsen powered it with a Wright J-4 Whirlwind that churned out two hundred horsepower at full throttle and the PA-5's aerodynamic qualities were that of a spirited but well-behaved steed—easy to handle, amazingly steady, and reassuringly strong. It was test-flown by a number of military pilots including an Army lieutenant named Jimmy Doolittle, who stunted the Mailwing the first time he flew it thereby giving Jim Ray a near-coronary. Another was Lieutenant Harold Elliott from the Naval Aircraft Factory, who was impressed by the whole Pitcairn setup as well as the PA-5 itself—he was to join the new airline when it got started.

Larsen's final contribution to the PA-5's success was a new landing gear, with a welded steel split-axle and struts cushioned by shock absorbers; landing-gear deficiencies were responsible for the failure of the Mailwing's predecessor, the PA-4, to go into production, and actually caused a serious rift between Larsen and Ray.

The chief pilot, from all accounts, had long felt that Larsen was a bad influence on Pitcairn—getting him involved, according to Ray's way of thinking, in too many visionary, far-out projects. Ray was totally committed to getting the airline under-way and he blamed Larsen for the delay, telling Pitcairn himself that they'd be flying the mail by now if it were not for Larsen's botching up the PA-4's gear. The result was an unhappy session between Pitcairn and his longtime colleague, with Larsen quietly announcing he was taking a month off to rest.

Larsen returned to Ithaca, where, at the old Thomas-Morse factory, he had once learned his trade, and loafed for two weeks before an associate at Pitcairn phoned him with the news that nobody had solved the gear problem yet.

"They want you back, Agnew," he was told.

Larsen's loyalty to Harold Pitcairn was stronger than his resentment toward Ray. He came back to Bryn Athyn and re-sumed work as if nothing had happened; in less than a month he came up with the new gear design that wound up on the PA-5 and an elated Pitcairn gave the go-ahead to build at least six Mailwings for the new airmail fleet. The Post Office Department awarded the CAM 19 contract February 28, 1928, and set a target date of May 1 for inauguration of service. It was met, but only after efforts that could have been included among the labors of Hercules—not the least of which involved the government's edict that the CAM 19 would have to be flown entirely at night.

This had come as dire news to Operations Manager Jim Ray, but fortunately it was not of the last-minute variety. With traditional foresight, not to mention optimism, Pitcairn had in-sisted on creating his airline long before the Post Office Depart-ment got around to making it official. Postal officials, of course, had approved the proposed route before any bid was filed and this alone required considerable advance planning. And they warned about the night operations right from the start, explain-ing that any New York–Atlanta mail service must be based on two factors: mail from the south had to connect with westbound transcontinental flights leaving New York early in the morning, and mail to the south had to reach Atlanta before seven A.M. for delivery that day.

The government would supply the necessary "lighted air-ways," which consisted of flashing beacons along the assigned flight paths and lighted emergency fields, also provided courtesy of Uncle Sam. But at the time Pitcairn and his associates began to flesh out what was merely a skeleton of an airline, some of the cities they intended to serve didn't even have airports. Three men took on the main organizational tasks—Pitcairn, Ray, and Geoffrey Childs, a close friend of Harold who had become vice president of Pitcairn Aviation. Like Pitcairn, he was quiet, religious, and astute in business matters, if inexperienced in aviation. Using promotional material prepared by Childs, the trio visited the cities that would become stations on the new airline's system, selling them on the immediate concept of airmail service and the longer-range prospects of commercial aviation. The *pièce de résistance* was Pitcairn's promise to build a six-thousand-dollar hangar at each field, offer various flying services at every airport in addition to regular mail service, and even join the local chamber of commerce.

One by one they fell into line. Richmond city officials approved an airport site selected by Ray, agreed to build a small terminal with offices and a pilots' lounge, and the mayor himself—J. Fullmer Bright—supervised the laying out of a pair of 2,000-foot runways. The city also accepted Pitcairn's offer to manage the airport, to be called Byrd Field after Virginia's most famous pilot, Commander Richard E. Byrd.

Ray expected trouble at Greensboro, North Carolina, where the route he laid out ran right through the middle of an area also embracing the cities of Winston-Salem and High Point. The three towns got together and decided to locate the airport on a site almost an equal distance from the three communities—and it still serves them to this day. Such intercity cooperation was not the case at Spartanburg, South Carolina, however; Charlotte and Greenville also clamored of airmail facilities and it took a congressman from Spartanburg to convince Pitcairn his hometown deserved the airport—his name was James Byrnes; he would one day become a senator and later Secretary of State under Harry Truman.

Pitcairn's ally in Atlanta was the colorful William Hartsfield, who stood second to no man in his support of and faith in aviation. Hartsfield, then an assistant city attorney, considered Florida Airways' demise a calamity ranked slightly below Sherman's siege; he talked a recalcitrant city council into appropriating $5,000 to improve decaying, dilapidated Candler Field, predicting during the course of his sales pitch that "someday Atlanta will rank right along with Chicago as an aviation hub." It was a forecast that was to become startlingly true and was typical of the man who as Atlanta's mayor did so much for aviation that the city's present airport is named for him.

The Post Office Department used Hadley Field, located at New Brunswick, New Jersey, as the terminus for transcontinental airmail in and out of New York—it should be pointed out that until the fall of 1927 the government continued to fly the mail from New York to San Francisco via Chicago; the private contractors merely fed their operations into the transcontinental route. Pitcairn thought Hadley an abomination and he had an even worse opinion of what passed as Philadelphia's municipal airport, but he agreed to use both because there were no alternatives. He did consider using his own superb facilities at Willow Grove, but postal officials reminded him that the Philadelphia field was an hour closer to the main post office.

He did balk when the government suggested that Pitcairn's mail planes utilize Washington's Hoover Field, located in Virginia on a site now occupied by the Pentagon. Ray had told him Hoover's short runways were unsafe even for the PA-5. The little Mailwing could land on the proverbial postage stamp but the field was surrounded by booby traps—power lines that made every night landing a lethal obstacle course.

"I agree Hoover is out," Pitcairn said, "but what else could we use?"

"Bolling Field just across the Potomac from Hoover," Ray suggested. "It's like a Louisiana swamp when it rains but otherwise it's a lot safer than Hoover."

So Bolling it was—an unsatisfactory but necessary compromise choice that completed Ray's route blueprints. The exact air mileage between New York and Atlanta, following the virtual straight line Ray had drawn on a map, was 792; the choice of cities to be served was largely dictated by the Mailwing's range—roughly averaging about one hundred miles between each stop. Some segments, such as New York–Philadelphia, were relatively short (only eighty-three miles). The longest leg ran between Richmond and the Greensboro/Winston-Salem/High Point joint facility—177 miles.

The chief pilot did the aerial route survey himself, in a Pitcairn Orowing (one of the PA-5's predecessor models). Ray flew a number of courses and finally picked one that had the fewest mountains, although from Richmond on south there was no way to avoid some hilly terrain. His next step was to mount an aerial camera on the Orowing and take strip photographs of the entire route—more than a thousand pictures pasted together in a mosaic which he could show his pilots. Not for several years did he confess a monumental goof—flying between Hadley Field and Bolling, he had forgotten to take the lens cover off the camera and had to fly the trip a second time.

The survey flights also included selection of the emergency landing fields. Ray scouted nearly two hundred possible locations and turned over to the government a list of about eighty recommended sites; almost fifty were finally chosen for clearing and lighting installation. All this was accomplished before Pitcairn actually won the right to operate CAM 19, largely because the thirty-year-old Scotsman had hoped to get his airline underway by the summer of 1927. He delayed filing the bid until September after Larsen's troubles with the PA-4 made it apparent they would not have an airplane meeting either Pitcairn's or Ray's specifications for reliable airmail service in time for the original target date.

Pitcairn was to admit later that it was not entirely Larsen's fault. It was Pitcairn himself who decided that the OX-5 engine which had powered the PA-1 would suffice for the PA-4. The result was an undersized, underpowered aircraft; yet despite these two deficiencies, it was regarded as a "hot" airplane—even with the OX-5, it was so light that it was almost completely unforgiving and required constant attention to keep its prima donna tendencies from killing somebody. The PA-5, by contrast, was docile and incredibly stable, its powerful Wright engine notwithstanding. No finer airplane could have been built for flying the mail at night, when a man and a machine had to become one entity, each reliant upon the other.

Like all their brethren of the twenties, Pitcairn's first airmail pilots were Characters—the capitalization is deliberate. The first eight Jim Ray hired were veterans for their day, but the two most experienced had logged not much more than 2500 hours of flying each—by modern airline standards, they'd be rated as greenhorns. Yet it is only fair to remember that in 1927, any airman with 2500 hours had to be not only good but lucky; the majority of those hours had been spent in primitive, unreliable aircraft operating in and out of inadequate fields and flying under conditions that made accidents probable if not inevitable. There were no such safety devices as two-way radios, antiicing systems, electronic navigation aids, nor even—with rare exceptions— paved runways. These facts of life, combined with the crystal-ball aspects of 1927 weather forecasting, gave them a life expectancy somewhat below that of lion tamers, steeplejacks, and racing drivers. They not only weren't required to know instrument flying (which didn't become a Federal regulation until 1932), most of them didn't even trust instruments. They were seat-of-the-pants pilots; the pressure on buttocks, the feeling in the stomach and bowels, the visual reference of horizons that could be as elusive as a mirage, and clouds that were beautiful enemies—all these were considered more reliable than crazily-dancing dials and vibrating needles pointing to unreadable numbers.

It was quite a collection Jim Ray enlisted for his Pitcairn "squadron": Verne Treat of California, the only nonsoutherner of the first group hired; John Kytle and Gene Brown from Atlanta; Amberse Banks of Texas; Don Johnston of North Carolina; Syd Molloy from Mississippi. Treat, at thirty, was the oldest and Kytle at twenty-four the youngest. In personalities, backgrounds, and appearances, they were as individualistic as seven men from seven different planets, sharing only two things in common: love of flying and courage, both requisites for their dangerous profession.

There was Johnny Kytle, whose forte was acrobatics. Army-trained, like so many pilots of his time, he was good—perhaps too good, for his confidence in his ability to fly the flimsy airplanes of that era eventually was to lead to his death.

Syd Molloy was another who loved acrobatics, but once he joined Pitcairn he turned conservative and never rolled or looped a plane again. He looked more like a young banker than an airmail pilot and ex-barnstormer; his clothes were impeccably tailored and, unlike the others, he wore his flying jacket or coveralls only when on duty—his colleagues appeared willing to sleep in them. Molloy's first name was Rutherford, which he disliked even more than Verne Treat did his middle name—Egbert. But Rutherford seemed to fit his personality; he had an air of dignity rather than dash, and even the Pullman-sized black-and-tan Chrysler roadster he drove seemed to be an extension of the man himself. (Curiously, big, flashy cars were an airmail pilot's trademark; a psychiatrist could have had a field day figuring out why.) Molloy's soft-spoken, almost diffident manner masked a sense of humor and an addiction to practical jokes—the latter a common denominator among the early pilots and typical of many of their later compatriots.

Verne Treat was either Pitcairn's luckiest pilot or the unluckiest, depending on one's point of view. He was not only the oldest but the smallest, and was hired largely because he had been an old flying buddy of Jim Ray's in their barnstorming days—he grounded himself after cracking up a plane and was working in a New Jersey garage when Ray found him and offered him a pilot's job. The diminutive Treat had more forced landings than the rest of the Pitcairn crew combined; he survived one monumental night when he cracked up one plane and then had to parachute out of another after he ran out of gas trying to find a fog-shrouded airport.

At the other end of the Lady Luck spectrum was big, handsome Amberse Banks, who resembled Jack Dempsey, seemed to court risk deliberately, and always got away with it. Banks also was Army trained, but the Army never taught him his instinct for sheer survival—to Banks, life was going against the odds. He defied the worst weather, ran every engine at full throttle as if daring it to falter, and rode planes down to blind landings when most pilots would have bailed out.

The most serious-minded of the original pilots was Gene Brown. He was neither prudish nor pompous, but to him flying was a profession and he regarded it through the eyes of a professional. When he was still in his early teens, he unloaded a Curtiss Jenny out of a packing crate and assembled it. A native of Atlanta, he worked around Candler Field doing odd jobs without pay and occasionally would be given rides by sympathetic pilots; they'd let him put his hands and feet on the controls, absorbing the techniques of flight as they maneuvered. It may seem unbelievable, but the first time Brown flew a plane himself, he took off and landed solo. At age sixteen he was part owner of two Jennies and he was as good a mechanic as he was a pilot. Brown, too, was Army taught and a former barnstormer.

So was Don Johnston, a pale-faced youngster with hair so blond it was almost white and gave him the appearance of an albino. When he first started flying the mail, he and Kytle were Pitcairn's "wild men" but Johnston decided to reform and turned conservative—a decision prompted largely by two near disasters, one of which involved almost hitting the Capitol Dome on a flight into Washington. Johnston used to boast that he would never die in an airplane, but his luck ran out during World War II; he was taking off from Miami in a military transport plane when an Army bomber, landing without clearance and no lights, collided with him head-on.

The seventh and eighth pilots were taken on as reserve or relief men. The first was Ed Morrisey, a likable, slightly older man who had learned how to fly in the Army and then did the usual barnstorming stints. The second, hired after Pitcairn began flying the mail, was to become an Eastern legend.

If Eddie Rickenbacker symbolized the airline in general, Henry Tyndell Merrill was "Mr. Eastern" in the air. His father was a railroader and Merrill became a railroad fireman before he became a pilot. If he had been a bit bigger and stronger, he might have made it as a baseball big-leaguer—Merrill actually played minor league ball as an ambidextrous pitcher while hurling for a Canadian team. He pitched southpaw in a morning game and won it, then threw righthanded in an afternoon game and won that one, too. He earned the nickname "Dick" after the brother of Frank Merriwell, the athletic Superman of early juvenile fiction. Dick Merriwell was known for throwing a baseball that rose a foot just as it approached the plate, but this "jump ball" was a prosaic feat compared with "brother" Frank's "double-shoot"—a pitch that curved twice in different directions. Not even Merrill could ever explain why he wasn't nicknamed Frank instead of Dick but whatever the reason, it stuck.

In later years Merrill loved to tell the story of how Pitcairn hired him. He had been barnstorming before Jimmy Wedell offered him sixty-five dollars a week to fly his new airmail route between New Orleans and Atlanta (one on which Pitcairn had bid unsuccessfully). Jim Ray was at Candler field one day in the spring of 1928 when the weather was of the "even-the-birds-are-walking" variety. Ray had just finished commenting to a companion that "a goddamned eagle couldn't find Candler in this slop" when a Wedell mail plane suddenly materialized out of the rain and fog like solidifying ectoplasm and made a perfect landing.

Ray made a point of introducing himself to the pilot. "That was one hell of a job of flying," he added admiringly.

Merrill shrugged. "Thanks," he said with false modesty, giving the distinct impression he considered such zero-zero approaches completely routine and rather dull.

"We could use guys like you at Pitcairn," Ray suggested.

"Wadda you pay?" the practical-minded Merrill inquired.

"Well, the base pay plus ten cents a mile for night flying could add up to almost three hundred bucks a week."

"Hell, that's a lot more than I'm making now. You got a deal."

Thus did Dick Merrill, an ebullient, absolutely fearless and enormously skilled pilot, come into the Eastern story. In a sense, however, he entered under false pretenses; not for a long time was he to confess to Ray that his impressive landing at Candler was 99.9 percent pure luck. He was hopelessly lost, and located the field only after he broke out of the overcast and found himself heading for a tall office building in downtown Atlanta. Fortunately he recognized a street he knew led to Candler and he followed this to the airport.

With five pilots and two reliefs lined up, Pitcairn was still not ready to roll on CAM 19. Even then, as it is today, the airborne operations of an airline were only the visible tip of the iceberg—what happens in the air is merely the culmination of what far more people have done on the ground to make each flight possible. Of Pitcairn's forty-one employees assigned to the airline, only seven were pilots, and the other thirty-four played vital if not as glamorous roles.

To Sterling Smith of Bryn Athyn went the honor of becoming Pitcairn's first employee; Harold Pitcairn had hired him as a mechanic in 1923 to assist Agnew Larsen in Pitcairn Aviation's infant stage. When the airmail route opened, Smith was sent to Spartanburg as assistant station manager and he was to stay with the airline until 1936; he was a sprightly seventy-four when Eastern celebrated its fiftieth anniversary in 1978, and living in his old hometown of Bryn Athyn.

While Smith was Pitcairn's first paid employee, technically speaking he had competition for the title. A feisty, cigar-smoking little man named Johnny Ray actually was the first one assigned to the airmail operation—before Smith got into the act via his Spartanburg assignment. Ray hailed from Buffalo, New York, and got his first aviation job there with the Curtiss Airplane and Motor Company. Curtiss trained him as a mechanic specializing in engines, and he had few peers in that area. His reputation was such that Harold Pitcairn heard about him and seduced him away from Curtiss.

Ray began working for Pitcairn June 21, 1925, at the Willow Grove field. As the time neared for Pitcairn to submit his mail bid, he called in Ray to brief him on his airline plans. "We'll be using Richmond as our principal maintenance base," he informed his top mechanic. "It's just about at the halfway mark for the system so you better go down there and set things up."

His first shop was a room the size of a small kitchen, located in one corner of a dirt floor hangar. He could be found there almost any hour of the day or night, working with tools that included some he had to make himself. He did his first engine overhaul personally, partially because he didn't trust anyone else to do the job properly and also because his handful of assistants could have recorded their collective knowledge of aircraft engines on a postcard. He literally was hiring mechanics off the street.

One day he spotted a young man wandering around the runway area. Ray, as usual shorthanded, stopped him.

"You lookin' for somebody?"

"Not somebody. Something. A job."

"What do you do?" Ray asked.

"I'm a sewing-machine mechanic."

"Well," Johnny growled, "if you can fix a sewing machine you must know how to use tools. You just got hired."

Ray recalls that the boy stayed with him eighteen years and finally quit only because he refused to join a union. It was strictly on-the-job training under Professor Ray, whose *modus operandi* was one-third improvision, one-third ingenuity, and one-third pure guesswork. But the little man was good; to Johnny Ray, airplane engines were living creatures to be cursed or coddled, disciplined or babied. If pilots were possessive about their airplanes (and the early Pitcairners each had his own assigned PA-5), Ray was equally so about his beloved engines. He once warned a pilot, "Take it easy with that engine—I just overhauled it."

The pilot took off for a brief test hop and roared at full throttle across the field just over Ray's head. In total but understandable frustration, Johnny fired his only available antiaircraft weapon—a big hammer which he threw in the general direction of the zooming plane. It missed the target by about a hundred feet and what made it worse was that Ray was never able to find that hammer again.

It was another early employee who gave Johnny Ray his most unusual chore in the nearly three decades he was to spend with Pitcairn/Eastern. That was the ex-Navy lieutenant Harold Elliott, who became assistant operations manager under Jim Ray after his discharge. Elliot had won his naval wings despite the handicap of a wooden leg. Johnny saw him limping around the Richmond field one day and asked if the artificial leg was bothering him.

"Yeah, Johnny," Elliott admitted. "The damned thing's killing me. I guess I need a new one fitted or something."

"Lemme see it," Ray said. He inspected the limb briefly. "If you can leave it with me, I'll see what I can do."

The upshot was the first overhaul of a wooden leg by a master of the overhauling of airplane engines—with special tools he handcrafted for the task. But that was Johnny Ray, who took special pride in the fact that no Pitcairn pilot ever lost his life in a crash blamed on engine failure. The pilots respected his single-minded devotion and some of them were a little bit afraid of the peppery little guy who didn't mind raising hell with anyone who mistreated one of his precious Whirlwinds—that included the redoubtable Mr. Banks, the worst offender of them all.

A common thread of motivation was woven through the minds and hearts of those Pitcairn pioneers: love of aviation and faith in its future. Typical was the story of Howard Weant, a Salisbury, North Carolina, youngster who had the flying bug planted in his bloodstream by watching itinerant barnstormers come into his small town and offer rides for five dollars a head. Weant borrowed the money for his first flight and was hopelessly hooked.

He was about to sign up for flying lessons at the Sweeney School of Aviation in Kansas City when he spotted a newspaper feature story about Pitcairn starting up a facility at the Tri-Cities Airport—the communal field serving Greensboro, Winston-Salem, and High Point. Weant wrote the new Pitcairn manager at Tri-Cities, Henry Rafus (a veteran associate of Harold Pit-

cairn), inquiring about the cost of flying instruction. Rafus replied it would run $30 an hour or $275 for a 10-hour course—the
money to be paid in advance. Weant had to borrow half the
amount from a friend and took the rest from his depleted savings.

He was working as a street cleaner in Salisbury at the time,
so he could take flying lessons only on weekends—doing the
town's business section early Saturday morning, then taking a
bus to Greensboro for his lessons. He talked Rafus into letting
him work at the field Saturday afternoon and all day Sunday,
selling tickets for sightseeing rides and fueling the Pitcairn
Orowings stationed there. This helped him pay back his loan and
take care of his Saturday-night hotel room at Greensboro, which
cost him the then considerable sum of $1.50 a night.

When Rafus was hospitalized from injuries received in an
Orowing crack-up, none other than Syd Molloy ran the airport
in his place. Weant was startled to discover that Molloy was the
barnstorming pilot who had given him his first ride, and Molloy
eventually qualified him for his first solo. Weant still wasn't experienced enough to rate a pilot's job, but Molloy liked him and
finagled a job for him as a Pitcairn mechanic under Johnny Ray
at Richmond. Weant remembered years later that Ray's shop was
clean enough to cook in.

"Johnny always wore a white shirt working on those engines and it stayed clean," he recalled.

Weant was to stay with the airlines forty-four years, mostly
as a dispatcher and occasionally as a reserve copilot in the days
when flight crew requirements weren't as stringent as they were
to become. His background and experience were rather typical
of the average Pitcairn employee—and his starting mechanic's
salary of $86 a month, for an eleven-hour day six days a week,
explained why Pitcairn's monthly payroll when the airline was
launched totaled less than $10,000; fifty years later it would
amount to $63.3 million a month.

CAM 19 went into operation May 1, 1928, with a starting
fleet of six airplanes—four to fly the line, one earmarked for Jim
Ray, and the sixth assigned to reserve just in case the Lord failed
Johnny Ray. Theoretically there were only seven pilots, but it

was surprising how many management personnel could be called on for cockpit duty if the need arose. Virtually every man in this emergency pool was assigned a station-manager's job—Rafus, for example, was a good pilot—and executives like Jim Ray and Harold Elliott could and did fly the mail on occasions.

May 1 was a Tuesday—cloudy over most of a nearly 800-mile route punctuated by sixty-two beacons and nineteen lighted emergency fields with additional strips being readied; before long there would be a beacon every ten miles and emergency fields every thirty miles. On inaugural day an estimated 100,000 persons crowded the six airports to be served (Spartanburg wouldn't open until September) and the volume of mail was so high that Jim Ray decided to operate a double schedule. Molloy flew one trip north out of Greensboro, while Kytle and Brown took a pair of Mailwings out of Atlanta; Treat and Banks piloted the southbound flights out of New York. Ironically, the latter picked up mail flown in two planes from New Orleans on Wedell's St. Tammany Gulf Airlines, one of them carrying Dick Merrill as the copilot—the ubiquitous Mr. Merrill thus played a role in the birth of his airline even before he went to work for it.

Pitcairn could only flash his shy smile when he heard about the mail load—Molloy alone took more than 23,000 letters out of Greensboro. Pitcairn was not smiling at the end of the day, however; Treat (who else?) cracked up landing at Philadelphia when one wheel hit a chuck hole the size of a moon crater—it was filled with rainwater and Treat never saw it. The Mailwing's prop bit into the soggy ground and the plane somersaulted, bursting into flames. Treat, shaken but unhurt, crawled out of the wreckage and a postal employee rescued the mail before the flames spread to the mail compartment.

With Treat *hors de combat*, Andy Banks won the honor of flying the first mail load into the nation's capital. Dressed more for dinner than an historic mail flight, Banks wore a business suit, white shirt, and tie in the cockpit; his helmet, goggles, parachute, .45 caliber automatic, and cartridge belt supplied jarring incongruity but not many people noticed in all the excitement of unloading the mail pouches and putting the Washington southbound mail aboard. A wiry, pixie-faced reporter covering the event described it in these words:

The Stage Coach of the 20th Century went through Washington last night on its initial flight. It ran before a crowd of 7,000 at Bolling Field, when a racy black and yellow mail plane came out of the night from the north, paused for a few minutes, then flew off into the southern sky again.

The reporter was from the Washington *Daily News*. His name was Ernie Pyle and a few weeks later he was to visit Richmond, staying almost a week interviewing Molloy, Treat, Brown, and Kytle and later doing a feature story on each. Ernie had what amounted to hero worship of pilots, numbering them among his closest friends and achieving a rapport that was unusual for a man who couldn't fly himself.

There was a lot of improvising that first night, Treat's mishap leaving them shorthanded. Molloy, Banks, Brown, and Kytle flew double duty, as Jim Ray frantically juggled schedules to keep the mail moving. They were turning the Mailwings around as soon as they landed, switching pouches, and changing directions, for the rest of the night—Ernie Pyle was to write later that Banks, Brown, and Kytle in particular flew longer on the first day of CAM 19 than most pilots did in a week. But they did the job, delivering more than fifty thousand pieces of mail in time for next-day distribution or early morning connections with transcontinental mail planes.

Neither Pitcairn nor Ray took any time off to congratulate themselves. Both already were immersed in plans to expand, for even before Pitcairn started operating CAM 19, it was evident that the airline had a chance to double in size virtually overnight. Seven months before Pitcairn launched the New York–Atlanta route, the Post Office Department had put the dormant CAM 10, Atlanta–Miami, up for bids. Pitcairn, whose original bid for CAM 19 has been described by one aviation historian as "half-hearted" (it is said that he actually was surprised when he won), definitely didn't feel that way about CAM 10. He wanted it badly, and his opposition was to find out how badly.

Said opposition was none other than Reed Chambers, who with a former partner in Florida Airways, had formed a new venture called Southeastern Airlines, which was battling to win the coveted Key West–Havana airmail route. The other aspirants were Juan Trippe and John K. Montgomery's Pan American; the latter won the contract but Trippe, in one of his patented end-runs, had wangled exclusive landing rights in Cuba from Cuban dictator Gerardo Machado—and without those landing rights, Montgomery's contract wasn't worth a Havana cigar.

Trippe then talked the other two companies into forming a coalition to be named Pan American Airways—not a difficult task inasmuch as he held the trump card. But even as the new Pan Am was getting off the ground, Chambers convinced Trippe that he should bid for CAM 10 to give him a route feeding into the foreign airmail operation. It was brilliant foresight on Chambers's part (Rickenbacker, disillusioned, had gone on to other fields when Florida Airways went under)—as it turned out, CAM 10 would be Pan Am's best shot at a domestic route for the next four decades, but Trippe got overconfident.

With Chambers urging him to bid low, all Trippe would do was cut five cents off the standard three-dollar-per-pound rate applied to the majority of airmail contracts. Pitcairn, wisely suspecting that his airline wouldn't be going very far with just CAM 19, submitted a bid of $1.46. The Post Office Department grabbed it with alacrity and the day after Pitcairn's pilots completed their first night of flying, Jim Ray was on his way south in a Mailwing, surveying the old Florida Airways route.

For two weeks Pitcairn operated routinely—until a spell of unpredictably horrendous spring weather suddenly turned routine into tragedy. It was the night of May 16 and pilot after pilot was reporting everything from fog to angry thunderstorms all along the East Coast. Johnny Kytle landed at Richmond and was informed that Treat had been forced down by a violent storm near Baltimore. Trying to squeeze his Mailwing into an emergency landing strip, he broke a propeller.

"Well," Kytle allowed cheerfully, "somebody's gotta go up there and get Verne's mail. I'll go but I don't particularly want to—I've seen enough thunderstorms for one day."

The station manager told him other arrangements already had been made: Ed Morrisey, the relief pilot stationed at Richmond, would ferry an empty Mailwing north.

"Ed, you're lucky," Kytle laughed. "I think I've used up all the bad weather."

Morrisey just smiled; this would be his first airmail run and it also happened to be his thirty-third birthday. He took off at 1:23 A.M. and disappeared into a thick patch of fog. A few minutes later Kytle and the others heard his engine—he apparently was coming back to Byrd Field, but Kytle was frowning. His airman's instinct told him something was wrong—there was a saying among pilots that "even an engine can sound lost."

The roar increased as if Morrisey were diving, then changed pitch. Kytle had just blurted, "Jesus—he's in trouble!" when they heard an explosion and then saw a bright orange ball of fire reflected eerily through the opaque fog. When they dug Ed Morrisey's body from the wreckage, they found his watch had stopped at 1:44—his first mail flight had lasted only twenty-one minutes. Disorientation of the pilot resulting in loss of control, the investigators said. For years Howard Weant couldn't forget the sight of Morrisey's parachute in a corner of the hangar, stained with blood.

Eleven days later disaster struck again. This time it was Jim Reid, the field manager at Philadelphia, who had been sent to Richmond as Morrisey's replacement. Reid, too, "bought the farm" on a ferry flight delivering a Mailwing to Banks, who was grounded in Washington with mechanical trouble. He took off at one A.M. on a flight that should have taken not more than an hour; they found his body and what remained of his plane in a Virginia farm field the next day. Reid apparently kept descending to keep under the lowering cloud cover, encountered fog, and flew the ship into a small hill.

Pitcairn, even at his youthful age a kind of patriarch who regarded every employee—and his pilots especially—as members of a close-knit family, was stunned. So was Jim Ray, to the extent that he wondered out loud if the treacherous CAM 19 wasn't too much for the then state of the art. It was one-legged Harold Elliott who put starch into their backbones, pointing out with almost brutal frankness that two men had died because they were unprepared—one lost control and the other lost his bearings.

"We have to face up to it," Elliott said firmly. "Our guys have to learn instrument flying and they'd better learn it damned fast."

Pitcairn wasted no time. He ordered Agnew Larsen to install a second seat with duplicate flight controls into a Mailwing, and he called an old friend—Paul Henderson, operations chief of National Air Transport and one of the best flight supervisors in the infant industry.

"I need to borrow one of your pilots," Pitcairn said. "A man who knows night flying and instrument flying. Someone who can teach our pilots to stay out of trouble."

Henderson answered without hesitation. "I'll send you Earl Ward. He's a veteran on CAM 17 [New York–Chicago], which we operate entirely at night. How long will you keep him?"

"I don't know. Couple of weeks, at least. Maybe longer. We need him, Paul."

"Yeah, I know. Keep him as long as you want."

Brotherhood of the air. It was no empty slogan.

Ward worked with Pitcairn's pilots for just two weeks before returning to his duties at NAT, satisfied that the boys had absorbed his sermons. Admittedly, for most of these rugged individualists raised on seat-of-the-pants flying, the Gospel according to St. Earl was close to heresy. But the Morrisey and Reid accidents had sobered them considerably, even the carefree Kytle and irrepressible Merrill. There was some grousing that orders to check out on instrument training in the two-seater Mailwing was like sending Einstein back to first grade, but on the whole they accepted the new discipline as professionals.

Pitcairn didn't start flying CAM 10 until December 1, 1928, giving Ray plenty of time to line up fresh airborne troops.

He needed reinforcements, for the Atlanta–Miami award had doubled Pitcairn's system to more than 1400 miles; only Boeing's Chicago–Seattle route surpassed it in length. The Mailwing fleet was expanded to sixteen airplanes, including the new PA-6 Super Mailwing, which was faster and slightly larger than its predecessor—Ray flew one nonstop from Miami to Atlanta in five hours and thirty-five minutes, almost twenty hours faster than the average train.

The airline had ninety-one employees, including thirteen pilots, as Pitcairn prepared to take over the new 619-mile leg that added Jacksonville, Tampa, and Miami to the system. The combined New York–Miami route was rechristened CAM 25.

Paraphrasing Murphy's Law, if anything can go wrong on an inaugural day, it will. And it did. Furman Stone took off from Candler Field in Atlanta at 6:55 A.M. (the Post Office was allowing Pitcairn to operate day flights over CAM 25's southern leg temporarily) and encountered such violent storms that he was forced down on an emergency field at Cochran, Georgia. A farmer gave him a ride into the local Post Office where a marshal arrested him for carrying a gun. A hasty phone call to Jacksonville, where a crowd of more than a thousand was waiting, got him released and he took off again an hour later—this time making it safely to Jacksonville. Don Johnston took over Stone's load but ran into brutal headwinds and came down at Vero Beach, where he had to spend several hours finding gas. When he finally reached Miami, it was dark and there were no runway lights. Johnston finally landed safely after a Pitcairn employee, A. K. Handey, borrowed emergency flares from a nearby railroad yard —he ran down the runway, sticking one in the ground every few feet and lighting it. Johnston's final guidance came from the airport beacon, which someone stopped revolving long enough to focus its beam on the runway edge.

Fred "Fritz" Schwaemmle had taken the first northbound load from Miami to Jacksonville without incident and that was the way the operation was to run for several months. By the end of 1928 Ray's "squadron" had completed 93.1 percent of its scheduled flights. In March, Daytona Beach, Orlando, Tampa, and Macon, Georgia, were added to the system. Unbelievably, although Pitcairn had yet to carry a single paying passenger (quite a few employees, however, were always hooking rides in the mail compartments if there was room), the airline was making money.

Ever the one to foster good morale, Pitcairn had given his approval for publication of a small company newspaper, the *NewsWing*, which first appeared in September 1927, seven months before airmail service began. Once CAM 19 was underway, *NewsWing* was the epitome of optimism as to Pitcairn's future and became absolutely ecstatic when CAM 25 was opened. Certainly the nearly one hundred employees had no reason to see anything but rainbows over the horizon; by mid-1928 Pitcairn was flying almost a third of the nation's total airmail mileage.

But there was a cloud ahead that no one could see, for it was in the mind of Harold Pitcairn.

Without confiding in even his closest friends and associates, he had decided to sell the airline.

To none other than Clement Keys.

CHAPTER TWO

END OF
THE BEGINNING

Why Harold Pitcairn sold his fast-growing, profitable airline just when it looked so promising will always be something of a mystery.

The evidence suggests multiple reasons. None is conclusive by itself but together they form a pattern that points to disenchantment with the airline business. Pitcairn's heart was really in the manufacturing end of aviation; his happiest hours were spent with Agnew Larsen discussing new ideas, technological problems, aerodynamic theories. Apparently he liked his airline endeavors only in the sense that the airmail service was an outlet for the aircraft he loved to build.

Nor was there any doubt that the deaths of those two pilots left scars. He came to dread the ring of his telephone late at night or early in the morning, fearing the worst and always half-expecting it. A pilot himself, he knew how thin was the margin for error, knew the risks that were far from being calculated, and the terrible vulnerability to weather compounded by lack of communications capability. He respected his gallant brood of primitive eagles—perhaps to the point where the association and the closeness became almost too painful; Pitcairn probably had put himself in the position of a wartime squadron commander who had grown to hate the task of sending his men on missions where fifty–fifty odds were considered a luxury.

Flying the mail wasn't that dangerous, of course, but it was no picnic. In combat an airman took off because he was following the inviolate rule of command. In the airmail service Pitcairn's pilots took off because they were following an inviolate rule of economics: You got paid a lot more if you flew than if you stayed on the ground. To which had to be added their fierce, almost foolhardy pride; they were a hotly competitive breed for the most part, with tremendous loyalty toward the company and their job. It was psychologically almost impossible to turn down a trip because of threatening weather when you saw your fellow flyers battling through the same storms—that hoary "The Mail Must Go Through" slogan was a legitimate challenge, not a publicity gimmick.

Exactly when Pitcairn decided to sell out was known only to him. Ray was indirectly responsible, for he kept pressuring Pitcairn to start carrying passengers and that meant bigger aircraft like the Ford and Fokker trimotors. Pitcairn kept evading the issue but Ray and everyone else might have known that their boss was losing interest in the whole airline business—even while they were preparing to start service on CAM 25, he suddenly took off for Europe and it was no pleasure trip. On December 11, 1928, he returned to New York accompanied by four huge crates and a signed agreement with Juan de la Cierva to build autogiros in the United States; inside the crates were the components of a disassembled autogiro which Pitcairn planned to test thoroughly before going into production. Under the terms of the agreement, Pitcairn would form a subsidiary of Pitcairn Aviation called the Pitcairn-Cierva Autogiro Company of America.

While Pitcairn disappeared almost daily into the hangar where Agnew Larsen supervised the reassembly of the autogiro, Jim Ray kept pressing for passenger service. "Mr. Harold," as everyone called him in those days, finally relented if only to get

Ray off his back; it may also have been that Pitcairn by then had made up his mind about selling out and really didn't care. Ray's chief ally in his crusade was Geoffrey Childs, the airline's vice president and general manager, who knew the operations manager was getting a lot of heat from the system's major cities to start carrying people as well as mail sacks.

There is reason to believe that this very pressure may have had some negative influence on Pitcairn. It would seem logical that if he constantly worried about his pilots risking their lives, he would feel an even deeper responsibility toward trusting passengers. Harold Pitcairn was sensitive; outwardly undemonstrative, he was capable of dark brooding and his feelings of personal responsibility toward those dependent on him ran deep.

He did go so far as to authorize the purchase of three Ford trimotors, the 4-AT model, but long before the first "Tin Goose" was delivered, Pitcairn dropped his bombshell.

In the spring of 1929 he went to Europe for more meetings with de la Cierva, taking Larsen with him. He was gone a couple of months and when he returned, he called what everyone assumed would be a routine meeting to hear about his trip, and to have his subordinates brief him on the airline's progress during his absence—and the progress had been impressive, what with Pitcairn turning in the highest profits in the industry and pleasing both the Postal Service and mail users with its reliability.

Mr. Harold walked into the conference room, exchanged greetings, and after a long silence cleared his throat nervously.

"I've been a bad boy," he said softly.

The others stared at him. There was another agonizing silence before Pitcairn, his pleasant face now grim, murmured, "I've decided to sell the airline."

It was Childs who managed to ask the obvious question. "To whom, Mr. Harold?"

"I don't know yet. I've just made up my mind."

Jim Ray muttered that finding a buyer might take months—a period in which word of the impending sale inevitably would leak out and wreck employee morale, not to mention the airline's own standing.

"I realize that, Jim," Pitcairn agreed. "As a matter of fact, Clement Keys of NAT once told me if I ever wanted to sell, he'd be interested. I don't see any reason why I shouldn't call him right now."

He put the call through from the conference room. The others heard only one end of the conversation and it chilled them. It took no longer than five minutes. Pitcairn informed Keys he was willing to sell and that he'd meet with Keys and the postmaster general to arrange transfer of the mail contract. Keys asked him how much money he wanted and Pitcairn, his hand over the mouthpiece, held a hurried conference with Childs.

"You've put almost a half million into the airline so far," Childs said with swift mental calculations. "We're grossing about a hundred thousand a month and netting around forty thousand. Equipmentwise, we're committed to ten more Mailwings and three Ford trimotors. It adds up—let's see—to roughly a million dollars."

Ray suggested asking for another half-million and Pitcairn was about to agree when Childs swallowed hard. "Make it two and a half million, Mr. Harold."

Pitcairn calmly gave Keys the $2.5 million asking price. No one knows what Keys said exactly but his answer was an unequivocal yes, for Pitcairn replied, "All right, we're agreed."

The conversation was over and so was Harold Pitcairn's commitment to the airline he had fathered.

A few days later the final arrangements were consummated in Pitcairn's downtown Philadelphia office. Turned over to Keys were the mail contract, airport rental agreements, and stock in both the airline and Pitcairn's associated aviation enterprises. Turned over to Harold Pitcairn was a certified check for $2.5 million.

Keys represented himself; he was used to conducting his own business and he seldom bothered consulting lawyers. He and Pitcairn exchanged copies of prepared statements to be issued to employees and the press on July 10, 1929. Both were brief; Pitcairn's simply said the airline had been sold for an undisclosed price and added:

The offer we have accepted is the most recent of several which have come to us as a result of the great success of our airmail routes and the growing importance of links in the national and international airmail system.

It has been increasingly evident that this expansion will continue and will be supplemented by passenger-line development on a large scale.

The Pitcairn manufacturing interests, Pitcairn Aircraft, Inc., and the Pitcairn-Cierva Autogiro Company of America are not affected.

Those three paragraphs contained two items of significance. Pitcairn never did disclose who else had offered to buy the airline; Ray, for one, always believed the reference to "several" other offers was something Mr. Harold thought up to make the deal with Keys more palatable; it would have been logical for him to try to give the impression he had not accepted the first and only offer made. Of more interest to the employees was the pledge for development of full-scale passenger service—at least they were assured that Keys, who at one time had discouraged passenger traffic on NAT by the simple process of doubling the existing fares, would carry through Pitcairn's expansion plans.

Keys' briefer statement contained a paragraph composed by Jim Ray with Pitcairn's approval. It read:

Mr. Pitcairn has reserved the services of Mr. G. F. Childs, business manager of the line, and of Mr. J. G. Ray, chief pilot. Apart from these positions we hope to make few, if any, changes in the personnel to carry on the line.

Childs, of course, would have followed Harold Pitcairn into an erupting volcano; he was a financial expert and it made no difference whether he was working for an airline or a company making airplanes. Ray's decision to stay with Mr. Harold was something of a surprise; in those embryonic days of the industry, he was regarded as one of the best operations men around. There is no doubt that he could have become president of a carrier if he had remained in the airline business; few of his position had better rapport with the pilots, broader knowledge in his field, or more sheer executive ability. Jim Ray was the perfect combination of stern discipline blended with compassion and appreciation of human dignity. It was the airline's loss and Pitcairn's personal gain when he decided to remain with the man who had given him his start.

And what of Pitcairn Aviation's new owner?

He wasn't to own it very long—and that probably sums up best the methods, personality, and philosophy of Clement Melville Keys, a wheeler-dealer type with a brilliant mind unfettered by any outward trace of sentimentality.

Unlike so many of the early airline chieftains, he could care less about the romantic, pioneering aspects of the young industry. Clement Keys was out to make money, acquire power, and achieve unprecedented dominance. "Ten percent of aviation is in the air," he once commented. "Ninety percent is on the ground."

A Canadian by birth, Keys joined *The Wall Street Journal* as a young reporter fresh from McGraw University in Toronto. He learned and listened, in sufficient proportions to leave and start his own investment-banking firm. World War I sparked his interest in aviation's commercial possibilities, for he saw in its hectic wartime activities a glimpse of inevitable postwar expansion. During the war he became financial vice president of the Curtiss Aeroplane and Motor Company and by Armistice Day he had acquired enough stock to gain control of the company. Then he began spreading his wings, for Clement Keys, basically, was an empire builder with vision.

While most aviation tomes describe him as cold, he could be charming, persuasive, and exceptionally courteous. Keys was tall, thin, and tougher physically than his pipe-cleaner frame would indicate. He smoked long black cigars incessantly, the thick smoke obscuring the penetrating eyes that squinted behind rimless glasses. His forte was a knowledge of the bond market, and his one-time investment clients included Glen Curtiss—Keys's entry into the dawning world of commercial aviation.

In 1925 Keys formed North American Aviation, a holding

company under whose banner were such aviation enterprises as NAT, Curtiss, Sperry Gyroscope, and Transcontinental Air Transport (TAT), forerunner of TWA. Pitcairn became part of this mushrooming empire capitalized to the then astronomical sum of thirty million dollars. It was a vast, interlocking masterpiece of slick organization with the airline subsidiaries serving not only as profitable entities on their own but also as outlets for the manufacturing branches like Curtiss and Sperry. Keys virtually wrote the book on this money-minting formula; unfortunately he couldn't copyright the plot and a rival entrepreneur was to use it against him.

Keys is an almost forgotten figure in aviation history, thanks largely to his own personality. He hated publicity and was strictly low profile; he listed himself as president of Pitcairn, something he hadn't done at NAT where his title was chairman of the executive committee, but the presidential designation was pure window-dressing. Paul Henderson ably ran NAT for him, yet the man he picked to run Pitcairn not only had absolutely no airline experience but had never been in an airplane. He had been recommended by Thomas Morgan, president of the Sperry division, whom Keys respected.

His name was Thomas B. Doe, a West Point graduate and a former captain of artillery. A tall, heavyset man wearing glasses, he showed up at Richmond two weeks after the Pitcairn sale had been consummated and introduced himself to Harold Elliott, the only survivor from previous management in the new Pitcairn hierarchy.

"I guess I'm going to be running things," Doe told Elliott pleasantly enough, "and I'd like to take a look at the airline."

"I'll fly you over the system myself," Elliott offered.

They used "old 61," Larsen's improvised training plane— first removing the hood used to cover one cockpit during instrument-check flights. Elliott had planned to go all the way to Miami but the inspection tour ended in Jacksonville at the ashen-faced Doe's request. He took a train back north and Elliott flew home alone, wondering how it would be working for a man who obviously was petrified of flying.

He found out quickly, for Doe to many was something of a

figurehead—the crack around Pitcairn for a time was that he should have been named John. Likable if a bit quick tempered, he was smart enough to enjoy the prestige of being president and turned much of the actual running of the airline over to Elliott and the other Pitcairn veterans. Doe was an able, decisive executive; he was a bit over his head in the airline business and he also was only too well aware that the domineering figure of Clement Keys was calling most of the shots. Doe's biggest asset was political clout of sorts—he had a number of Washington connections and he got along with politicians.

This actually was a transition period in the airline's history. The whole industry was maturing fast and Pitcairn was no exception. The year 1929 brings to most minds the terrifying catastrophe of the stock-market crash and the beginning of America's worst depression; to aviation it was a year of expansion and technological innovations. Keys's Sperry subsidiary came up with the first practical directional gyro, which was tested in a Mailwing that took off with the cockpit completely hooded, flew a 15-mile course, and landed blind at the starting point. The test pilot was Jimmy Doolittle, who had just been photographed standing nonchalantly on the wing of another biplane being flown by a new electronic gadget, one denounced loudly by all redblooded airmen: an automatic pilot.

Coming to an end were the days when so many airmail pilots seemed to rely mostly on prayer for navigation—and there was one who used a cigar. This worthy flew the New York–Cleveland route and would light a cigar at a specified time after takeoff. When it had burned down to one inch, he would descend through the overcast and usually would find Bellefontaine, Ohio, his checkpoint, just below. Now the U.S. airlines were flying 90,000 miles every 24 hours over more than 10,000 miles of lighted airways and into 275 lighted airports and emergency fields. There were 1,352 rotating beacons to guide the night flyers and the aircraft themselves were getting better—the sturdy Fords, first flown in 1926, provided new dimensions of safety, reliability, and comfort—although the latter virtue was diluted by the fact that the Goose was by all odds the noisiest airliner ever built. And just around the corner that same year was the huge Curtiss Condor, the last word in airborne luxury; Pitcairn's employees heard scuttlebutt that the Ford was just an interim airplane until the Condors (built, naturally, by a Keys subsidiary) could be delivered.

Yet until Pitcairn actually began carrying passengers (it would not happen until mid-1930), the airline operated much as it had from that first day in May, 1928—it was still flying single-seat biplanes under primitive conditions. A safety revolution was in the making, but it would be some time before all the technical goodies found their way into the cockpit. Items, for example, like Elmer Sperry, Jr.'s artificial horizon and direction indicator; Sperry was the son of a brilliant inventor who had perfected gyroscopic controls for ships. Another son, Lawrence, had been lost in a flight over the English Channel and the elder Sperry had pledged to devote the rest of his life to making flying safer. The father and the surviving son became partners in this crusade, but not until Keys bought out their rather tiny company did they have the financial muscle to develop markets for their flight aids. In Pitcairn, Sperry found not just a market but a flying laboratory.

Considering the varied adventures of Kytle, Banks, Merrill, Brown, and the others, improvements couldn't come too soon. They still were all taking too many chances and too often missing tragedy by inches or seconds. Part of the motivation, of course, was money—most of them lived fast, loved highpowered automobiles and expensive clothes, and being fatalists as a whole, theirs was a philosophy of "be happy today because tomorrow you might buy the farm" (an ancient airman's saying traced to the necessity of paying farmers for damage to crops caused by a forced landing in some field).

To his everlasting credit, Harold Pitcairn had tried to remove some of their monetary motivation. Shortly before he sold the airline, he told a group of pilots "there's no sense in killing yourself for dough—from now on we'll pay night rates for all trips." Gene Brown remembers that the accident rate declined after this gesture.

"He was a fine gentleman and a great boss," Brown adds. "And Jim Ray—well, he was tops. They both knew why we got into trouble. We were after the money and sometimes we didn't know when to stop."

It was only too true. Kytle commented once that on a night flight, "every time I passed a beacon my cash-register mind would ring up a dollar."

The earliest Pitcairn pilots had a life expectancy averaging only two years from the day they began flying the mail. Syd Molloy was the first of the original five to die; he hooked a wing tip on a radio-tower wire while approaching Atlanta in a fog. No one was surprised because Molloy had a phobia about bad weather. Unlike Merrill and Kytle, for example, who took a perverse delight in challenging the odds, Molloy despised weather problems to the point of brooding about them—it was almost as if he had a premonition that the weather would kill him.

Kytle seemed to lead the proverbial charmed life. He walked away from several crashes, his most miraculous escape occurring one foggy night when he flew right into the side of Stone Mountain near Atlanta. His Mailwing hit a clump of brush, cushioning the impact just enough to keep it from going over a two-hundred-foot cliff; Kytle got off with a split lip and broken finger. He hit another mountain only three months later and the same thing happened—the plane was slowed down by scrub brush and Kytle climbed out unhurt. On his third close call he ran out of fuel battling severe storms south of Richmond and had to use his parachute.

Kytle's Achilles Heel was his inability to resist acrobatics. He flew one Mailwing inverted for so long that the battery acid leaked and ate through the fuselage skin.

"I'd like to be flying," he told Dick Merrill, "when planes are so fast that if I stuck my finger into the slipstream it would peel off the skin."

Johnny would never live to see that day. His obsession with speed and stunting had its inevitably tragic result: He was doing acrobatics in a stubby-winged G-B racing plane one day over the Atlanta airport when the aircraft disintegrated. Kytle had a parachute but the G-B came apart so fast he never had a chance to use it.

Gene Brown had remonstrated with him one day after Kytle had insisted on flying the Mailwing on its back—the Pitcairn was almost totally unstable when inverted.

"You're going to kill yourself some day," Gene warned.

"I know, Gene," Johnny had sighed, "but I just can't resist it."

Flying was a tough enough way to make a living without begging trouble as pilots like Kytle and Banks so often did. Yet the compensation was not always found in a paycheck—there were moments when a pilot felt ten feet tall. Such as in October of 1929, when flood waters marooned thousands in Georgia and South Carolina, and Pitcairn's pilots flew emergency food and medical supplies to stranded areas.

And to a man, they knew how lucky they were. Brashness was as frequent a commodity as skill, and they got away with misdeeds and illegalities which today would have been a one-way ticket out of the airline business. Fritz Schwaemmle, for example; he was to become a senior captain at Delta and later Delta's director of public relations, and he still remembers the day Jim Ray hired him.

He had walked into Ray's office at Willow Grove.

"I'm a pilot," he informed Ray.

"You're hired," Ray said.

Some months later Schwaemmle was called on the carpet for stunting an Orowing with two passengers aboard.

"Fritz, you pull that again and you'll lose your license," Ray warned sternly.

"What license?" Schwaemmle gulped.

Andy Banks was about the most incorrigible of all. Like Kytle, he couldn't resist stunting the Mailwings and he also could be meaner than a constipated bear when he had a few drinks. One night he went out to Byrd Field and announced he was going to do a little "private flying." It was fairly obvious he didn't need an airplane to get him off the ground and a mechanic named Bob McKee bravely took matters into his own hands.

"Fine, Andy," he said. "I'll go get your ship ready."

McKee quickly fixed the engine on Banks's ship so it wouldn't start. After a few minutes of loud cursing, Banks marched into the office waving his Smith and Wesson .38 and proceeded to shoot up the place. For months the bullet holes were covered up by pictures. That wasn't the only time Banks pulled a gun in a fit of inebriated temper—he splattered the walls of another airport office after discovering that a fellow Pitcairn pilot had borrowed his plane without permission. They got the gun away from Andy before he could use it on the transgressing airman.

When the new post-Pitcairn regime took over, the pilots had to give up their personal planes. It was a black day when the order came down; the pilots babied their Mailwings, even washing and waxing them during off-duty hours—not even the redoubtable Johnny Ray was allowed to perform *those* chores.

"A dirty airplane was a reflection on the pilot assigned to it," Ray recalls. "Hell, now you can't get a pilot to knock a fly off the windshield."

The boys fixed up their ships any way they pleased. One had the then-popular comic strip character Felix the Cat painted on his plane, and another adorned the rudder with a shamrock. There were Mailwings with extra cockpit lights controlled by a button switch on the stick, and Gene Brown installed in his plane a special air cushion that supported his back as well as his buttocks. Don Johnston was one of several who attached sirens to the landing gear; they were driven by the propeller and controlled by a switch in the cockpit. Johnston cut loose with the siren one night while flying over the Marine base at Quantico, Virginia, and woke up every Marine in camp—it was shortly after this incident that the siren operators were told to get rid of their contraptions.

Almost every week added to the legends of close calls, miracles, and humor. The terrible-tempered Mr. Banks contributed one classic that could have ended in some of the blackest headlines in the history of aviation. He was flying the mail from Richmond to New York on a dark night and spotted what appeared to be a large gray cloud directly ahead. He was just about to fly through it when instinct told him something was wrong. At the last second he pulled back on the stick and zoomed over the cloud—which suddenly lit up like a giant Christmas tree.

What he had almost rammed was the Navy's giant dirigible *Los Angeles.*

Dick Merrill was the source of countless stories. It was Johnny Ray who cured him—temporarily—of a hedge-hopping habit; Merrill had landed one day, stoutly insisting that the weather had caused him to fly lower than usual.

"Damned near hit some pine trees with my gear," he chortled.

Ray said nothing, but went outside, cut off some small pine boughs, and stuck them in the landing gear of Merrill's Mailwing. Then he went back to the office. "Come outside, Dick—I wanna show you something."

Merrill followed him out to the plane and took one startled look at the boughs.

"Jesus, I didn't think I was *that* low," he muttered. Four years were to pass before Ray mustered the nerve to tell him where the boughs had come from.

Almost from the day he came to work for the airline, Merrill had an uncanny gift for attracting publicity. He was almost as much a promoter as a pilot, yet no one resented it because Merrill was a headline hunter and publicity hound only in the sense that he would do anything to promote aviation. He had a flair for attracting attention, but his flamboyance was deftly aimed at getting people to talk about flying, the airlines, and Pitcairn itself; he was a kind of goodwill ambassador who frankly enjoyed the limelight yet never became blinded by it.

Reporters covering the airports around Pitcairn's system quickly learned that Merrill made good copy. His pets, for example—at one time or another he owned a lion, monkey, squirrel, various dogs, and other assorted animals he often took with him on flights when he knew there might be photographers around. The lion was always his favorite although he was forced to give it away to a zoo after two unfortunate incidents. Gene

Brown issued one "get rid of the damned thing" after Leo tore off his pants while he was walking through the hangar at night. The mayor of Richmond issued the other, declaring that Merrill and his tawny beast were a menace to automobile traffic: Dick used to drive around the city in his flashy black Packard touring car with the lion sitting next to him in the front seat.

Once Merrill took a flight out dressed in his bathing suit, over which he had strapped his parachute and pistol belt. He claimed he had been swimming at a beach and didn't have time to change, but this didn't explain why there were photographers conveniently waiting for him when he arrived at the field. Ironically his fellow pilots considered this gimmick good sense; a number of them began flying in swimsuits during the hot summer months. A pilot named Pete Branson neglected to take his swim apparel on one flight, and when the heat became too bad, he took off his pants to cool off. Disrobing in a Mailwing cockpit required the ability of a contortionist and Pete was not quite up to it—his pants blew out of the cockpit during a sudden downdraft. It was an embarrassed airman who phoned Atlanta from the next stop, Spartanburg, and asked his wife to meet him at Candler with a pair of trousers.

Underneath all the horseplay and publicity appetite, Merrill was a solid and dedicated pilot who worked hard on his instrument flying. In truth, he was more of a gambler on the ground than in the air; Merrill would have bet on one of two water drops trickling down a windowpane—he loved playing the horses, poker, dice, slot machines, blackjack, and anything vaguely resembling a game of chance. It is said that he knew every floating crap game on the east coast and he once walked out of a crap game in Atlanta with $58,000 won in fourteen consecutive passes. He blew the whole bundle the next day at a racetrack but this yo-yo financial existence never bothered him. Curiously, he had a reputation for having the slowest draw east of the Mississippi when it came to picking up a dinner check, but he was constantly lending his friends money with no questions asked. Merrill always seemed to be at the apogee and nadir of finance— he either had a wad of bills on him capable of choking a tyrannosaurus or he was so broke that he had to borrow against his next month's salary.

Like his brethren, he was not averse to a few shenanigans in Pitcairn's earlier days. It became a routine ritual to do a few rolls and at least one loop at the end of a mail flight—a practice which at first Jim Ray mildly discouraged and then flatly prohibited. The latter fiat was prompted by an incident at Richmond when the mail compartment came open during the customary loop. It took postal inspectors three days to retrieve all the mail from the woods where the sacks had fallen and split open.

Virtually every man flying for Pitcairn regarded a trip cancellation as the equivalent of insulting motherhood and spitting on the flag, but Merrill and Johnston were about the worst. If either heard the other was flying, it made no difference how bad the weather was—he had to go, too. One particularly foul night, Merrill was in Atlanta trying to decide whether to take off a southbound mail flight. He knew Johnston was in Jacksonville and sweated out word as to Don's intentions.

Departure time approached and Merrill called Jacksonville operations on the long line. "Ask Johnston what he's gonna do."

There was a short pause. "He says he'll cancel," Jacksonville finally informed him. "He doesn't like the weather."

"That's good enough for me," Merrill sighed, and went outside to supervise the loading of the mail sacks onto a truck which would deliver them to the railroad station. A few minutes later he was back in Atlanta operations shooting the breeze when the Pitcairn teletype began chattering. Merrill was sitting next to it and glanced at the incoming message.

"That dirty, double-crossing ————!" he roared. "He left Jacksonville on schedule—get that mail back!"

It was too late, but Merrill himself was not immune to an occasional practical joke of that kind. He came into Greensboro one night on a smooth, uneventful northbound trip and bumped into a junior pilot about to leave for Atlanta.

"How's the weather to Atlanta?" the younger pilot asked.

"Terrible," Merrill said soberly. "The worst I've ever seen.

The lightning was so bad I could have read a newspaper by it."

"That bad?"

"I wouldn't go through it again for a million dollars," Dick assured him, resorting to one of his favorite expressions.

For a long time no one except Merrill knew why the southbound trip was canceled that night.

Throughout the airline's youthful years the pilots developed a kind of camaraderie with people along the route system—the farmers near the emergency strips who would always welcome these goggled visitors from another world with hot coffee and sizzling food . . . the night clerk at a Havre de Grace, Maryland, hotel, who furnished en-route weather reports . . . the families in isolated homes who could set their watches by the roar of the Mailwing passing overhead.

The emergency fields were near farmhouses and the owners of the latter became part-time employees who were used to communicating with the mail planes. They were given flares for this purpose; one flare meant that the destination field had been closed down and that the pilot should land at the emergency field and phone in. Two flares meant that destination weather was worsening and that the pilot should act at his discretion: Either proceed with caution, or land on the emergency strip and call in.

There are a number of stories to the effect that the airmail pilots several times saved the lives of farmers by buzzing their burning homes and awakening them in time to escape. This may have happened (Gene Brown spotted twenty-seven fires in the six years he flew the Mailwings) but the life-saving aspects may be largely apocryphal.

"If you dove, you were automatically a hero," Brown chuckles. "I saw one once and went down for a closer look—the firemen were already there but later I read in the papers that I had saved their lives."

In those glory days, a pilot could get away with almost anything short of mayhem provided that the mail was delivered. Incredible as that may sound today, when the airline pilot's life is so regimented, disciplined, and rule-dominated, it was true. Witnesses once reported seeing Andy Banks stunting his mail plane over a girl friend's house in New Jersey. The complaints reached the ears of a postal official who said he didn't care what a pilot did so long as the mail arrived on schedule.

Now, as the new regime took over Harold Pitcairn's airline, the halcyon times were over.

The first official action was to move the airline's headquarters out of the Philadelphia area—to Brooklyn, where Sperry had its home offices.

The second was to change the name of the airline. It never has been recorded who was precisely responsible for the new designation (Keys, probably), but the choice was obvious: Eastern. The full title was Eastern Air Transport, and it came into official being on January 15, 1930.

The third was to take a good look at Pitcairn's overall operations, from airport conditions to personnel and aircraft. Keys, his previous anti-passenger policy at NAT notwithstanding, had become convinced that the days of airline feeding at the airmail trough were coming to an end—a new postmaster general named Walter Folger Brown had assumed the post in the cabinet of Herbert Hoover, and Brown was publicly proclaiming that the industry's real future lay in transportation of people, not mail.

Keys had a high opinion of Harold Elliott, and made him vice president and operations manager—the only other vice president was Thomas Morgan. But he evidently thought Elliott may have been too close to the old Pitcairn crew to form any objective opinion as to what, if anything, Eastern Air Transport needed in the way of improvement.

The new president, Tom Doe, was more an employee of North American Aviation than head of Eastern Air Transport—a liaison man between the parent company and the airline. He was assigned mostly the task of developing political contacts in what —under Postmaster General Brown—was fast becoming a political atmosphere, for Brown had his own ideas on what the air transport industry should look like. Doe's name at the top of EAT's officers' list in the 1930 *Official Aviation Guide* (it is now the *Official Airline Guide*) came close to being an honorary gesture; the *Guide* carried him as "Captain Thomas B. Doe," incidentally, making him the only airline executive in the United States at the time to retain his old military rank in his civilian capacity.

So Clement Keys went shopping for what could be termed a "troubleshooter," and he found one in the person of Charles H. Dolan, quite literally a soldier of fortune with a background that could have been made into a half-dozen movies.

Dolan had once worked for Sperry in the firm's London office, but quit to join the French Foreign Legion. There he learned to fly. When the U.S. entered World War I, Dolan had somehow attracted the notice of Billy Mitchell, who had him transferred to his staff. After the war Mitchell talked him into flying Curtiss-built planes in China, and here he established a reputation as a daredevil pilot—he once crash-landed a Curtiss on the Great Wall and fortunately for Dolan both he and his lone passenger escaped without a scratch; the passenger was Secretary of the Navy Edwin Denby.

Dolan's previous employment at Sperry and his stint flying Curtiss planes in China had brought him to Keys's attention. Keys met him in Peking. Dolan helped him work out a deal for half interest in the Chinese airline that was operating the aircraft.

Dolan by this time had had his fill of the Orient and sailed for Hawaii, where he got involved as a consultant in starting up an interisland airline. He sold his stock in the Chinese carrier at a fat profit and wound up back in the U.S., wealthy enough to relax until a good airline post opened up. It was Keys who supplied the opening, arranging a meeting at which he tentatively offered Dolan the job of assistant operations manager, working directly under Elliott.

"Where?" Dolan asked.

"Atlanta. We've already moved operations headquarters to there from Richmond. Bigger facilities and a more central location for the route system."

Keys went on to explain that he wanted to start passenger service as soon as possible. He had assigned Eugene Vidal (the father of author Gore Vidal and a man who someday would become the government's director of air commerce in the pre-FAA days) to survey passenger traffic potential on CAM 25. Vidal, he added, had recommended a number of airport improvements before any service could start but Keys said he didn't think things were as bad as Vidal had painted.

Actually they weren't. What Vidal had encountered was a dubious Harold Elliott, who thought the airline was unprepared for what Keys had in mind and acted accordingly. With dubious intentions he had flown Vidal over EAT's system but picked the worst weather and the roughest fields for most of the survey trip; Vidal based his conclusions on what he had seen, and what he had seen was the bottom of the barrel. When the three Fords Pitcairn had ordered were delivered in the fall of 1929, Elliott assigned them to promotion flights—the majority on behalf of airmail service—and figured he had delayed passenger operations indefinitely.

Delayed, yes—but not indefinitely. Dolan's first task was to study CAM 25 himself and he didn't have Elliott along as a subtle saboteur. Elliott gave his new assistant a Pitcairn for the route survey and waved him good-bye. Three months later, after visiting every point on EAT's system and talking to virtually every employee, Dolan turned over to Keys more than one hundred and fifty recommendations adding up to a single conclusion: Passenger service could start anytime, if on a limited basis at first, and the potential for profit was there.

His report landed on Keys's desk in mid-November, but not until late December did Dolan hear from anyone at EAT. The long-awaited call came from the brusque Doe, who told him to "get your ass over to the Sperry Building—I want to see you."

Their meeting was brief. Doe simply gave Dolan carte blanche to translate his long list of recommendations into action —the order actually was relayed from Keys, who had been named chairman of the board. Dolan did, and the resulting shock waves reverberated throughout the airline. His first act was to end the practice of pilots being assigned their own personal aircraft—they screamed like wounded panthers but the edict stuck, along with Dolan's refusal to tolerate such activities as stunting mail planes at the end of trips, or buzzing everything from frightened drivers to romantic couples in canoes.

"You're going to grow up or get out," he told a meeting of sullen-faced pilots.

A handful—Brown, Treat, and even Merrill were among them—accepted the inevitable. Treat, in fact, walked away from two more minor mishaps that weren't his fault and asked to be transferred to the new Fords. And resentful as the others were, they knew they were coyotes howling futilely at an unhearing moon. They were well aware that the likable but stern Dolan had brass-hat support and they also recognized the inevitability of an event that demanded regulated professionalism in every cockpit: passenger service. It was coming not only because Keys wanted it, but because the United States Government was insisting on it.

In April of 1930 Congress passed the Watres Act—introduced by Representative Lawrence Watres of Pennsylvania and Senator Charles D. McNary of Oregon, both Republicans, in reality bore the fingerprints of Walter Folger Brown. The legislations accomplished two things:

1. It scrapped the practice of paying the airlines by the weight of the mail they were flying. In its place went a system based on payment by space offered—at a maximum rate of $1.25 regardless of whether the space was filled. The change had two effects: It ruined smaller airlines with relatively little mail capacity, and it reduced mail revenues for the larger carriers to the point of forcing them to get into the passenger business quickly and seriously—which was Postmaster General Brown's chief intention all along.

2. It gave any airmail contractor with two years' operating experience permission to exchange his current authorization for a ten-year route certificate, including recognition of pioneer rights. One had to read the small print in the bill, because the Watres Act defined pioneer rights as applicable to any airline

being "the lowest responsible bidder who has owned and operated an air transportation service on a fixed daily schedule over a
distance of not less then two hundred and fifty miles and for a
period of not less then six months prior to the advertisement for
bids." Eastern Air Transport was well qualified under this provision (assuming, of course, it wound up as the "lowest responsible
bidder") but the small airlines flying minuscule routes were dis-
qualified and Brown's plans to restructure the nation's entire
airline system were becoming most apparent.

Less than a month after the Watres Act became law, Brown
added a rule which wasn't even in the legislation: He announced
that no mail bid would be considered unless the submitting airline had compiled at least six months of night operations over
routes of not less than 250 miles. Again this was fine for EAT,
whose ex-Pitcairners hadn't done much else except fly at night,
but it was a death blow for companies with little or no night
experience.

In May 1930, Walter Folger Brown took a final step
toward his goal: to weed out all marginal operators and turn air
transportation over to a relative handful of carriers with the financial muscle and operating skill for developing a passenger-
carrying system. He summoned to Washington the heads of various airlines for a series of meetings later dubbed "spoils conferences." The "guest list" was indicative of Brown's plans—he invited only the largest carriers and ignored the smaller ones.

The meetings ran from May 19 to May 30 and Tom Doe
represented EAT. Basically what Eastern got out of it were pioneer rights to CAM 25, and Doe almost swung a deal to go into
partnership with Southern Air Transport, a division of the Aviation Corporation (AVCO), which was the holding company for
what eventually would become American Airlines, for the coveted southern transcontinental route. When this suddenly fell
apart, Doe came close to an alliance with Erle Halliburton, a
tough-talking oilman from Oklahoma whose Southwest Air Fast
Express (SAFE) operated out of Tulsa with routes to Texas,
Missouri, and Kansas.

Halliburton agreed to set up a new company which would

operate SAFE's old routes as a subcontractor to EAT. But Halliburton made two mistakes: He announced that William Gibbs McAdoo, son-in-law of Woodrow Wilson, would be head of the new company, and, without consulting the autocratic, thin-skinned Keys, he ordered ten new Ford trimotors to operate the route's western legs. McAdoo's name was anathema to Republican Brown and the Fords were anathema to Keys, who was planning to reequip both Eastern and TAT with a fleet of Curtiss Condors.

The Halliburton-Doe deal collapsed, and so did one Doe worked out with C. E. Woolman, the general manager of tiny Delta, which was operating between Birmingham and Dallas. Woolman had laid stake to this leg as part of the southern transcontinental route, and when Doe objected, a tentative compromise was reached—extend Eastern's New York–Atlanta route to Birmingham and sublet Birmingham–Dallas to Delta. Most of the other conferees were agreeable but AVCO got Brown's ear and it was American which wound up with the southern transcontinental route.

Monday morning quarterbacking being a fascinating albeit futile pastime, it is interesting to speculate how the history of both Eastern and Delta would have been changed if the Woolman-Doe partnership deal had been consummated. Delta, instead of becoming Eastern's most bitter rival, probably would have been swallowed up by the larger carrier and Eastern itself would not have become a predominantly north–south airline for the next three decades. One historian claims that the Eastern-Delta feud dates back to the aborted Spoils Conference deal, but this is stretching matters beyond belief; both Doe and Woolman wanted the partnership and were disappointed when Brown scotched it.

A more accurate long-range view would be the conclusion that Clement Keys was the biggest loser when Brown arbitrarily rewrote the U.S. airways map. For the very compressing of the airline industry into a handful of giants was the start of a squeeze play on North American Aviation.

This was not the Postmaster General's intention. History

has tended to paint him as something of a villain. Cold-blooded, ruthless, dictatorial—he was all that. But he also was a totally sincere, well-meaning man with intense convictions. Brown was an Ohio attorney who became chairman of the Republican National Committee and served as Herbert Hoover's campaign manager in the 1928 election. A close friend of Hoover, he received the traditional reward for a successful presidential campaign chief—a place in the cabinet as postmaster general.

He was tall, lean, always immaculately dressed, and wore steel-rimmed glasses that somehow fitted his austere personality. He also happened to be a scrupulously honest and dedicated man who took his job very seriously. As soon as he took office, he carefully studied the black leather portfolio then presented to new cabinet officers, containing an outline of their duties. His own portfolio listed one of the main tasks of the postmaster general to be the encouragement of commercial aviation, an assignment to which he applied a startlingly broad interpretation.

As of the day he joined the Hoover administration, the airline industry resembled the economy of a South American country—either wealth or poverty. There were no fewer than forty-four carriers, ranging from the huge conglomerates like Keys's North American, AVCO, and United, to the tiny, undercapitalized operators who could exist only with mail contracts. Brown's blueprint amounted to nothing more dastardly than a desire to develop passenger traffic by reducing the reliance on mail pay, even if this meant forcing out the smaller airlines.

Just before the Spoils Conference, Keys had lost control of NAT in a bitter and bloody fracas with William Boeing and Fred Rentschler, the brains behind the aviation conglomerate known as United Aircraft and Transport Corporation. Boeing had merged his aircraft-manufacturing company with his airline, Boeing Air Transport, and then had married the joint firm to another giant: Pratt & Whitney, the engine manufacturer headed by Rentschler. In swift succession they had added to the United family Stearman Aircraft, Chance Vought (builder of Navy planes), Hamilton Propeller, and Sikorsky Aviation, creating a colossus with a whopping $146 million capitalization.

Even Keys stood no chance against this formidable crew when Bill Boeing cast coveted eyes on NAT's New York–Chicago route. Acquisition of NAT would give United a transcontinental route stretching from New York to San Francisco, and Boeing took a page right out of Keys's own book. United Aircraft staged a secret raid into NAT's backyard, getting its hands on one third of NAT's stock from many of the Chicago backers who had helped Keys start the airline.

Keys countered by changing the corporate bylaws just before a showdown meeting of NAT shareholders; he reduced the quorum limitation by one third, then issued three hundred thousand new shares to North American Aviation which, of course, he controlled himself. The move enabled him to win the shareholders' fight, but in winning this battle, he lost the war; United took him to court, his last-ditch maneuvering was declared illegal, and NAT went under the United flag.

Keys, still calling signals at the twelve-day marathon in Brown's conference room, came up with a new strategy designed to make up for NAT's loss. He proposed that Brown authorize a merger between Transcontinental Air Transport and Harris "Pop" Hanshue's prosperous, fast-growing Western Air Express, then the country's largest single air carrier with a route system that stretched from Los Angeles to Kansas City.

It was an attractive proposition for Brown, who envisioned three transcontinental routes—south, central, and north. United would operate the northern route, American (AVCO) the southern, and TAT the central. Hanshue, already with plans of his own for going transcontinental, adamantly refused and was promptly shafted. Brown called him in for a private session and presented a compromise: TAT and Western would form a new airline, taking over the assets of both carriers on a fifty-fifty basis over the routes on which they were competing.

"Including Los Angeles–San Francisco?" Hanshue asked unhappily. Western had pioneered passenger service between the two cities and was still dominant despite competition from Maddux Air Lines, which Keys had just acquired and merged into TAT's system.

"Including Los Angeles–San Francisco," Brown said firmly. He added the final solar plexus blow: "If Western wants to get in on any transcontinental route, *any*, mind you, the merger I've suggested is the only way you're going to do it."

"All we ever wanted was the Kansas City–Los Angeles leg which we're already operating," Hanshue said bitterly, "but under your plan that's impossible."

"That's correct—impossible."

Hanshue caved in. The two carriers were merged to form Transcontinental and Western Air Express, today's Trans World Airlines. As a sop to Hanshue's pride, Keys named him president of TWA—a post he was to hold for less than a year. He continued to run what Brown and Keys had agreed to leave untouched—Western's route between Los Angeles and Salt Lake City—and on that thin foundation Western stayed in existence as an independent carrier.

But once again Keys had won a Pyrrhic victory. He now controlled two airline giants whose routes totaled some five thousand miles, one stretching coast to coast and the other covering almost the entire eastern seaboard, but he had sown the seeds for overexpansion at a time when the Depression was changing from an unpleasant dream to a nightmare. His downfall, of course, was to come later, and, the sagging national economy notwithstanding, his plans for EAT as well as TWA were grandiose.

He gave Doe the green light for Eastern's most ambitious equipment splurge to date: six Curtiss Condors, fourteen smaller Curtiss Kingbirds, and a fourth Ford trimotor, plus a pair of Fokker trimotors leased from TWA.

On August 18, 1930, Eastern began carrying passengers for the first time in its history.

CHAPTER THREE

PASSENGERS
ARE PEOPLE TOO

Considering what was to come later, inauguration of passenger service was not merely modest in scale but minuscule. It consisted of a daily-except-Sunday Ford trimotor round trip between New York and Richmond via the intermediate stops of Newark, Philadelphia, Baltimore, and Washington. If there was one thing Harold Elliott had inherited from Harold Pitcairn, it was caution; nursed on the risks and uncertainties of the airmail service, Elliott wanted no part of such vagaries when it came to carrying people.

Thus there was virtually no promotion or advertising of the new service. Elliott may have lost his battle against any passenger service, but he won from Keys, Doe, and Morgan their promise to go slow for the rest of the year. He insisted on about six months of experimenting, testing, and developing whatever had to go into a successful passenger operation, and they also let him travel around the country to see how other airlines were handling passengers.

His survey trip didn't accomplish much except to reinforce his doubts and fears. There were no standardized fares, baggage handling, ticketing, or arrangements for ground transportation; the industry in those days was informal to the point of chaos, each carrier setting its own rules and procedures. Haphazard it was, but understandable inasmuch as traffic was so light that the airlines actually ran their own air traffic control system—not until 1936 would the federal government assume the task of handling traffic on the nation's airways.

Slowly and painfully Elliott began assembling the human and mechanical components going into the service. He hired a chief pilot, Navy-trained like himself and with a reputation for conservatism to match his own—Erlon "Pete" Parker, whom he seduced away from the real-estate business and sent to the Ford flight-training school at Dearborn. The second pilot-in-command (they weren't called "captains" yet) was Frank Jerdone, who had acquired impressive experience flying multiengine aircraft while working with the government's Bureau of Air Commerce. Elliott picked his three copilots ("assistant pilots," they were designated) from the ranks of management—R. E. Lee from Atlanta, D. G. Hendrickson from Philadelphia, and J. B. "Army" Armstrong from Richmond; significantly, they were all station managers at their respective cities because Elliott hadn't reached the point where he could trust his maverick airmail pilots with a load of trusting passengers. Even Verne Treat, the first of the ex-Pitcairners to qualify on the Fords, wouldn't be allowed to fly passenger schedules for some time.

Only one of the three EAT-owned Fords was available for the start of service; the other two had been loaned to another airline which was operating them between the U.S. and Cuba. Elliott borrowed a trimotor from an almost defunct carrier to use until Eastern's own Fords could be retrieved from Cuba. For the northern terminus it was decided to use the old Glenn Curtiss Airport at North Beach, New York, because Hadley was too far from downtown Manhattan. The North Beach runway was cinder covered and what would become Eastern's first passenger terminal building was a hastily erected shack nailed together just in time to board the pioneering customers on that August 18 date.

The first ticket office was improvised as quickly as the terminal. It consisted of a single desk parked forlornly in a corner of the Sperry offices in Brooklyn, and none other than Elmer Sperry bought the first two tickets—one for himself and the second for Arctic explorer Hubert Wilkins, a close friend.

There were eleven passengers on the inaugural flight; all were accompanied to the airport (reached by a leased motorboat boarded at the East Forty-second Street pier) by the head of the Traffic Department, Ralph Westing. Mr. Westing refrained from disclosing that he was not only the head of the Traffic Department but its only employee.

The Elliott-compiled fare of seven cents a mile amounted to $21.50 for the full New York–Richmond flight; it was $5.75 to Philadelphia, $12.50 to Baltimore, and $14.50 to Washington, and the free-baggage limit was thirty pounds—you were allowed up to fifty pounds for half the regular fare. Scheduled flight time: five minutes less than four hours, for a trip of slightly more than three hundred miles.

Both the inaugural flight and the return trip were on time and uneventful; there were eleven customers on the latter, too. In the first five days Eastern Air Transport carried one hundred and two persons and it was beginning to dawn even on Elliott that there was money to be made flying "live cargo," as he had disparagingly phrased it. EAT's public relations man, Ed Jones, was instructed to compose an advertisement which *The New York Times* subsequently carried; it quoted Thomas Doe as announcing a "study to determine the most desirable equipment for increased passenger service which on December 1 will be extended to Atlanta and shortly thereafter to Miami, making all intermediate stops."

The "study," of course, already had been made; Eastern was committed not only to the giant Condor but a smaller Curtiss-built transport plane, the Kingbird. The Fords and the TAT-borrowed Fokkers were interim aircraft, for Clement Keys was betting not just his shirt but his underwear on the Condor.

As airplanes go, it wrote an almost forgotten page in aviation history—eclipsed by such greats as the Tin Goose, the DC-

3, and even the little Mailwing. Undeservedly so, it might be added, for the Condor in its own way was a revolutionary airliner that was the first to bring an American-designed, American-built transport aircraft up to the passenger-comfort standards of European planes. The Ford trimotor won fame because of its strength, safety, and reliability, but in terms of passenger luxury it was an abomination with its small, noisy, drafty cabin and relatively low cruising speed.

The Ford might be compared with France's LeO (for Lioré et Olivier) 21, a twin-engine transport carrying eighteen passengers—six in a forward lounge area and twelve in the main cabin. The most Spartan model boasted a bar and bartender, and one version had a twelve-seat restaurant! And there was the Fokker F-32, another Ford contemporary, a four-engine giant of unusual spaciousness; in one configuration, the cabin was divided into individual compartments seating four persons each.

Not until the Condor did America's air travelers enjoy such accommodations in a U.S. designed transport. Its big cabin held eighteen persons who reveled in such unaccustomed accoutrements as upholstered reclining seats, toilets with hot and cold running water, and the first soundproofing ever installed on a U.S. transport—seventy pounds of noise-deadening material; this, plus the use of engine mufflers and three-bladed propellers enabling the Condor to cruise at lower rpms reduced the interior noise level to about the same as a Pullman car. The Tin Goose was approximately thirty percent noisier.

Both Keys and Curtiss had great hopes for the airplane, although some aeronautical experts considered its military ancestry a potential drawback. The original Condor, known as Model 18, was a derivative of the XB-2 Condor bomber and was almost a twin of the military craft, inheriting most of its faults as well as its virtues. Powered by two twelve-cylinder Curtiss Conqueror engines, it was built at the Curtiss plant in Garden City, Long Island, with three respected aeronautical engineers supervising the task of transforming a bomber into a passenger-carrying airplane. The chief designer was George R. Page of Curtiss, assisted by Alexander Noble and a brilliant M.I.T. graduate named Theodore Wright who would one day become the government's top civil aviation officer. Some historians give Wright most of the credit for developing the Condor's civilian version but he didn't go around claiming it because the Model 18 was a turkey.

Keys envisioned it as the ideal plane for TAT's and later TWA's transcontinental route, what with its interior plushness and 150–160 mile per hour cruising speed, about forty-five miles per hour faster than the Tin Goose. It lacked the Ford's tough all-metal construction—the Condor was a fabric-covered biplane with a fuselage of aluminum tubing and steel wing spars —but all-metal construction was the exception to the rule in those days; Boeing's highly regarded Model 80 and Tony Fokker's big transports were all built of wood, as were Lockheed's "plywood bullets," and one contemporary airline president was publicly quoted as saying that a wooden transport was cheaper to maintain than a metal aircraft.

Keys even tried to sell the Condor to Pop Hanshue of Western, who scornfully rejected it with a classic and painfully accurate appraisal of the vaunted airliner. Asked if Western could ever use a transport like the Condor, Hanshue snorted, "Not until they build a tunnel through the goddamned Rockies!"

That was the Condor's chief drawback—the Model 18's Conqueror V-12's were about as powerful as egg beaters at anything vaguely resembling high altitudes; in truth, the Condor *couldn't* climb over the Rockies, and this left Eastern Air Transport as the only available customer for the Model 18. In 1932 Page—with considerable input from Wright—completely redesigned the aircraft, installing two Wright Cyclone engines. Curtiss named the new plane Condor II but it bore only a superficial resemblance to the Model 18; the landing gear was partially retractable, the whalelike fuselage was even more buxom, and the original twin fin and rudder design was scrapped in favor of a single tail. Technically known as the T-32, the revised Condor was to become an important part of Eastern's fleet and also American's.

But in 1930 what EAT acquired as the queen of its fleet was an airplane half-bomber and half-airliner—not the most satisfactory of choices, as the Russians have proved with so many transport designs that were mere facelifts of military aircraft. Frank Kern, one of Eastern's first Condor pilots and a former Curtiss test pilot, remembers the plane with fond nostalgia that falls short of outright admiration. The Condor's huge fabric wings made it the largest plane for its weight ever built in the U.S. and gave the ship a landing speed of only forty-five miles per hour.

"It was fun to fly," Kern recalls. "Just a big box kite, really. Landing it was an experience. It would float all over Hell's half-acre. The only way you could get it down was to put it right on the edge of a stall and let it mush in. If you ever got the nose down, you could never get it up again. Its best feature was the cockpit visibility—it was a damned greenhouse."

Transitioning from a Mailwing to a Condor was like going from a racing car to a Cadillac. Few Eastern pilots ever flew the Fords or Fokkers—there weren't enough of them. But a great many were checked out on the Condors and Kingbirds, the latter referred to occasionally as "the poor man's Condor." The Kingbird, built in St. Louis, was a twin-engine ship carrying six to eight passengers, and the pilots were never enamored of it. It flew fairly well on two engines and like an iron bathtub if you lost an engine; Curtiss eventually installed bigger power plants but they didn't help performance that much.

Equipment inadequacies notwithstanding, Eastern began integrating first the Condors and then the Kingbirds into its system. In mid-December two additional round trips were scheduled between New York and Washington, preceded five days earlier by Condor service from New York to Atlanta—the latter at a fare of just over $57. On January 1, 1931, Eastern inaugurated passenger service between Atlanta and both St. Petersburg and Miami; by the end of 1930 EAT's planes were flying more than 10,000 miles daily.

The pilots were wrestling with a new gimmick installed initially on the Condors and then throughout the entire fleet: radios. Scientists still hadn't perfected ground–air voice communications and the radios actually were just a key for sending and receiving Morse code. Only a handful of the crews mastered Morse; most of them merely learned to send the letters ZAA which mean the flight was "on course and on schedule," but this was quite an improvement over the old days of no communications capability at all.

The radio installation proved the undoing of one pilot. He had a girl friend at Charlotte, and quickly learned that the pretty North Carolina community was a good place to cancel a trip. Charlotte was on the Southern Railway's double track from Washington to Atlanta, and the airport was close to several good downtown hotels. Not many passengers complained about canceling in Charlotte and our airman took full advantage of this situation—he'd cancel if there was dirt on the cockpit windshield.

He came in on a Kingbird one day and told Station Manager Howard Weant he had engine trouble and couldn't complete his northbound trip. Weant by now suspected that the pilot's libido and not the engine was involved, but station managers did not argue with captains. Weant was getting ready to make alternate arrangements for the stranded passengers when the radio receiver began clicking away—another Kingbird on a ferry flight was reporting its presence in the vicinity of Spartanburg.

Weant contacted the pilot and asked him to land at Charlotte. Then he broke the news to the first pilot.

"We got a break," he announced—trying valiantly not to smirk. "There's an empty Kingbird being ferried north and we flagged him down. You can take his ship and we won't have to cancel."

"Yeah," the pilot muttered in a tone implying he had just been stabbed in the back.

Charlotte was not Eastern's biggest or busiest station by a long shot, but it earned the somewhat dubious distinction of providing the airline with the first oversale in its history. Oversales today are rarer than Ralph Nader would ever admit yet they do happen; in 1931, when a full passenger load warranted the kind of headlines usually reserved for a declaration of war, an oversale was the impossible suddenly happening.

Weant had just taken over as Charlotte station manager when Frank Kern brought in a Kingbird northbound to New York, with six passengers occupying the six available seats. Nobody got off—they were all bound for New York—and Weant had personally delivered a Charlotte–New York ticket to a Mr. Z. B. Phelps, who was at the airport ready to board.

"I've got troubles," Weant confided to Kern. "Your trip's full and I have a passenger holding space to New York."

Kern was sympathetic but not very helpful. "That's your problem, Howard. All I can do is fly the damned thing. I can't kick anybody off."

It was axiomatic among all young station managers and agents that an airplane always looks better going than coming, but in this case Weant dreaded giving Kern clearance to leave. When the Kingbird took off, Weant confronted the boiling Mr. Phelps.

"I'll refund your thirty-four dollars and seventy-five cents, Mr. Phelps," Weant said unhappily.

"The hell you will. I'll lose money if I'm not in New York tonight."

"I'm sorry, sir, but the ship was full. All I can do is give you back your dough. After all, if the weather had been bad, we would have had to cancel the trip and you wouldn't have been in New York tonight anyway."

The logic of this argument escaped the irate passenger. "If you'll just look outside, young man, you'll see that the weather is not bad. I'll just keep this ticket and see what can be done about it."

It sounded like the beginnings of a lawsuit and the end of Weant's airline career, so Howard did what comes naturally to all twenty-two-year-old station managers—he passed the buck. He telephoned Division Superintendent Harding at Richmond and told him the story.

"I think he may sue," Howard concluded, "and if he does, he could wind up owning Eastern Air Transport after he collects."

Division Superintendent Harding allowed that while Mr.

Phelps was not likely to be awarded that much money, he probably would get enough to cause Clement Keys to climb walls.

"Look, Howard, can you charter a plane there and fly the guy to Richmond? I'll get him to New York from here."

"I'll fly him myself," Weant promised. He scrounged up a Curtiss Robin monoplane from a Charlotte doctor who owned it, for seventy-five dollars—more than double the price of Phelps's ticket. Phelps became a valued and veteran Eastern customer and Weant likes to think that in a sense he originated the concept of guaranteed space that was to become part of Eastern's famed Air-Shuttle thirty years later.

No one was truly happy with the early Condors, Elliott and Dolan included. Johnny Ray was sent to the Curtiss factory in Buffalo where the Conqueror engine was made, to see if he could help the engineers work out the numerous bugs—this was after Keys admitted to Elliott that an expert had urged him not to buy the airplane. Keys might have ignored most technical opinions of an aircraft that Curtiss itself insisted was the world's greatest flying machine, but he couldn't ignore this one: His name was Charles Lindbergh.

Ray came back from Buffalo; Johnny didn't have any degree in aeronautical engineering but he knew his engines like Gray knew his anatomy, and he began rebuilding the Conqueror according to his own ideas of an efficient, reliable airplane power-plant. He couldn't do much about the Condor's flying qualities, which left something to be desired in anything suggesting turbulence and/or icing. Condor's advertisements on the plane claimed it was "as safe as a tethered balloon," which drew the comment from one pilot that "it also flew like one."

One of Johnny's tasks was to modify the Conqueror's carburetors, which were prone to icing—Ray never did achieve complete success in this, nor could he do anything about another pilot complaint: The landing lights were mounted in the nose, and in any kind of haze, snow, rain, fog, or blowing-dust conditions the beams reflected back into the cockpit and were virtually useless. (The Condor's deficiencies in this respect led to the general practice of installing landing lights in the wings of later transports; the first DC-2 models were the only exception.)

But while the Condor left several things to be desired technically, it was a passenger's dream. The Model 18 and the slightly earlier Fokker F-32 were the first "wide-bodied" airliners introduced to the American public. EAT's Condors had carpeting, reading lights, curtains, a galley with an ice box, detachable tables, and one section of the cabin was designated as a "card room" with facing seats on either side of a coffee table. The final and most welcome touch was a flight attendant—female.

United had introduced women cabin attendants in the spring of 1930 and it didn't take the rest of the industry long to realize that United had stumbled on the greatest air travel promotion gimmick since Kitty Hawk. Eastern's hierarchy was divided on its desirability: Elliott straddled the fence, Dolan—speaking for virtually every pilot—was adamantly opposed, Keys leaned to the affirmative, and Doe's mind was made up for him by his wife. She was a forceful and positive woman, from all accounts, and she not only convinced her husband to hire flight attendants but went out and recruited one of the first candidates herself—Mildred Johnson, the debutante daughter of a friend.

Eastern's own records, however, list Marion Cook of Meadville, Pennsylvania, as the first hiree; Miss Johnson was among the initial seven and so was a Mildred Aldrin whose nephew Buzz would someday walk on the moon. There was considerable debate over what to call the girls—among the suggested job titles were airess, airette, airaide, courierette, and hostess. Eastern finally followed United's practice of designating them as stewardesses. (Some early company records refer to hostesses but apparently this designation was temporary.)

There were some ten thousand applicants and only twenty-two were chosen, all but the original seven ending up with ground jobs until flight positions opened up. The qualifications were stiff—a lot stiffer than the training, which was nonexistent. Eastern accepted only unmarried women under twenty-eight; the height limit was five feet four inches and weight 123 pounds. An applicant had to be either a registered nurse or a college graduate—a prerequisite which few of them understood once they went to work on the menial tasks assigned to flight attendants in the 1930s.

Cook got an inkling of what to expect the day she was hired.

"There's only one thing you have to know," she was told. "Treat the passengers as if the airplane was your living room."

"That's all?"

"Of course that's all. What the hell more do you need?"

"Well, I assumed there'd be some training and . . ."

"You've just finished your training, Miss Cook."

That wasn't quite true—the girls had on-the-job training. The basic tasks were simple. They handed out gum, cotton for the ears, and newspapers. Also ammonia capsules when they were needed, which was only too frequently inasmuch as fainting ran a fairly close second to airsickness. Meal service in the initial days of Condor service was limited to coffee and doughnuts, spurned by most passengers because they were afraid of getting airsick.

Even refueling became an occasional stewardess duty. If a station was shorthanded, the girls would become part of a bucket brigade—fuel trucks were not always available. They helped load and unload baggage, punched tickets, cleaned cabins (which could look like a postinvasion beachhead after a particularly rough flight), and always carried railroad timetables for those who decided air travel was for the birds and wanted to transfer to a train at the next stop. A stewardess never knew when she might even be asked to help push a plane into a hangar after a trip.

The Condors carried a large clock, air-speed indicator, and altimeter in the cabin for the information of passengers who might be interested in knowing that at one P.M., they were cruising at 130 miles an hour at the astronomical altitude of 3,000 feet. The stewardesses had to set the clock before every trip and adjust the altimeter to the proper barometric pressure. For all this they were paid $125 a month and their flying time was limited to not more than forty hours a month—a schedule which today would send every flight attendant straight to his or her union with a major grievance.

The pilots, or most of them, resented them at first but gradually resentment turned to grudging respect and even affection. They discovered, for example, that the girls were blessed with a collective sense of humor and this was a major virtue in a world where crisis and adversity were a way of life.

Dolan was a tough but fair boss; promoted to operations manager in 1931, he assumed full responsibility for hiring new pilots for Eastern's growing fleet and generally he picked well. One of them was John Halliburton, who rose to become vice president of flight operations. Another was Howard Stark, one of the best instrument pilots who ever flew—Dolan hired him, in fact, when it became apparent that the government was going to require instrument ratings for all airline captains; he gave Stark the job of preparing Eastern's pilots for that inevitable day.

Stark had flown for three other carriers before joining Eastern: NAT, Colonial, and NYRBA (New York, Rio and Buenos Aires Airlines), which Pan American absorbed. A booklet he wrote on instrument flying was the first ever published on the subject, but for all his seriousness he actually was a deadpan humorist like so many of his brethren.

Halliburton was in Atlanta one night when Stark was getting ready to climb into a northbound Mailwing. They exchanged pleasantries, punctuated by Stark's usual discourse on the importance of instrument flight.

"You cannot call yourself an airline pilot until you have been instrument-rated, John," he lectured sternly. "Well, I guess I'd better be leaving."

Stark started his engine, taxied to the south side of Candler, where he poised the Mailwing on the edge of the red clay runway, and then suddenly waddled back to the ramp. Halliburton and agent Dempsey Brown ran over to see what was wrong. Stark poked his head out of the cockpit.

"Engine troubles, Howard?" Brown shouted.

Stark shook his head.

"Which way is Richmond?" he yelled back.

The puzzled Brown pointed to the northeast. Stark nodded and taxied out again.

Expert airman though he was, the one thing Stark could

never master was the Condor's landing idiosyncrasies. Says Halliburton:

"Some of his landings at the old Washington Hoover Airport were so spectacular that whenever he was coming in, the word was passed around and employees would gather on the wooden steps of the little building that served as our terminal to watch the show. On one occasion the Condor stopped with its nose about five feet from the blast fence. It had to be pulled back by a tractor before it could proceed to the ramp."

Quite unexpectedly Stark suddenly began making perfect landings even with the Model 18 and lost his usual audience. Halliburton met him in operations one day and complimented him on the landing he had just seen him make.

"You've sure improved, Howard," Halliburton observed. "Frankly, I don't understand how you did it."

"Simple," Stark explained. "I've been letting my copilot make all the landings."

The flight crews were called pilot and copilot in those days; eventually Dolan changed these designations to captain and first officer, following Pan Am's nautical terminology, as did most of the carriers. Along with the revised nomenclature went new uniforms—at Elliott's insistence—which featured navy-blue trousers and jackets plus visored caps. The pilots hated them, the general consensus being that the outfits closely resembled the latest fashions for streetcar motormen. Dolan solved this dilemma by adding stripes: two for the captain and one for the first officer. Supposedly this also added dignity along with sartorial splendor but twenty stripes wouldn't have dignified some of the boys.

There was Ervie Ballough, for example, by any standard of measurement a Character worthy of the glorious traditions created by such as Merrill and Banks. Ballough was almost totally bald except for a fringe of gray hair around the lower part of his head, giving him the appearance of a Trappist monk. He was a master at quick repartee, a fine example being the day another pilot ran his hand over Ervie's bald head.

"Ervie," he observed, "this feels just like my wife's fanny."

Ballough placed his own hand on the smooth, glistening dome.

"Well, I'll be damned," he said seriously. "It sure does."

Ervie was one of Eastern's better joke-tellers, a meaningful accolade on an airline thickly populated with this breed. He acted out each story with great embellishment, a keen sense of the dramatic, and realistic dialects—and this skill almost cost him his job. He was waiting for his flight to leave Jacksonville one day and got to telling a barroom story to the ramp personnel at the departing gate.

The joke involved a drunk and Ballough played the inebriate's role to awesome perfection, using his plane's stabilizer as the imaginary bar. Unfortunately he failed to notice that his audience included more than just Eastern employees—the passengers for the flight were standing by the ramp gate, listening to every slurred word. When the flight was called, not one passenger would board. Agent Tom Caldwell had to ask Ervie to come out of the cockpit and convince the frightened customers he was sober.

Ballough had cut his teeth on the Mailwings; an excellent pilot, his chief weakness was a rather vague notion of where he was at any given time. He got away with this failing in the pre-radio days of the Mailwings, but came the day—in 1931—when Eastern finally got two-way radios with voice capability instead of the Morse key. It so happened that Ervie took out the first radio-equipped Kingbird and was briefed carefully on communications protocol: A ground station would contact him, calling his flight number every ninety minutes, at which time he was to give his position.

Orlando was the first station to request position. It took four calls before Ervie would answer, innocently inquiring, "You calling me?"

"Yeah, Ervie. What's your position?"

There was a long pause while Captain Ballough pondered the situation. Finally his answer came in loud and clear.

"Well, right up ahead of me I can see the lake where I landed last year when my Mailwing engine quit and . . ."

It was a matter for debate whether the stewardesses were unhappier with their uniforms than the pilots were with theirs. Reportedly, Mrs. Doe had a fairly large hand in choosing what the girls wore, so any griping was private, particularly after the word got out that the president's wife considered the Eastern uniform a Paris creation compared with United's. It consisted of a ruffled white shirtwaist, a blue silk polka-dot jacket and skirt, and a matching hat—attractive or not, at least it was a departure from the severe look adopted by other airlines whose taste wavered between Florence Nightingale and General Pershing.

And Eastern *was* trying amid the industry's overall growing pains. Polka-dot jackets and two-way radios, rank stripes and instrument ratings—it was a long way from the hit-and-miss airmail days. A big terminal hangar was built at Newark which became EAT's northern terminus serving the New York area, and the points on the route system were multiplying. Atlantic City, Norfolk, Raleigh, Savannah, Greenville, and Florence were among the cities added in 1931—a St. Petersburg–Tampa leg had been created shortly after Keys bought out Pitcairn. By the end of that year Eastern Air Transport had nearly five hundred employees, operated more than forty airplanes over routes totaling 2,876 miles, and carried 24,378 passengers—approximately 23,000 more than in the previous year.

Passenger business was so good, in fact, that the seven-cents-per-mile rate was scrapped in favor of a new tariff—six cents for one-way flights and five cents for a round-trip ticket.

That same year also saw Eastern's first acquisition of another carrier. It purchased New York Airways, a Pan Am subsidiary that had been flying between New York and Atlantic City, giving EAT a triangle route with Philadelphia providing the third leg. Access to Atlantic City, then a booming resort area, was what Eastern wanted; no aircraft were involved and only one New York Airways employee came over to EAT—Max Goodnough, who became station manager at Newark—actually an important post, inasmuch as Newark by 1931 had emerged as the country's biggest and busiest airport.

Those were the days, of course, when any airline passenger was courted and coddled; each was a VIP, for service and courtesy were the sole antidotes to inevitable fear. Pampering was the only way to entice most people into an airplane; speed was a doubtful selling point to anyone worrying whether he'd get there in the first place, and flying itself was considered so dangerous that the majority of life insurance policies were automatically suspended for the duration of any flight.

Eastern, as did most of the bigger airlines, tried just about everything to make air travel more enjoyable. One gimmick was furnishing enroute stock-market reports; Howard Weant recalls that one of his duties was phoning a Charlotte stockbroker for the latest quotations—he would type thirty or forty on a preprinted form and hand them to the stewardess for distribution to passengers aboard a northbound Condor flight each morning.

The station managers literally were jacks-of-all-trades. If they were licensed pilots, they might even have to fill in as copilots in an emergency—as Weant did many times. Gender made no difference; the first station manager at Raleigh when it opened was Mrs. Elmer Myers, whose husband ran the airport. A capable and exceptionally pretty woman, she worked as hard as her male counterparts and was expected to. So were the pilots themselves—they wore many hats, particularly the younger copilots, as the following bulletin indicates:

Operations Department
Service Bulletin No. 26

Oct. 15, 1931

BAGGAGE, RESPONSIBILITY OF

On ships carrying copilots, the copilot will be held responsible for the checking of all baggage on and off the planes. The back of form E.A.T. #27 will be used temporarily.

On ships not carrying copilots, the pilot will check the passengers' baggage on and off and make a report on the back of form E.A.T. #27.

They will also inquire, prior to the time the ship leaves, if a passenger has all his baggage and has it properly tagged.

C. H. Dolan
Operations Manager

Another Dolan memo of that era offered evidence that the Pitcairn peccadillos hadn't quite been eradicated.

SUBJECT: PASSENGER PILOTS LEAVING & APPROACHING FIELDS

Passenger pilots are getting lax once again in their methods of leaving and approaching fields. We have continually warned pilots about "S-ing" and side-slipping and banking at 45 and 90 degrees on their turns and rushing into a field and then remaining on the field for fifteen minutes because they are ahead of schedule.

This is lack of thought and must be corrected.

C. H. Dolan
Operations Manager

In general, however, the flight crews were maturing along with the airline itself. The government's rule that all aircraft commanders (i.e., captains) had to be instrument rated went into effect in 1932, and even the rugged individualists and the mavericks were accepting a more regulated existence. Safety and economics were interlocked—a crash on any carrier affected all, and there was a noticeable and even drastic traffic slump after every accident. This escalation of fear was to be prevalent until the jet age, but at no time was it more damaging than in the early thirties when the airlines, their mail pay diminished markedly, were terribly vulnerable to anything that depressed passenger traffic. The Depression was bad enough without "AIRLINER CRASHES—ALL ABOARD PERISH" headlines.

It was a tribute to the pilots that no airline had a better safety record than Eastern, and the pilots in turn knew who deserved a large share of the credit: Charlie Dolan, a kind of benevolent tyrant who was simultaneously their father confessor and top sergeant, totally impartial whether he praised or punished. It wasn't easy for Dolan, either—inevitably there were economy moves that somehow Dolan prevented from directly affecting safety. Things got so bad at one point that Doe ordered the teletype system removed; the station managers handled dispatch duties via Morse code, with certain times set aside for communications that normally would have gone via teletype.

Along with such measures went general salary cuts; Howard Weant, for example, saw his monthly check drop from $180 to $160 and even the pilots took pay slashes.

Clement Keys had every expectation of living out the Depression-spawned adversities. Compared to other carriers, Eastern Air Transport was relatively healthy. The addition of Atlantic City was a bonanza, for the New Jersey resort city was the biggest tourist mecca in the United States—far more so than Florida at the time. Keys also had going for him the friendship and support of Walter Folger Brown, who openly admired EAT, rode on it frequently, and even more frequently urged further expansion.

In 1931 Brown awarded Eastern its permanent certificate for CAM 25—including mail and passenger rights between New York and Washington, a segment for which Doe had submitted a bid of eighty-nine cents a mile. It was more than three times higher than the twenty-five-cents-a-mile bid by the Ludington Line, incorporated under the name of the New York, Philadelphia and Washington Airway Corporation. That one award was later to ignite a conflagration that destroyed Brown's entire airline structure, prompted a headhunting Senate investigation, cost the job of virtually every major airline president in the country, and caused corporate upheavals cataclysmic in their far-reaching effects.

Ludington was a small carrier that had started out modestly in 1929. Its "angel" was C. T. Ludington, a wealthy Philadelphian who knew little about the aviation business but was smart enough to hire two men who did: Gene Vidal and Paul Collins, both experienced airline people who had worked for Keys at TAT until they earned his displeasure by insisting that passenger traffic deserved a higher priority than mail. After experimenting with a small-scale operation, Vidal and Collins in 1930 began an on-the-hour, every hour (8:00 A.M.–5:00 P.M.) passenger-only service between Philadelphia and Washington using Stinson trimotors with Lockheed Vegas as backup planes. Tickets were sold and passengers picked up at Pennsylvania Railroad stations.

In the first three months Ludington carried some 15,000

passengers and by the end of the year showed a small but significant profit of slightly over $8,000—the first time an airline had
made money without a cent of mail pay. It was only too natural
that Vidal and Collins figured they could make even more with a
mail contract, but Brown personally tossed their low bid aside
for Eastern's larger one. He was to explain later that Ludington
sought only a Philadelphia–Washington mail route, whereas
Eastern offered mail service covering the entire eastern seaboard
—and for Walter Folger Brown, this was compatible with his
concept of a few airlines providing one-carrier service to large
areas rather than a hodgepodge of smaller companies operating
multiple, chopped-up segments.

Failure to win a mail contract eventually proved fatal to
Ludington, for EAT pitted its Condors against the Stinsons and
stepped up its own schedule frequencies. The competition remained heated for two years and Ludington even expanded with
a Philadelphia–Washington–Roanoke–Nashville service. But
even as Ludington fought for its existence and EAT fought for
dominance, events on another front were forging a crisis for
Clement Keys and the empire he had so diligently erected.

The stock market crash had hit Keys and North American
Aviation hard—not in direct losses but in the overall effects of
the market collapse on the general economy. Of all the Keys's
enterprises, only Sperry and Eastern Air Transport were in the
black, and there wasn't enough ebony on their books to dilute
the blood-red figures pouring from the other companies. Keys, a
man of unimpeachable integrity, decided on what seemed to be a
judicious strategy designed to protect North American's financial
stability: He put all the holding company's earnings into his own
investment firm where they were put out on call loans at interest
rates of up to twelve percent. Theoretically it was a wisely conservative move and a profitable one, but it was Keys's own faith
in aviation's future that led to his downfall.

Late in 1931 he decided to go to Europe; like Juan Trippe
of Pan Am, he had visions of a global aviation empire and the
European voyage seems to have been intended as a preliminary
planning expedition. Exactly what he had in mind was never

made clear, for shortly after he arrived in France, he received a cablegram from Thomas Morgan to return immediately. Morgan rode out on the pilot boat and met Keys aboard the *Aquitania*, where he broke the news that spelled ruin for Clement Keys.

In the brief time he had been in Europe, Keys's associates at his investment company had diverted millions of dollars into the still-plunging stock market. The first diversion was more than $1 million from North American's funds, and this was followed by futile transfusions from those of Keys's clients. The stocks they had tried to bolster with the diverted money kept sinking and it took Keys little time to add up what all this had cost him: Even if he liquidated everything he owned into cash, he was a million dollars short.

Keys had no choice. He moved swiftly to contact all the sources he knew in the financial world, and to save North American he let them exact the grim price—he traded his resignation for a promise from a syndicate of five banks to replace most of the misappropriated funds; loans he got from close friends made up the rest. In time he was to repay every cent, not only to those friends but to the syndicate that had forced him out. He even had to pawn his wife's jewels to help him start a comeback, but he redeemed these, too. He was seventy-six years old when he died in 1952, wealthy again but an almost obscure figure in the annals of an airline industry he helped create.

The Eastern Air Transport he left behind him was still headed by Doe, with Tom Morgan wielding the real power. Although the parent company showed signs of demoralization, the airline remained viable and apparently untouched by all the corporate convulsions stemming from the Keys ouster. The year 1932 was one of consolidation and improvement rather than expansion; Johnny Ray's engine shop at Atlanta, no longer a drafty room with a dirt floor, provided one example of progress —EAT was averaging nearly two million miles between engine failures, a record in an industry where engines had to be inspected after every twenty-five hours of operation because malfunctions were so frequent.

And that was par for the course in 1932; for both Eastern

and the industry as a whole, it was something of another transition period, the final pages of one chapter in aviation history containing overtones of what might be written next. Just around the corner was an aeronautical revolution involving aircraft, government regulatory influence, and airline management itself —the last of these taking on the proportions of a major upheaval. And to understand the significance of the forthcoming new era, one must look back on 1932, the year that marked the end of an old era.

As of January 1, 1933, there were some 450 transport planes flying, but eighty percent of them were single-engine aircraft; the average seating capacity per plane in this mighty fleet was slightly under six. The maximum distance any single plane could fly before a refueling stop was only 300 miles. Manning these transports were 507 captains but only 147 copilots—indicative of the relatively few planes in service big enough to hold two pilots, let alone warrant them.

The insurance statistics showed that a pilot's chances for getting killed on the job were roughly 300 times greater than they are today, which explains why they wouldn't be able to purchase life insurance for another five years. One must smile wryly at the airline advertisements of 1932, one of them boasting that the pilots on this particular airline averaged 4,500 hours of flight time—an impressive claim in 1932, but one which might be compared with an experience yardstick of 1979: Few airlines will even look at an application from a pilot with less than 2,000 hours logged.

The industry was composed of twenty-four airlines offering nearly 700 daily flights, an impressive total until it is placed alongside that of 1979 when Eastern alone operated 1,600 daily flights and the industry all told flew some 13,000. And the twenty-four carriers was a somewhat misleading figure, inasmuch as only four—United, American, TWA, and Eastern—were carrying almost ninety percent of the traffic. Some of the names operating in 1932 are still familiar, such as Braniff, Pan American, Northwest, and Western, but the others have become historical footnotes: Bowen . . . Gilpin . . . Gorst . . . Hanford . . . Hunter

. . . Inter City . . . Ludington . . . Mamer . . . Martz . . . National
Parks . . . Pennsylvania . . . Portland . . . Rapid Air . . . Trans-
american . . . United States Airways . . . Varney Speed Lines . . .
Wyoming Air Service.

For most of them, meeting a payroll was more difficult than
flying airplanes. In 1932 no fewer than seven carriers resorted to
putting card advertisements on their aircraft cabin walls, similar
to those carried on streetcars and buses. The practice underlined
how desperate they were for revenue, but pressure from the rest
of the airlines forced them to abandon the cards in less than a
year—it was too undignified, argued the protestors; airliners
should not look like streetcars.

Some anachronisms remained from the old days—such as
pilots carrying pistols to protect the mail and special forms au-
thorizing passengers to obtain railroad tickets in the event of a
flight being grounded or canceled. This happened often enough
for the airlines to be one of the railroads' best customers, although Eastern ran counter to this common industry occurrence
—EAT in 1932 boasted an operating efficiency performance of
93.2 percent, not a bad record considering its varied route structure and the comparatively large number of cities served.

Its safety record was far above average, too; 1932 happened to be one of the safest air travel years on record, but this
fact has to be greeted with raised eyebrows because what was a
good record then would be considered rightful cause for a full-
scale Congressional investigation today. There were 108 accidents, 16 of them involving fatalities—in terms of deaths per 100
million passenger-miles flown, the rate was a horrendous 14.96;
by contrast, the fatality rate per 100 million passenger miles
flown has stayed below 1 since the jet age began.

Accidents were inevitable considering the tools the pilots
worked with—or rather, the lack of tools. In 1932 there were no
such aids as reversible propellers, efficient deicers, extinguishing
systems for in-flight engine fires (although some later-model
Condors had a crude, not-too-successful device for putting out a
midair engine blaze), Instrument Landing Systems for poor-
weather landings, high-intensity runway approach lights, or

static testing to determine airframe structural strength—a common method for ascertaining ability to withstand stress was to push one's foot against a piece of tubing to see if it would hold. Static testing—the deliberate destruction of key structural components—would not be adopted until Boeing and Douglas introduced the 247 and DC-2 respectively. Research in this phase of safety progress had been stepped up after the death of Notre Dame's Knute Rockne on March 31, 1931, when the Fokker F-10 in which he was a passenger lost a wing in what apparently was moderate turbulence.

Of course, things *were* getting safer in 1932, and the Condor's low landing speed was considered one of the outstanding steps forward—particularly when it was recalled that a prominent aviation official of the day had issued a warning that it was dangerous to land any airplane faster than sixty miles an hour. And even sixty was considered fast, inasmuch as the average cruising speed of 1932 transports was only 109 miles per hour; no one could foresee three decades ahead when jets were landing routinely and safely at 120 miles per hour.

By the end of the year the government had installed beacon lights every eleven miles along 18,000 miles of airways and the airlines themselves had a radio station about every 300 miles. Eastern alone had a network of eleven ground stations strategically located along some 3,100 miles. Federal expenditures on the nation's airways system that year amounted to a whopping $7.5 million, a sum which today wouldn't be enough to purchase a single jetliner.

Those aforementioned twenty-four airlines carried a half-million passengers and United, the biggest of them all, justifiably bragged in advertisements that in 1932 it had flown 96,567. Four and a half decades later Eastern's annual passenger total was nudging the 35-million mark, or about 100,000 a day.

Still, for passengers 1932 marked new luxuries and convenience. The big Newark airport was one of several facilities experimenting with restaurant concessions, some airlines put radios in their cabins so passengers could hear the Yankees whipping the Chicago Cubs in the World Series, a few planes were testing a newfangled device called a cabin public-address system, and one carrier actually beamed a television picture to a plane in flight. Eastern, along with the rest of the industry, changed its short-lived no-smoking policy after an industry nationwide poll of passengers showed that the majority wanted to smoke aboard planes—cigarettes only, however.

Eastern's new T-32 Condor models scheduled for delivery in 1933 were ordered with sleeping berths—and this feature pointed to what Walter Folger Brown had been urging on the airline for a long time: development of passenger service to Florida on a much broader scale than ever before. This was one of the reasons both Morgan and Doe proceeded cautiously on further route expansion; the only new route added in 1932 was a 172-mile leg between Columbia, South Carolina, and Augusta, Georgia, that provided through-plane service from Camden, New Jersey, to the Georgia city.

But even as Eastern consolidated its gains, history came close to repeating itself. In strategy strikingly similar to the maneuvering that had wrested NAT from Clement Keys and North American, United Aircraft suddenly moved to gain control of Eastern Air Transport. Brokers acting for the nation's largest air carrier quietly bought sufficient shares of North American to take over EAT. The attempt was nothing but a counterattack against Postmaster General Brown's plan to create as much competition for United as possible, and it would have succeeded if Brown hadn't reacted like an infuriated bull. He declared United's stock acquisition illegal and ordered the big conglomerate to sell every share it had purchased.

Normally, North American would have bought back the stock itself, but the colossus Keys had forged out of brains, daring, and determination was crumbling toward bankruptcy. There was only one taker—and it was a reluctant one: giant General Motors.

GM had wedged into the airline industry on a modest scale in 1931 when it saved the Brown-truncated Western Air Express from oblivion by acquiring 60,000 shares of WAE stock for the bargain basement price of $900,000. The purchase gave General

Motors not only control of the airline but also of Fokker Aircraft —owned largely by a group of WAE stockholders. Most GM officials, unimpressed by tiny Western's performance and a sorry Fokker sales record since the Rockne crash, were lukewarm toward getting further involved in the stormy, politics-ridden world of commercial aviation—so totally dominated by Walter Brown. It took one man to interest them in taking over North American—and at the time he not only wasn't working for GM, he was jobless.

His name was Edward Vernon Rickenbacker.

CHAPTER FOUR

THE RICKENBACKER ERA BEGINS

In all the historical accounts written about Eastern, there is a curious gap between 1930 and 1934—almost as if the airline didn't exist in that period.

There is voluminous material on the Pitcairn days and even more starting with Captain Eddie Rickenbacker's assuming command. But the interim years between Pitcairn and Rickenbacker have not only been neglected but almost forgotten—and unfairly so. For without the loyalty and dedication of Eastern's employees in the pre-Rickenbacker years, there might not have been any airline for the Captain to take over.

John Halliburton, Eastern's vice president of flight operations until he retired recently, wrote the author during the course of researching this book—commenting on the attitude of employees in the early thirties.

"Back in those days," he observed, "few outside the industry felt the airlines would survive, and most people felt it was a fad stemming from the Lindbergh hysteria. But the employees felt differently and were determined that the company would succeed."

Continued Halliburton:

Most of them spent much of their spare time at the airport to keep in touch with what was happening and to see if they could be of help. Many times I have seen mechanics who had already put in an eight-hour day continue until midnight or beyond if a mechanical difficulty was threatening a delay the next day. I was a licensed mechanic as well as a pilot and often filled in in the former capacity if Maintenance was shorthanded or extra help was needed. This was not unusual; similar things were done by all.

Frequently I would run a check on the plane I was to take out later. And all of this was long before anyone heard of overtime pay. We looked upon it as part of our responsibility to the company.

Without this attitude on the part of employees, Eastern might not have survived the crucial first years. . . .

It is important to emphasize that selfless spirit before beginning the incredible saga of the Rickenbacker years. The Eastern he was to dominate to such an extent that the airline and the man became a single entity numbered among its chief assets that intangible yet so very real sense of loyalty to which Halliburton referred. It is only too easy to assume, as so many have done, that Rickenbacker actually founded Eastern. He didn't; he merely inherited a legacy founded on faith in aviation and built up by the devotion of some five hundred men and women. But it also must be admitted that this remarkable man did more than inherit. What he took over, he branded with his own special kind of personality and courage.

Which was only to be expected, because Captain Eddie was a very special kind of person.

It is not true that Eddie Rickenbacker inspired Horatio Alger's stories of Poor-Boys-Who-Made-Good, Rising-From-Poverty-Through-Diligence-and-Hard-Work.

But it should have been true.

For no man in American history personified the American Dream better than Rickenbacker; his name belongs with those of the Edisons and the Fords and all the others who turned the Horatio Alger fable into fact. In later years, when it was fashion-

able to jeer at Rickenbacker's patriotism, flag-waving, and jin-
goism, or to lambast him as a political and economic reactionary,
his critics ignored the ethics and mores that molded his character. His background was strictly late nineteenth and early twentieth century, a time when parlaying hard work into opportunity
was as natural as breathing—and almost as essential. Imbedded
in his genes was allegiance to God, family, and country, perhaps
old-fashioned virtues today but philosophical cornerstones at the
turn of the century, the sturdy pilings upon which the edifice of a
man's life was built.

He was born in 1890, the third child of William and Elizabeth Basler Rickenbacher, who had emigrated from Switzerland;
his father was of German stock, his mother had French blood—
one account claims the family name originally was Reichen-
bacher and another has it as Richenbacher, but Rickenbacker
himself always used the "Rickenbacher" spelling before he
changed it, during World War I, apparently to rid it of any
German connotation.

His parents gave him no middle name—he added the "Vernon" later, choosing it from a list he had drawn up mostly because, he explained, it sounded classy. That word was not
applicable to his boyhood; in 1979 terminology, Eddie Rickenbacker belonged in the juvenile delinquent category. He smoked
cigarettes in the first grade, was ringleader of a gang of young
toughs who specialized in stealing coal from railroad yards, was
constantly getting into fistfights, and quit school at the age of
twelve.

Rickenbacker's father was a construction contractor who
built with his own hands the house in which the family lived for
years, a small frame dwelling in Columbus, Ohio, with two
rooms on the ground floor and two smaller, unheated rooms in
the attic. There was no running water, no electricity, and the
only heat came from the kitchen stove—this was home for Eddie,
his four brothers, and three sisters.

Rickenbacker's autobiography, published in 1967 (Prentice-
Hall), contained some poignant memories of those tough yet
tender early years. It is an admittedly self-serving account with

definite overtones of "I never made a mistake," but reading it provides ample clues to the source of his conservatism, respect for simple virtues, and canyon-deep sense of responsibility. When he writes of selling newspapers for a dollar a week, selling eggs from the family hens for seven cents a dozen, and working as a stonecutter for a dollar a week, one can see when the seeds were planted and the mold carved.

Rickenbacker's father died when Eddie was only fourteen. He had been an affectionate yet stern parent—the children never knew whether to expect a pat or a razor strap. Both William and Elizabeth spoke halting English, and German was the language used regularly at home—the result being that Eddie in his youth had a decidedly Teutonic accent that led to such school nicknames as "Dutchy" and "Kraut." From his father came ambition and stubbornness; from his mother an abiding faith in religion. Theirs was a closeknit family, achieving a togetherness that served as a rampart against adversity—even the death of William Rickenbacher in an accident at a construction site.

There was no life insurance—the father's only legacy was the roof he had put over their heads. Eddie, a scrawny, somewhat belligerent little boy with big dreams, went to work at night in a glassmaking factory for $3.50 a week. This was only one of his jobs; he also rose early every morning and went out to peddle eggs and the milk from goats he had raised himself. He would nap a few hours in the afternoon and then trudge off to the glass works for a twelve-hour trick six nights a week.

He was willing to take on anything that paid a little more money; he left the glass factory to labor in a foundry, then a brewery, a shoe factory, and a monument works where one of his tasks was to carve a tombstone for his father's grave. His sixth job in the three years following his father's death was in a combination machine shop and garage, and it was here that he began his love affair with automobiles and the internal combustion engine.

Rickenbacker was only sixteen when he met Lee Frayer, manager of the Frayer-Miller Automobile Company and a top racing driver. Frayer liked the skinny, feisty, but personable youngster and took him to Garden City, Long Island, to ride with him in the Vanderbilt Cup Race as his mechanic. Eddie worked for Frayer over the next six years, learning much about automobile manufacturing and marketing, and accumulating enough experience to strike out on his own as a full-time race driver. The big prize—first place at Indianapolis—always escaped him (he never finished higher than tenth) but he won plenty of other honors, including a new world's speed record of 134 miles an hour, set in a Blitzen-Benz at Daytona Beach.

Rickenbacker was making $40,000 a year when the U.S. declared war on Germany, and it was typical of him that he didn't wait to be drafted—he volunteered, was sworn in as a sergeant (thanks to his racing fame he was a headline figure), and went overseas as a staff driver attached to General Pershing's headquarters. At this stage of his life he came to a crossroads: He was assigned to Colonel Billy Mitchell as the flier's personal driver and pestered him incessantly for a transfer to aviation.

"How the hell old are you, Eddie?" Mitchell once asked with justified suspicion—Rickenbacker actually was on the fringe of turning twenty-seven and was almost two years over the age limit for Army Air Service flight training.

"Twenty-five," was the prompt, straight-faced reply.

Eddie always suspected Mitchell knew he was lying, but doubts notwithstanding, the colonel had him transferred. Rickenbacker got another break when the doctor who gave him his flight physical turned out to be an auto-racing buff and put down the false age. Eddie soloed after seventeen days of training, was commissioned a second lieutenant, and joined the 94th Aero Squadron. He was never to forget what Billy Mitchell had done for him—eighteen years later he was among the handful of relatives and friends listening to a bugler play taps over the freshly dug grave of air power's greatest advocate.

The 94th was composed largely of college graduates who at first took a dim view of the rather crude, unpolished, and uneducated newcomer—Rickenbacker's formal education had stopped short of high school and all he had managed in the years he had worked under Frayer was an International Correspondence Course in engineering and drafting. To these unspeakable shortcomings was added the fact that when Eddie joined the squadron, he looked more like a mechanic than a commissioned officer wearing fighter-pilot wings. It was unusual to find him without oil stains on his face and grease under his fingernails, and his personality could be abrasive.

Rickenbacker, of course, knew engines better than most of the squadron's mechanics, and he was never one to indulge in false modesty. He was quick to give advice even when it wasn't asked, and in general he was a lemon on an orange tree; Reed Chambers, who became his best friend, once described him as "a tough, uneducated bastard who threw his weight around the wrong way." But Chambers also became aware of an unsuspected quality in Rickenbacker—he was a natural leader, not to mention that this pea-green rookie also turned out to be the squadron's best all-around combat pilot.

The 94th's commander was Captain James Norman Hall, later to win literary fame as coauthor of *Mutiny on the Bounty*. He, too, recognized Rickenbacker as a diamond in the rough who was rapidly being polished—Eddie even began wearing pink britches, a tailored nonregulation tunic, and boots you could see your face in.

More to the point than this appearance was his perfection of flying techniques. He was not really a skilled pilot but his combat effectiveness was deadly. He checked out his own guns before every patrol. He developed a technique of cruising just above stall speed to save fuel and be assured of maximum engine performance when needed. His years on the race track had given him judgment of distance and speed that few pilots possessed, and he made sure that he and not the enemy had the advantage of position and altitude before he attacked like a striking hawk. No one ever knew how good a marksman he was, because he held his fire until some of his squadron mates were convinced he was going to ram an opponent instead of using his machine guns.

He gradually won not only the respect but the affection of the 94th—in sufficient proportions to be named squadron com-

mander after Hall was shot down behind enemy lines and captured. It was Captain Rickenbacker now, and he celebrated the
first day of his promotion by taking off at dawn and wading into a
formation of seven German planes single-handed. He shot down
two, a feat that earned him the Congressional Medal of Honor.
By war's end, he had been credited with twenty-two enemy
planes and four observation balloons—the best record of any
American fighter pilot in World War I. He never asked any of his
men to do anything he wasn't willing to do himself; he flew up to
seven hours a day and had two Spads assigned to him, the mechanics doing hasty repairs and patching on one while he was
flying a mission in the other. Under Rickenbacker the 94th became the most famous U.S. squadron in the war and its hat-in-
the-ring insignia (an Uncle Sam striped top hat in the middle of
an oval) the most widely recognized symbol.

Rickenbacker entertained no illusions about his hero status.
"When I was in racing," he said wryly, "I learned that you can't
set stock in public adoration or your press clippings. I heard
crowds of a hundred thousand screaming my name but a week
later they couldn't remember who I was. You're a hero today
and a bum tomorrow—hero to zero."

He had no intention of going from hero to zero—not this
self-made man with his infectious, ingratiating toothy grin, his
king-sized ambition, and his determination to be a leader and not
a follower. The Armistice didn't bring disillusionment to Eddie
Rickenbacker as it did to so many of his fellow airmen; to him,
peacetime meant opportunity for anyone with the guts and
brains to answer the knock on the door. Except that being Eddie
Rickenbacker, he didn't wait for the knock.

He showed no interest in postwar aviation development as a
career, although he was to make many speeches about the importance of aviation and air power. No one could blame him, for it
definitely was no prime labor market. As of Armistice Day the
Army Air Service had almost 3,000 trained pilots and more than
15,000 skilled airplane mechanics. The only real aviation job
outlet for this manpower pool was the U.S. Post Office Department's airmail service, which at its height operated less than 100

airplanes—as the only game in town, it offered woefully limited employment chances for veterans wanting to get into civil aviation.

The alternative was barnstorming, and Rickenbacker wanted no part of this precarious existence—precarious not only in terms of risking one's life but also in making any kind of a decent living. He knew his first taste of financial security had been as a race driver and it was to automobiles that he eventually turned when he took off his uniform for the last time.

As a genuine war hero—only the legendary Sergeant York won as much public adoration—he came home to enticing offers and deals, all of which he knew were predicated on some fast-buck artist trying to cash in on the Rickenbacker name. What with his background of childhood deprivations that came close to poverty, the temptations must have been enormous, but he possessed willpower along with a sense of integrity and good taste. He said no to countless enticements—such as endorsements of cigarettes, chewing gum, clothing, and numerous other products. Carl Laemmle, head of Universal Studios, offered him a certified check for $100,000 to appear in a movie. When Rickenbacker refused, Laemmle sent his persuasive young assistant to follow the Captain around the country; he booked adjoining compartments on trains and in hotels and became such a pesky shadow that Rickenbacker finally threatened to sue for invasion of privacy. It was one of the few times in his highly successful life that Irving Thalberg had to admit defeat.

At the time Rickenbacker was almost broke; he had sent all his wartime savings to his mother and, for all the public adulation, nobody had offered him what he considered a legitimate job with a future. His only income came from a forty-day combined Liberty Bond and lecture tour (for a fee of $1,000 per appearance) and before he undertook this venture he had to take elocution lessons and hire a ghost writer—a young newspaperman named Damon Runyon.

One published account claims that Rickenbacker hired the tutor and the writer after an embarrassing experience at a mammoth testimonial dinner held in his honor at the old Waldorf-Astoria Hotel. According to this story the captain got a bad case of stage fright and delivered an almost incoherent, mumbling response loaded with grammatical errors. This was not the way Eddie described the occasion; he admitted he was extremely nervous, but saved the day when he took the jeweled rings that had been given him and presented them to his mother, who was in the audience. He remembered the spontaneous gesture prompting a standing ovation but he also was to admit that his speaking technique left much to be desired.

He had known Runyon during the latter's stint as a war correspondent, and it was Damon who recruited the elocution instructor—a voice teacher for the Metropolitan Opera. Between the two of them they managed to smooth out the rough edges and make him an effective speaker—Rickenbacker's own forceful personality and bluntness did the rest. The subject of his nightly, coast-to-coast sermon was aviation and air power—in that respect he was a Billy Mitchell disciple. His first appearance was in Boston before an audience of 6,000, and Rickenbacker later confessed to being "scared to death"—until the governor of Massachusetts introduced him with a delivery that made Eddie's sound like William Jennings Bryan at his oratorical finest. He told that story to the governor a few years later, when the governor was President of the United States, and wrote, "It was one of the few times I saw Silent Cal laugh."

As the tour progressed, he learned to think fast on his feet —something he was to demand from his airline subordinates. One introductory speaker rambled on for thirty minutes, in essence delivering the same speech Rickenbacker was going to make; he had to hastily improvise most of his own remarks. To forestall any repeat of this disaster he would plant a few friends in the audience; when the speaker was showing signs of long-windedness, he would uncross his legs—that was the prearranged signal for his friends to start chanting, "We want Rick!"

It was while he was undergoing the pressures of the tour that he discovered he was subject to a terrifying affliction: sleep-walking. He was to have recurrences for years until one night he fell off a twenty-five-foot balcony. That was the last incident; he claimed he cured himself through "mental discipline."

Rickenbacker thought he had found his future when the

tour ended and he made contact with an automotive engineer and former racing driver named Harry Cunningham. He was an old friend of Rick's and like the Captain, he, too, had dreams of designing and producing his own automobile. They enlisted the talents of three other veteran automobile men in their project: Walter Flanders, a production expert who had helped design the Ford assembly line; Barney Everitt, who had been instrumental in designing what eventually became the Studebaker: and William Metzger, another veteran Studebaker executive nearing retirement.

The venture was incorporated under the name of the Rickenbacker Motor Company, with Everitt as president; contrary to legend, Captain Eddie never headed the company that bore his name. He was vice president and director of sales—and being Rickenbacker, he refused to accept what could have been an empty title, with his partners merely trading on his name. While the company was still being organized, he got a job as California distributor for the Sheridan, a new four-cylinder car built by General Motors. He sold Sheridans for two years, and his record was not lost on GM executives—by the time the Rickenbacker was ready for introduction, Captain Eddie had established more than fifty Sheridan dealerships in California, and he also had established a reputation for being a tough boss who wasn't averse to chewing out a dealer for wild trades or poor service.

Even while he was working for General Motors, he was secretly road-testing the Rickenbacker prototype. It was a six-cylinder in the middle-price bracket, between $1,500 and $2,000; Rickenbacker and his partners wanted no part of competing against Henry Ford's Model-T nor the higher-priced market dominated by Cadillac and Packard. For its day, it was a revolutionary vehicle, probably ahead of its time. The Rickenbacker's outstanding feature would be its four-wheel brakes, the first American car to be so equipped with what was to become a taken-for-granted item (Duesenberg introduced the first in 1920); the brake concept was Eddie's major design contribution, although it was not adopted until the third year of production.

Thirteen thousand persons bought some $5 million worth of

stock in the new company, Rickenbacker and his four partners retaining about twenty-five percent. Three models went on display for the first time at the 1922 New York Automobile Show —a $1,485 touring car, a coupe priced at $1,885, and the top of the line: a $1,995 four-door sedan. "A Car Worthy of Its Name" was the company's slogan and the name was magic, for the orders began piling up at the Detroit factory.

When he was a GM distributor, EVR had leased a Bellanca cabin plane in which he toured California, setting up and then visiting his dealerships. He did the same for the Rickenbacker, flying around the country in a German Junkers piloted by Eddie Stinson; he did it for the sake of saving time, but it also was a way to promote aviation. Such promotion was the major role he played when he invested in Reed Chambers's Florida Airways; Chambers had bought stock in the Rickenbacker Motor Company and Captain Eddie was not one to forget a favor by a friend. Even when the Rickenbacker began to have sales problems of alarming proportions, Rick never let Chambers down— he'd fly anyplace to put in a plug for Florida Airways in particular and commercial aviation in general.

It was at this time that everyone began calling him "Captain Eddie." In truth, he could have been called "Major Eddie"—that was the rank he held at the time of his military discharge. But Rickenbacker, who could be disturbingly egotistic, was also refreshingly modest; this was one of the many contradictions that made up his character. He felt he had earned the rank of captain but that promotion to major had been a last-minute gesture of gratitude on the Army's part and as such, undeserved.

In September 1922 he married Adelaide Frost Durant, former wife of millionaire racing driver Cliff Durant; they had met in California before the war, and bumped into each other at a New York party while the motorcar company was in the organization process. Eventually they were to adopt two boys, David Edward and William Frost; curiously, Rickenbacker's autobiography never mentioned that they were adopted, EVR simply writing that "we have been blessed with two boys," giving their birthdays with the implication that he and Adelaide were their natural parents. The omission is strange, for Eddie was extremely proud of them and from all accounts was a loving, albeit stern father.

It was after his marriage that another woman came into his life, in a completely professional sense, and not even Adelaide was to give him more devotion or personal loyalty. Her name was Margaret Shepherd; she was a Canadian who came to the U.S. seeking secretarial employment and answered an ad in a Detroit newspaper for "girl with secretarial experience to work with automobile manufacturing firm." Rickenbacker was in Europe attending an auto show and Miss Shepherd was interviewed by an office manager at the Rickenbacker Motor Car Company. Diminutive, assertive, and personable, she made a good impression and he hired her, assigning her to advertising manager Roy Pelletier on a temporary basis.

Pelletier knew the ad was aimed at recruiting a personal secretary for Rickenbacker but he was so taken with her efficiency that he tried to talk her into staying with him—admitting to her that she was supposed to go to work for the Captain when he returned. Margaret sought the advice of a friend at an employment agency who told her, "Wait until Captain Rickenbacker gets back." She did—and thereby changed the course of her own life. She was to stay with EVR just three months short of fifty years.

With Captain Eddie she achieved the ultimate in a boss-secretary relationship: He trusted her implicitly, and she never betrayed that trust. At first it was "Miss Shepherd," then "Margaret," and finally "Sheppy"—the nickname the Rickenbacker boys gave her. In years to come she was Sheppy to everyone and some people at Eastern never knew her real first name. Only once did she come close to leaving and that was shortly after she became his secretary. She began getting other job offers—some of them extremely attractive—and Sheppy was a girl of the spade-calling variety.

"Do you think I'm going to be satisfactory?" she asked EVR pointedly.

She still remembers that he seldom answered a question

directly; his usual response was to ask a question himself. Thus:

"I'll ask *you* a question. Why do you want to know?"

"Because I'm being offered other jobs at more money."

He looked at her from under those bushy awnings that passed for eyebrows. "I can't promise you a raise, young lady— not in three months, six months, or even a year. But if you continue as you are, you'll have no regrets."

She never talked of quitting again. Not even when she discovered that galley slaves had shorter work days than either Captain Eddie or the people who worked for him. He always came in at eight A.M. sharp and expected her there, too. (Later, when he moved to New York, he would issue profane imprecations against the Gothamites' work habits, which called for never getting to one's desk earlier than nine A.M.)

He was traveling almost all the time and this necessitated working on most Sundays, the only chance he had to catch up on correspondence and other matters that had piled up during his absence. When he was in Detroit he liked to have his desk completely clear by ten A.M., giving him the rest of the day to meet with people or handle unexpected business. Sheppy geared her own schedule to his, and this meant spending many a weekend in the second-floor office of the old Rickenbacker factory building in the Polish section of Detroit. This was when he would dictate his letters and write his many speeches—he was in constant demand for personal appearances, and even when someone else composed a talk for him, it always bore the stamp of his editing and revisions.

At first Adelaide would travel with him, anxious to help him in any way she could. But in just one respect they were totally incompatible—he liked to get up early and she liked to sleep late, so gradually she stopped accompanying him. Sheppy describes her as a "marvelous person—very attractive, talented, popular though opinionated." Sheppy was almost as close to Adelaide as she was to the Captain, becoming her confidante and friend, but EVR always took priority—particularly in times of great stress when he tried so hard not to show concern that she so easily sensed.

Stress became a way of life as the motorcar company ran into increasing difficulties. The truth was that the Rickenbacker was too good an automobile, and when the 1924 models came out with four-wheel brakes, the competition set out to deliberately destroy it. There was nothing surreptitious about the anti-Rickenbacker campaign, either; Studebaker went so far as to run full-page advertisements in hundreds of newspapers, attacking four-wheel brakes as inherently dangerous. General Motors, Ford, or Chrysler didn't get that tough, but in addition to the direct assault by Studebaker there were plenty of rival dealers and salesmen who were providing potential customers with such tidbits as "if you apply your brakes on a curve, the Rickenbacker will flip over" and "I know a Rickenbacker driver who jammed on his brakes and went right through the windshield."

All this was malarkey, of course; privately every automobile manufacturer had four-wheel brake systems on his drawing boards and Buick would feature them the year after the Rickenbacker went out of production. But the Studebaker-led propaganda unquestionably affected sales, and this was compounded by the 1925 recession. When sales slumped, Rickenbacker dealers began folding and this was a death sentence for the company itself. Then Walter Flanders was killed in an accident, an irreplaceable loss at a crucial time. Captain Eddie borrowed money to help shore up faltering dealers but it was a lost cause. The Rickenbacker Motor Company went into bankruptcy in 1927: EVR himself was a quarter of a million dollars in debt and his friends pleaded with him to also declare bankruptcy.

"I owe the money and I'll pay it back," he growled.

He did, although on the day he spoke those brave words he was flat broke, unemployed, and with assets that consisted mainly of a boxful of war medals and a loyal wife. Sheppy remembers his last day with the Rickenbacker Motor Company; he had come from a creditors' meeting, walked into his rather sparsely furnished office, and calmly dictated a letter of resignation. From the expression on his face he might have been dictating a letter to some dealer; only Sheppy knew how torn up he was.

At age thirty-five he apparently was a failure, although Eddie Rickenbacker always said that "failure is the greatest word in the English language."

"Here in America," he was to write in his autobiography, "failure is not the end of the world. If you have the determination, you can come back from failure and succeed."

One of the few men who bothered to call him after his resignation was Frank Blair, president of the Union Guardian Trust Company of Detroit. Blair said he wanted to see him and Captain Eddie went over to the bank.

"You're a young man," Blair told him, "and knowing you as I do, I'm sure you'll find a new line of endeavor. When you find it, and if you need financing, come in and see me."

Rickenbacker was to take him at his word only a few weeks later. He was tipped off that the Indianapolis Speedway was up for sale; he went in to see Blair and came out with a financing agreement: The bank underwrote a bond issue to raise the necessary $700,000, EVR keeping fifty-one percent of the common stock as a bonus and the bank retaining the rest as payment for marketing the bonds. On November 1, 1927, Captain Eddie took over the Speedway as its president—he was to stay in that capacity until after World War II when he sold his interest for exactly what he had paid for it, writing off the considerable sum he had put in for improvement over the years. After the first year the presidency had become more of a nominal position anyway —subsequent to 1928 Rickenbacker devoted only a couple of weeks a year to the Speedway's operation and this left him plenty of opportunity to take on other jobs.

His chief goal was to pay off his debts down to the last penny, and he even started a comic strip called *Ace Drummond*, for which he wrote the continuity based partially on his own wartime experiences. It was a modest success, syndicated to some 135 newspapers at the height of its popularity. He also wrote a book of World War memoirs, *Fighting the Flying Circus*, which sold well (it was reissued in 1965).

Neither writing project occupied enough of his time nor earned enough money to satisfy him. His relations with General

Motors had always been good, even when the Rickenbacker car was a GM competitor, and in 1928 he accepted an offer to go with GM, first with the Cadillac Division and then as sales manager for the new La Salle. Yet he also kept up his drumbeat of speech-making, usually preaching the gospel of civil aviation— for even then he was quietly urging General Motors to get into commercial aviation. The message reached the receptive ears of big Bill Knudsen, then president of Chevrolet, who privately suggested to GM chief Alfred P. Sloan that Rickenbacker might have something.

The outcome was his appointment as head of Fokker Aircraft, acquired by GM when it bought control of Western Air Express. The new position brought him to New York, where Fokker's headquarters were located, and somewhat to his surprise he found he liked the big city—if not its work-starting hours. While with Fokker, he got GM further involved in aviation by negotiating the purchase of the Pioneer Instrument Company, Sperry's chief rival in that field; Pioneer eventually became Bendix Aviation.

Rickenbacker was happy with General Motors but he was still, in the spirit so representative of a fighter pilot, something of a maverick. When the 1929 stock-market crash sent the economy reeling, GM decided it would be cheaper to move Fokker to Baltimore. Rickenbacker had brought his family from Detroit, he enjoyed living in what was then the pleasant suburb of Bronxville, and he balked. It was no contest; on March 31, 1932, he resigned from General Motors and was once more unemployed.

He stayed unemployed for less than a month, accepting an invitation from W. Averell Harriman and Robert Lehman to join American Airways, major air carrier property of the big holding company known as the Aviation Corporation, or AVCO. There is some confusion as to EVR's exact title with American; several historians listed him as vice president of public relations, but Rickenbacker's autobiography says he joined American as simply a vice president, adding that one of his major duties was to visit Washington frequently "to develop and maintain governmental goodwill." In today's airline lexicon, this would have made him a vice president of government or public affairs, not public relations, and Captain Eddie seems to have had virtually nothing to do with handling publicity for American Airways.

It didn't make much difference, because he found himself devoting little time to whatever duties Harriman and Lehman had in mind for him. It was shortly after he joined American that he came up with an idea to merge the airline with Eastern Air Transport, with AVCO buying out terminally-ill North American. Such a deal made complete sense to Rickenbacker; he told Harriman and Lehman that American, primarily an east–west carrier, did its best business in the spring, summer, and fall, whereas Eastern, operating north–south, carried its most profitable traffic in the winter.

"Eastern flies to Florida," Captain Eddie pointed out.

"From what I've heard," Harriman commented dryly, "it doesn't carry many passengers there."

"But it will," Rickenbacker predicted. "Someday Florida is going to be the greatest winter air travel market in the country. Who the hell wants to spend thirty hours getting there on a train when they can fly from New York to Miami in a third that time? Look, if we merge American and Eastern we'd have a year-round peak. In warm weather we can concentrate most of our equipment on American's routes. In the winter we can transfer equipment over to Eastern's Florida trips."

He was at his persuasive best, but Harriman and Lehman didn't agree with him solely because of his arguments—they had another motive for going along with the North American purchase. They themselves were facing a struggle for control within AVCO, the challenge coming from Erret Lobban Cord, who like Rickenbacker had come up the hard way. Cord got his start running a small car-wash business in Los Angeles—EVR had known him then—and from there on to automobile manufacturing with the famed Auburn and the front-wheel-drive Cord. He also founded Century Airlines, an all-passenger operation serving St. Louis, Chicago, Detroit, and Cleveland with fourteen-passenger Stinson trimotors and airport transportation furnished by sixteen Auburn limousines. It was successful enough for Cord to start a subsidiary, Century Pacific Lines, Limited, between San Francisco and San Diego via intermediate points, at fares below those of the railroads.

Cord's *modus operandi*, however, didn't endear him to the Commerce Department's air safety officials, who considered his cut-rate operations potentially dangerous. They were instrumental in blocking his admittedly low bid for a mail contract, and he was further hampered by a pilots' strike called by the newly formed Air Line Pilots Association (ALPA). Cord figured he couldn't hack it without a mail contract and sold both his airlines to AVCO; the price was 140,000 shares of American Airways stock.

AVCO had invited a wolf into the fold. As a major stockholder, Cord immediately began making waves. Lamotte Cohu, an able airline man, was in the process of reorganizing the sprawling, haphazard American Airways system, regarded as one of the most inefficient in the industry (it was operating a half-dozen types of aircraft and its pilots didn't even wear a standard uniform), but Cord didn't wait for Cohu's broom to do much sweeping—he wanted his own broom.

Harriman and Lehman, the financial brains behind AVCO, saw in Rickenbacker's merger proposal a chance to block Cord's increasing influence. Their strategy was simple; AVCO had some $30 million in cash reserves, but instead of using this money they planned to issue an additional two million shares of AVCO stock. This would not only provide them with the funds necessary to buy out North American, but would reduce the voting power of Cord's stock.

E.L., as Rickenbacker and everyone else called him, was infuriated. He threatened to take the issue of American's alleged mismanagement to the public, and added the ominous hint that maybe the whole airline industry deserved to have some dirty linen washed in the open—a view which Captain Eddie himself privately thought justified. But Rickenbacker recoiled at the idea of a public exposé, fearing it might lead to a congressional investigation loaded with political overtones; there were too many rumors about Walter Brown's manipulations, about too much Wall Street influence throughout the industry. And Ricken-

backer also knew that Brown's days were numbered in a discred-
ited administration about to be voted out of office by a
Depression-disillusioned country.

He tried valiantly to serve as a peacemaker between the
Cord and Harriman/Lehman/Cohu factions, but E.L. wanted
blood, not peace. He waded into an all-out proxy battle based on
his opposition to AVCO acquiring North American, a move
which he declared would be reckless and ruinous. Rickenbacker
had to choose sides, and as an American vice president, he cast
his lot with Harriman and Lehman—knowing, he said later, that
Cord was going to win. Between them, Harriman and Lehman
held only seven percent of AVCO's outstanding stock and Cord
had been buying up every share he could get his hands on.

When the firing stopped, Erret Lobban Cord was in control
of American Airways. His first move was to fire the old board of
directors and put in his own board. His second was to oust Cohu
as president, naming in his place Lester Seymour, who thus
earned the dubious distinction of becoming the only airline president so petrified of flying that he always took the train. His third
was to accept Rickenbacker's resignation—interestingly enough,
with reluctance.

Captain Eddie went in to see him immediately after the
proxy fight and went right to the point.

"Well, E.L., when do you want it?"

"Want what, Eddie?"

"My resignation."

Cord looked at him—perhaps remembering Rickenbacker's
reputation for total honesty, his war-hero status, and their past
friendship.

"Eddie, I don't want it."

EVR smiled. "You've got to take it, E.L., if you want to
retain any esprit de corps in your personnel. You know and they
know I was on the other side. If you keep me on, your people
would lose confidence in you."

Cord sighed. "Well, I see your point. But I'd appreciate it if
you'd stay around for a couple of months to finish up what
you've been doing."

EVR agreed. There is reason to believe that Cord, a tough

old rooster who respected toughness in other men, had the notion of talking Rickenbacker into staying with American, and this raises the fascinating possibility that had things turned out that way, the story might have been Captain Eddie of American rather than Captain Eddie of Eastern; certainly Cord would have considered him as a logical replacement for an ineffectual Seymour. But Cord's next major decision was to end any chance of Rickenbacker remaining—he moved the airline's headquarters from New York to Chicago and that was EVR's excuse to leave.

He walked out of his office at American for the last time on February 29, 1933, only four days before the man with whom he was to feud so bitterly came into another office for the first time—at 1600 Pennsylvania Avenue, otherwise known as the White House.

As usual, he didn't stay out of work for very long. While the contestants in the AVCO proxy battle were jockeying for votes, Rickenbacker had been talking to an old friend at General Motors—tiny but sharp and powerful Ernest R. Breech, at the time the assistant treasurer at GM but a man with more influence than his title suggested. In addition to his GM post he already was a director of TWA, a North American company, and he had been instrumental in reorganizing TWA internally and putting it in the black for the first time in its history.

Eddie and Adelaide were guests at the Breech home in Larchmont, New York, on Christmas Day 1932, an occasion on which Rickenbacker managed to get Breech off in a corner for a private discussion. The subject was North American in general and Eastern Air Transport in particular, and the Captain urged Breech to engineer a GM takeover of North American. Breech reminded him that AVCO seemed to have North American in its corporate hip pocket, but Rickenbacker shook his head.

"Cord's going to win that proxy fight," he informed Breech, "and E.L. wants no part of North American. He hung his hat on the deal being a bad one and that's the reason he started the proxy business. General Motors could pick up North American for a song—and believe me, Ernie, Eastern's the real plum. It has potential that's never been realized."

Breech was more than interested; he was excited, and wasted no time in going to GM's hierarchy with the Rickenbacker proposal. There was a temporary roadblock in the person of Colonel Edward Deeds, a major stockholder in United Aircraft who had also—through United Aircraft—purchased 330,000 shares of North American. Deeds was enough of a leading financial figure to warrant his getting an appointment with Alfred P. Sloan of GM, and he informed Sloan that United in effect had already gained control of North American.

"I have enough North American stock to prevent your taking over," he advised Sloan. "General Motors has no business in air transport and I suggest you call off your Mr. Breech."

Sloan said cautiously he would think it over. He conferred with Breech, who defended the deal Rickenbacker had urged, and Sloan told him to go ahead. When Postmaster General Brown, in one of his last official acts, declared United's planned acquisition of North American illegal, that was all Ernie Breech needed.

The GM-North American merger negotiations, nevertheless, were rocky and approached such acrimony that Rickenbacker lost hope. At one crucial moment he sighed to Breech that "you guys are never going to agree—I'm gonna go take a leak."

While he was in the sanctuary of the men's room, Breech broke the impasse by suggesting a compromise—a split of North American "at market price on the basis of net asset value of the remaining companies." This financial verbiage simply meant that General Motors would acquire control of only part of the North American empire. Sperry and Ford Instruments would be spun off and listed separately on the New York Stock Exchange; GM would get Eastern Air Transport plus the comparatively small interests North American held in Pan American Airways and the Douglas Aircraft Company.

When Rickenbacker returned, the deal had been unofficially consummated. EVR didn't object, although he confided to

Breech he had misgivings about letting Sperry go—for an agreed-on price of two dollars a share.

"That's like giving it away," Captain Eddie complained. "Sperry Gyroscope has almost as good potential as Eastern itself."

"You can't have everything, Eddie," Breech soothed. "We had to give up something to get Eastern Air Transport and Sperry was the price."

Breech's reward was his being named president of the new North American subsidiary; Rickenbacker, at Breech's insistence, became vice president, although not immediately. Control of Eastern Air Transport passed over to General Motors on February 28, 1933—the same day Rickenbacker left American —and not until the following June did Captain Eddie officially join North American as general overseer of its aviation activities. Tom Doe remained as EAT's president, with Harold Elliott as vice president and general manager, and Charlie Dolan as vice president of operations. Rickenbacker's role was that of a consultant, and he made little or no effort to interfere with the airline's operations even though he saw much that worried or displeased him.

There is no doubt that he would have taken over Eastern sooner or later anyway—he stood high in Breech's estimation and it has always puzzled some why Breech didn't let him start running the airline from the moment it became part of the GM family. Quite possibly Breech wanted him to gain some additional experience in civil aviation before entrusting Eastern's destiny to him; Rickenbacker's brief stint at Fokker hadn't included much exposure to airline problems, and, as far as CM was concerned, his background was more automotive than aeronautical.

Whatever plans Breech had for him, they were speeded up when the seeds that Walter Folger Brown had planted at his unforgotten Spoils Conference suddenly sprouted into a scandal. For Eastern, 1933 had been a rather uneventful year, the top event being the inauguration of Condor sleeper service between New York and Atlanta—an innovation that proved so popular, Eastern had to increase the two berths originally offered to six berths. Simultaneously, Eastern began one-day, thirteen-hour Condor service between New York and Miami, upping its Condor fleet to fourteen aircraft. The other major development was the acquisition of the Ludington Line, up for grabs after its bid to win a mail contract failed. The price was a bargain $260,000 which included Ludington's seven Stinsons—it would have been even lower except for the fact that Brown had let Eastern know he wouldn't approve a figure that was embarrassingly low. Actually, it *was* embarrassingly low but Ludington was about bankrupt and had no bargaining power.

Yet it was Eastern's takeover that ignited the Spoils Conference scandal. And the man who lit the match was a young reporter from the Hearst papers named Fulton Lewis. He had happened to be lunching with a minor officer of Ludington who mentioned quite casually that Ludington was in trouble because it hadn't been able to win a New York–Washington mail contract.

"We thought we had it cinched with a bid of twenty-five cents a mile," he added.

Lewis sympathized but thought little about it until he read a Post Office Department release announcing the award of a New York–Philadelphia–Washington mail contract to Eastern Air Transport for eighty-nine cents a mile. He remembered his conversation with the Ludington man and smelled a distinctly non-kosher odor.

He got the personal approval of William Randolph Hearst to dig further, devoting full time to the behind-the-scenes activities of Walter Brown and the Spoils Conference. His report was sent straight to Hearst, who recognized it as political dynamite and refused to approve its publication—thereby leaving Lewis with a bag full of apparent skullduggery and no place to air the contents.

The reporter found one man interested in the whole affair: Senator Hugo Black of Alabama, chairman of a special Senate committee established to investigate ocean mail contracts. Black, an ambitious small-town lawyer with inbred prejudice against so-called Big Business, saw in the Lewis report a chance to reap some headlines—the ocean mail probe had been buried amid the want ads in most newspapers. He expanded the scope of the committee's original investigation to encompass the alleged illegal awarding of airmail contracts.

These were the early quick-trigger days of the New Deal and someone like ex-PMG Walter Brown was a fat, inviting target. The special committee became the Black Committee, thanks to Washington's propensity for giving unwieldy committee titles the name of whoever happened to be chairman, and there was no shortage of candidates for the honor of scuttling Brown's reputation—virtually every small-airline operator whom the postmaster general had knifed ran to Black with numerous allegations of under-the-table dealings. Black figuratively drooled, for all this fitted perfectly his own preconceived image of giant corporate sharks feeding on helpless small competitors.

The roof blew off even before the Black Committee started its hearings in March of 1934. Black had met with President Roosevelt late in January, pouring into FDR's willing ears a tale of chicanery and back-alley intrigue—most of it based on the material Lewis had supplied. The senator urged FDR to cancel all mail contracts immediately because, he said, they had been obtained by fraud and conspiracy. And Black had done his homework; he pointed out to the President that the postal laws gave the postmaster general punitive powers if conspiracy to obtain the contracts was apparent.

Roosevelt was impressed by Black's fervor and intensity, even though he knew little about the awarding of mail contracts. And statesman though he undoubtedly was, the politician in him saw a chance to embarrass even further the already humiliated Hoover administration. He promised to think it over for a few days and Black, encouraged by this response, turned his files over to U.S. Solicitor General Carl Crowley.

Crowley, in turn, condensed the data, allegations, and still-incomplete evidence into a 100-page report which he presented to Postmaster General James Farley. Big Jim thumbed through the verbose copy and growled, "I can't wade through all this—just tell me about it."

The Solicitor General orally condensed the written condensation which, stripped of all his gobbledegook, simply recommended cancellation of all airmail contracts. Farley was shaken by the implications—he agreed to set up a meeting for the following afternoon with the President, Black, Crowley, and himself, but he also warned Crowley he had misgivings. He never read the voluminous material in Black's files nor Crowley's lengthy summary, and neither did FDR. Roosevelt apparently took the word of both Black and Crowley as gospel and decided to cancel the contracts as they had recommended.

Farley tried to talk him out of it, at least for the time being. He urged FDR to delay cancellation until the Post Office Department could invite new bids for all routes; he not only was overruled but became the scapegoat for the tragic mess that followed. Farley bluntly informed the President that he had doubts whether the Army was capable of flying the mail without special training. Roosevelt's answer was to summon Brigadier General Benjamin Foulois to the White House. There the chief of the Army Air Service was asked a direct question: Could the Army start flying the mail in ten days?

Foulois found himself in a terrible position. He had been under constant attack from Billy Mitchell, who had been claiming that in its current state of preparedness the Air Service couldn't have licked a South American banana republic, or words to that effect. For Foulois to tell FDR the Army wasn't ready to fly the mail would have added at least some credence to Mitchell's charges. He also may have underestimated the difficulties of airmail operations in winter weather—Foulois met with the President the afternoon of February 9. Whatever the reasons, his reply to Roosevelt's question was an immediate and confident "Yes, sir," thus setting the stage for one of the most dramatic and tragic chapters in aviation history. If Foulois had hesitated even a few seconds, that history might have been changed.

At four o'clock that same afternoon a grim and unhappy Jim Farley announced at a White House press conference the cancellation of all airmail contracts effective at midnight February 19. Three days after Farley broke this shocker, FDR himself announced that the Army Air Service would start flying the mail on February 20—adding that he had the assurance of General Foulois that the Army was prepared to do the job.

It was not prepared. The young military pilots were not well trained in instrument flying (some of the Army planes first used weren't even equipped with the navigation aids airline pilots took for granted), they had virtually no experience in night operations, most of them didn't know the mail routes to which they were assigned, and few had ever been exposed to the horrendous weather conditions which hit the nation almost simultaneously with the start of their mail flights.

Charles Lindbergh was just one of many prominent men in aviation who wired or wrote the President that he was making a terrible mistake. Captain Eddie put his protest onto the front pages of every major newspaper in the United States—he met with reporters in his office at the General Motors Building on Broadway (they had been moved there from the Sperry Building after GM took over North American). It was a foggy, rain-sodden day and Rickenbacker looked out his window, waving at the dreary view as he spoke.

"The thing that bothers me is what is going to happen to these young Army pilots on a day like this. Their ships are not equipped with blind-flying instruments and their training, while excellent for military duty, is not adapted for flying the airmail. Either they are going to pile up ships all the way across the continent, or they are not going to be able to fly the mail on schedule."

Rickenbacker knew what he was talking about. As of the day the Army took over the airmail, there were only three pilots in the entire Air Service who had logged as much as 5,000 hours. A parsimonious, shortsighted Congress had emasculated military appropriations to such an extent that the Army's airmen were restricted to approximately 175 hours a year—almost every minute of it in good weather. The average airline pilot flew that much in three months, at night and in all kinds of weather.

Most of the Army's equipment consisted of open-cockpit aircraft. And to compound all these weaknesses, Foulois could

THE RICKENBACKER ERA BEGINS

assign only 200 officers and less than 400 enlisted men to do a job that had kept some 7,000 airline pilots and technicians busy. The nation was shocked at what followed, but it didn't surprise any airline man, Captain Eddie included.

The industry staged one last act of defiance—a flying symbol of proof that regardless of the airlines' past mistakes, commercial aviation still belonged in the hands of private enterprise. In Santa Monica, California, Donald Douglas was in the final test stages of a new airliner, the DC-1—prototype of a twin-engine transport already ordered by TWA, American, and Eastern as the DC-2. It had been designed largely to TWA's specifications, with American and Eastern contributing some of the developmental funds.

TWA vice president Jack Frye called Rickenbacker from his office in Kansas City the moment he heard about the mail cancellation order. "Rick," he said without preamble, "we've got to do something that will show the public we're better qualified to fly the mail than the Army. Maybe there have been some past deals, but I see by the papers they're also criticizing our pilots, operational procedures, and our equipment. Let's show the bastards they don't know what they're talking about."

"I couldn't agree with you more," Rickenbacker said. "What the hell do you have in mind?"

"We were gonna try for a transcontinental speed record in March—as a publicity gimmick. Let's fly the damned thing the day before the Army takes over. Burbank to Newark. You were going with me in March, anyway. We'll do it a few weeks earlier, and we'll carry the last load of mail."

"You've got a deal," Rickenbacker snapped. "When do you want me on the west coast?"

"We'll have to arrive in Newark before midnight of the nineteenth. I'm figuring on a flight of less than fifteen hours so we'll have to leave Burbank accordingly. Get yourself out there before the eighteenth, the earlier the better."

"How about press coverage?"

"We'll need every inch of space we can get. Round up some newspapermen we can trust and bring 'em with you."

Rickenbacker arrived in Los Angeles with a small journalistic contingent on February 17. At a press conference he and Frye announced that takeoff would be at nine P.M. the following night—revealing at the time that meteorologists were predicting a blizzard would strike Newark only twenty minutes after their scheduled arrival time.

"Hadn't you better leave Burbank earlier?" a reporter asked.

"The purpose of this flight is to demonstrate the efficiency of a privately-run air transportation system," Captain Eddie said. "I want the American people to know that air transport has progressed to the point at which we can call our own shots. We'll leave on schedule."

Actually, they left even later than planned, not earlier—the trim, sleek DC-1 left the ground at ten P.M. Burbank time, delayed by the loading of the unexpectedly heavy mail shipment. Frye, a former TWA line captain, occupied the left seat and Rickenbacker served as his copilot; he already had made the headlines hours before they left—at a press breakfast that morning.

Just as they had sat down, someone brought in a copy of the *Los Angeles Times* and showed Rickenbacker the black headlines: Three Army pilots had been killed flying to their assigned airmail stations. Two had died when their plane hit a mountain in Utah and the third crashed trying to land his plane in a heavy fog in Idaho. Rickenbacker's hawklike face flushed with anger.

"That's legalized murder!" he blurted.

"Jesus, Eddie," one reporter said, "can we quote you?"

"You're damned right you can quote me," the Captain said tersely.

The "legalized murder" line preceded the DC-1 across the country, but even before Frye and Rickenbacker took off, Captain Eddie was involved in another donnybrook. NBC had asked him to deliver a fifteen-minute speech prior to the flight, and still burning over the death of the Army fliers, he had asked an old friend, Harry Chandler, publisher of the *Times*, to assign his best editorial writer to help him compose his remarks. He enlisted a writer from the *Herald-Examiner* to assist, too, and among the three of them they turned out fifteen minutes of the most blistering attack on the White House cancellation order yet made.

Just before Rickenbacker left for the Burbank airport, he was advised that NBC would cut him off the air if his remarks were too controversial. EVR was so mad he tore up the speech and no record of it exists. He calmed down enough to go through with a brief extemporaneous talk, toned down considerably but still containing barbs at the Roosevelt administration that would have to have been printed on asbestos. It was the start of a long EVR-FDR feud that was never resolved, Rickenbacker earning a place in the president's affections similar to those FDR felt toward Lindbergh.

Certainly the president couldn't ignore what Frye and Rickenbacker accomplished in the way of publicity that stormy night. The new DC-1 flashed across the country in thirteen hours and four minutes, setting a transcontinental speed record for transport-type aircraft. But thrilling a feat though it was, it couldn't outrace the course of events that was to remold the airline industry.

The Army's gallant try was doomed from the start, as the deaths of ten pilots demonstrated. In truth, it was not as bad as some historians have painted; of the ten who died, only four perished while actually flying the mail. Rickenbacker's "legalized murder" crack was an impulsive bit of hyperbole, understandable but not entirely justifiable. The passage of time has created a kind of opaqueness, exaggerating our memory of the past into an image of planes "dropping out of the sky like acorns," as one writer so colorfully but inaccurately put it.

More to the point is a judgment of how efficiently the Army flew the mail, and this is where the politicians who made the decision must equally be faulted. The undermanned, inadequately equipped military force trying to perform a civilian job could operate only 16,000 miles of airmail routes compared to the 27,000 the airlines had served. It cost the government $2.20 to fly every pound of mail that the airlines had been carrying for less than sixty cents. To its everlasting credit, the Army showed marked improvement as it gained experience—its last fatal accident was March 31 and from that date until June 1, 1934, when the airmail routes were turned back to the airlines, its safety record was spotless.

It was also to FDR's lasting credit that he tacitly admitted he had made a mistake. The Army had been flying the mail for slightly over a month when Roosevelt gave Farley a green light to invite new bids for temporary airmail contracts—emphasizing that the awards would be good only for three months, plus two additional three-month extensions at the discretion of the postmaster general. Not even the airlines themselves could argue against the temporary conditions—the Black Committee had started its hearings and it was obvious that major regulatory legislation was inevitable.

Before the carriers resumed airmail service, they had taken cancellation on their respective chins. Eastern was as hard hit as any of them, forced to reduce its daily route mileage from 11,000 to less than 6,000 with only seven cities receiving regular service—Newark, Washington, Richmond, Greensboro, Atlanta, Jacksonville, and Miami. Cities like Philadelphia, Baltimore, Charlotte, Greenville, Florence, Charleston, Savannah, Vero Beach, Macon, and Daytona Beach became flag stops. Howard Weant, for example, was the only employee left on the payroll at Charlotte. The stewardess department was eliminated and the total payroll dropped from 534 to 287 in just one month, but even with all these economy moves the airline was losing a quarter of a million dollars a month—a sum which just about equaled what Eastern had been getting in mail pay.

As far as sensational revelations were concerned, the Black Committee laid one large egg—it produced a lot of fireworks but no solid evidence that Walter Folger Brown or any airline official had been technically guilty of anything. All the hearings accomplished was to show that Brown, in his zeal to obtain air-transportation efficiency, had unfairly favored large operators over small ones; he had carried his airways master plan to the point where the three giant aviation holding companies—United Aircraft, AVCO, and North American/General Motors—wound up holding twenty-four of the twenty-seven government airmail contracts.

In the climate of the recent Depression, with millions of average Americans still embittered by the loss of savings in failed banks and crumbled stocks, it was only too easy to make a scapegoat out of Walter Folger Brown and the aviation barons to whom he had been so generous.

And out of this climate came the Air Mail Act of 1934, which turned America's civil aviation world upside down. It required the separation of airlines from all aircraft manufacturing companies, reopened all airline routes to competitive bidding, and banned any air carrier executive who had attended the Spoils Conference from holding office in his respective airline. To the industry the act spelled total chaos, but it was the much maligned Jim Farley who came to the rescue.

The administration came under strong pressure from smaller carriers hungry for the routes flown by the big boys. Farley placated them by getting Congress to insert a provision into the act forbidding any airline which had been represented at the Spoils Conference to bid for new route authorization. Taken at face value it would have meant demolition of the air transportation system, but Farley wanted only to ease the pressure for punitive measures against the large carriers.

Privately he advised them that his provision was simply a face-saving device. All an affected airline had to do, he suggested, was reorganize so it would no longer bear the name it held at the time of the Spoils Conference. Thus Eastern Air Transport now became Eastern Air Lines, American Airways changed to American Airlines, United Aircraft & Transport shifted to United Air Lines, and Western Air Express organized a dummy operating company called General Air Lines in which it held all the stock.

Figuratively speaking, Farley had put them in jail and then handed them the key. But he could do nothing to save the jobs of those airline chiefs suddenly deposed under the terms of the Act. Tom Doe was one of them, and Ernest Breech's choice to succeed him was Ernest Breech. The most tragic figure in all this head-chopping was Pop Hanshue of Western; his crime had been to attend an infamous meeting at which he had been mugged; he was the only major airline president who had tried to block Brown and for this he lost his airline.

Rickenbacker suggested to Breech that he give Hanshue a job at Eastern, and for a brief time Hanshue served as a kind of general manager with virtually no duties and even less authority. Pop was ailing with high blood-pressure and a bad heart and left Eastern after only a few months, during which time he showed little interest or initiative. Nor was it any wonder; during the last six months of that hectic year, Eastern itself was in a kind of limbo; Breech was too busy with a multitude of other General Motors projects to pay much attention to the airline and for a while it seemed to be running itself.

There *was* growth—a new route from Chicago to Atlanta and another between Atlanta and New Orleans. There was exciting new equipment: The first of nine DC-2's EAL had ordered went into service and Rickenbacker himself flew the "Florida Flyer" inaugural from New York to Miami, advertised as the "dawn-to-dusk" flight providing ten-hour service to and from the Florida vacation mecca.

What was lacking, however, was leadership; the airline was a ship without a captain, being run by its crew with no sense of direction or cohesion. Despite the new routes and the award of a new mail contract, EAL was losing money at a frightening pace and Breech had had enough.

Late in December he called in Rickenbacker.

"Eddie, do you want to run the airline?"

"Yeah, but on one condition. I'll tell it to you now and I'll tell it to the board of directors. Eastern's being propped up by government subsidy. I think it can stand on its own two feet. If it continues to live on the taxpayers' money, I don't want the job. Because I'll tell you right here and now, Ernie, I'm going to pledge all my efforts and energies to making it self-sufficient."

On January 1, 1935, Edward Vernon Rickenbacker was named general manager of Eastern Air Lines.

CHAPTER FIVE

THE CAPTAIN
TAKES COMMAND

His first major act was to cancel every pass that Doe had been awarding regularly to various politicians; his second was to fire nineteen station managers.

It was just one manifestation of how he intended to run Eastern Air Lines—putting it briefly, succinctly, and accurately, like a benevolent tyrant. He was many things to many people; he could be generous and ruthless, considerate and arbitrary, amiable and intolerant, but he left no doubt whatsoever that he was running the show. He generated fear and respect, hatred and affection, in equal proportions, and Breech, a strong person himself, gave him a nearly free hand.

Without any question, however, he chafed under the unspoken, unwritten restrictions of his title as general manager of EAL and vice president of North American. Significantly, his autobiography devotes very little space to his first three years at Eastern—so long as General Motors retained control of both North American and the airline subsidiary, he felt he lacked complete authority.

Yet Rickenbacker made substantial progress in those three years, turning Eastern around profitwise; the airline had lost $1.5 million in 1934 but the following year netted a modest $38,000—with "scrupulously honest bookkeeping," he found it necessary to point out. It was not to lose money again for a long, long time. He ordered five more DC-2's, bringing the total Douglas fleet up to fourteen airplanes, and at the same time began to phase out the airline's obsolete equipment. Before 1935 ended, he had sold every Condor, Kingbird, and Stinson along with the gallant old Mailwings. Added to the DC-2 fleet were five Lockheed Electras, a twin-engine, all-metal transport carrying ten passengers—an ideal aircraft for EAL's low-density routes. And on October 16, 1935, the curtain rang down on the airmail era —Captain J. Shelly Charles flew Eastern's lone remaining Pitcairn from Chicago to Atlanta, the last open-cockpit airplane to carry the U.S. mail. The Mailwing veterans like Merrill had no time to shed tears—they were too busy mastering the idiosyncrasies of the DC-2, truly a revolutionary airliner but one possessing a few undesirable characteristics. Its sleek and powerful appearance belied the fact that it was a lot slower than it looked; advertised as a 200-mile-an-hour transport, it needed a brisk tailwind and a shallow dive to achieve such speeds. It had an extremely stiff gear which made every landing an adventure—if a pilot failed to plant the DC-2 firmly on the ground the first time, he had to log the subsequent bounces. It was not only hard to land but even more difficult to taxi. The classic description of this exercise in frustrating futility came from pilot/author Ernest Gann in his *Flying Circus* (Macmillan, 1974):

When taxiing, the braking system in a DC-2 was activated by heaving on a horn-shaped handle protruding from the left side of the instrument panel. By simultaneous use of rudder and handle the desired left or right brake could be applied. Since there was inevitably a lag between motion and effect, the DC-2 was stubbornly determined to chase its own tail on the ground and in cross-winds, sometimes switching ends to the embarrassment of all aboard.

Like its successor, the far more renowned DC-3, the DC-2 also suffered from the tendency of the cockpit windshield to leak. All DC-2 crews, Eastern's included, adopted the practice of wearing raincoats while flying—it was the only way to stay dry in anything vaguely resembling precipitation. Perhaps the most famous in-flight weather report ever transmitted came from a DC-2 pilot who was asked what kind of weather conditions he was encountering.

"Light rain outside, heavy rain inside," he radioed back.

No pilot ever became enamored of the DC-2, in contrast to the love affair most airmen had with the DC-3. Its noisy and inefficient steam heating system, operated by a small boiler in the forward baggage compartment, had to have been designed by an engineer who hated the human race. The earlier models had a landing gear deficiency of such proportions that five of Eastern's first nine DC-2's suffered a gear collapse while taxiing or sitting peacefully on the ground. One of the latter incidents occurred in a hangar at Washington's Hoover Field while Rickenbacker was in the plane. It is said that Donald Douglas didn't need a long-distance telephone in his Santa Monica office to hear Captain Eddie's opinion of the DC-2 uttered 3,000 miles away that day.

No one who ever flew a DC-2 can forget the physical effort required to raise the landing gear. It was a mechanism activated largely by the copilot's biceps working on a hand pump, a task that might have given pause to Tarzan of the Apes. It took a full minute to get the wheels up on a normal day and in cold weather the crews were positive the gear had been lubricated with frozen molasses. Some copilots started working the pump before the wheels left the ground.

Another DC-2 drawback was its lack of an antistatic device, which resulted in frequently inoperative range receivers. Some DC-2 flights got lost because the pilots got nothing but crackling sounds through their earphones; they would have to land at some available airport, often not even on their assigned route, to find out where they were. Douglas put an antistatic loop under the nose of the DC-3 and corrected the problem, but it was a miracle the DC-2 didn't have an accident record worse than it actually compiled.

The other side of the coin, however, was the DC-2's reliability and ruggedness. There is a picture in the Douglas files showing a steamroller being run over the prototype DC-1's wing without popping a rivet. The DC-2 was underpowered and too small, carrying fourteen passengers compared to the DC-3's twenty-one, but its operating costs were the lowest of any transport built up to that time and the record showed it. Thanks to the DC-2 and Rickenbacker's close-to-the-vest operating methods, Eastern in 1935 carried almost twice as many passengers as in '34 and flew nearly three million more revenue passenger miles in a fleet numbering twenty-eight fewer aircraft. And this was accomplished with only a hundred more people on the payroll. The Rickenbacker way of running an airline already had been stamped on what had been a largely demoralized, discouraged group of employees.

Nor was Captain Eddie afraid to spend money if he had to. He approved establishment of a twenty-four-hour meteorological service, moved the main operations base from Atlanta to Miami, set up a new system of twenty-three ground radio stations, and kept the DC-2 in the public's eye by breaking the transcontinental record he had set with Jack Frye. He personally commanded the demonstration flight which covered the Los Angeles–Newark route in twelve hours and three minutes, landing only at Kansas City for refueling.

The press loved him. He was always good copy, easy to see, and the rapport was mutual. Sheppy remembers the time when a reporter wrote a derogatory story about the Rickenbacker Motor Company's troubles that EVR considered unfair and untruthful. He called the newspaperman and every third word was a different form of profanity—"I never heard him talk to anyone like that," she marvels.

Yet when he was through venting his wrath, he added, "I'm sorry I had to talk to you like that but you should have come to me first before you printed all that garbage. You'll always have access to me anytime you want."

He maintained this open-door policy to the press all his life, although he frequently talked to reporters off the record. Only once did a newsman violate such remarks and it was during World War II when he held an off-the-record press conference—the *New York Post* printed verbatim what he had said and Captain Eddie's wrath activated every seismograph east of the Mississippi. The truth was that although he liked newspaper people, he didn't quite trust them; he had a stenographer record every interview and news conference (except for an occasional impromptu session) so he could challenge anything he considered a misquote.

The change in command inevitably had its casualties. Even before Rickenbacker had taken over, Breech had cleaned house—gone not only were Doe but also Harold Elliott and Charlie Dolan. The August 1934 edition of *The Official Aviation Guide* listed such unfamiliar names as Charles W. France, vice president of operations, and George R. Cushing, vice president and general superintendent. L. Edwin Gill, vice president of traffic, was the only holdover from the Doe regime.

But Rickenbacker was not the type to be satisfied with key aides chosen by someone else—and that included Breech as well as Doe. Early in 1935 he cleaned house—not with a broom but a bulldozer. He dispensed with the services of Cushing and Gill, took away France's title as vice president, demoting him to simple "operations manager," and hired as his second-in-command an able and experienced airline executive, Paul Brattain of TWA. He had been a consultant engineer in Washington for several aircraft manufacturers, served briefly with Western Air Express, and then gone to TWA first as assistant to Jack Frye and later as a vice president.

Rickenbacker named him Eastern's assistant general manager and general traffic manager. Incredible as it may seem, Brattain came over to Eastern sans his vice presidential title and he was not the only top EAL official who lacked that status. Not until 1938 did Captain Eddie have a vice president on the airline's roster of officials.

The Rickenbacker axe also swung in the direction of the

stewardesses—EVR simply refused to hire back the girls who had been furloughed when the airmail contracts were canceled. As a temporary economy move he assigned cabin service to the copilots—a task which they welcomed with all the alacrity they would have displayed toward an engine fire—and it took another year before Captain Eddie relented to the point of hiring forty male flight attendants. He announced this move by explaining that men were better equipped to anticipate the needs of passengers and were not only superior in providing service but had the physical strength to help with such chores as baggage loading and unloading. His final and most telling argument was that Eastern spent one thousand dollars training each stewardess, only to have her quit in six months to get married.

The first steward uniform issued in 1936 consisted of a white double-breasted jacket with red piping, dark-blue trousers, blue tie, white-and-blue cap, and the words "flight steward" embroidered on the jacket's breast pocket. Rickenbacker thought they looked great but his chauvinistic policy left Eastern the only major domestic airline in the U.S. which didn't have stewardesses. At one pilots' meeting, he was asked why.

"Because," Captain Eddie roared, "you bastards are making enough dough to buy your own pussy!"

For years Eastern's aircraft interiors were a combination of cream white and an almost bilious green, forming a color scheme that psychologists claimed would tend to increase the chances of air sickness if not actually induce it. But in the Captain's mind cream and green were restful colors and no one could convince him otherwise.

"The Captain was bigger than life itself," a veteran employee observes, "but so were his blind spots."

Slowly but surely his grip on the corporate control yoke tightened as he began to form the team that was to help him run the airline for more than two decades. Persuasive and personable when he had to be, he was not by a long shot the worst recruiter in the industry. One man he enlisted at this time was an engineer named Charles Froesch, whom EVR had met a few years before when he was running Fokker Aircraft. One thing Rickenbacker had noted with misgivings was a discrepancy between airplanes sold versus spare parts sold—Fokker had peddled $11 million worth of aircraft the year before Captain Eddie took over, but sales of spare parts amounted to less than $70,000.

He asked Fokker to assign one of its engineers to work with him on marketing of spares, and Froesch was the man picked, under duress.

"I'm an engineer," he protested in his soft voice slightly tinged with a Teutonic accent. "I've had no sales or service experience—I've spent my whole life in design."

"I don't give a damn," Rickenbacker told him. "What I'd like you to do is visit all Fokker operators, see what their problems are, and maybe we can sell 'em some spares. The first thing you do is go over to Cadillac for two weeks and see how they do it."

Froesch did a good enough job for EVR to tag him as someone to watch. When General Motors sold Fokker in 1935 and the plant was moved out to the West Coast, Froesch confided to the captain that he didn't want to go.

"Fine," Captain Eddie said. "Come over to Eastern with me."

It was Froesch that talked Rickenbacker into disposing of what he called "a junk fleet"—the Condors, Kingbirds, Stinsons, and Mailwings. It was Froesch who recommended purchase of the five Lockheed Electras purely as an interim airplane to operate until the DC-3's were ready. EVR trusted his judgment as much as he did that of any man who ever worked for him— many years later, when Rickenbacker wanted to buy the British-built, prop-jet Viscount "so bad he could taste it," as one contemporary recalls, it was Froesch who argued him out of the purchase pointing out that the plane couldn't fly nonstop between New York and Miami. Froesch was to have a major hand in Eastern's aircraft purchases right through the Boeing 727, which he helped design.

Another 1936 enlistee was Beverly Griffith, whom Rick had known from his prewar racing days when Bev was a movie cameraman. He was to become a legendary and much beloved figure in Eastern's history, but he was close to having already achieved the legendary category when EVR hired him as the airline's director of public relations. Griffith was the first man to shoot a newsreel film from an airplane, photographing General Pershing's campaign against Pancho Villa in 1917. Until he joined EAL, Bev had spent his adult life in the motion picture industry and at one time had been general manager of both Universal and Fox, jobs that had taken him to Cuba, Britain, Mexico, Spain, Japan, and China.

He had just returned from China when he visited Rickenbacker in New York.

"Captain," he confessed, "I've had all of China I can take. How about my going to work for you?"

"I don't have anything open right now, Bev," Rickenbacker said, "but I'll keep you in mind. Come back and see me in a few days."

The next day Eastern's PR director resigned and EVR summoned Griffith.

"You're our new director of public relations," he informed Bev.

"My God, I don't know a damned thing about public relations."

"That's all you've been doing since you were a cameraman," Rickenbacker assured him. "You'll do just fine."

Griffith was the personification of the ancient "everybody loves a fat man" axiom. And he *was* on the stout side: He was five feet ten inches and weighed close to three hundred pounds. Rickenbacker used to plead, scold, threaten, and demand that he take off weight and Bev would solemnly promise to try. His prodigious appetite, however, kept getting in the way of his resolve—he would average five meals a day and it was not until some years later, when the Captain's personal physician threw the fear of God into him by predicting every calamity from a heart attack to diabetes, that Griffith actually went on a diet. He lost 120 pounds and stayed healthy enough to remain with Eastern for some thirty years.

In the process, it must be noted, he also stayed loyal to

Rickenbacker. He worshiped Captain Eddie, who could do nothing wrong in Bev's eyes. Griffith was the Captain's idea man, his Boswell, almost his alter ego. To Bev, Eastern was Edward V. Rickenbacker and vice versa; saying something derogatory about either the airline or its leader was like violating all ten commandments. He dedicated his life to making both look good in the eyes of public and press alike, and in view of Eastern's splattered reputation in years to come, that was no mean assignment. What made it easier in the darker days was Bev's own reputation for honesty. Everyone liked him and he seemed to like everyone, although it was said that the worst thing anyone could do was double-cross Bev Griffith because he would double-cross you right back.

He was a true gourmet, relishing unusual food, and he knew the maitre d' at every good restaurant on Eastern's system. A magazine editor once called him "an idea factory" and this describes him perfectly. He was particularly adept at promoting airmail service, a task at which he was indefatigible—the stunts he pulled in this department would fill a book. Bev was the instigator for National Air Mail Week and had a Mailwing parked in the middle of the sunken plaza at Rockefeller Center for two weeks.

There are many at Eastern who credit Griffith with originating Easter's falcon symbol, with the exception of American's eagle the most enduring insignia in the industry. But the falcon wasn't Bev's idea at all; it was the brainchild of a non-Eastern employee named Brad Walker whose advertising agency, Campbell-Ewald, began handling Eastern's ad account shortly after EVR became general manager.

Few EAL employees knew Captain Eddie as well as this man who wasn't even an official member of the airline family. He might as well have been, because Rickenbacker not only trusted him but listened to him. Walker knew how to handle him, how to sell him on some new idea—and also when not to even try. Ernie Breech introduced Brad to the Captain, recommending Walker's agency as one that had done good work for General Motors. Walker's input was immediate: He came up with the "Great Silver Fleet" gimmick—words that would be painted on every EAL airplane until the sixties—and naming flights, like the "Florida Flyer" for the New York–Miami DC-2 trips and "Atlanta Flyer" for New York–Atlanta flights.

Giving Eastern a new image actually was Walker's scheme. He came into EVR's office one day with a recommendation that Eastern scrap its symbol—a black map on an orange background vaguely resembling the eastern seaboard that the airline served.

"What's wrong with it?" Captain Eddie grumbled.

"The damned thing looks like it belongs on the side of a freight car," Brad said stoutly.

"It looks fine to me," Rickenbacker said stubbornly. "The hell with changing it just to change it."

To virtually any new proposal, the Captain tended to agree with the Marx Brothers' song "Even If It Was Good, I Wouldn't Like It," but Walker went ahead anyway. He did considerable research on various birds, particularly members of the hawk family, and came up with a single choice: the duck hawk, also known as the peregrine falcon. He had his art department draw up several symbolic impressions of the bird before picking a simplified version, then combined this with his "Great Silver Fleet" slogan and the plan for naming major flights into a single "new image'" package.

Brad first laid the campaign in front of Paul Brattain, who loved it but was worried.

"You can take it into Eddie but he'll probably throw the whole damned thing out if he's not approached right," Brattain warned.

"You go in first, Paul. I think I know how we can handle it. The one thing we can't do is tell him we want to make drastic changes. Don't talk about changes, talk about modernizing— that we're going to make the airline bigger and better. That way we'll have a chance."

Walker knew his Captain. Brattain did go in first and launched his subtle sales pitch. "I've got Brad Walker outside, Eddie, and he's got some ideas about that symbol of ours"—

EVR's bushy eyebrows shot up like twin warning flags—"he wants to modernize it," he added, putting a slight emphasis on the word "modernize."

"Well, tell him to come on in," Rickenbacker said gruffly.

When Walker entered, Rickenbacker impaled him with a look that said, you're wasting my time and yours; but Walker went into his act.

"Eddie, I've got some things that'll go with your modernizing this airline. For one thing, I'd like to use this falcon as our new symbol." Before Rickenbacker had a chance to react, Walker continued hastily, "The reason I picked the falcon is because it's the fastest-flying bird in the world."

He put the falcon sketch in front of EVR, who never changed expression.

"Okay, Brad, what else have you got?"

Walker put the entire package in front of him: sketches of DC-2's with the words "The Great Silver Fleet" emblazoned above the window line drawings of nameplates on cabin doors reading "Florida Flyer." Rickenbacker didn't spend five minutes studying the layout. He handed it back to Walker and simply said, "Go ahead and do it." (In his autobiography, which never mentioned Walker, EVR claimed credit for thinking up the "Great Silver Fleet" slogan and the falcon symbol as well. John Halliburton, who truly loved him, simply comments, "Modesty was not his strongest suit.")

So long as Walker handled Eastern's advertising account— and this was to be for many years—that was the way Captain Eddie did business. Brusque, tough, a man who could make up his mind in the length of time it takes to bat an eyelash. Walker's recollections of him consist of deep affection tinged with awe.

"He was very selfish about his prerogatives," Brad remembers. "He felt, dammit, he was head of Eastern and that was it. He ran it from his office and he worked a seven-day week. In many ways Sheppy was the only one who could tolerate him. Yet in all the years I knew him, he was fair. He'd eat out your ass constantly and at any place at any time—in private or in front of five hundred people. But he always was loyal and once he reamed you, he ended it right there and would never bring it up again. That's why he, in turn, commanded such loyalty toward himself."

Walker was one of the few persons whom Rickenbacker trusted with the airline's money. He would go in to EVR with some project in mind, tell him, "Eddie, I'd like to do this and it'll cost such-and-such"; the Captain seldom, if ever, turned him down. Yet for years no one at Eastern could spend more than fifty dollars without EVR's personal approval, and when the airline got too big for such one-man monetary control, Rickenbacker grudgingly raised the limit—to a hundred dollars.

He seemed to have developed an unquestioning trust of Walker because Brad never took advantage of his connection with Eastern to throw his weight around. It would have been easy for him to do it, for EAL officials and employees alike knew that when Walker asked for something, it had EVR's approval. Rickenbacker used him as something of a sounding board, insisting that Walker accompany him on his frequent system-inspection trips, and never thought it unusual that his companion wasn't an airline employee but an ad-agency representative.

On one occasion Rickenbacker told Walker to make some kind of demand on an airframe manufacturer. Brad balked.

"Eddie," he said, "I can't tell Douglas or Lockheed that— I'm not with the airline."

"Goddammit!" Rickenbacker retorted. "You're *my* man and don't give me any of that crap!"

Theirs was an unusual relationship, perhaps unique in the industry, and it withstood Rickenbacker's own abrasive personality and stubborn prejudices. For a long time Walker operated Eastern's advertising program on the proverbial shoestring—the ad budget in his first year with the account was only $225,000. Walker was to see it rise to $13.5 million but the upward climb was strewn with Rickenbacker rocks—he was a hard man to please, convince, or sell.

Once Walker came up with a proposal to put buttonholes in napkins—something Western had pioneered on the logical assumption that it provided the only means of keeping a male passenger's tie clean while he was eating an in-flight meal. When he brought it up to the captain, EVR went into a rage.

"For Christ's sake—a buttonhole in a napkin? Are you crazy?"

Walker argued that it would cost only a penny per napkin —which was the wrong argument. Rickenbacker for as long as he ran Eastern had one ringing slogan: "Don't count pennies, count the mills." The buttonhole idea was discarded for a while.

Although he was a man whose vocabulary would fry eggs, Captain Eddie was something of a straight arrow when it came to ads. When Walker was trying to promote air travel to Florida in a campaign featuring pretty girls in skimpy bathing suits, Rickenbacker turned him down.

"No broads in bathing suits," was his edict. "Look, Brad, I don't want a flood of mail from rabbis, priests, and ministers."

One day Walker brought him in an ad proof with the picture of a baby crawling over a sandy beach, his tiny bottom wet with cool surf.

"Absolutely not!" he informed his ad manager.

"Eddie, nobody's gonna make waves about a baby's fanny," Walker protested.

"I don't give a damn," EVR declared firmly. "I'll get letters."

The ad ran, but only after Walker had the baby's bottom retouched by adding a diaper. Yet while the captain vetoed portions of ad campaigns or ordered changes in style and emphasis, he never actually turned down a Walker campaign—including that first one in 1936 when, in addition to the new symbol, the flight names, and the "Great Silver Fleet" logo painted on aircraft, Walker put out one of the first schedules in the industry to be printed on slick paper using red ink to mark prime flights. It was a long way from the old mimeographed schedules and was indicative of Rickenbacker's determination to put the airline at the top of the industry. He was not yet the shortsighted monolithic leader who demanded so much in employee loyalty while forgetting there was such a thing as passenger loyalty, too.

Despite his frequent throbs of parsimony, he was in those

days as progressive an airline president as there was in the United States. And parsimony may well be too strong a word; actually Rickenbacker was simply a devotee of tight cost controls, recognizing that in the airline industry the margin between profit and loss may well be a decision involving an item that might cost a few pennies per unit but a few million dollars if adopted for mass usage. And when it came to safety, Captain Eddie's wallet was wide open.

His establishment of a meteorology department under Joseph J. George was one example; George was a disciple of Irving Krick, the young scientist who was the first American meteorologist to employ the Norwegian method of forecasting weather by charting the movement of the upper air masses. Another case in point was Rickenbacker's hiring of Dr. Ralph Greene as the first full-time medical director in the airline industry. Captain Eddie had known him during World War I.

Rickenbacker, who always had closer rapport with his pilots than with any other group of employees, had become concerned over their health problems—he had heard that some were bribing doctors to give them passing grades in their medical tests, and he also knew that most airmen in the thirties had no other profession to fall back on if they were grounded for medical reasons.

He looked up Greene in Jacksonville, where the doctor had gone into practice, and discussed one of his pet theories: It was time to apply the same preventative maintenance to people, pilots especially, as Eastern was applying to its flight equipment. Greene became interested and accepted Rickenbacker's offer to establish his own aeromedical laboratory in Miami; suspicious at first, the pilots came to accept him as a friend and confidant, much as they would a regular family doctor.

The pilot–Rickenbacker relationship stemmed largely from the fact that EVR was one of them—he understood their thinking and they shared that common bond of directness, quick decisiveness, and sense of mixed mysticism and fatalism so prevalent in airmen. Certainly his pilots got away with a bit more than most employees because of the relationship. The crews had

feuded bitterly with Breech and regarded EVR as a kind of
buffer zone between them and the president's somewhat intrac-
table attitude toward pilots. Captain Eddie wasn't around to
referee their first clash—when the mail contracts were canceled,
Breech wanted to fire all copilots but was finally talked out of it
after the pilots agreed to take a pay cut instead.

Eastern's pilots were among the first to join the new Air
Line Pilots Association even though, being largely southerners,
they were not exactly union minded. Gene Brown, who was the
first EAL chapter chairman, remembers that the move to unionize
in 1932 had followed Harold Elliott's order for a twenty percent
pay reduction right after he already had eliminated per diem
expenses. Pilot-company relations weren't improved under
Breech, who didn't like the way ALPA was lobbying for labor
legislation in Washington and suddenly ordered all Washington-
based crewmen transferred to New York.

Breech then threatened another twenty percent cut in 1933,
on top of the still-in-effect twenty percent slash imposed when
the mail contract was voided. The pilots responded by voting to
strike if the additional cut was put into effect, and a walkout was
narrowly averted by a last-minute compromise that actually
stemmed from a con job on the usually wily Breech. The near
strike occurred while a government board was trying to settle the
so-called Decision 83 dispute. The airlines had proposed
monthly flying limits of 140 hours for captains and 160 hours for
copilots; the pilots asked for an 85-hour limit and also a new pay
formula based on mileage hours, and base pay.

Eastern's negotiators, led by Brown, agreed to take the new
cut if the labor board voted against the pilots and Breech promised to rescind it if the board voted against the airlines. What
Breech did not know at the time the compromise was reached
was that Gene Brown had a telegram from Washington in his
pocket advising him that Decision 83 had been approved, giving
ALPA everything it was seeking.

The Eastern pilots had no trouble with Rickenbacker as far
as Decision 83 was concerned, but those flying for other carriers
did. The law's chief weakness was its lack of enforcement provi-

sions and some airlines went their own merry way. One was Braniff, which had a deal with a flight school in Dallas—students were paying up to $4,000 to obtain a transport-pilot's license and part of the curriculum was for a student to fly copilot on Braniff for a couple of months of "on-the-job" training without pay. Technically it was perfectly legal but Dave Behncke, ALPA's first president and its principal organizer, protested.

When Braniff told Behncke to go fly a kite or words to that effect, he went to see Jim Farley. The outcome was Farley's ordering Braniff to comply with Decision 83 within fifteen days or lose its airmail contract. Farley's intervention helped Behncke to get Congress to incorporate Decision 83's provisions into the Air Mail Act of 1934, which gave it enforcement teeth.

Even under Decision 83 life wasn't really easy for any airline pilot. Eastern's crews still weren't able to buy life insurance, there was no such thing as sick leave or paid vacations, and the 85-hour limit was more fiction than fact. Pay started when the wheels left the ground and stopped when they touched the ground; not for quite a while would "block-to-block" time be figured into pay computations, along with driving time to and from airports and the hours spent in operations planning a flight.

Jerry Wood, a now-retired veteran EAL captain, estimates that 85 hours by today's standards would add up to about 100 hours of on-duty time.

"We were limited to a thousand hours of actual flight time a year," he points out, "and we couldn't fly more than eight hours a day. But those eight hours usually meant you were on duty for as much as seventeen hours a day."

The bad blood between the crews and Breech fueled Rickenbacker's burning desire to assume full control, yet his authority was such that it was almost taken for granted that he *did* possess such control. Breech played virtually no part in Rickenbacker's move to acquire another airline—the Wedell-Williams Transport Corporation, operating a small but important route between New Orleans and Houston. It was the highlight of 1936, a year in which the airline's payroll jumped to more than 800 and Eastern had taken delivery on the first two of the ten DC-3's

Captain Eddie had ordered. He could hardly wait to put the new Douglas airliner into service; he never had been completely enamored of the DC-2.

The Wedell-Williams purchase was to prove one of Rickenbacker's most sagacious moves, for it not only gave Eastern its first entry into Texas but was to make possible a later route expansion into Brownsville, Texas, where Eastern's flights would connect with Pan American's service into Mexico, Central America, and South America. It also fed EVR's dream of eventually becoming a transcontinental carrier via a southwestern route system.

Rickenbacker was well acquainted with Harry P. Williams, Jimmy Wedell's partner in the small but moderately prosperous little airline. Williams not only had bought a Rickenbacker roadster a few years back, but also had purchased three Lockheed Vegas on EVR's recommendation. Wedell was killed in a crash before Captain Eddie flew down to New Orleans and the way Rickenbacker described the negotiations, they were conducted solely with Williams and involved fifteen separate meetings before Williams finally agreed on the price: $160,000. According to Smythe Gambrell, then a young Atlanta lawyer whom EVR had talked into becoming Eastern's general counsel, that wasn't quite the way it happened.

Gambrell accompanied EVR to New Orleans and swears that Captain Eddie did more of a selling job on Wedell's widow than on Williams himself. Whatever the case, both the widow and Williams finally caved in and Eastern had a potentially potent route addition—not as potent ultimately as Rickenbacker envisioned it initially, but still a landmark in the airline's history. And even the hard-to-please, tough little Ernie Breech couldn't argue with success. Eastern was making money—not much, but at least it was in the black. Rickenbacker felt confident enough in the future and grateful enough for the past to institute a bonus system, awarding a Christmas "appreciation fund" to all employees earning less than $200 a month.

Spontaneous generosity was one of the many sides of the multifaceted man. Eastern's salaries were among the lowest in the industry, but there wasn't a man or woman working for EVR who didn't have access to the company checkbook (or his own) in any kind of a jam. There wasn't any sick leave, but heaven help the supervisor who took a needy underling off the payroll when he was sick. In some cases Rickenbacker himself picked up hospital bills while simultaneously threatening instant dismissal if the employee told anyone. Any employee with a legitimate hard-luck story found the Captain a soft touch, yet he could be ruthlessly arbitrary, firing people in a fit of temper over mistakes, omissions, or transgressions that often were minor. He had a deep, genuine feeling of pride and gratitude toward his airline family, but it was diluted by his short fuse and heavy-handed methods. He was more of a stern patriarch than a paternalist, the difference being that he was unpredictable.

His reaming jobs on erring employees were classic—"Eddie invented the proctoscope," one once commented with a certain amount of admiration. But he could spring to their defense, too, even if it meant losing a customer. He heard of one passenger who delighted in making life miserable for Eastern personnel, and quite by coincidence happened to sit next to him on a flight. The minute Rickenbacker heard the man give his name, the alarm bell rang and the Captain opened fire.

"I've been looking for you, you sonofabitch." The passenger's mouth dropped like a drawbridge gate. "You've been browbeating every person on this airline you've come in contact with and by God, they don't deserve it. They're doing the best they can and frankly I don't care if you never ride this airline again."

"Who the hell are you?" the passenger finally asked.

"My name's Rickenbacker and I'm the general manager."

The passenger apologized.

Eastern's mechanics ranked just behind the pilots in affection for the captain who had once been a mechanic. They were the first group of employees to be given paid vacations, and Johnny Ray was always one of EVR's favorites—he had access to Rickenbacker almost anytime he wanted and could even get him to spend money—if he could prove the need. He marched into Captain Eddie's office one day, chewing on his ever-present cigar, and announced, "We gotta buy a lathe."

"A lathe? What the hell do you want a lathe for?"

Ray handed him a list of every outside machine-fabrication job done in the past six months, along with the cost, length of time it took, and the name of the part involved.

"A lot of this stuff we could do ourselves," Ray suggested.

"Cheaper?"

"A lot cheaper," Ray assured him.

"Go ahead and do it."

On another occasion Rickenbacker was sitting next to a young mechanic in the employee lunchroom and noticed a bandage on his hand.

"How'd you get hurt, son?" he inquired pleasantly.

"On a jack, Captain Eddie. If you want to know the truth, our jacks are no damned good."

By the end of the week the jacks had been thrown out and better ones purchased.

Yet these two incidents must be contrasted with EVR's renowned tightfistedness. For years Eastern was the only airline whose pilots were not allowed to use autopilots—Rickenbacker considered them unperfected and dangerous, claiming that if something went wrong while an autopilot was engaged, the crew lacked sufficient time to take corrective action on their own. Inasmuch as an autopilot can be disengaged in the time it takes to blink an eye, his reasoning was suspect but no one could convince him otherwise. A captain from another carrier once asked an EAL pilot why Eastern's planes lacked certain technical equipment that was fairly standard throughout the industry.

"If it wasn't on a Spad," the Eastern captain said dourly, "we can't have it."

Nor was it a case of his being shortsighted, miserly, and guilty of tunnel vision. One of the major quirks of his character was his unyielding faith in aviation's future, far greater than that of many of his contemporaries, yet offset by an almost pathological fear of the technological advances molding so much a part of the future. Some of his closest associates believe firmly that this fear had its roots in the failure of the Rickenbacker automobile, with its advanced design features such as four-wheel brakes.

Certainly Rickenbacker, during Eastern's formative years

under the volatile Captain, displayed courageous ingenuity and astuteness. His reputation for being blindly antiunion was not entirely justified. True, he had the paternalistic conviction that he could do more for an employee than any labor organization, and throughout his airline tenure he remained stubbornly opposed to classifying workers—he considered this union policy nothing but stagnation of ambition. In November of 1937 he broke an attempt to organize EAL mechanics at Newark by encouraging dissidents to keep working. The day before a planned strike he brought a number of antiunion mechanics into Newark and when the men walked out, his loyalist platoon moved in—along with cots and food. They were at work before the picket lines were up, and the strike fizzled.

Yet it was so typical of this untypical man that once the strike ended, he walked into the office of George Brown, president of the International Association of Machinists, and calmly announced: "I want to unionize my mechanics—how the hell do I go about it?"

Rickenbacker explained this 180-degree turn by saying he had come to realize that most mechanics felt more secure with a union behind them and he had no objections—provided the union wasn't dominated by Communists or racketeers. He picked the IAM as the bargaining agent after conducting a quiet investigation of its background and reputation.

It was in the area of route expansion that friction first seems to have developed between the Captain and Breech. As far back as 1934, when the new airmail contracts were awarded, EVR had suggested to Breech that the airline apply for new routes as well as get back its old ones. He proposed what he called a "figure-eight pattern"—a system embracing Chicago and New York in the north, New Orleans and Miami in the south, and Atlanta in the center of the pattern. Supplementing this would be a direct New York–Miami leg and, eventually, a transcontinental route through the southern tier of states.

Breech bought only part of his expansion blueprint, refusing to go along with one key segment: New York–Chicago. He adamantly forbade Rickenbacker to apply for the route, informing EVR that he believed it would be impossible to take it away from American. The captain disagreed and to his dying day insisted that Eastern could have won New York–Chicago away from American. The Captain disagreed and to his dying day in-American submitted when it won the route, and the outspoken Rickenbacker never stopped reminding Breech of this fact.

He could not have completed his "figure-eight pattern" anyway, because Eastern would not win a New Orleans–Miami route for years. It ended up with an "X" pattern plus its old New York–Miami aerial gold mine. Nevertheless, his argument with Breech over New York–Chicago seems to have caused some dissension and hard feeling between the two men, mostly on Breech's part. For what Rickenbacker did not know was that Breech for some time had been trying to talk General Motors chief Alfred Sloan into selling Eastern—to himself.

Ernie Breech was no neophyte in the airline business. He had been largely responsible for putting TWA back on its feet, and the able Jack Frye was his protegé. Breech had finally become dubious about GM's involvement in air transportation. In fact, almost on the heels of the airmail contract cancellation of 1934, he had obtained Sloan's blessing to peddle Eastern right then and there—something of which Rickenbacker had been totally unaware. Breech had phoned Alvin Adams, a young official at National Aviation (an investment firm specializing in airline stocks).

"Alvin, my friend," Breech said, "I'm going to give your outfit an option to buy Eastern."

"How long an option?" Adams wanted to know.

"Sixty days."

"I think we'd be interested," Adams allowed cautiously. "I'll get back to you."

The deal fell through when Adams couldn't get his two superiors, President Edward McDonald and Board Chairman Richard Hoyt, to agree on which one would become head of the acquired airline. They still were arguing when the option expired and Adams, who later became president of Western, had to inform Breech reluctantly that National wasn't interested.

Breech bided his time for three years, but late in 1937—again without EVR's knowledge—he went back to Sloan with another interesting proposition. He informed Sloan that James "Dutch" Kindelberger, whom GM had installed as the new president of North American when Breech became Eastern's president, was perfectly willing to dump the airline as a wholly owned North American subsidiary.

He explained that Kindelberger had confidence in Eastern, but was unhappy over the provision in the Air Mail Act forbidding any company holding an airmail contract to pay any top executive more than $17,500 a year. Kindelberger, Breech added, also had moved North American's corporate headquarters to the West Coast where it was doing well as an aircraft manufacturing company, and thus had little interest in an east-based carrier.

What Breech was now proposing to Alfred Sloan was a simple two-step process: North American would distribute all Eastern stock not held by GM to North American's stockholders, then allow Breech to purchase GM's interest in Eastern. This would give Breech thirty percent of the airline's shares, with individual North American stockholders owning the rest. It made sense to Sloan, who promised to recommend the plan to the General Motors board.

Breech then went to John Hertz, a partner in Lehman Brothers since the sale of Hertz's Yellow Cab Company to GM (a deal, incidentally, which Breech helped engineer). From Hertz he received assurance of financing and at this stage, the end of 1937, Ernest Breech was inches away from taking over control of Eastern in a move that probably would have cost the unsuspecting Rickenbacker his job. This is speculation, of course, yet Hertz and the Captain disliked one another intensely and if Breech's deal had been consummated, the odds were overwhelmingly in favor of EVR's being ousted.

Breech had every reason to believe he had Eastern in his hip pocket; when he reported back to Sloan that he had the financial support of Lehman Brothers, the GM chairman offered to loan Breech the money himself, with the airline stock as security. While Breech was pondering this unexpectedly generous offer, however, Sloan presented the plan to his board and ran into a storm of opposition. The directors felt that Sloan, in effect, had offered Breech an attractive inducement to leave GM and they were convinced Ernie was too valuable a man to lose. The next day Sloan informed Breech that the board wanted him to stay at General Motors—as a vice president.

That killed Breech's airline-owning ambitions, although he still felt obligated to Hertz and Lehman Brothers. While he accepted Sloan's request to remain at GM, he also talked him into giving Hertz an option on GM's Eastern stock for three million dollars—and so advised Hertz.

In January 1938, Rickenbacker received a phone call from Leslie Gould, a financial writer for the Hearst newspapers and an old friend of the Captain's.

"Eddie, I've just learned that John Hertz has taken an option on Eastern for three million dollars. What can you tell me about it?"

By his own account, Rickenbacker turned pale. He could only mutter, "I can't tell you anything about it, Leslie, this is the first I've heard of it."

Fully aware that Hertz never would let him remain at Eastern's helm, EVR's dilemma was devastatingly simple: He didn't have three million to match the Hertz option, nor did he even have Sloan's promise that GM would consider a matching offer, provided he could raise that kind of money. He tackled the latter roadblock first, rushing over to see the general counsel of General Motors and North American, Henry Hogan.

Hogan confirmed Gould's report.

"How long is the Hertz option?" Rickenbacker asked.

"Thirty days."

"Do you see any reason I shouldn't talk to Mr. Sloan about this personally?"

"No, I don't, Eddie. Whether seeing him will do you any good is something else."

Rickenbacker quickly arranged an appointment with the GM board chairman and wasted no time getting straight to the crux of the matter.

"I've done a good job with Eastern and I think I'm entitled

to as much of an opportunity as any outsider to bid," he said quietly. "If I can't outbid John Hertz then I'll accept defeat. But isn't it fair to give me a chance?"

Sloan privately thought Rickenbacker, who was making not much more than $12,000 a year as the airline's general manager, had about as much chance of outbidding Hertz as he had of serving in FDR's cabinet. But he did promise to "look into it" and suggested that the Captain come back in a few days. EVR spent that time canvassing some of GM's top officials for support, and while he received no commitments, he did get assurance that no one was committed to Hertz either. He didn't bother to see Breech; he was too angry and hurt at Breech's failure to inform him of the stock sale, knowing that it meant Rickenbacker's corporate death sentence at Eastern.

How much of Hertz's anti-Rickenbacker feelings were shared by Ernie Breech will never be known. The evidence points to a considerable amount; Rickenbacker himself told of an incident that occurred months before there was any hint of GM selling its Eastern stock. Captain Eddie was at home one night when his phone rang. It was John Hertz.

"Eddie?" Rickenbacker thought he said.

"Yeah."

Hertz had mistakenly dialed Rickenbacker's number instead of Breech's; he hadn't asked for "Eddie" but "Ernie," and when the Captain answered in the affirmative, Hertz went into a tirade against Rickenbacker and how he was going to "get that s.o.b. out of Eastern." EVR let him rant and rave for almost thirty minutes and when Hertz finally wound down, Rickenbacker said gently, "John, this is Eddie Rickenbacker you're talking to."

Sloan summoned Captain Eddie back to his office a few days after their first talk and handed him some encouraging if not conclusive news: General Motors was willing to give Rickenbacker the same thirty-day option that Hertz held carrying the same price tag—$3 million, with $1 million in cash and the remainder in long-term notes.

Rickenbacker was thinking fast. . . . It wasn't enough to

match the Hertz bid—he had to top it, in terms so advantageous
to GM that Sloan and the directors couldn't turn it down. That
$3 million asking price was high—only two years before there
had been talk of selling Eastern for a paltry $1 million—and if
he could sweeten the pot a little more . . .

"Mr. Sloan, if I could offer you $3.5 million *in cash* for
Eastern before the option runs out, would you sell it to me?"

"Yes, Eddie, I would," Sloan replied promptly.

He didn't have the money—he was to tell one friend, "I was
about three million, four hundred and fifty thousand dollars
short"—but he was Captain Eddie Rickenbacker and he had
contacts.

He made the rounds of everyone he knew in banking and
financial circles, and struck a lode at Smith, Barney and Company, a Wall Street investment-banking firm where one of his
oldest friends, William Barclay Harding, was an associate. Harding was aviation-minded; he told EVR that his firm didn't have
the muscle to underwrite the Eastern purchase, but he thought he
knew who did. Harding arranged for the Captain to meet with
three top officials of Kuhn, Loeb and Company—John Schiff,
Hugh Knowlton, and Frederick Warburg.

This trio spent three weeks investigating Eastern, Rickenbacker's methods of running an airline, EAL's future prospects,
and every other aspect pertaining to a $3.5 million investment.
They came back to EVR with the verdict: Kuhn, Loeb and
Company would advance the cash for Rickenbacker's purchase
of EAL. The plan was to set up a new corporation with Captain
Eddie as president and raise enough money by public subscription to repay Kuhn, Loeb and Company. Rickenbacker's joy was
tempered considerably by the realization that time was running
out.

His option agreement with General Motors would expire at
six P.M., Sunday, April 22. The preceding Thursday he met with
GM and North American directors in the General Motors Building at Fifty-seventh and Broadway, accompanied by his attorneys
and financial backers. The marathon session lasted all day, with
the Hertz-versus-Rickenbacker arguments batted back and forth

in a verbal Ping-Pong game. The big stumbling block was the diminutive but powerful figure of Ernest Breech, who fought openly for John Hertz.

Rickenbacker angrily attacked Breech for "your outright favoritism toward Hertz" and Breech just as angrily retorted that he had a perfect right to speak his mind. When the meeting adjourned for supper with no decision reached, Captain Eddie went to a phone and called Bill Knudsen, GM's president.

"Breech has no goddamned business taking sides," he complained. "And even if he did, our bid is better than the Hertz offer and Ernie knows it."

"Go back to your meeting, Eddie," Knudsen said gently. "I'll ask Mr. Breech to refrain from participating."

What Knudsen said to Breech will never be known, but Knudsen obviously reminded him that his loyalty had to be toward GM and not John Hertz. When the negotiations resumed, Breech remained silent, and shortly after three A.M. the Rickenbacker offer of $3.5 million cash was accepted. It was now, of course, Friday morning and Rickenbacker still wasn't home free—he didn't have the cash on hand yet and he told Schiff and Warburg he didn't know where they were going to collect $3.5 million on a weekend.

"The option expires at six Sunday evening," he worried.

"We'll do our damndest, Eddie," Warburg assured him.

All day Saturday and through most of Saturday night Rickenbacker waited in vain to hear from them. At eleven P.M. he panicked and phoned Alfred Sloan.

"I know it's late, but could I come over and see you for fifteen minutes?"

Sloan said yes and less than an hour later Rickenbacker was at Sloan's residence, unloading his concern. "I don't think Warburg and Schiff are going to have that money by Sunday night. Would you give us a ten-day extension?"

Sloan, still in his pajamas, merely smiled.

"Eddie," he said, "if I were you, I'd stop worrying."

Rickenbacker went home and spent a restless night; Sloan's advice not to worry sounded reassuring, but he hadn't granted any ten-day extension, either. Early Sunday morning Warburg called.

"Where do you want me to deliver your three and a half million dollars?" he asked calmly.

"How about ten o'clock tomorrow morning at the Eastern hangar at Newark, Freddy—if it's convenient?"

"I'll be there," Warburg promised.

Rickenbacker then phoned Sloan again to inform him that he would be in his office before noon on Monday with a certified check.

"I know it's past the six o'clock deadline today," he added, "but Fred Warburg assured me he had the money."

"Monday will be fine," Sloan said. "Just stop worrying."

Twenty-four hours later Rickenbacker handed Alfred Sloan a certified check for $3.5 million. Sloan put the check down on his desk and held out his hand. "Congratulations, Eddie, and God bless you. I wish you every success in the world."

Under Rickenbacker's agreement with his backers, the new corporation—Eastern Air Lines, Incorporated—was to have a half-million dollars in working capital. In addition Captain Eddie was given an option on ten percent of the capital stock; some 400,000 shares would be sold to the public at ten dollars a share. The latter was to present some problems, because the day the stock went on sale Germany invaded Austria and the subscription was only half sold. Rickenbacker himself would have to go on a stock-selling tour to raise the rest of the money.

But this was a mere foothill compared to the mountain he had just climbed. As of April 22, 1938, Edward Vernon Rickenbacker became president of Eastern Air Lines, for better or for worse.

And there was to be a lot of both.

CHAPTER SIX

GROWING PAINS

He was forty-eight years old when he fused his own personality, policies, and philosophy into an inanimate object known as an airline.

His official title was president and general manager. Unofficially he was "the Captain," and that title was synonymous with absolute authority; no airline chief executive had more autonomy or greater power. He was a dictator with the saving grace of sentimentality, a corporate potentate with a conscience, an egotistical autocrat with a strange streak of humility, a feudal baron demanding total allegiance, yet not quite capable of suppressing both affection for and a sense of responsibility toward the serfs.

They quailed under his wrath, feared his mercurial temper, and still managed to love him for the very qualities that made him so difficult to work for. In so many ways, his was the quintessence of leadership in an industry struggling not just for profits but for respect, trust, and recognition. It is too easy to forget in these days of three hundred million passengers a year, when the airplane has become a means of mass transportation, that the airlines of the late 1930s needed their Rickenbackers with their heavy-handed strength, their single-minded determination, their dogged resilience under the worst adversity.

Eastern was no exception. In 1938 it had just over a thousand employees and twenty-two airplanes—ten DC-2's, ten DC-3's, and a pair of single-engine Stinson Reliants. The payroll was only $180,000 a month, which averaged out to $180 per person; one had to be dedicated to work for an airline, but that was the name of the game in those days and it was definitely true at Eastern, where the average employee wore five hats in constant demonstrations of job versatility. Eventually EAL would be the first airline to work a forty-hour week and also the first to have a pension plan—Rickenbacker had that much in common with Delta's C. E. Woolman in staving off unionism by staying ahead of labor's demands—but the industry owes an incalculable debt to the gung-ho spirit of its men and women during the crucial growing years before World War II.

And they were precisely that—growing years. In 1938 Congress completely overhauled the Air Mail Act of 1934 and forged a new operating blueprint for the U.S. airlines known as the Civil Aeronautics Act. It was a commercial aviation milestone that ended the quarrelsome, clumsy system of dividing regulatory authority over the airlines among three federal agencies: the Post Office Department (mail contracts and routes), Interstate Commerce Commission (mail rates and fares), and the Bureau of Air Commerce (safety, operation of airways, and pilot and aircraft licensing).

The Act created a five-member Civil Aeronautics Authority which took over all of the aforementioned functions; the once all-powerful Post Office Department retained only its authority to approve airmail schedules, but not contracts. The legislation also established within the CAA a three-man safety board charged with the responsibility of investigating air accidents and armed with complete independence. Experience quickly showed that the new law concentrated excessive power in a single agency, and within two years the act was amended—the CAA became the Civil Aeronautics Board, regulating routes and fares, while a separate Civil Aeronautics Administration was established within the Commerce Department, assuming authority over civil aviation operating matters. The Safety Board lost its independence and became part of the CAB.

Overall, however, the 1938 act brought stability and reasonable regulation to an industry that had been walking a tightrope between czarlike controls and government permissiveness. Preceding its passage was a $7 million allocation for airways modernization, an exchange for which the airlines gladly welcomed stricter safety rules and more efficient accident investigation. And perhaps the act's major significance lay in the Post Office Department's almost total removal from airline regulatory matters—it was tacit recognition that people and not mail packs controlled the industry's destiny. Passenger revenues were steadily approaching the level of airmail income and in two years would surpass them. (Today passenger revenues are sixty-five times greater than those from mail.)

Without any doubt the DC-3 was the instrument of this revolution that ended airline dependence on mail pay—it was, as American's C. R. Smith put it, "the first airplane that could make money just carrying people." Rickenbacker himself was not slow to grasp what Donald Douglas had achieved in this technological miracle of symmetrical metal that provided so much more reliability, safety, and economic efficiency. Not until the DC-3 did flight insurance become available to air travelers—$5,000 worth of protection for twenty-five cents, a development on which *Time* commented:

"That insurance companies can now bet $5,000 to two bits against a passenger being killed on a flight of some eight hundred miles is one of the best pieces of publicity the U.S. airlines ever had."

Rickenbacker's DC-3 orders lagged considerably behind American and TWA numerically, to such an extent that for a while Eastern's advertisements referred to its DC-2 equipment as "giant Douglas airliners" in apparent hopes that nonaeronautical-minded customers might assume they would be riding in a new DC-3. From the standpoint of public confidence, the DC-3 didn't

arrive on the scene any too soon—in late 1936 and 1937 there
had been five fatal crashes and passengers had canceled reservations by the thousands. United's passenger revenues alone
dropped from $25,000 to $5,000 in a single day, a decline attributed directly to the alarming headlines.

Rickenbacker wisely refrained from boasting about Eastern's own safety record, which happened to be the best in the
industry. In 1937 it became the first airline in U.S. aviation history to receive a special award from the National Safety Council
for operating seven consecutive years (1930–1936) without a
single passenger fatality. It was cited again for completing in
1937 its eighth consecutive year with a perfect record, but the
framed commendation certificate had been on the wall of Captain Eddie's office for only three months when tragedy struck.

The date was August 10, 1938; Rickenbacker got the word
while he was a guest on Alfred Sloan's yacht at Newport—a
message delivered via ship-to-shore telephone informed him that
an Eastern DC-2 had crashed at Daytona Beach, Florida. EVR
immediately headed for New York, where he caught the first
flight to Florida and was in Daytona Beach that same evening.
Station personnel gave him a quick briefing and his reaction
would have burned through chrome steel.

His anger was totally justified. The DC-2, bound from Chicago under the command of Captain Stuart Dietz, had landed in
Daytona Beach at four in the morning. Passengers and mail were
unloaded and Dietz took off, unaware that the runway had been
booby-trapped. The day before, a severe thunderstorm had hit
the Daytona Beach area and had caused a short circuit in an
underground transmission line located at the end of the field. A
repair crew had effected temporary repairs by erecting two poles
and stringing a power line between them to bypass the inoperative conduit. One of the poles had been put up smack at the end
of the runway—with no warning light. To compound this deadly
mistake, no one at the power company had bothered to inform
airport officials that the unlighted poles had been erected.

Dietz took off on what he assumed was an unobstructed
runway and flew into the power line; he and three passengers

were killed. Rickenbacker blamed the airport manager as much as he did the electric company—"He should have known everything that went on at his field," he fumed. EVR couldn't bring back the dead, but he contacted every city Eastern served, advised them of the Daytona Beach circumstances, and urged them to make sure a similar accident could not recur. As proud as he was of the airline's safety record, however, he had a fatalistic attitude toward crashes. He told Brad Walker never to use the word "safe" in an Eastern advertisement.

"We can say air travel is reliable," he explained, "but there's no such thing as absolute safety. The only time anyone is really safe is when he's completely static. If you move, there's always a possibility of an accident."

He ordered five more DC-3's for delivery in 1939 but Florida traffic was booming to such an extent that he had to lease three of United's for the peak winter season—something that stabbed his pride, for he hated to ask his peers for anything. He was always something of an industry maverick and loner, resented by other airline executives partially out of envy for Eastern's money-coining monopoly Florida routes—so profitable in winter months when most of the other airlines were losing their collective shirts—but also because what they considered his arrogance irritated them like fingernails on a blackboard.

His unpredictability was something competitors feared. The classic example was his bid for a Houston–Brownsville mail contract, submitted before the Civil Aeronautics Act of 1938 became law. There was great pressure on the Post Office Department not to award any more new contracts while the new act was pending, and to circumvent this possibility he talked Congressman Richard Kleberg of Texas into introducing a special bill that authorized bidding for the Houston–San Antonio route via Brownsville. Much to the dismay of virtually the entire airline industry, the Kleberg bill sailed through Congress and Rickenbacker had his foot in the door.

His opposition was Braniff, owned by Tom and Paul Braniff, whose influential Texas friends included Jesse Jones, later to become chairman of the Reconstruction Finance Corporation and a power in both Texas and national politics. Rickenbacker knew him, too, and because of his own friendship with Jones committed a boner that almost cost him the Brownsville award. He had stopped in to visit Jones at the latter's Washington office and Jones, almost casually, asked him what he was going to bid on the route.

Just as casually, EVR replied, "Well, if we have to we'll go as low as a cent per mile."

Not until Rickenbacker had left did he realize what he had done—Jones was almost certain to relay Eastern's planned bid to Tom Braniff. He confessed what he had done to Paul Brattain, who sympathized but couldn't offer any suggestion for undoing the damage.

"I've really loused it up," the Captain muttered. "All Braniff has to do is bid less than a cent. Or just match us—with Tom Braniff's political clout, he could damned well win it if we bid the same figure."

"Less than a cent is zero," Brattain pointed out.

Rickenbacker's eyes flashed. "Paul, I think I'll ask Smythe Gambrell and the rest of our legal brains whether we could get away with a zero bid."

The aforementioned legal brains unanimously concluded there were precedents for the government accepting services from private contractors for exactly nothing. On the day the sealed bids were opened in the office of Charles Graddick, superintendent of airmail for the Post Office Department, Rickenbacker was present with Brattain. Tom Braniff also was there, along with officials of other carriers seeking the route. Bids were opened alphabetically, and Braniff's was first.

$0.00001907378.

There were a few laughs and an equal number of groans—the latter from representatives of airlines which obviously hadn't dared to go *that* low.

Assistant Postmaster General William Howe then opened Eastern's bid, and did a fast double-take.

"Eastern bids zero-zero-zero cents," he gulped.

Tom Braniff jumped to his feet. "That's illegal!" he roared.

"The hell it is," Rickenbacker said with the satisfied expression of a crapshooter who has just rolled his tenth consecutive pass.

It was very legal, of course. So legal that when Braniff went as high as President Roosevelt in an effort to hold up certification of the Brownsville award until the new act could go into effect, the Post Office Department's own lawyers informed Jim Farley that he had no authority to delay the Eastern award.

Braniff refused to surrender, getting community leaders in the cities involved to protest to FDR and Farley. Rickenbacker was making a speech in Brownsville when he got word that Tom Braniff was going to appear before the Houston Chamber of Commerce board of directors later that afternoon. He cut short his Brownsville remarks and flew to Houston, arriving just as Braniff was winding up his own talk. Rickenbacker listened outside the board room and grimaced when he heard Braniff argue that Eastern would destroy Braniff Airways, "a Texas operation," he kept repeating.

EVR finally talked his way into the room and was permitted to deliver a rebuttal. He opened up by reminding his audience that Braniff was based in Oklahoma City, not Texas, then concluded with this promise:

"Gentlemen—and that includes you, too, Tom—you simply do not realize the vast potential of your own state and community. There is enough business here for both Braniff and Eastern to prosper. If you really seriously feel that additional air service would destroy the existing service provided by Braniff, let me make this statement: I am willing to guarantee you and Tom Braniff, here and now, that should the day ever come that he is carrying one passenger less on an average than he has been carrying all along, then I will take our own sales force off the job here in Houston and turn them over to Braniff Airways. I make that guarantee in good faith, before witnesses."

The board voted to support Eastern, and the new Texas route made EAL the nation's third biggest carrier in terms of route mileage.

That Houston incident was pure Rickenbacker, vintage

1938—an audacious gambler with the courage of his convictions. The time would come when he would not be so generous toward competition, when he would blame everyone but himself for his own mistakes. But in the first year of his regime and in subsequent years, before a changing industry left his ilk wallowing in the mud of outmoded thinking and methods, he was one giant of a man. It is an almost forgotten and vastly underrated historical fact that in 1938 Eastern became the first U.S. airline to go off Federal subsidy—Rickenbacker had kept the promise he had made to Ernie Breech.

Gradually he was building up his own handpicked executive cadre. One key newcomer was a former station manager at Richmond, big, heavyset Sid Shannon, whom EVR promoted to operations manager while finally giving Brattain the title of vice president of traffic and sales. He still insisted on keeping executive salaries as low as possible, but this policy he also applied to himself. The carrot he dangled at the end of a stick for potential officers was the stock option. When the new airline was organized, EVR had insisted that his own option on ten percent of the capital stock be held for him for five years at the issue price of ten dollars a share. If the stock increased in value, as Captain Eddie justifiably expected it to, he would be well rewarded. But he suddenly decided to split his option with Eastern's employees, working out a formula by which they could purchase the bargain-priced shares in amounts varying with their jobs and seniority. Executives and pilots were given top priority.

He set his own salary at $50,000 a year, not an immodest sum in 1938. But for the next twenty-five years, his salary stayed at $50,000—and by the sixties he was the lowest-paid chief executive of any trunk airline in the U.S. despite Eastern's status as one of the nation's four largest carriers.

Only Rickenbacker could have attached a minor condition to his largesse with stock options. Shortly after he announced the stock availability, he told a staff meeting he was going to monitor any share sales.

"If it develops that selling these shares will bring in a profit and you need that money to buy a home or pay medical bills or take care of some extreme emergency, then I won't object," he advised. "But if I find anybody selling his stock to buy a big red automobile or something equally frivolous, I warn you right here and now I'm going to get mad as hell!"

He was congenitally unable to keep his brand of paternalism from overflowing into his employees' private lives. There was no direct interference (although Sheppy claims he prevented at least five divorces among EAL executives), but a constant flow of stern advice, usually through the medium of the company publication, *Great Silver Fleet News*. In one issue he came out forthrightly against installment buying in these words:

If you cannot afford it, do without it. If you cannot pay cash for it, wait until you can; but do not in any circumstances permit yourself to mortgage your future and that of your family through time payment plans or other devices.

His column at first carried the caption *Captain Eddie Says* and later was changed to *Captain Eddie Reminds You*. It was more of a sermon than a means of informing the rank and file what was going on at the higher levels; a few random samples will suffice:

None of us here is doing so much work that he cannot do more.
You cannot bring about prosperity by discouraging thrift.
You cannot strengthen the weak by weakening the strong.
You cannot help the wage earner by tearing down the wage payer.

It is not unreasonable to assume that nobody followed all his advice and probably few even paid attention to part of it. Yet Captain Eddie unquestionably was the only airline president who could have foisted these homilies on the more or less cynical rank-and-file and still retain their respect. His beliefs may have been anachronistic, old fashioned, or noble depending on one's point of view, but employees put up with them because Rickenbacker gave them a full-size, grand-scale father image—he was, indeed, Big Daddy, the family provider. And what he was providing was a prosperous airline, solid security (if you didn't cross him), and quick recognition if you did an above-average job. If he demanded loyalty, he also gave it, although there were some who felt this was not always in equal proportions.

"You either were for him or against him," one veteran official remembers. "With Captain Eddie, there was no middle ground."

Employees were sure of one thing, however: The Captain worked as hard as anyone and usually harder. No detail was too minor for him to oversee, no task too menial for him to perform himself, no problem too small for him to try and solve personally. For a long time he insisted on answering all passenger mail —another reason why Sheppy seldom took a weekend off, because weekends he often used to clean up correspondence. When Eastern began putting "write us and tell us how you liked your flight" forms in seatbacks, Rickenbacker had to see all responses.

He even struck up an extended correspondence with one passenger who kept submitting suggestions for improving service. Rickenbacker answered each proposal politely and in friendly fashion, although for obvious reasons not one was adopted.

"On night flights," the passenger wrote, "pilots ought to be given 'sweet potatoes' or ocarinas to lull your customers to sleep."

When this was rejected, he came back with "How about hanging a trapeze in the middle of those big Douglas cabins so we overworked businessmen can exercise as we fly?" It got so that EVR used to ask Sheppy, "Anything in the mail today from old so-and-so?"

J. J. Mehl was company treasurer, but there were times when he might as well have been answering reservations phones. Rickenbacker rode herd on virtually every penny spent—it may be apocryphal but reportedly EVR once saved four thousand dollars in pennies for his sons over a twelve-year period. Not even his favorite employees were safe from his wrath if he found they had circumvented his standing orders that even small purchases had to have his personal approval.

Johnny Ray almost lost his job when he shelled out $250 to build the airline's first engine test-stand. He did most of the work himself and the money went largely for materials, but Rickenbacker was on one of his base-inspection tours when he spotted the stand.

"What the hell did that cost?" he asked sternly.

"Two hundred and fifty bucks," Ray said, his heart sinking.

"That's two hundred above my fifty-dollar limit!" the Captain exploded. "Are you trying to break this airline?"

"No, sir. We needed it and I thought . . ."

EVR stalked angrily away, leaving a trail of invectives behind him. For days Ray expected to get his dismissal notice, but Rickenbacker never brought it up again.

As the DC-3 fleet grew, he sold the five Lockheed Electras; they had been in service less than two years but were hopelessly antiquated by the new planes. Rickenbacker had been impressed with Lockheed, however, and especially with Bob Gross, its president—their relationship was to lead to future purchases that would make Eastern one of Lockheed's biggest customers. For the time being, though, there was nothing coming out of any aircraft factory that could match Donald Douglas's masterpiece. Route expansion paralleled the gradual DC-3 additions—in the 1938–39 period, EAL's route system increased by more than eleven hundred miles, with extensions from Atlanta to Tallahassee and Tampa, Houston to San Antonio, Memphis to Tallahassee via Montgomery, Birmingham, and Muscle Shoals, and Houston–Brownsville via Corpus Christi.

One airport Eastern didn't move into was the spanking, brand-new La Guardia field—not right away, anyway. La Guardia opened in 1939 but Rickenbacker wouldn't let EAL start operating there until the following year—exactly why became a matter of speculation that is still unresolved.

One theory was that Captain didn't dig the liberal politics of the man for whom the airport was named: feisty Mayor Fiorello La Guardia. Another involved an incident that occurred in 1934 when the New York mayor was a passenger on a flight that landed in Newark. The DC-2 came to a stop but La Guardia refused to budge from his seat. The stewardess asked him what was wrong.

"My ticket says Chicago–New York," the mayor said, "and this is Newark. I want to go to New York."

"We don't fly to New York," the flustered flight attendant explained. "Newark serves the New York area."

"I paid for a ticket to New York," La Guardia said testily, "and that's where I'll get off this plane."

The Captain came back, got nowhere, and retreated to the terminal, where he did some hasty consultation with the airline brass. La Guardia won the battle—the DC-2 took off again, with the mayor the sole passenger, and landed at Floyd Bennett Field, the only New York field capable of handling a DC-2.

Years of retelling embellished the story until it was assumed that Eastern was the airline that had to fly La Guardia from Newark to Floyd Bennett—with the accompanying assumption that this was the reason Rickenbacker refused to use La Guardia when it opened. The DC-2 was a TWA ship, however, and the flight to Newark had originated in Chicago—a route EAL didn't serve. A more logical explanation is that Captain Eddie simply stayed loyal to the Newark airport which had been part of Eastern's system for so long. He finally agreed to start operating out of La Guardia when passenger preference for the more convenient airport forced him to make the move—and even then Newark was to remain a major EAL base for many years.

Use of La Guardia was inevitable, at any rate, for by 1940 Eastern was booming and needed new facilities. It was serving eighty percent of the population east of the Mississippi, a figure achieved when St. Louis joined the system. Total route mileage had jumped from 3,358 miles in 1934 when EVR became general manager, to 5,381 miles. Employee ranks had swelled to just under 2,000 with an annual payroll of almost $4 million. The bottom line was profit: Eastern netted more than $1.5 million in 1940.

On the sidelines watching this progress was a man destined to play a major role in Eastern's history—a handsome, erudite scion of a distinguished American family. He had joined the board of directors in May of 1938 at Rickenbacker's own invitation and would someday own a huge chunk of EAL stock. He became Captain Eddie's close friend, confidant, and advisor, possessing more influence on the volatile Rickenbacker than anyone alive. He was born to wealth but also was blessed with a social conscience—something Laurance Rockefeller shared with his brothers.

By this time the Captain was chafing in the cramped space of the General Motors Building. The airline had outgrown its quarters and Rickenbacker began looking around for larger offices. One day he was tipped that Pan American was negotiating for space in the new Rockefeller Center—heresy to Captain Eddie, who quickly called Lawrence Kirkland, in charge of handling the Center's leasing contracts.

"You're an Eastern stockholder and Laurance is on our board," EVR pointed out. "What the hell are you negotiating with Trippe for? Come over to Eastern—we need new space."

What the Captain had in mind was an airline building in the new complex. He met with Kirkland and Rockefeller, agreed to sign a ten-year lease for top-floor quarters, and got them to go ahead with his other scheme: The skyscraper housing EAL's offices would be called The Eastern Air Lines Building. Bev Griffith had another idea—he talked Rickenbacker and the Rockefeller interests into signing the leasing agreement in an Eastern DC-3 cruising over Rockefeller Center.

Rockefeller himself recalls those exciting glory days with fond nostalgia.

"Eastern was the blue chip of the airline industry then," he says. "Eddie had inherited from General Motors their accounting system so he really did talk in mills when others were talking about pennies. His forte was his ability to analyze costs—that was the key to his early success. He and three other men ran the airline. Brattain, who used to be a schoolteacher, lectured like one. Sid Shannon was an excellent technical man. Charlie Froesch was, too, but he often tended to wind up rationalizing whatever Eddie wanted. It was quite a team, though."

That it was—lean, hard, and tough like the man who

headed it. Rockefeller didn't mention another member, however; that was Tom Armstrong, a big, friendly, square-jawed bear of a man who had started out with Pitcairn as an apprentice book-keeper and worked his way up the executive ladder until he became company treasurer in 1939, replacing Mehl. Not many took much notice of an employee who came with EAL in 1940, fresh out of Fordham University, who was hired as a junior accountant but quickly discovered there was no such animal as a specialist at Eastern—Charles Simons found himself loading bag-gage and working behind ticket counters when he wasn't adding up columns of figures. He would be heard from later.

The shock waves from the European war already were roll-ing over the United States, and included in the U.S. defense buildup was a stringent priority system for ordering new airline aircraft. Rickenbacker had the funds; he had swung a deal with a group of investment bankers to underwrite a $3 million stock issue—over the objections of his own board of directors, inciden-tally. The board had wanted to give Eastern's stockholders pref-erential rights but EVR warned that if the war continued to go badly for the British and French, the stock market would dive.

"Our stock's selling right now for forty dollars a share," he argued. "If the Germans keep going the way they are, that price is going to drop. The banks are willing to underwrite the issue at thirty-two fifty—and we couldn't get that figure from our own shareholders if the market takes a plunge."

The directors went along, some of them reluctantly, but EVR was proved right—shortly after the stock issue agreement was signed, Belgium collapsed and the rout of the French army was in full swing. This obstacle hurdled, Rickenbacker then won priority authorization for ten new DC-3's by selling all ten of EAL's remaining DC-2's to Australian carriers. In that one transaction, he proudly reported to his directors, Eastern had doubled its passenger capacity.

High-finance manipulating, of course, is just one facet of the air carrier industry. The people of an airline are another—especially their collective sense of humor, so essential in a busi-ness involving constant exposure to an occasionally unreasonable, irascible public . . . in an atmosphere where crisis becomes a way of life, and death a reminder of the frailty of man and machine; a peripatetic kind of existence in which the deepest roots must be planted not in homes or communities but in tradition and comradeship, often the only solid, real common denominator in a world of flights, transfers, and job changes.

It was truer in the old days than it is now, and it was more applicable to flight crews than to anyone else, because of their nomadic lives. Pilots in particular were prime sources for the stories and anecdotes that have become part of airline history; the yarns and the characters are interchangeable, for airmen—regardless of which airline uniform they're wearing—are a breed apart anyway. A wonderfully wacky individualist at Eastern would have a counterpart at American, Western, Continental, and just about every other carrier.

And Eastern *did* have its Characters, especially in the DC-3 days when the unsophisticated equipment seemed to generate uninhibited pilots. An all-time EAL favorite was Herman Wilhelm, known to all as "Herman the German." He was a huge, gruff man and his vocabulary was populated largely by the finest collection of four-letter words east of Dodge City.

Herman was based in Chicago and had a farm in nearby Joliet. He once put a DC-3 down on a landing strip he had carved out close to the farm and invited all twenty passengers aboard into his house for hot coffee—"My wife makes better coffee than what you'd get on the plane," he explained with devastating logic. Nineteen of his guests considered this unscheduled landing a commercial aviation highlight, but the twentieth reported Captain Wilhelm to the company and he got two weeks off without pay.

He never landed an Eastern plane on his farm again, but he flew over it—at low altitudes—countless times. When radar came along, the Chicago controllers invariably would see Herman disappear from their scopes right after takeoff. Normally this would have rung every alarm bell in the ATC system but not when it was Captain Wilhelm—they knew he was heading for an aerial check of the farm. He never identified a flight by its as-

signed number and never had to; every controller knew his
booming voice, capable of producing more decibels than a
champion hog caller's.

He'd radio, "What's doing down there?"

And the answer would come back, "Hi, Herman—do you
need a clearance?"

The controllers loved him and he was one of the comparatively few pilots who appreciated the job they were doing and the
difficulties under which they labored. He staged an annual corn
roast on his farm and invited every controller in the Chicago
area—whoever was off duty showed up. In gratitude they named
a radio checkpoint after him: Wilhelm Intersection.

When Eastern eventually got stewardesses back, Herman's
vocabulary caused immediate problems—to call it salty would be
a hopelessly inadequate description. One flight attendant,
warned in advance, told him not to use bad language in front of
her.

"What's wrong with my language?" he demanded indig-
nantly.

"I've heard it's full of profanity."

"Now who the hell told you that crap?" Herman roared.

Art St. John was another Eastern pilot cut out of the Wilhelm mold. He was death on newly married copilots, who would
confide shyly and proudly, "Art, I just got married to a wonderful girl."

"Great," St. John would reply. "Got any dirty pictures of
her?"

"Of course not!"

"Wanna buy some?" Art would leer.

Then there was a captain named Max Marshall who had
suffered through an unhappy love affair with a girl who had
always worn a distinctive perfume. When the romance ended,
Marshall suddenly acquired a phobia about *any* perfumed
aroma. No stewardess assigned to his flight dared wear any and
every copilot quickly learned to abstain even from after-shave
lotion. A new first officer's first glimpse of Captain Marshall was
startling: He would enter the cockpit and sniff the throttles to

check on any residue of odor from the previous occupants' hands.

A longtime favorite was Ervie Ballough, whose career with Eastern dated back to the Mailwings. When EAL meteorologist Joe George wrote a pamphlet on the new air-mass method of forecasting weather, copies were put in pilot mailboxes. Ervie took his out and tossed it in a wastebasket.

"Aren't you going to read it?" an agent asked him.

"Hell no," Ervie said. "There'll be days you can fly and days when you can't."

Slim Babbitt was another Character. Unlike Wilhelm, he spent his long and honorable airline career feuding with Air Traffic Control and used to wage a particular vendetta against the Jacksonville tower personnel. One night he deliberately turned off the landing lights on his DC-3 and as he neared Jacksonville he began radioing, "Eastern twenty miles out . . . fifteen miles . . . ten . . . five. . . ."

The controllers peered into the blackness, trying in vain to spot him. Finally Babbitt messaged, "Eastern one mile from field," and turned on his lights.

"Roger," Jacksonville acknowledged. "You're cleared to land."

And they turned out every light on the field.

It is customary today for many pilots to live in one city but fly out of bases hundreds and even thousands of miles from their homes—air travel has reached such a stage of reliability that such commuting is entirely feasible and quite common. It wasn't that reliable in the DC-3 era but some pilots did commute, including one EAL captain named Bob Boswell, who resided in Philadelphia but flew out of the Newark base. Boswell was reported for sneaking aboard several American Philadelphia–Newark flights without a pass and John Gill, then chief pilot at Newark, called him in.

While Gill was chewing him out, Boswell kept glancing nervously at his watch.

"Quit that," Gill snapped. "What the hell's wrong?"

"I wish you'd hurry up, Johnny," Boswell pleaded. "American's got a flight leaving in ten minutes."

The roll call could go on and on. . . .

Gil Waller looked more like a jockey than an airline captain with his five-foot-six-inch height. He used to punish himself if anything went wrong on a flight—such as the time he walked up and down a ramp with a parachute strapped to his back, like an Air Corps cadet doing a fifty-demerit punishment tour. If he thought he had flown a bad trip, he would walk all the way from the airport to his layover hotel carrying his suitcase and "brain bag" containing navigation maps. Once he forgot the brain bag when he was halfway downtown, and trudged back to the airport for it.

Olin King had a high, rather effeminate voice completely out of keeping with his burly physique—he was built like a butcher, which he actually had been once. Copilots hated to fly with Olin on any DC-2 trip. He always would assure his DC-2 cockpit companion, "Now, today I'm gonna let you do the take-off." They'd start rolling, the happy copilot clinging to the yoke. Just as they broke ground, he'd yell, "Gear up," and King would reply, "Okay, I've got the yoke"—leaving the other to perform the hernia-inducing job of raising the gear. After struggling up to cruising altitude, Olin would wrap himself in a blanket and instruct the copilot, "Wake me up when we're ready to land." Most copilots tried to let him sleep so they could make the landing but King seemed to have an altimeter planted in his brain—he would always wake up before final approach.

The favorite of the younger pilots was Dick Merrill. He was one of the easiest-going captains who ever commanded an airplane and never seemed to get mad at anybody. No matter how inept, erring, or outright stupid the greenhorn, Merrill would slap him on the back after a trip and solemnly assure him, "You're the best damned copilot I've flown with." It must be added, however, that the inept, erring, and stupid either shaped up fast or they were finished—not every captain was as tolerant of mistakes as Merrill, and Eastern's pilots overall ranked high in the industry.

"Maybe I'm a bit prejudiced," John Halliburton says, "but I honestly believe we had a reputation for having the best bad-weather pilots in the country."

Tom Button, now senior vice president of flight operations and a line captain before he went into management, agrees with Halliburton.

"Eastern always was a pilots' airline," he maintains. "The brass hats from Captain Eddie on down let each captain run his own show and to some extent that's still true—I think an Eastern captain has more control over his flight, more freedom of operation, than on any other airline. They were and most of them remain rugged individualists because that's the way Captain Eddie wanted it. Hell, I can remember other pilots standing with their noses against operations windows and watching Eastern planes landing when they were grounded. It was all legal—if the tower gave you an indefinite ceiling, it meant you could make one pass at the runway."

Halliburton and Button may be biased, but it is a fact that Eastern really was known for its ability to operate safely in the worst kind of weather. At any airport EAL served, it was not uncommon to find planes of the Great Silver Fleet landing and taking off while agents at the counters of other carriers were posting "canceled due to weather" or "delayed because of weather" on their flight-information boards.

But reputations, like records, are things of fragility, made to be broken—as Rickenbacker himself found out on the night of February 26, 1940.

He never regarded himself as clairvoyant or possessing ESP, but some of his associates wondered—and Sheppy was one of them.

On the afternoon of the twenty-sixth, she noticed he was unusually restless, wandering around his office and sometimes staring aimlessly off into space. He was scheduled to leave for Birmingham that same night and at first she blamed it on his reluctance to make the trip; he had previously agreed to be in the Alabama city on the twenty-seventh for a speech before the Birmingham Aviation Committee, and just that morning had asked his hosts to postpone his appearance, explaining that he had a directors' meeting scheduled in Miami on February 28.

"I just can't squeeze Birmingham in," he had complained to Sheppy. "Let's call 'em and I'll explain my schedule's too crowded—I'll go down there later."

The Aviation Committee wasn't too happy, and Rickenbacker got the impression they thought he was snubbing them. The more he dwelled on their phone conversation, the more he began to fret until he finally summoned Sheppy.

"Get those Birmingham people back, Sheppy," he ordered. "What the hell—I won't get much sleep but there's no point in offending anyone."

The Birmingham speech ranked below the board meeting in priority—he planned to ask his directors to approve a $5 million expenditure for additional DC-3's. But Eastern had applied for authority to operate a Chicago–Birmingham–Miami route and EVR wanted the support of civic leaders—it was this more than anything else that weighted his decision to make a trip he really didn't want to make.

He packed a briefcase with papers for the directors' meeting and then began his pacing. It was late in the afternoon when it suddenly dawned on Sheppy she had seen him this way before—the day preceding the Daytona Beach accident. She said nothing but the disturbing word "premonition" sprinted through her mind.

His plane left New York at 7:10 that night—Flight 21, the "Mexico Flyer" bound for Brownsville with intermediate stops at Washington, Atlanta, Birmingham, New Orleans, and Houston. Rickenbacker was pleased to find that the aircraft was one of EAL's five brand-new DST's—Douglas Sleeper Transport, the designation for DC-3's equipped with berths. He didn't intend to sleep, but Eastern's DST's had a small private room just behind the cockpit; called the Sky Lounge, it afforded privacy and a chance for Rickenbacker to read over his notes for the Birmingham speech.

The flight was over Spartanburg, South Carolina, when the

captain—Atlanta-based Jim Perry—came out of the cockpit and stopped by the lounge to talk to his boss.

"The weather in Atlanta isn't too good," he confided. "We might have some trouble getting in."

Rickenbacker recalled later that he made some remark to the effect, "You're the captain—do what you think best." Perry nodded and continued his way through the cabin, chatting pleasantly if briefly with passengers—in those days all airlines expected their captains to perform this public relations gesture.

The last weather report Perry received before starting his letdown showed low but legal ceiling and visibility, and he continued a normal instrument approach—in this case, following the range beam on a path that would take the flight over and past the airport, then making a 180-degree turn and riding the beam back toward the assigned runway. They were in that final turn, left wing low, when Rickenbacker felt a shudder as the wing scraped the tops of some pine trees. Simultaneously Perry jerked the wing up in a move so violent and sudden that Rickenbacker, sensing trouble, jumped out of his lounge seat and started toward the back of the plane. He was still in the aisle when the right wing crunched into the trees and ripped off.

The impact was severe enough to somersault the twelve-ton airliner, nose first. It landed upside down on its tail. The fuselage ruptured into two pieces, the break occurring in the middle of the cabin where Captain Eddie had been standing. Rickenbacker was hurtled toward the ceiling as the DC-3 flipped over, coming down so hard on the armrest of a seat that the impact crushed his left hip.

Miraculously there was no fire—Perry had cut the ignition and light switches the minute the right wing hit the trees, and the fuel pouring out of the torn wing tanks somehow failed to ignite. Rickenbacker found himself lying on top of the dead body of steward Clarence Moore—they had been talking in the lounge just before the crash, Moore sitting in the aisle seat next to Captain Eddie, who was by the window. EVR never did know whether the steward followed him down the cabin aisle or whether the violence of the somersault propelled him rearward.

Moaning was the only thing Rickenbacker heard after the terrible sound of tearing metal ceased. He was soaked in his own and probably Moore's blood, and with a throb of terror he discovered he was virtually paralyzed. Then some voices, mostly dazed and pained. Eleven of the sixteen persons aboard had survived the crash, but several subsequently died of injuries. Both pilots were dead. Rickenbacker remembered later that some survivors were stumbling around the wreckage in night clothes or underwear—they had been in their berths. He himself was drenched not only with blood but gasoline.

It was raining and Rickenbacker heard one man call out, "Let's start a fire so we can keep warm."

"For God's sake, no!" Captain Eddie managed to rasp. "The spilled fuel will explode."

"Who the hell is that?" the voice asked.

"Rickenbacker. Don't light any matches. Just sit tight and somebody will come get us."

It was dawn before a search party reached the crash site. Rickenbacker was in untold agony—his pelvis was smashed, a nerve in his fractured left hip severed, his ribs broken—some in three places—and he had sustained serious head injuries. Included in the first rescue group was John Halliburton, who was based in Atlanta at the time—a dispatcher had called him with the news that Flight 21 was down, with Captain Eddie aboard.

Halliburton helped carry the crushed body of his boss out of the wreckage, prying loose the jagged metal that had pinned him between a bulkhead and a fuel tank.

"I wouldn't have given a plugged nickel for his living another twenty-four hours," he says grimly. "One eye was hanging out of its socket, all the way down to his cheekbone. It was lucky we found the plane just when it began to get light—farmers in our search group were carrying kerosene lanterns and the ground was saturated with gas. We put Eddie on a stretcher with a defective catch; it was the folding kind and kept coming loose. I can still remember him cussing, even though he was only semiconscious. Some bastard of a newspaper photographer shoved a camera in his face just as we got him on the stretcher, but he never got a chance to snap a picture. Somebody from Eastern, I don't know who, damned near knocked him off the ridge where the plane had hit."

Rickenbacker was alert enough to notice that the first ambulance to arrive was loaded with the bodies of the dead.

"What the hell's going on here?" he mumbled through swollen lips. "They're taking corpses when they've got injured people to move."

Halliburton said he didn't know but someone else volunteered the information that the state law allowed a twenty dollar fee for transporting dead bodies but only ten dollars for live ones. Rickenbacker and the other injured had to wait an hour for the second ambulance and the doctor accompanying the search party finally gave him two shots of morphine to ease the excruciating pain.

All the injured were taken to Atlanta's Piedmont Hospital. An intern took one look at Rickenbacker and ordered the stretcher bearers to move him out of the way.

"He's more dead than alive," he ruled. "Let's work on the live ones first."

Rickenbacker was so weak he couldn't open his mouth to protest—until a priest came into the emergency room and asked a nurse if the Captain was Catholic. EVR figured he was about to receive the last rites and with that his speech came back.

"I'm a damn Protestant like ninety percent of the people!" he protested.

He was to spend four months and two days in Piedmont, and for the first ten days was given up for dead. Rickenbacker had always been convinced of the benefits of osteopathy and he refused to let surgeons operate on his crushed hip—so badly smashed that the ball of the joint had splintered the socket, leaving his left leg four inches shorter than the right. Until he was able to take osteopathic treatment, he remained in such pain that morphine was the only relief and at one dark point he decided that the agony was preferable to becoming an addict. The drug had caused periods of hallucination that frightened him.

Once, when his two sons were in the room, he had invited

them to take some of the grapes and cherries he saw hanging from a bar over his head. His oldest boy, David, looked at him with mixed bewilderment and fear.

"I don't see any grapes or cherries, Dad," he told his father.

This and other moments of delirium led to his finally ordering Dr. Floyd McRae, Piedmont's chief surgeon, to "quit giving me morphine."

"Eddie, you won't be able to stand the pain," McRae warned.

"The hell with the pain. Promise me—no more drug!"

"I'll take you off morphine for twenty-four hours," the doctor compromised, "but you'll regret it."

Only Rickenbacker's willpower pulled him through that particular crisis. The entire staff marveled at his will to live—he was an obstreperous, cantankerous patient, especially when he was hallucinating and imagined that the doctors and nurses were mistreating him, but they had to admire his iron courage. While he was hovering between life and death, Adelaide turned on the radio in his room and Rickenbacker heard Walter Winchell's staccato voice:

"Flash! Atlanta! It is confirmed that Eddie Rickenbacker is dying and is not expected to live another hour!"

Adelaide started to laugh but Rickenbacker didn't think it was funny. He grabbed a water pitcher and fired it at the radio. Glass, tubes, knobs, water and splintered wood flew all over the floor; his wife knew then that he simply refused to die.

He walked with a limp for the rest of his life (the irreparable residue from the smashed hip) and his once ramrod-straight frame had a slight but permanent stoop. The severed hip nerve prevented him from putting any pressure on his left leg so he gave up driving a car—a rather minor penalty inasmuch as this veteran of hundreds of high-speed automobile races had never bothered to obtain a driver's license. (For that matter, he never had a pilot's license, either.)

His convalescence took longer than he had expected or wanted. He had hoped to go back to work full-time by September but he was constantly in pain and not until late fall was he able to go to his office for even a few hours a day. The telephone became his only contact with the airline during the long summer, and he talked frequently with Brattain and Shannon, who kept him posted on problems, programs, and policy decisions—most of the latter, it must be added, being kept on the back burner until his return.

Captain Eddie took particular delight when Shannon told him how Eastern had ruined American's plans to become the first carrier to land a plane at Washington's new National Airport. It was a showplace that rivaled La Guardia in modern facilities, and before it was built the government had boasted that its main runway would be as long as the distance between the Washington Monument and the Capitol Building. Convenience was its principal feature—National is less than four miles from the heart of downtown Washington. Construction involved dredging the Potomac River to land-fill some 500 of the 750 acres constituting the airport site.

The official opening was scheduled for just after midnight of June 19, 1941, a time at which American had a flight scheduled to land, thus winning the honor of being the first. American naturally made much of the occasion publicitywise—perhaps too much, because Bev Griffith took due notice of the hoopla American was planning and decided to try to short-circuit the celebration.

Eastern had a DC-3 flight in the area at the same time, scheduled to land just behind American. Bev probably could have done nothing without the help of whatever gremlins afflicted the American DC-3, but the flight was delayed and Griffith moved quickly.

He was in the control tower at National when the word came that American would be a few minutes late. He knew Ray Tucker, commanding Eastern's DC-3, was holding until American got landing clearance, so he began badgering the controllers.

"You can't make Eastern wait just because American's screwed up its arrival!" he shouted. "Let us go ahead and land."

"We promised American . . ." a controller started to explain.

"The hell with American! Captain Rickenbacker won't stand for this injustice!"

Whether it was Bev's persistence or the mention of the stricken Captain Eddie that did the trick, nobody knows, but the chief controller finally sighed, "Okay, tell Eastern they can come in."

Aboard Tucker's plane were a number of chorus girls— Griffith's ace-in-the-hole for stealing at least some of the photographers away from American's ramp area. As it turned out, Bev got practically all the attention anyway.

The Captain spent that summer at a Connecticut lake where the greatest dividend of his enforced leisure was a chance to be closer to his boys. David, the oldest, was more mechanically inclined than Bill and already had spent a summer working for his father's airline at Newark. EVR had passed the word that he was not to be shown any favoritism and Dave found out he meant it—he was assigned the job of cleaning "honey buckets," meaning aircraft toilets. Rickenbacker always called the boys "pal Dave" and "pal Bill" during their younger years, took them to baseball games, and genuinely enjoyed their companionship.

But even being with his sons couldn't compensate for the long days spent away from his other family: the airline. Brattain and Shannon did a good job of running it, the latter being rewarded with a vice presidency. Rickenbacker's parsimony in doling out vice-presidential plums had more good sense behind it than mere stinginess; he was one of the few airline chiefs who recognized quite early that an airline's real strength lay in the caliber of middle management. Added to this awareness, it must be admitted, were two other factors: the fewer the vice-presidents, the smaller the executive payroll and the number of potential crown princes with ambitions of succession.

He had taken on, in 1940, the services of Leslie P. Arnold, a World War I pilot he had known in France, naming him to the newly created post of assistant to the president. Arnold had been a vice president of Pennsylvania Central Airlines, but this was another case in which EVR resisted any increase in the vice-presidential ranks.

He also continued to resist hiring stewardesses, although by this time the burgeoning defense effort had put ten percent of Eastern's male employees into the military reserves, half of them in the Air Corps. The pressure to add girls became so pronounced that Captain Eddie had one of his personnel officials write an article for the *Great Silver Fleet News* defending the all-male flight attendant policy.

The article disclosed that EAL's stewards ranked above average in educational background—ten percent were college graduates, forty percent had attended college, and virtually all were high school graduates. Seventy percent were married, and the article pointed out that a married flight attendant was a more valuable employee because his stability increased—in direct contrast to the short job-tenure of the average stewardess.

"The steward profession has great stability," the article continued. "This is demonstrated by the fact that resignations and dismissals are very rare, indeed. A flight steward knows that all departments of air transportation are open to him if he is willing to study and prepare himself during his leisure, whereas the stewardess realizes there are very few places she can go in her company."

This was the polite if chauvinistic way of putting it. Another way was expressed by Rickenbacker when Laurance Rockefeller mildly questioned the all-steward rule.

"If passengers want to fool around with girls, let 'em do it at their expense, not mine," EVR declared.

Rickenbacker apparently never had the fear that either Brattain or Shannon was in back of him with a hidden knife. He took their loyalty for granted, perhaps Shannon's to a somewhat greater extent. Shannon in some ways was a lot like him—rough, gruff, good rapport with employees and especially the pilots who were under his direct supervision. Rickenbacker made him responsible for negotiating labor contracts with ALPA and the self-educated Shannon, who played the piccolo for relaxation, made them about as informal as possible.

Sid took a dim view of formal education anyway, and used to bristle at the younger members of the negotiating committee whose vocabularies produced a large supply of erudite phraseology and legalistic definitions. Mike Fenello, now vice president of system operations and safety, was one of them and still chuckles at the memory.

"You're using a lot of fancy words that don't mean a goddamned thing," Shannon would complain to Fenello. This inability to communicate resulted in many fruitless and futile daytime sessions in which the major agreement was a decision to adjourn until the next day. The younger pilots would leave to plan the strategy for the next session while Sid and the older members like Jerry Wood and Slim Babbitt retired to the nearest bar.

"The following day," Mike recounts, "we'd march in loaded with bristling arguments, devastating statistics, and impassioned pleas, only to find that Sid, Jerry, and Slim had settled the whole contract at the bar the night before."

Someone once half-convinced Shannon to give new pilot applicants a highly touted psychological aptitude test. Sid agreed but only conditionally—he decided to first give the test to fifty senior Eastern captains. When half of them flunked it, Shannon scrapped the testing program—much to Captain Eddie's pleasure.

For Rickenbacker really loved the rugged individualists who flew the line. It was typical of him that he never uttered one word of blame, not an iota of recrimination, against Captain Perry. On the contrary, he insisted that the crash probably was caused by Atlanta Approach Control giving Flight 21 an erroneous altimeter setting—and he may have been right. The DC-3 obviously was lower than Perry thought but it was never determined whether the aircraft's altimeters had been set to the right barometric pressure. One of EVR's first orders after he recovered was the installation of two barometric altimeters on the captain's side of the instrument panel—one set to sea level pressure and the other to actual airport pressure—on all DC-3s.

Curiously, the *Great Silver Fleet News* never mentioned Rickenbacker's crash until he was well on the road to recovery, and even then the reference was somewhat oblique, in the form of a poem written by Captain Dick Dice.

The captain who runs the Great Silver Fleet
doesn't know the meaning of the word defeat.
At the moment they've got him off his feet
but he has a spirit you just can't beat.
As his ships day and night keep churning the air,
in the heart of each pilot he knows there's a prayer
for speedy recovery and a complete repair
of the skipper who labors to keep them there.

As 1941 drew to a close, Rickenbacker finally got to the directors' meeting he had missed in Miami the previous February. His report to the board, after it approved the purchase of eleven more DC-3's, showed 2,280 employees on the payroll—331 of them pilots and more than 500 mechanics. It was no accident that more than a third were in the operations side of the airline; ground personnel substituted productivity for numerical strength.

The payroll itself was $4.7 million, with Eastern serving forty cities in seventeen states and operating a fleet of just under forty DC-3's. Three Stinson Reliants were used for instrument training and the airline also owned a Kellett autogiro used briefly to fly mail between the airport at Camden, New Jersey, and the roof of Philadelphia's main post office. EAL by the end of the year would have carried more than 300,000 passengers, placing the airline sixteenth in terms of people transported on common carriers—seven railroads ranked ahead of American, United was tenth, and TWA twentieth.

The airline showing underlined the industry's growth—no air carrier, Eastern included, was anywhere near the status of a transportation giant, but the outlook was promising. It was a satisfied if not entirely happy Captain Eddie who sat in his office one Sunday afternoon in early December, dictating letters to Sheppy.

The date was December seventh.

CHAPTER SEVEN

THE WAR YEARS

Eddie Rickenbacker was an avowed isolationist, an indefatigable foe of Franklin Roosevelt, and an unrelenting critic of organized labor during the war years.

But he also was a patriot who sincerely loved his country, and like so many Americans who opposed involvement in another European war, once we were in it he went all out for the war effort. His isolationist beliefs did not stem from any admiration for Hitler, whose rise to power he had predicted. The only Germans he knew personally were his former aerial enemies, and he made no secret of the fact that he had met a group of them after the war—including Goering, Ernst Udet, and Erhardt Milch—at a dinner they arranged for him.

He was visiting Germany at the time and was shaken by the poverty and suffering he saw. When he returned to America, he was one of the few Americans who publicly urged a more charitable treatment of the foe he had helped conquer. Harsh reparations, he warned, would merely result in some dictator taking over Germany and making it a worse menace than she had been under the Kaiser.

He was only fifty years old when the U.S. entered World War II and he briefly may have envied fellow airline chiefs like C. R. Smith and Bob Six who donned uniforms. Still badly crippled from the Atlanta crash, however, he had no illusions about going back into active military service. He did want to do something—even as he had preached isolationism, he also had preached preparedness; in his autobiography, interestingly enough, he spoke proudly of the latter but never mentioned the former. He was absolutely convinced that if the nation's leaders had listened to him in the prewar years, Hitler would have never dared launch a war and neither would Japan. For Rickenbacker above all else was a Billy Mitchell disciple, believing that an all-powerful air force would have been a major deterrent.

He made a point of reminding people that he had given up his commission as a reserve colonel in 1934, as a protest against FDR's "legalized murder" orders to Army mail pilots. When Bill Knudsen of General Motors donned the three stars of a lieutenant general to take charge of war production, Rickenbacker told him that by accepting the commission "your usefulness to the country will be cut in half." Yet Rickenbacker leaped with alacrity at any wartime job or mission Washington suggested to him—including one that almost cost him his life—and for a man in almost constant pain, his ready acceptance was almost foolhardy.

In March of 1942 he willingly agreed to go on a nationwide tour of Air Corps training bases, at the suggestion of General H. H. "Hap" Arnold, who told him morale was poor. Accompanying him was General Frank "Monk" Hunter, an old buddy from the 94th Squadron; Hunter had suffered a serious back injury in a crash, so another member of the tour was a masseur to keep the old warhorses reasonably upright and mobile.

The war was the first time in Rickenbacker's airline career that he did not devote his entire time to Eastern. This was not surprising, for during World War II there was no need for normal marketing and sales efforts, there was a virtual moratorium on route expansion, and the main task for every carrier was to keep its emasculated fleet in the air, covering prewar schedules with about half its prewar aircraft.

Eastern alone lost more than fifty percent of its fleet, either selling the planes outright or leasing them to the Army. In a technical sense it could have lost every plane, for President Roosevelt wanted the government to take over the airlines and operate them for the duration. FDR had even signed an executive order to that effect but tore it up after the president of the Air Transport Association (ATA), Edgar Gorrell, went to bat for the industry and convinced Roosevelt he didn't need to nationalize it to provide an efficient military transport system.

Gorrell, a tough ex-Army colonel himself and a vastly underrated figure in U.S. aviation history, had had the foresight to blueprint that system as far back as 1936 and it had been updated well before Pearl Harbor. In essence, the Gorrell plan created a civil air reserve that could be turned over to the military almost overnight in the event of a major emergency, furnishing not only transport planes but flight crews and ground personnel.

And that was to be Eastern's principal role during the war, flying a military airlift with more planes than it had given up to the Army. They were mostly big Curtiss C-46's, a twin-engine transport with one main virtue—huge cargo capacity—and a myriad list of technical faults. To operate them Eastern established a separate Military Transport Division (MTD) and its aircraft, painted in that peculiar Army drab that can't seem to decide whether it's olive or brown, naturally were dubbed "The Great Chocolate Fleet."

MTD was in existence for three and a half years, a period in which it carried some 45.5 million pounds of war cargo and 130,000 passengers on flights covering nearly 33.5 million miles —most of them over open water or primitive jungles. In some respects it had the finest operational record compiled by any airline during the war; not one scheduled flight was ever canceled and only one aircraft was lost—Eastern's reputation for being a "bad weather airline" was carried over into MTD.

Headquarters were in Miami, and at the height of its operation the MTD had more than 500 EAL employees assigned to it. It began on a modest scale with the conversion of six DC-3's from passenger to all-cargo configuration and these flew only domestically for a month. On April 14, 1942, Sid Shannon and a number of senior pilots took off on a survey flight over the route that would be Eastern's prime responsibility by 1944—a 6,500 mile hop from Miami to Accra, Africa, via San Juan, Trinidad, Georgetown, Belém, Natal, and Ascension Island. The Trinidad–Georgetown–Belém–Natal legs were flown over uninhabited jungles while the other legs involved overwater hops.

Eastern had no previous ocean-flying experience and only pilots with at least 10,000 hours of logged flight time were assigned to MTD. The logistics and handicaps were enormous. The Trinidad air strip, for example, was surrounded by jungle and was located at the base of a mountain range whose peaks were usually obscured by clouds; there was no such luxury as a missed approach at Trinidad—a pilot had to be right the first time. Maintenance was a problem, particularly at the start when there were no facilities along the route. In the early days a mechanic went on each flight, but this proved impractical as the Army began beefing up the Chocolate Fleet with new C-46's and Eastern found that the aircraft outnumbered the available mechanics.

A temporary solution was to station two mechanics at Borinquen Field, Puerto Rico. One would work on two planes each morning, board the second aircraft, and then fly with it down to Trinidad where he would service the same two planes for their return trip the next day. He would come back to Puerto Rico on the second aircraft, service the two ships all over again, and then get some sleep while the second mechanic went through the identical grueling schedule.

This arrangement lasted only until Eastern received enough C-46's to extend its operations beyond Trinidad. MTD then had to station mechanics at each stop and few mechanics today would or could work under such horrendous conditions. The fields at Georgetown in British Guiana, and Belém and Natal in Brazil, were airports only in the sense that they had runways.

Atkinson Field at Georgetown was a case in point. Located halfway between Miami and Natal—it was 2,000 miles from each point—Atkinson's runway was nothing more than a narrow clearing hacked out of the jungle. For a time Eastern's sole and very lonely employee at Atkinson was a mechanic whose living quarters consisted of a mud hut with a roof made of dung and palm leaves. Not until later in the war was a crude barracks built for the additional men assigned there.

The pilots had to avoid flying over French Guiana, which came under German control after France collapsed. They usually stayed five miles offshore, but more than one EAL plane came home with bullet holes in the fuselage because it had wandered closer than the five-mile limit.

Eastern's base at Belém was Van de Cans Field, located twelve miles from the Amazon delta town. This Brazilian facility, like the field at Georgetown, had been carved out of solid jungle and some of the trees towered as high as two hundred feet—it was another "airport" where no pilot dared try a missed approach in a heavily laden C-46. Overnighting pilots stayed in Belém's Grande Hotel and so did the mechanics—occasionally. The latter worked on an average of four aircraft a day, starting early in the morning and often finishing up close to midnight. At that hour a mechanic was usually too tired to make the twelve-mile trip over a road that was more of a wide path, so he would curl up on top of some cargo inside a plane and grab what sleep he could. His breakfast consisted of emergency rations he got out of the aircraft, and no pilot ever begrudged this appropriation of supplies.

Things were slightly better at Natal, where there also was a Grande Hotel some fifteen miles from Parnamirim Field. At least the weather was a bit drier and cooler than at either Belém or Georgetown; the biggest problem was the field's soil, fine-grain sand which a stiff South Atlantic breeze could whip into a first cousin of a Sahara sandstorm. The hotel beds were straw mattresses plunked on top of wood planks, but these sleeping quarters were palatial compared to the food service. The meals ran from poor to unbearable and the waiters spoke no English. Reporter Bill Wooten, later to become public relations representative in Miami, was assigned to cover some MTD flights where he witnessed firsthand the language-barrier problem.

"If a guy from Eastern wanted an egg," he reminisces, "he almost had to lay one. He'd flap his arms and cackle until the waiter got the message. Until the boys got to pick up a little Portuguese, they had to work out some ingenious sign language to get served."

Wooten also found out how difficult the flying conditions were. When the Army finally got permission to bypass French Guiana entirely, Eastern began operating a more direct course over the Brazilian interior. Wooten reported what this involved in these words:

"Although the direct route saved time, it also brought hazards not confronted on the coast. In the first place, the entire thousand-mile stretch was over almost solid jungle as wild and dense as any in the world. There were no dependable radio aids over most of the route and the maps pilots had to use were neither complete nor accurate. Many high mountains in the area were not even indicated on the maps and many of those shown were higher or lower than indicated, and frequently as much as fifty miles from their designated locations. The intertropical front, a barrier of cumulus, turbulent clouds often towering to the stratosphere and extending to within 500 feet of sea level, frequently blotted out most landmarks and made flying at about 9,000 feet a necessity. . . ."

Late in 1942 the Army took over the bases at Belém and Natal and Eastern's MTD became a quasi-military operation. Employees were required to wear uniforms and be subject to Army regulations, including trial by court martial for violation of the Articles of War. There was even a system of rank—a captain or top administrative official wore three shoulder bars; a chief mechanic, station manager, or copilot two bars; and radio operators, navigators, mechanics, or assistant station managers one.

The "troops" liked the C-46's five-ton load-carrying abilities, twice that of the DC-3, but their admiration stopped right there. The fat-bellied Commando—its military nickname—had more bugs than a Sunday picnic. Its hydraulic system was abysmal, so seriously faulty that Eastern grounded every C-46 it was operating for two weeks while technicians in Miami solved its troubles. Hydraulics wasn't the only problem: Its fire-extinguishing system "couldn't have put out a match in a high wind," as one mechanic bluntly phrased it. Before EAL's experts finished their improvement program, they had made more than 300 modifications to the Commando and turned it into a pretty reliable airplane—good enough to take over the major share of flying the "Hump" and good enough to put a gleam into the eyes of Captain Eddie, who even then had visions of what Eastern's postwar fleet might need.

The Miami–Natal flights began in the fall of 1943 and a few months later the War Department asked EAL to extend its aerial pipeline from Natal across the South Atlantic to Accra. There was some brief concern—the Commando was a long-legged bird but its single-engine performance left a lot to be desired, especially with the heavy loads it would be carrying. Thanks to MTD's incredible maintenance performance and the skill of the pilots, the operation came off without incident, although there were some hairy moments when, according to one crewman, "only my laundry knew how scared I was."

Ascension Island, just under 1,500 miles from the Brazilian coast, was the refueling stop, and landing a C-46 there was like trying to park a Greyhound bus in a phone booth. Hills lapped each side of the runway, which constituted an obstacle course in itself. It was humped, making the middle fifteen feet higher than it was at the approach end and forty-five feet higher than at the other end. The result was that pilots landed uphill until they reached the top of the hump and then rolled downhill the rest of the way. The crews had to get used to the illusion that they were running out of landing strip until they could see the downgrade.

Flights always left Natal at night in order to land in daylight —Ascension had no field lights. There were no night takeoffs from the island either, for besides the unlighted runway there was the problem of terns—birds roosting by the landing strip with the unpleasant habit of conducting takeoffs of their own as soon as darkness fell. There were thousands of them and they had wrecked one airplane before EAL began operating there.

Eastern stationed only one employee at Ascension, a mechanic who lived with Army personnel; he got along fine with the military boys but always welcomed the sight of an MTD flight carrying letters, fresh reading material, and maybe some special food treats. MTD was closeknit, a proud wartime fraternity that quickly built up its own traditions and esprit de corps. Their living and working conditions were abominable but griping was at a minimum, boredom being the worst enemy.

Accra was as bad as any other place on the route. It was malaria infested, and its population was heavily weighted with giant mosquitoes so voracious that M.P.'s checked cots every night to make sure the men were sleeping under nets; if they found someone in bed without a mosquito net it was a court-martial offense. The airfield was in bush country inhabited by primitive natives, and while they were harmless and even friendly, nobody felt much like straying away from the base. Maintenance work was done in the open—under almost unbearable heat or teeming rain in the daytime. Nights were cooler but darkness brought forth hordes of mosquitoes; the insects, Wooten observed, waited until perspiration washed away the repellent the men had to wear, then attacked.

For anyone assigned to MTD, laughs were few, the work hard, and the hours long—a fifteen- or sixteen-hour day was the norm, not the exception. The flight crews didn't pull duty to that extent, but they had their own brand of fatigue and tension. No pilot who ever flew the Natal–Ascension leg can ever forget the difficulties of finding a dot in the middle of the ocean, with no other land within 700 miles and the nearest alternate landing strip at least 1,000 miles away. Navigation was celestial and by dead reckoning—plus, on more than one occasion, the power of prayer. A mistake of a couple of degrees meant a flight would miss Ascension and make a ditching inevitable, but even this strain was no worse than over the rest of the route where a forced landing gave one a choice between the ocean and the jungle.

But there were compensations—the chief one being the knowledge that MTD was not only a way to help win the war, but was infinitely better than getting shot at. Plus the discovery so many provincially smug Americans had made when exposed to life in other than a prosperous democracy: There is a human urge for dignity and pride no matter how primitive or uneducated a man may be. The MTD contingent met such people, and gave them dignity through jobs.

The station managers, whose chief duty was to serve as liaison men between the airline and the Army, hired South American natives for about thirty cents a day. To many of them, the pay was secondary to the satisfaction of working around airplanes—it gave them a sense of responsibility and importance they had never known before and quite possibly would never know again. Wooten remembers one tall, dark-skinned native who seemed lackadaisical until the station manager gave him a title: *Jefe de los Lavoratorios*. From then on, he literally strutted through his chores, menial though they were—his translated title was Supervisor of Lavatories, which meant that, like David Rickenbacker, he was cleaning the honey buckets.

At Borinquen Field a young Puerto Rican was assigned the task of waking up the flight crews overnighting in the barracks. Some of them, worn out by hours of tough flying, would have slept through a major earthquake. The youngster would shine a flashlight in their faces and shake them until they opened their eyes, but this often proved inadequate—a weary pilot would fall back to sleep after the boy left and then would blame him for almost missing his flight.

A few such scoldings forced him to take drastic action. He would draw up a list of those to be awakened the next morning and take it with him when he made his before-dawn rounds. The minute a pilot stirred into semiconsciousness, the boy would deliver the one English sentence he had memorized—"Sign de paper!" The flashlight stayed on until his bleary-eyed man had signed next to his name, and if he went back to sleep, the "alarm clock" was in the clear of any negligence.

Eastern's C-46's hauled anything that could be fitted into a Commando's cavernous, dirigible-shaped hulk—including, on one occasion, a disassembled Army observation plane. The cargo ranged from a $750,000 cash payroll to medicine, vaccine, and blood plasma. The story of World War II was written in the

MTD manifests: cryptograph machines, spare engines, ammunition, guns, food, mail, soap, and technical specialists whose presence was needed in some combat zone in a hurry. One flight carried railroad engineers bound for Iran and another had aboard "sappers," men trained to detect land mines.

The return flights didn't come back empty. They hauled mica and quartz crystals from Brazil to the U.S. when a shortage of these critical materials threatened to halt production of radio and radar tubes. They flew tons of crude rubber, captured German equipment to be tested and evaluated by U.S. ordnance experts, and Army ferry pilots going back to pick up more planes.

The latter often performed their ferrying operations over Eastern's MTD route but their safety record was alarming. They were young and inexperienced, with very little instrument training, and for a time scores of them were victims of violent and usually unexpected tropical storms they were ill-equipped to handle. Army officials discussed the problem with MDT personnel and the result was the use of Eastern's planes as "weather ships." Many southbound flights began carrying Army weather observers, radioing their firsthand en route weather information back to ferry bases. If there was no Army observer aboard, EAL's own radio operators provided weather data to military aircraft in their area, and if a ferry pilot needed an up-to-date report he could call the nearest Eastern plane.

In only two weeks after the program went into effect, the ferry accident rate dropped dramatically and stayed low for the duration of ferry operations over the route. Impressed, the Army also contracted with Eastern to operate a school in Atlanta for military pilots, navigators, and flight mechanics. Nearly 1,200 men went through the school, which included instrument and transitional training for pilots. A subsequent on-the-job training program qualified almost 800 pilots to fly heavy cargo planes.

Eastern's wartime educational assignments involved one unusual task: giving additional training to none other than Pan American's veteran crews. One of the instructors was ex-EAL Captain Ernie Burton, now a highly successful home builder in Miami and the Washington area, who gives a logical explanation of why it was necessary to work with men who had far more ocean flying experience than any Eastern pilot.

"The trouble," Burton says, "was that Pan Am had been operating mostly big flying boats which always had to take off or land in daylight—nothing was more dangerous than moving a seaplane in water at night where you might never see a half-submerged log. The Pan Am guys were damned good, but few of them had done much night flying and for that very reason they hadn't had a great deal of instrument experience. When the war came and Pan Am began operating its own military cargo missions with land planes, we had to teach their crews a few things in operational areas with which they were unfamiliar. It was no reflection on Pan Am—just a fact of life they had to face."

More than the MTD went to war from Eastern, of course. By 1944 there were more than 800 EAL employees in uniform, not including the Military Transport Division. The first Gold Star went up in memory of Roger Owen, twenty-seven, a former reservations clerk in New York, who was killed in combat while with the Royal Canadian Air Force; by the end of the war EAL's Gold Stars totaled forty-two.

Captain Eddie also temporarily lost the services of Leslie Arnold, who went back in the Army in 1942 and was assigned to military cargo operations—Rickenbacker argued in vain that he could have done the same job by going with MTD but Arnold, who had been one of the Army's round-the-world flyers in 1924, was a soldier at heart. The Captain also had to abandon his antistewardess policy as Eastern's steward corps went into the service almost en masse.

Stewardesses replaced them and even when the stewards returned after the war, the girls were on EAL's flights to stay. Not many had to be hired at first because Eastern's fleet in early 1944 was down to only twenty DC-3's—aircraft operating, incidentally, at a whopping eighty-seven percent load factor (percentage of available seats occupied by paying passengers). No airline had to go out and sell tickets—the government/airline priority system put seats at a premium and the average would-be air traveler, if he or she wasn't on urgent defense business, might as well not have even tried to get space. The *Great Silver Fleet News*, reporting on the effects of the fleet reduction, mentioned that "many details of the passenger service were reduced correspondingly in quantity," then added this comment on the 180-degree course change from the no-stewardess policy:

"One very pleasant and outstanding exception to this reduction is the addition of Flight Stewardess Service, supplementing our Flight Stewards aloft."

The scarcity of airline seats taxed the patience of reservations personnel, but there was still time for an occasional laugh. Toward the end of the war, when space was loosening up a bit, A. J. McNickle of New York Reservations got a call from a young girl who wanted to know how she could make a reservation, where to buy a ticket, how was baggage handled, would a meal be served on the plane, and "suppose I decide not to go?" McNickle answered every question in detail, she thanked him, and hung up.

The next night she called him back.

"I'd like to read you my high school theme on how to get an airline reservation," she offered.

Stewardesses weren't the only distaff breakthrough resulting from the shortage of able-bodied males. Women were hired in ever-increasing numbers and they were assigned tasks supposedly beyond their female capability. One was a young lady named Margaret "Maggie" Robinson and her story is the story of all. Maggie, now Eastern's manager of consumer affairs, joined EAL's St. Louis reservations staff in 1944 and gives a vivid account of what it was like to work for an airline in the war years:

"Eastern had stopped serving St. Louis temporarily when service was cut back but the station was reopened in 1944—with a station manager, a chief agent who was like a supervisor, and five girls. We had a small office on the second floor of the Lambert Field terminal. Our reservations table was borrowed from the coffee shop downstairs and covered with a green oilcloth. We recorded all reservations on three-by-five cards and filed them in a cigar box, arranged by days of the month, alphabetically and current.

"Eastern was very strict about our wearing correct uniforms. I remember we had to have blue shoes and sometimes we had to borrow ration coupons from friends in order to buy a pair. And we figuratively had to wear many hats—even if you were assigned to reservations, you were also expected to work the ticket counter prior to a flight departure.

"Forty-five minutes before a flight left, you rushed from reservations down to the counter and began to check in passengers. We had big limousines bringing people from the downtown hotels and I always wondered how we could ever take care of a full planeload—twenty-one passengers! Actually, there was almost as much to do checking in twenty-one as there is today checking in 200. There'd be a long manifest on which you had to record each passenger's weight, destination, and baggage—how many pieces, their weight, and the check numbers. Plus whether he'd need limo service when he arrived. You started talking to passengers the minute the first one came up to the counter and you could never stop talking because if you did, you were dead. We used to keep one eye on the clock, seeing how close we were to flight time. After everyone was checked in, you'd lock up the counter, put on a uniform hat, and run outside to help load last-minute baggage—after you made the flight announcement.

"When the last bag was loaded and everyone on board, you'd pull back the steps, salute the captain, and run back to reservations where you'd start teletyping information to down-line stations—how many limos would be needed at each stop, who's making connecting flights, and so forth. We had three flights in a day and three flights out so you were kept pretty busy.

"St. Louis was a terminating and originating point on the system, with the first inbound flight arriving at five thirty in the morning. I worked from 4:00 A.M. to noon, six days a week. There were no such benefits as shift differential pay, overtime pay, or holiday pay. On your day off you'd usually come out to the airport to see how things were going and invariably you'd wind up helping out. All this for a starting salary of $125 a month. But the airlines were like that, not just in the war years but before and for a while after the war.

"The training program for reservations consisted of reading

Eastern's traffic manual. There was only one desk in reservations so I'd have to study in the terminal lobby. Once you read through the manual, you were considered trained. We did have a training school in New York and I wanted to go there badly, but once I had read the traffic manual, they figured I had enough of an airline education."

Rickenbacker himself gave her the nickname of Maggie—she met him four weeks after she started working in St. Louis and will never forget *that* experience. The station manager had warned her, "Don't say anything to him unless you know what the hell you're talking about."

Captain Eddie arrived and, as usual, began chatting with the employees on duty. For some reason the topic of conversation centered around the difficulties of landing at certain airports, and Rickenbacker mentioned one that presented a particular problem because "the beam sways"—meaning the electronic range signal.

Maggie didn't know a range signal from a spark plug but she was positive she was well versed on beams—after all, Lambert had one that revolved from the top of the control tower.

"I know just what you mean, Captain," she blurted. "I come to work every morning at four o'clock and I see it going around and around."

There was dead silence. The station manager mentally crossed himself. Rickenbacker gave Maggie a long look—and then started to laugh. He never let her forget the incident, either.

His reaction to another late wartime boo-boo was never recorded, and it is possible he never heard about it, although what happened became a classic airline story. Eastern had a brand-new young woman employee assigned to the ticket counter at Washington National, and came the day when she was allowed to make her first flight-departure announcement. She was scared stiff and cleared her throat three times before she began.

"Ladies and gentlemen," she chirped bravely if nervously, "Eastern announces the departure of Flight 420, Silver Falcon service to New York City. Passengers will please show your tickets to the plane as you board the stewardess."

The Captain's attitude toward his airline during the war became close to detachment, at least through the first years. This was natural, inasmuch as he couldn't order new planes, start new routes, nor press for increased traffic. He came out strong for Thomas E. Dewey in the 1944 presidential election, which didn't surprise anyone—in 1940 he had handed out Willkie buttons to EAL employees and while he hadn't actually ordered anyone to wear them, quite a few interpreted the distribution exactly that way. At times he almost seemed determined to make his own political views Eastern's policy; perhaps he didn't really want to go that far, but years later one of his successors was to comment:

"Rickenbacker was always complaining the government was prejudiced against him, blaming politicians for the airline's route troubles. What the hell did he expect when he handed out Republican campaign buttons while a Democratic administration was handing out route awards?"

But at least Captain Eddie was consistent. He claimed to have voted for FDR in 1932 but he quickly became disenchanted with the New Deal and he remained an unyielding enemy of Roosevelt as long as FDR lived. Yet the President never tried to keep Rickenbacker out of the war effort, as he did with Charles Lindbergh. One reason was that Captain Eddie had a "friend in court," so to speak—Secretary of War Henry Stimson, who admired EVR's frankness and dedication if not his open hatred of Roosevelt, not to mention Rickenbacker's close friendship with Hap Arnold.

Arnold had told Stimson of Captain Eddie's rapport with rookie pilots on his tour of flight-training centers, and Stimson was impressed enough to suggest another mission. In September 1942 he wrote Rickenbacker suggesting that the Captain visit England "as a nonmilitary observer" of Army Air Force bomber and fighter commands—evaluating the morale situation at these overseas stations.

Captain Eddie accepted immediately, but at a subsequent face-to-face meeting with Stimson, the Secretary of War enlarged considerably on what he wanted EVR to accomplish in England. Look at two things, he told Rickenbacker—the conduct of the air war in general and evaluation of U.S. aircraft and personnel specifically. Stimson, a conservative but not nearly as right-wing as EVR, never bought the claim of so many liberals that the Captain was a hoary anachronism, the 110-percent American who would gush forth praise and platitudes about any piece of U.S. equipment because to criticize it might seem unpatriotic. Rickenbacker had his faults, but he was unwaveringly honest and brutally frank.

Both Arnold and Stimson offered him a brigadier general's commission. When he refused, they upped the ante to a major generalship and got the same answer.

"You pay me the same as you did when I toured the domestic bases," he told them. "A dollar a year. And I'll pay my own expenses."

"You might be more effective as a high-ranking officer," Arnold suggested. "Some people might clam up to a civilian— even somebody as well known as you."

"No, sir!" EVR declared. "When I get back, I want to be able to pound the table, point to the facts, and get some action."

He was in England several weeks, meeting with a number of British officials including Churchill, but spending most of his time observing and studying U.S. air bases. His most comprehensive report concerned the B-17 bomber, on which he submitted more than twenty criticisms and seventeen recommendations for improvements—such as improved oxygen masks, installation of armor plate under the pilots and navigator (in 1918, he had placed a stove lid under the seat of his Spad), and more electrical power to gun turrets to keep them from freezing at high altitudes.

His written reports to Arnold and Stimson were made public after the war, but what he told them verbally he steadfastly refused to reveal—and neither the Stimson nor Arnold memoirs mentioned this phase of his findings. The logical supposition is that Rickenbacker was much more critical in his verbal briefing than he ever wanted anyone to know. He did bring back with him one set of plans for the North African invasion, the other two sets going by special courier via airplane and on a U.S.

cruiser—Rickenbacker was prouder of this messenger role than of anything else he did in the war.

Figuratively speaking, Stimson told him not to bother unpacking—six days after he returned from England, EVR was heading for a similar mission to the Pacific theater and carrying in his head a carefully memorized, confidential message from the Secretary of War to General Douglas MacArthur—Rickenbacker later described it as something "of such sensitivity that it could not be put on paper." What the message concerned was never disclosed.

He left San Francisco October 17, 1942, on a Pan American Clipper, accompanied by Colonel Hans Adamson, the Army public relations man who had been with him on both the U.S. and England tours. At Honolulu, after a brief rest period and inspection of Air Force bases in the area, he changed over to a B-17 for the long flight to MacArthur's headquarters at Port Moresby, New Guinea.

There apparently was a clash of personalities the minute he met the aircraft commander, Captain Bill Cherry, a tall Texan who had been an American Airlines copilot before the war. Rickenbacker was to comment later that he was "a little surprised" at Cherry's appearance—the Texan sported a goatee and cowboy boots. The rest of the crew was somewhat more military: First Lieutenant Jim Whittaker, whom EVR thought looked a little old to be a copilot; the navigator, First Lieutenant John De Angelis; Sergeant Jim Reynolds, the radio operator; and Private John Bartek, the freckled, red-haired mechanic who was only three months out of mechanics school.

There also was a third passenger—Sergeant Alex Kaczmarczyk, a young crew chief who had been hospitalized in Honolulu with appendicitis and jaundice and was on his way back to his unit in Australia.

The B-17 ground-looped after blowing a tire on takeoff and the party had to shift to another Flying Fortress. This time departure was uneventful and the B-17 grumbled peacefully toward the first stop—tiny Canton Island, 1,800 miles southwest of Hawaii. The estimated flying time was ten hours, and for what transpired in that airplane and what went wrong, we have only the accounts written later by Rickenbacker—in his autobiography and in an earlier book, *Seven Came Through* (Doubleday, 1943).

They were scheduled to land on Canton at 9:30 A.M., and at 8:30 Cherry began a gradual descent. For the next two hours they kept squinting for the first sight of the island, only eight miles long and four miles wide. At 10:15 Rickenbacker asked Cherry about the fuel supply and was told there remained a little more than four hours' worth. Rickenbacker suspected they had overshot Canton because of a navigation error and wanted to know how much tailwind they had. Cherry said about ten knots.

EVR was to say later he had the feeling the tailwind was much stronger and that his hunch was confirmed by a navigator of another plane that had left Hawaii for Canton only an hour before Rickenbacker's aircraft. This navigator, Rickenbacker wrote, told him he'd had the same ten-knot forecast that Cherry had been given but after shooting the stars had allowed for a tailwind of more than thirty knots; his calculation had brought him straight into Canton.

Rickenbacker informed Cherry they probably had overshot the island and suggested they get cross-bearings to establish their exact position. Radioman Reynolds asked Canton, which reported it couldn't take bearings—it seems the necessary equipment, delivered weeks before, hadn't been uncrated.

There was a radio station on Palmyra Island, midway between Honolulu and Canton, and Reynolds contacted it with a request for a continuing radio signal which might give the B-17 a bearing. Meanwhile, young navigator De Angelis, understandably flustered, took a sun shot with his octant and gave Cherry a new heading. Thirty minutes later he changed it and then brought up the possibility that the octant, which he had transferred from the first B-17 to the second plane, might have been damaged in the ground loop. The entire flight, Rickenbacker wrote, could have been predicated on erroneous readings and it was possible they were as much as a thousand miles off course.

Palmyra suggested that they climb to 5,000 feet and circle

while the station took a bearing. This was done and Palmyra gave them another heading which Cherry followed, but there was still nothing but open water ahead of them. They tried everything, even requesting (at Rickenbacker's suggestion) that Canton fire antiarcraft shells timed to go off at 7,000 feet so the B-17 might spot them. Another idea was to "box the compass" —fly west for an hour, then north, east, and finally south, hoping they would stumble upon the island. The trouble was that they didn't have enough fuel to complete all four legs even though Cherry was running the engines on their leanest mixture and had cut the outboards to conserve gas.

Canton advised that the antiaircraft guns were being fired and that search planes had taken off. There was no sign of the shell bursts and by now they were down to an hour's fuel—at which point Cherry ordered Reynolds to send "Mayday." There was no response to these emergency signals and Cherry told his crew and passengers to start lightening the B-17 for a ditching. Captain Eddie, limping on his cane, went back to the tail with Sergeant Kaczmarczyk and began throwing out everything that wasn't bolted to the airframe—including Captain Eddie's expensive Burberry coat he had purchased in England, the suitcase EAL employees had given him for Christmas two years before, and his briefcase.

He took a carton of cigarettes out of the suitcase before dumping it, putting three packs in his pocket and distributing the rest to his planemates. When Adamson suggested that they should drink all the water they could before the ditching, EVR said no—they'd need it more later. They tossed out everything but two mattresses they needed to help cushion the shock of ditching, and various emergency supplies—water, thermos jugs with coffee, and food rations. Most of them took off their shoes and some even removed their trousers, but Rickenbacker stayed fully clothed and kept on his special high-topped shoes which he was required to wear after the Atlanta accident.

They donned Mae West lifejackets and waited for Cherry to ditch—one of the riskiest procedures any pilot can face. There was a heavy swell below and this made the ditching even tougher.

The trick was to descend parallel to the swell and land in the trough, using the swell to reduce speed and lessen impact, for hitting water at high speed is worse than colliding with concrete.

But Cherry timed the landing perfectly and with incredible precision. The shock, nevertheless, was violent; Adamson hurt his neck and back and Reynolds smashed his face against the radio panel, but the already crippled Rickenbacker was just shaken up. Private Bartek managed to get three rafts released and the B-17, filling rapidly with water, was abandoned— Cherry, Whittaker, and Reynolds climbed into one raft; Rickenbacker, Adamson, and Bartek occupied the second; and De Angelis and Sergeant Alex—he had told Captain Eddie not to bother trying to pronounce his last name—were in the third.

A sudden breeze blew the rafts away from the sinking plane, at which point the survivors discovered that all rations, including water and coffee, had been left aboard. They debated going back aboard to salvage it but decided against it because the aircraft might sink at any moment—which was a mistake because the B-17 stayed afloat for another six minutes.

The rafts themselves were half full of water and Rickenbacker began bailing theirs out with the old gray felt hat he always carried—no one, including Adelaide Rickenbacker, had ever been able to talk him into buying a new hat. The cane he threw overboard, explaining that "the Lord never taught me to walk on water with it."

They were to stay in those rafts for twenty-two days of torture, suffering, near starvation, and—in one tragic case— death. Young Sergeant Alex died on the thirteenth day of the ordeal; he had begun the flight still in a weakened condition from the surgery and jaundice, he had swallowed seawater getting into the raft after the ditching, and his constitution was just not strong enough to sustain him. At one point Captain Eddie held him in his arms, trying to warm the boy's shivering, emaciated body.

Most accounts, including Rickenbacker's, claim it was he who took command, almost from the first moments after Cherry's

brilliant ditching to the day they were rescued. *Time* described
him as "the flotilla's Captain Bligh." Still dressed in his business
suit, he cajoled, comforted, taunted, scolded, and led them in
prayer, although Adamson was the ranking officer and Cherry
had been the aircraft commander.

The only food in the raft consisted of four oranges which
Cherry had stuffed into his leather flight jacket. Rickenbacker
had taken a Hershey bar off the plane and Sergeant Alex had a
half-dozen chocolate bars, but the saltwater had made the candy
inedible (it also had ruined the cigarettes). They had no water
for eight days, until it rained and they managed to catch the
precious moisture in whatever was handy—bailing buckets,
EVR's ancient hat, canvas, clothing, and even handkerchiefs.
The rain came in a vicious squall that almost cost lives even as it
provided the life-saving water, for it flipped over Cherry's raft;
Rickenbacker himself was to say he always wondered how
Cherry, Whittaker, and Reynolds mustered the strength to get
the raft righted and haul themselves back in.

Until they encountered the squall, their only liquid and
food came from the oranges, which Rickenbacker doled out. Not
until the fifth day was the third orange divided among eight men,
and the last one was consumed the next day because Captain
Eddie figured it was the only way to keep Sergeant Alex alive.
They were haunted by culinary memories of things they had
taken so much for granted. Reynolds kept talking about soda
pop and Cherry swore that if he ever got back, he was going to
gorge himself on chocolate ice cream. Rickenbacker, for reasons
he couldn't explain, began thinking of chocolate malted milk,
something he hadn't tasted for twenty-five years.

Tempers flared under tension—jostling a raftmate stinging
with sunburn was enough to touch off cursing. Rickenbacker, as
the self-appointed leader, became a natural target for a kind of
sullen hatred—yet after they were rescued, most of them said it
was his strong willpower that had kept them alive. One man tried
to commit suicide to make more room in the crowded raft; Rickenbacker hauled him back into the raft and cursed him for cow-
ardice. When he heard someone praying for death, Captain

Eddie lashed him with invectives. Long before they were rescued, some of them were swearing they'd stay alive just to "get
even with the old sonofabitch." And at least one man reportedly
never stopped hating him—Bill Cherry.

The man who commanded the ill-fated B-17 returned to
America after the war and became a respected senior captain,
retiring at the mandatory age of sixty. Through the years he has
adamantly refused to be interviewed about the raft ordeal, talk
about Rickenbacker in any way whatsoever, or, according to
pilots who flew with him, even discuss the events of those twenty-
two terrible days.

"You couldn't even mention the name Rickenbacker to
him," one of his closest friends says. "I think Bill Cherry will go
to his grave carrying inside of him his own version of what happened in that plane and on those rafts. If you brought up the
subject, he'd just walk away. Someone who knows him pretty
well had a theory that Rickenbacker may have been the one who
got them lost over the Pacific, by getting panicky when they had
trouble finding Canton and issuing the wrong orders. But that
was to be classed as scuttlebutt and I never heard Bill himself say
anything like that."

Even if Cherry or any of the others on the rafts were justified in hating Captain Eddie, their feelings and emotions about
his guidance had to have been affected by this ordeal. Certainly
the evidence points to his powerful leadership, his indomitable
will, and to a courage that had to spring from his faith in God.
The Rickenbackers and the Pattons of this world can inspire
hatred, but they also can inspire men to do things of which they
had never dreamed themselves capable.

The famous seagull incident occurred on the eighth day.
Rickenbacker was dozing when the gull suddenly landed on his
hat. Instinctively he grabbed the bird, wrung its neck, and calmly
defeathered it—carving up the body, dividing the raw, stringy,
fishy-tasting meat into equal shares, and saving only the intes-
tines, which provided fishing bait.

They weren't out of trouble yet, of course. The rain water
was finished the night before Sergeant Alex died and they went

another forty-eight hours suffering horribly from thirst. A fish caught on the ninth day was the last for a long time—they lost the lines and hooks trying for more—and they found they couldn't even eat the one they had caught. It was a small shark, and even hunger pangs weren't enough to overcome the foul, rancid taste of shark meat—all they could do was chew a little bit of it and then spit it out, gagging.

Sharks were constant and unwelcome companions, coming up under the rafts and jolting them so hard they would be raised out of the water. Another enemy was the salt water, corroding watches, compass needles, and even the Army automatics Cherry, Whittaker, and Adamson carried—they had tried to shoot seagulls with them but the quick corrosion froze the guns' mechanisms and they finally were thrown overboard.

Physically, Adamson was in the worst shape of those who survived. His ditching injuries were extremely painful and these were aggravated by saltwater sores and blistering sunburn over almost his entire body. The miracle man was Rickenbacker, whose already battered frame grew thinner and thinner until he achieved the appearance of a living skeleton and his prominent nose took on the shape of a big meat hook. By the fifteenth day they were all cursing each other, and at Rickenbacker more than anyone else. The rafts were roped together and it was only too easy to hear what was being said.

"You're the meanest, most cantankerous sonofabitch who ever lived," one man swore at him. EVR heard another tell a companion, "I swear I'll live so I can have the pleasure of burying that old bastard at sea."

The only moments of calmness, even lucidity, came at night when they prayed together, taking turns reading out of a Bible Bartek had brought off the plane. Yet even the prayers led to bitterness, mostly directed toward Captain Eddie. As the days and nights passed and hopes for rescue faded, some of the men questioned the existence of a God they felt had abandoned them —and such sentiments were enough to stir angry rebuttals and recriminations from Rickenbacker, whose devoutness never wavered.

They all dreamed fitfully, of rich foods, homes, loved ones, and the days when pain had been nothing more than a mild toothache. The dreams became nightmares when they awoke to the realities of slow death in cramped rubber coffins—Rickenbacker's raft held three men in a space less than seven feet long and a little more than two feet wide, and one of the other rafts was even smaller.

On the seventeenth day, overcast with the sea running rough, Cherry heard the sound of airplane engines. They began shouting when they saw the plane, a single-engine scouting seaplane too far away to spot the seven men yelling and waving their arms. The letdown was demoralizing, but at least it had been the first sign of human life they had seen for two and a half weeks—a ship had to be close by, or perhaps even land.

The next afternoon two more aircraft were seen in the distance but flew away without spotting them. On the nineteenth day the same frustration—four aircraft appeared with identical results; the rafts were a bright yellow but were so small that a plane had to be virtually on top of them to see anything. It was at this point that Rickenbacker and Cherry had their most serious confrontation.

Cherry wanted to take the smallest raft and try to make land by himself, putting De Angelis into one of the two larger boats. De Angelis, alone since Sergeant Alex's death, was objecting and Captain Eddie sided with him after Cherry said there was no use in staying together.

"You're crazy," Rickenbacker rasped to Cherry. "You don't know what direction to take—those planes we saw came from the north, south, east, and west. And if they couldn't see three rafts bunched together, how the hell are they going to spot just one?"

"I still think our only hope is to scatter," Cherry insisted. "It'll give us two chances to be seen instead of only one. But I won't go unless you agree it's right."

"It's wrong!" Rickenbacker snapped, "but I don't see any use in prolonging the argument."

De Angelis got into the raft holding Whittaker and Reynolds, the latter so weak he could hardly speak. Cherry, alone in the smallest boat, drifted away. As he disappeared from sight, Rickenbacker heard De Angelis and Whittaker murmuring that maybe Cherry was right about splitting up and the Captain blew his top. Some angry words were spoken before fatigue itself ended the argument—even Captain Eddie lacked the strength to carry it on and when Whittaker and De Angelis said they would take off on their own, as Cherry had done, he told them to go ahead.

Rickenbacker watched gloomily as the second raft faded from view. He was now alone with Adamson and Bartek, both more dead than alive, and for the first time he began to doubt their chances for being saved. They had drinkable water, laboriously gathered from the occasional rain squalls they had encountered, and before the rafts split up the survivors had been able to scoop up with their hands some small, sardinelike fish they found swimming close to the surface. But Rickenbacker knew that every man's condition was steadily weakening; when he doled out the morning ration of water, the equivalent of a whiskey jigger, his two companions were almost too weak to raise their heads.

He just about gave up hope the afternoon of the twenty-first day when two more planes appeared and flew by only a couple of hundred yards away without seeing them—by this time Captain Eddie was the only one with enough strength to wave and he had to do this while sitting down. That was their last chance, he thought.

The miracle happened thirty minutes later. Two aircraft came out of the sun and headed straight for the bobbing raft, one flying so low that Rickenbacker saw the pilot waving and swore he also could see him smiling. The planes flew off but other aircraft appeared just before the sun went down and a seaplane picked them up. The pilot, Lieutenant W. F. Eadie, told Rickenbacker that Cherry's raft had been sighted the afternoon before by a Navy plane on routine evening patrol; Cherry's rescue had sent every available search aircraft into the air—the rafts had drifted an estimated five hundred miles southwest of Canton to the Ellice Islands, a chain where the Navy had a base. Whittaker, De Angelis, and Reynolds reached the beach of an uninhabited island but were spotted by natives on a nearby island where an English missionary had a small radio transmitter. The missionary notified the Navy and the last survivors were picked up as soon as a plane could be flown there.

Captain Eddie had weighed 180 pounds at the start of the Pacific trip; he was down to 126 pounds when he was rescued. When they were undressing him in the small base hospital, his clothes fell apart. He saw his face in a mirror—he had a dirty brown beard with hair almost two inches long and a drooping mandarin mustache—and promptly demanded a shave. He admitted later he wished he'd had a picture taken of the beard but the impulse to get rid of it fast was almost as if he were ridding himself of the nightmare.

Officially they had been lost for twenty-two days, although by Rickenbacker's reckoning he was picked up on the twenty-first day; the discrepancy stemmed from the fact that the rafts had drifted across the International Date Line, losing a day— Rickenbacker thought they had been rescued on Wednesday, November 11, but the pilot's calendar showed Thursday, November 12.

EVR could have gone home to a hero's welcome but, typically, he insisted on finishing his mission as soon as he recovered. On December first he was heading back over the Pacific to deliver that message to General MacArthur and complete his inspection tour—but not by way of Canton Island. Twenty years later, however, he did visit Canton—he and Adelaide were returning from a trip through the Orient, and at his request their Pan Am jet made a special stop at Canton so Rickenbacker could finally step foot on the island.

When he got back to the U.S., he laid on Stimson's desk more than a report on the Pacific assignment—he wanted something done about survival equipment and methods and he wanted it done fast. Bill Cherry already had been assigned the task of working with the designers of new survival gear. Captain Eddie added his own input, frequently with expletives reflecting his opinion of current equipment. He told Stimson rafts should be bigger and equipped with some kind of sheet that could be used as a sail, sun shield, and rain catcher. One of his key recommendations was perfection of a small chemical water distiller —a project which became a personal crusade. It was at his instigation that a group of scientists launched extensive distillation experiments culminating in a practical apparatus now standard equipment on ship lifeboats and aircraft life rafts.

Stimson arranged for EVR to speak to a group of military air officers at the Pentagon, where Captain Eddie delivered his salty views on what was being done wrong. In the audience was a young Air Force colonel who was impressed not only with Rickenbacker's arguments, but the force with which they were delivered.

"It was the first time I had ever seen Rickenbacker," he recalls. "Frankly, I had been one of the guys who had to implement an Air Force order to strip everything possible off our life rafts so we could save weight. The theory was that if you went down in the ocean, your chances of ever being found were too slim anyway. But when Rickenbacker came back from his ordeal, he showed up at that Pentagon meeting and read us the riot act—every fourth word had four letters. Actually, we already had started putting survival gear back on the rafts, including chewing gum, but I have to admit we felt like little school kids getting reamed out by a teacher."

The name of that colonel, incidentally, was Floyd Hall, who would one day take over an Eastern Air Lines sinking toward bankruptcy while Rickenbacker stood helplessly on the sidelines, his own reputation in shreds and his name anathema among some disillusioned employees and stockholders.

This turn of events was far in the future, however. In the war years Rickenbacker was riding the crest of general popularity, prosperity, and power. He seemed to have a golden touch for doing the right thing. Henry Luce offered him $25,000 to write a full account of the Pacific experience to be published in *Life* over three installments; Rickenbacker agreed on the condition that the money go to the Air Force Aid Society, which Hap Arnold and his wife had created to help the widows and children of airmen killed in action. When Doubleday wanted to publish the installments of *Seven Came Through* as a hardback book, Captain Eddie again specified that all royalties go to the Society—and Doubleday clinched the deal by agreeing to donate its entire profits from the book to the same organization. At the time Rickenbacker was negotiating with Luce and Doubleday, the Society had raised slightly over $500; EVR's generous gesture ignited a bonfire of support that brought in hundreds of thousands of dollars just from the aviation industry, and by 1967 the Hap Arnold Educational Fund, administered by the Society, would be worth some $25 million—sending a thousand sons and daughters of Air Force parents through college annually.

Rickenbacker wasn't through carrying out Stimson's assignments, either. He spent three months after his return from the Pacific touring U.S. war plants, and in the Spring of 1943 the Secretary of War dispatched him to Russia by way of South America (Eastern's MTD route), North Africa, India, and China. He left April 26 and didn't return until August 7—with a briefcase full of notes for Stimson (mostly on Russian use of American equipment) 55,000 more miles of flying under his belt, the satisfaction of having spoken to approximately 300,000 American airmen, and a fresh feud with Franklin Roosevelt.

The latter involved an attempt by Gil Winant, U.S. ambassador to Great Britain, to have Rickenbacker confer with FDR. Captain Eddie had stopped in England on his way back from Russia and at a meeting with Churchill, at which Winant was present, warned the Prime Minister that Stalin was going to be a postwar problem unless the U.S. and Britain reached some realistic agreements with him before the war ended. EVR said Russia would demand ten times more after the war than she dared ask for while the fighting was still on. Winant was so impressed that with Captain Eddie's permission he cabled the White House, suggesting that the President see Rickenbacker as soon as he returned.

When Captain Eddie did get back, he learned that FDR hadn't answered the cable. Winant, also back in the U.S., wanted to make one more try at a Roosevelt-Rickenbacker meeting, but EVR refused.

"I wouldn't see the s.o.b. now if he asked me," he told Winant.

It is interesting to speculate on what would have happened to Eastern if Rickenbacker's raft had never been found. Paul Brattain, who with Sid Shannon's help actually ran EAL during the war, probably would have been his successor, although he never would have been EVR's own choice—Shannon would have been a more likely selection. Rickenbacker liked and trusted Brattain but not to the extent he did Shannon—there was some friction between EVR and his executive vice president which stemmed from Captain Eddie's battle to win control of the airline away from Breech. Rickenbacker felt that Brattain had done some fence-sitting during the fight and this, more than anything else, was to keep Brattain from ever achieving a successor's role.

Brattain was short, stout, and rough, with a number of enemies both inside and outside of Eastern. When it came to business he could be as tough and abrupt as the Captain himself, but away from the office—particularly when he had consumed a few belts—he could be extremely funny. During the war he moved his office to Washington and ran the airline mostly from there while EVR was away.

Brattain was an unusual person. Only five feet seven inches in height, he weighed 225 pounds and had the booming, jolly laugh of a fat man. He had once been a chemistry professor and held a patent on a form of resin used on early biplanes. Unlike some of his colleagues, he was never afraid of the volatile Rickenbacker and used to fight with him bitterly at meetings—something EVR respected even though he obviously didn't like it. What also killed Brattain's future chances of succeeding the Captain was something EVR learned when he returned from the Pacific—an unnamed director had organized a group to run Eastern with Brattain as its titular head. It was in power for the brief time EVR was missing, but Rickenbacker felt this succession machinery was as premature as his burial. Brattain actually had had nothing to do with the group's formation, but Captain Eddie suspected he had and he began to fear him as a potential threat to his power. He had a candidate for a "crown prince," but it wasn't Paul.

In truth, EVR had no reason to fall victim to the "uneasy is the head that wears the crown" phobia. As the war drew to a conclusion, he came back to Eastern with the same total control and absolute authority he had always held. Even before the war ended, he was planning for the postwar years, and whatever he wanted, his directors were ready to approve. Eastern was the only airline in the U.S. that had to pay an excess profits tax, an achievement of which the Captain was inordinately proud—he credited it to "our frugal, conservative, dependable management." He was right, but his philosophy of successful management contained a fatal flaw—successful it was, yes, but to such an extent that it solidified into rigidity of policy and became unable to adapt to change.

This failing would, like a dormant but deadly virus, not be apparent for a long time. For the time being there were nothing but rainbows on Eastern's horizon. When victory appeared assured in 1944, the airline industry began returning to normal in a hurry. EAL got back fourteen of the twenty DC-3s it had given up to the Army and when the Civil Aeronautics Board ended its moratorium on new route awards, Eastern won authorizations for New York–St. Louis and New York–Boston; the latter put Rickenbacker in head-to-head competition with C. R. Smith's American Airlines.

In that same year the Board of Directors gave EVR a green light for a $25 million fleet-expansion program—fourteen new four-engined Lockheed Constellations and ten CW-20s, civilian designation for the C-46. Rickenbacker said the new planes were part of an overall five-year aircraft modernization plan which also would include postwar purchase of the DC-4, another war-proven four-engine transport built by Douglas, whose development Eastern had helped finance and whose design included input by Charlie Froesch.

The extent of the program surprised a lot of people, including those who were predicting that Captain Eddie would stick with the DC-3 until every one in the fleet wore out. He had no intention of abandoning the gallant old plane—by July of 1945 Eastern had forty-three either back in service or in the process of being converted back to passenger configuration. But he recognized that its days as queen of the nation's civil air fleet were numbered; the pressures of war had accelerated aviation technology so much that research which normally would have covered a decade had been compressed into two or three years.

Rickenbacker was cautious about new technology but seldom blind to its possibilities. This, again, was part of his complex, contradictory nature—he figuratively was farsighted in one eye and astigmatic in the other. He could tread softly one minute and be perilously impulsive the next. He knew only too well, for example, that commercial aviation's postwar expansion might be more of an explosion, and that every airline in the country would be scratching for new routes and invading old markets. Yet he seemed to go out of his way to antagonize the powers-that-be in Washington, refusing to admit that route awards were often tinged with politics. His contemporaries in the industry learned to live with this fact of life, but Rickenbacker's distrust of politicians and bureaucrats was blatant. It's very possible he couldn't help himself—that was the kind of person he was, and there is something admirable about a man devoid of hypocrisy. But there is no doubt he carried his personal prejudices too far, to the point of hurting the airline.

In 1945 he arrived in Havana to represent Eastern at an international air conference. Before the sessions opened, Rickenbacker was invited to speak informally at a civic luncheon and just before he began, word was received that President Roosevelt had died.

Unbelievably, he began his speech by remarking that FDR's death was the best piece of news he had heard in a long time. The audience was incensed, so much so that EVR was asked to leave Cuba and Brattain had to rush to Havana to represent Eastern.

Eastern was to have many glory years under Captain Eddie's strong leadership. But in that Havana incident one can see the seeds of self-destruction he had planted himself. He gave conviction so high a priority that compromise—which is a long way from surrender—became impossible.

And that was how Eastern entered the postwar era—with a time bomb buried in the inflexible personality of the man who ruled the Great Silver Fleet.

CHAPTER EIGHT

THE MID-FORTIES—
OF CONNIES,
CATASTROPHES,
AND COMMERCIALS

Back they came from the war—to an Eastern Air Lines that was not the lean, hungry company they had left. Like a human counterpart to whom prosperity and growth also has brought a pot belly, EAL had become somewhat flabby.

Within one year after V-J Day the payroll had soared to some 6,000 employees, the route system to 9,000 miles, and the fleet to forty-nine DC-3's and nineteen DC-4's—civilian version of the four-engine C-54's that the Air Force had operated so successfully as cargo planes during the second half of the war.

The signs of flabbiness were there despite Rickenbacker, not because of him. In effect, he, too, was a returning veteran, his wartime missions now pages in history, and he hadn't changed one bit in his penchant for running a one-man show. Yet this was one of Eastern's troubles—the airline industry, expecting a post-war air-travel boom, had not yet matured enough to handle all the problems that such a boom had to involve. Virtually every carrier, like a starving man suddenly exposed to the luxury of a full-course, gourmet meal, went off the deep end in ordering new equipment. And Rickenbacker, with his awesome authority and inflexible mind, had to be right because there wasn't really anyone who wanted to challenge him.

As it turned out, he could be wrong. Not even Charlie Froesch had been able to talk him out of ordering the C-46, and Froesch—who agreed with Rickenbacker more often than he disagreed—had bluntly warned him that the big Curtiss transport, despite the fine job it had done for MTD, was not what Eastern needed for the postwar period.

"I'd like to know why, Charlie," EVR grumbled.

"Eddie, it was never really designed for airline operations. I've seen their shop facilities in Buffalo—they're not too hot. Second, the airplane's too damned slow. Third, their engineers don't have the transport aircraft design experience we get at Lockheed and Douglas. And let's face it—every postwar transport airplane will have a tricycle landing gear except the CW-20. It'll be a 'come-down.' "

"Well, Curtiss assures me it'll do a great job for us," Rickenbacker muttered. "I'll have to think it over."

Froesch knew the real reason Captain Eddie had gone for the Curtiss sales pitch—his friendship with Guy Vaughn, head of Curtiss-Wright. And on paper the airplane did look promising. Its big cabin was to be configured for at least thirty-eight passengers and the mockup included a feature that today's flight attendants would welcome—a divanlike seat with a folding desk for in-flight paperwork.

Froesch was to have his way in the end, Rickenbacker's loyalty to Vaughn notwithstanding. When Curtiss-Wright moved its engineering department from St. Louis to Buffalo, the company advised Eastern that the shift would cause some delivery delays. Then manufacturing facilities were relocated in Columbus, Ohio, which caused further delays, and the impatient Rickenbacker had had enough—he canceled the contract for an aircraft that Froesch described as "an inferior one that could not be delivered on time."

Froesch had always liked the DC-4, whose original prewar design had carried his input and that of his counterparts at four other carriers—Bill Mentzer of United, Walter Hamilton of

TWA, Bill Littlewood of American, and Andre Preister of Pan Am. Those five airlines contributed fifty percent of the development costs and dictated many of the design specifications, but when it came time to actually order the big plane, Rickenbacker balked.

After the war the Navy offered to lease a number of its DC-4's to the airlines and EVR jumped at the chance. He was a bit too eager, because the Navy suddenly reneged and asked Eastern either to return the already-delivered planes or buy them outright. The price was a relatively modest $130,000 for a transport that had had a $200,000 price tag when it was brand new, but EVR thought $130,000 was too high. He may have been right— some war-weary C-54's were going for as low as $10,000—but there were other factors to consider. Eastern already had spent a considerable amount redoing the interiors of the Navy planes and adding EAL's instrumentation to them. Froesch and John Halliburton, among others, tried to argue with the Captain but he wouldn't budge.

When the C-20 order was canceled, the airline badly needed equipment bigger than the DC-3 and the four-engine Douglas was all that was available for immediate delivery. But when Eastern tried to buy surplus DC-4's in good condition from other sources, the cost was higher than the Navy's $130,000 and that didn't include the refurbishing expense. The nineteen EAL eventually picked up averaged nearly $170,000 apiece.

One EAL employee who didn't need much transition training on a DC-4 was steward Rod Robitaille, whose wartime job in the Air Transport Command culminated in assignment to the "Sacred Cow," the C-54 which became the first Presidential aircraft. His passengers included such luminaries as FDR, Eisenhower, MacArthur, Stillwell, Marshall, Bradley, Molotov, Baruch, Truman, and Harry Hopkins. Truman's ninety-two-year-old mother had flown in the "Cow" and accused Robitaille of spiking her orange juice. Robitaille's stories about the flying White House were the source of great interest throughout the airline—particularly his description of the galley facilities from which he could serve fifteen full-course dinners. The item that drew the most envy from his fellow flight attendants was the three-cubic-foot refrigerator which he kept stocked with frozen sirloin steaks and, once, caviar for Soviet diplomat Molotov.

There were countless yarns from the returning pilots whose wartime duties had involved everything from deadly combat to chauffeuring the famous. Four EAL captains had wound up in the ATC's "Brass Hat Squadron," the 503rd—Dick Dice, Bill Johnson, Frank Bennett, and John Loveless. Dice seemed to gravitate to the most glamorous missions; his passengers ranged from Chief of Staff Marshall and Hap Arnold to presidential advisor Hopkins. He flew the exploratory flight to Yalta prior to FDR's Crimean trip and because of weather and adverse winds detoured over Crete. Coming out of the overcast, he ran into antiaircraft fire which put two shell holes in his fuselage.

Another EAL captain flying for the Air Transport Command was Cliff Zieger. He encountered something slightly worse than antiaircraft fire—the stubbornness of General Charles de Gaulle. Zieger was assigned the job of taking De Gaulle from Casablanca to Paris, a flight carefully timed so that the leader of the Free French would land near France's capital just as the Germans pulled out of the city.

The ceiling and visibility at Paris would have challenged Superman's X-ray vision. Zieger went back into the cabin and broke the news to the general's English-speaking aide.

"I guess you'd better tell General de Gaulle we may have to land in England and wait for the weather to clear," he announced.

Zieger didn't understand French but from the look on De Gaulle's haughty face he didn't need the verbal torrent translated.

"The general says he took off from French soil and he will land on French soil," the aide said, and Zieger could almost hear the strains of the "Marseillaise." They landed in Cherbourg, and arrived in Paris only two hours after the Germans left.

Zieger's aircraft, incidentally, was a Constellation—ATC operated a number of them during the latter stages of the war, although the plane had been designed specifically for airline use.

Both the Constellation and DC-4 were prewar designs whose civilian use was precluded by America's entrance into the hostilities; TWA, which had played a major role in the triple-tailed Lockheed's design, had ordered the aircraft and both United and American had top priority on DC-4 deliveries as soon as the war ended.

Charlie Froesch's lack of enthusiasm for the CW-20 didn't apply to the Constellation, and he urged Rickenbacker to buy it. There was one large stumbling block, however, and that was Howard Hughes—the Connie had been built largely to his specifications and TWA's requirements for a long-range transport plane. Hughes had put $1.5 million of his own money toward the development of a long-range airliner that would carry forty-five passengers from New York to London and in return for this investment he wanted TWA to be the only airline operating it for at least a while.

The Constellation's chief rival was the Douglas DC-6, in which Rickenbacker wasn't interested. Although it was pressurized, like the Connie, he considered it nothing more than a stretched DC-4, and in a sense it was; Douglas through the years has had a reputation of building "rubber airplanes"—new transports which are enlarged, improved versions of existing designs. Thus the DC-4 became the DC-6, the latter begot the DC-7, and when Douglas began building jets it stayed with the original DC-8 through a number of larger models all the way up to the DC-10. Likewise, the twin-engine DC-9 is still being stretched, to the point where the new DC-9 Super 80 is only a few feet shorter than the first DC-8.

So Rickenbacker had his heart set on the Constellation. He originally ordered twenty, then decided Eastern didn't need that many and cut the order to fourteen. Bob Gross, president of Lockheed, informed him that the twenty-plane contract was firm and couldn't be reduced unless Eastern paid a penalty.

"Okay," the Captain said, "but if I have to take the six I don't really want, I'll just sell them for whatever I can get. Do you want me underselling Lockheed? Think it over, Bob."

Gross thought it over and let EVR off the hook without

penalty. But a new obstacle arose when Lockheed couldn't give Eastern firm delivery dates because of Hughes. Rickenbacker went to see the brilliant but eccentric billionaire, and came back with Hughes's permission for Eastern to buy fourteen Constellations at $2 million per aircraft. Rickenbacker gleefully told his officers that when Hughes balked at first, the Captain had asked him if he was sure he wanted TWA to be the only airline using such a new plane.

"I said if the Constellation had any accidents, TWA would be the sole sufferer, but that if Eastern also flew the plane, the repercussions would be spread out," Rickenbacker reported.

There is no reason to doubt his version of the meeting, although he was not always accurate in his historical accounts—whether because of ego, poor memory, or rationalization, no one knows. In his autobiography, for example, he claimed that Eastern was the first carrier to put the Constellation into scheduled service. The basis for that boast is unknown—TWA was the first, by a wide margin, and EAL's only legitimate claim to Constellation pioneering was that it was the first to put an improved model into service (TWA's initial Connies were the L-049 and Eastern ordered the L-649, which had different engines and a slightly larger wing)—at the insistence of Froesch, incidentally.

Froesch was one of the few officers whose advice EVR occasionally took, but Paul Brattain apparently gave him too much—Rickenbacker kicked him upstairs to the high-sounding but meaningless post of first vice president. It was a title sometimes bestowed on men slated to inherit an airline presidency, but in Brattain's case it was more of a demotion. His influence within the airline waned perceptibly as Stanley Osborne, a young and ambitious man with considerable advertising experience, succeeded Brattain as vice president of traffic and sales. Brattain, his pride but not his loyalty hurt, was to stay on the sidelines for five years.

It was one of Rickenbacker's greatest strengths that he could recruit top executive talent; it was one of his greatest weaknesses that his own personality would seldom let him utilize that talent to its fullest capability. Hugh Knowlton, one of the three men who had helped him obtain financial backing for his takeover of the airline, had joined Eastern during the war to help Captain Eddie establish an economic-planning department. It was an area in which EVR finally got around to admitting was an Eastern weak spot—drawing up blueprints for future route aspirations and coordinating them with equipment and personnel needs. American had no fewer than fifteen experts in such a division; EAL started out with four in a department Knowlton headed.

Knowlton, although he liked and admired the Captain, simply couldn't last it out for more than a year. He never had any angry confrontations with Rickenbacker; he just got tired of debating a stone wall. A case in point was Knowlton's carefully composed outline for several big merger possibilities, something he had worked out with the aid of Laurance Rockefeller and William Barclay Harding. They included mergers that involved two transcontinental routes and a half-dozen new north–south routes, but when Knowlton laid the various proposals before EVR, the Captain summarily rejected them all.

"The trouble with you fellas from Wall Street," he commented, "is that as soon as you get something good going, you want to sell it."

There was no more talk of mergers for several years, and when Knowlton left the airline he had no hard feelings but no regrets, either. The subject was to come up again during the 1948–1949 recession; practically every airline in the U.S. was operating in the red except Eastern. Several EAL officials brought up merger possibilities again but Rickenbacker shook his head.

"Don't rush it," he advised. "I'm gonna pick 'em off one by one like sitting ducks—they're all heading for bankruptcy."

Perhaps he may have been fundamentally right, but his timetable was thrown off by an unexpected event that caused an economic boom and a return to industry profits: the Korean War. And even without the war, EVR certainly knew that the airlines are a cyclical industry, with economic peaks and valleys —it made little sense for him to assume that his rivals would never be capable of climbing out of a valley. Yet just when underlings would automatically anticipate his quick rejection—and maybe a five-megaton explosion—EVR would stun them by an equally quick acceptance of a proposal everyone expected would fire him into orbit. In the 1940s he yielded to the IAM's request for a closed shop without so much as a murmur; the union couldn't have been more surprised if he had joined the Communist party.

He pulled another shocker right after the war when Eastern became the first airline to introduce the forty-hour work week—blessed by a man who insisted that all executives be at their desks every Saturday morning, and who himself worked almost every weekend. He followed this up two years later by approving the airline's first retirement plan—he announced it in a speech at the Miami base and only Captain Eddie would have bestowed this bounty on employees with a simultaneous warning not to let the largesse go to their heads.

"There are only three places where absolute security exists with free clothing, food, and lodging," he told them. "In jail, behind bars, and the poorhouse."

A decade later he would fire another surprise by making Eastern the first U.S. airline to hire divorcees as stewardesses. His unpredictability could be frustrating at times but it was never dull, because his behavior was so often contradictory.

He was fond of proclaiming the glories of the free enter-prise system, yet his reaction to any opponent's route application which challenged an exclusive Eastern domain was an angry, "We pioneered that route—they're our cities and that's our market!"

Like so many airline presidents, he was all for competition when it came to invading someone else's territory, but cried foul if anyone invaded his. He was almost paranoic in his belief that the government would stop at nothing to hurt his airline, and there were times when it did seem that way, but other carriers certainly should have had every right to be paranoic about him. Against a competitor he truly hated, he could be ruthless. A case in point is his feud—bloody vendetta would be more like it—

with National's George Baker. At various times he tried to buy out National, did everything in his power to keep it from growing, and at one stage—in 1948, when National was reeling with financial troubles—Rickenbacker reportedly tried to engineer the purchase of outstanding loans several banks were holding on his Florida rival.

EVR's attitude toward route expansion in the 1940s was the same cautious one he had held toward mergers. He talked about applying for a transatlantic route but did nothing about it—even after a friend told him, "Eddie, the Atlantic's Eastern's ocean." His biggest and most serious bid for major international authority came in 1942 when he actually filed for a route from Miami through Central America, across Brazil, and down both coasts of South America. The chief opposition was Braniff, and the principal objector was Juan Trippe, who regarded both Braniff and Eastern as interlopers threatening his South American empire.

Thousands of dollars were spent preparing for the case—legal fees, impressive exhibits, and even a handsome brochure. The advance planning took two years but suddenly, without warning, Rickenbacker scuttled the venture. It was a Sunday night in a Washington hotel and EVR was meeting with his top executives to go over final arrangements for the CAB hearings scheduled to open the next day.

"I think we ought to drop the whole damned thing," he declared with absolutely no warning.

There was a stunned silence, broken finally by Sid Shannon's incredulous "For God's sake, Eddie—why?"

"Because we've got too many problems here at home. Let's face it, Sid—and all you guys—Eastern doesn't have the managerial experience to be operating foreign routes. We'll get our tits caught in the well-known wringer, so my mind's made up—we'll concentrate on our domestic system at least for a while."

There was no use debating or arguing with him, and it was Braniff which walked away with the pot. In retrospect, however, Rickenbacker's case of cold feet probably kept Eastern out of some hot water, for it took years for Braniff to develop its South

American service into a profitable operation. As it turned out, Eastern probably couldn't have absorbed international route deficits at a time when its domestic system was in deep trouble.

Eastern was to make one more rather vague stab at South America in 1947 when EVR took a new Connie loaded with dignitaries on a thirty-one-day Latin American tour—for reasons known only to himself. It was big news in the company newspaper, which devoted eighteen pages to the trip, and the speculation was that he was going after South American routes. This was a theory one astute observer seriously doubts. Wayne Parrish, a knowledgeable aviation writer (he founded *American Aviation* and *Aviation Daily* and has been a respected critic of the airline industry throughout his career), was on the plane as an invited and most curious guest.

"That trip was one of the biggest mysteries of Rickenbacker's life," Parrish says. "Nobody to this day can figure out why he made it. He stuck Lockheed for fifty percent of the bill and the National City Bank of New York, which had branches in South America, paid for receptions and other arrangements. It wasn't a press trip—I think I was one of the few reporters along—and it wasn't an inaugural flight. It was a flight without any purpose, unless it was a way to needle Juan Trippe into believing that Rick wanted to invade his province.

"Bert Holloway of Lockheed and I used to sit in our hotel room at night and wonder what the hell the trip was all about. Arthur Godfrey was on the plane and after the first two stops, he was ready to go home."

Whatever influence Hugh Knowlton might have had on the Captain's route plans was diluted by the war, and by the time postwar expansion was possible Knowlton already had departed the premises, although he later became an influential director. But one of his legacies to both Rickenbacker and Eastern was a peppery young man who had been a Wall Street broker before Knowlton hired him for the new economic-planning department. His name was Maurice Lethridge; everyone called him Lefty and, like Brattain, he was one of the few men around EAL who wasn't afraid to argue with the Captain. He joined the airline in 1943 and didn't retire until 1975—a period in which he held

nine executive posts and served under six different EAL presidents.

Lefty was asked once which of those six was the easiest to work for. Without hesitation he picked Rickenbacker.

"I knew exactly what the man wanted," he explains. "You never had to play games with Captain Eddie because he'd never play games with you. He was the most demanding person I ever knew, but he never asked you to do something he wouldn't do himself. He could bawl the living bejesus out of you but then he'd always pick you up and pat you on the back. I remember once he got mad at me and told me to close my goddamned mouth or he'd drive a Mack truck into it. I thought he was going to fire me right then and there, but all of a sudden he grinned, slapped me on the rump, and said, 'Nothing personal, Lefty.' "

One of Lethridge's first assignments was to serve as secretary of EAL's advertising committee, a group which worked closely with Brad Walker. The committee met once a month on a Saturday morning to review advertising plans for the following month—Saturdays meant nothing to Captain Eddie and he expected his executives to have the same attitude. As he did at all staff sessions, Rickenbacker had two ways of running an ad meeting: He might start off gruffly, putting everyone on his mettle and making them very defensive, or he'd open up very casually, almost gently, which invariably was the prelude to raising hell for about three hours.

Lefty was at one ad meeting which began with the Gruffness Method—he had spotted an error in the advertising copy and obviously didn't have the patience for the Delayed Barrage Approach.

"Who's responsible for this stupid mistake?" he demanded.

There were several vice-presidents present but not one dared open his mouth. Finally Lethridge cleared his throat.

"Captain, I saw the ad last so I guess it's my fault."

Rickenbacker gave him a hard, long look, but this time, as Lethridge described it later, "he took me to the woodshed rather gently." When the meeting broke up and everyone started to leave, Rickenbacker called out, "Wait a second, Lefty."

Someone whispered to Lethridge, "Boy, now you're going

to get it." The room emptied except for EVR and his grim-faced prey.

"Lefty," EVR said, "which son of a bitch are you protecting?"

"I can't tell you that, Captain."

Just the trace of a smile touched Rickenbacker's stern lips. "Okay, then—get the hell out of here."

Lethridge remembers that incident of so many years ago as if it had happened yesterday. "No, I didn't tell him and he really didn't want to know. But he did want *me* to know that *he* knew I was protecting somebody. And that's why I can't think of him in any way except with affection and respect—even love. Hell, there were times I wanted to kill the cantankerous, unreasonable old bastard, but there were other times when I thought he was about the greatest man I ever knew. Because that's what Eddie generated in almost anyone who really understood him: a love-hate relationship."

How much of Rickenbacker's rocky past affected the decisions he made in his later life only a psychiatrist could tell, but the trials of his youth helped create the man who ruled Eastern. His phobia against taking the lead in new equipment, traceable to the unhappy experience with the pioneering automobile that bore his name, already has been mentioned. His early poverty, the scarring failure of the Rickenbacker Motor Company that left him a quarter of a million dollars in debt—these were other major factors shaping the man.

At a staff meeting once, EVR was listening to some of his officers bemoaning postwar inflation, the high cost of living, and uttering other personal financial complaints.

"You fellas think you've got it tough?" he snorted. "I was in the gutter in 1927 when my car company went bankrupt. Hell, I was *below* the gutter—I owed two hundred and fifty thousand bucks and didn't have a job."

His personal frugality and dread of money troubles led to the incongruity of his being generous with individuals but niggardly toward the company—and, eventually, the customer. Lethridge told him one day that a young employee in the public-relations department had just learned his wife had terminal cancer.

"Got any kids?" EVR asked.

"Three—and they're only babies. Ages one to four."

Rickenbacker summoned the young man. "Joe, I just heard about your wife. How much money do you need?"

This was the same Rickenbacker who summarily fired Walter Sternberg, one of the best traffic and sales men in the industry, after someone told him Sternberg didn't think much of Eastern's in-flight service plans for the new Constellations. EVR assigned this criticism to the category of disloyalty, but his impulsive decision to fire Sternberg was to come back to haunt him. Sternberg wound up at National Airlines, which had just started competing with Eastern on the New York–Miami route.

Rickenbacker regarded National in the same way the Pittsburgh Steelers would look on a forthcoming game against a high-school team: total disdain. He also detested George Baker, the trigger-tempered wheeler-dealer who ran National exactly the way EVR ran Eastern, but in dismissing Sternberg he unwittingly armed Baker with a devastating competitive weapon. Sternberg knew Eastern's service weaknesses and aimed his guns at those inviting targets.

It was Sternberg who launched National's effective campaign as "The Airline of the Stars" and instituted such amenities as filet mignon dinners and attractive aircraft interiors, not to mention the policy of hiring the best-looking stewardesses in the industry. National was still too small to challenge EAL's domination of the prime New York–Miami market, but it began making inroads; among former and present Eastern officials who were with the airline in the mid-forties and early fifties—including those who admired Captain Eddie—there is unanimous opinion that Eastern's public-image problems started in the early postwar years.

To give Rickenbacker his due, the Captain's policies were based on more than simply a miserly and indifferent attitude toward passengers. He honestly believed that the public mainly wanted safe, reliable air transportation and he made every effort to provide exactly that. Conversely, he looked with disdain on fancy in-flight service gimmicks; he thought it was ridiculous and wasteful for any airline to furnish expensive gourmet meals complete with wine, free cocktails, and fancy linen when it should be concentrating on getting people from point A to point B as swiftly and safely as possible. It was hard for anyone at Eastern to argue with this logic, except that it never dawned on him that other carriers were providing good service *and* reliability.

Tragically for Eastern, the effects of this shortsightedness were long-range and not readily apparent when the Rickenbacker regime was at its postwar zenith. Maybe passengers didn't like Eastern's five-abreast seating in the new Constellations—for the same fare National was charging in DC-6's with four-abreast configuration—but EAL was big enough to offer the advantages of more frequent scheduling, greater capacity in the peak winter months, and, what was closest to Captain Eddie's heart, professional, on-time performance with as good a safety record as there was in the industry.

Rickenbacker, in fact, insisted on pegging EAL's entire advertising campaign to this theme for as long as he headed the airline. He told Brad Walker that was the only thing he wanted to emphasize in any ad—sell the public on Eastern's experience. Long before Pan Am hitched its wagon to the "World's Most Experienced Airline" slogan, it was the message and the battle cry of Rickenbacker's airline. Dependability. Confidence. Experience. Those were the magic words, and for quite a long time they worked.

In Madison Avenue terms, Captain Eddie demanded hard-sell advertising, which meant voluminous copy without too much leeway for originality or visual attractiveness. As Brad Walker explained it (with some reluctance, because he was an excellent ad man) to EAL officers, "The captain abhors white space in an ad like nature abhors a vacuum." EVR loved to clutter the ads with all the pertinent information he thought should be incorporated—with large black, block lettering and with a picture of a large airplane in each ad. Much to Brad's unvoiced displeasure, the style caused Eastern to be labeled "the S. Klein of the airline industry"—S. Klein being a high-pressure clothing store that sold suits off the rack near Union Square and whose ads were of the hard-sell variety.

Walker actually was a creative man trying hard to live with Rickenbacker's advertising prejudices. In 1946 he bought fifty-five percent of Campbell-Ewald's stock and changed the name of the firm to the Fletcher Richards Agency, after his partner. Eastern was his principal account and he even consulted Rickenbacker before he bought the agency. EVR's reaction was expressed in one sentence: "I never liked that goddamned Ewald anyway—go ahead and buy it."

The new 1946 slogan was "Tried and Proven." Its effectiveness was debatable, but it did draw a letter from a Harvard professor of English who said "Tried and Proven" was poor rhetoric and that the slogan should be "Tried and Proved." The letter wound up on the desk of Lefty Lethridge, who by now was assistant to the vice presidents of public and personnel relations and traffic and sales. Lefty showed it to Captain Eddie.

"What's this fancy word 'rhetoric'?" Rickenbacker said. "Tell that big brain from Harvard the slogan is selling seats and we're keeping it."

The theme was revised slightly through the years but the message was the same. It was "Double Dependability—Dependable Personnel and Dependable Equipment" in 1948, "Fly Eastern with Confidence" in 1952, and "There's No Substitute for Eastern's Experience" in 1955. "Tried and Proven" was still being used when the Constellation was introduced in 1947. For an airplane that was the newest bird in the skies and the new queen of EAL's fleet, the interior was rather mundane but EVR couldn't have cared less about cabin decor at the time.

His initial concern about the sleek Lockheed giant was the nickname that came so naturally: "Connie." For reasons no one could really fathom, EVR blew his stack every time he heard the word and even sent out a memorandum forbidding any Eastern employee to use it. Lethridge finally mustered up the courage to ask him, venturing the opinion that "Connie" sounded affectionate and refreshingly informal.

"The pilots are calling it 'Connie,' " Lefty added. "Frankly, I don't understand why you're making an issue out of it."

"Because it's just like calling your wife a floozie," the Captain snapped.

Not even a Captain Eddie memorandum could rid the Constellation of that nickname, however. But as far as the pilots and mechanics were concerned, the nickname at first was preceded by one other word: goddamned. Like virtually every new airliner, the Connie had its share of bugs—including a faulty electrical system that caused two fatal in-flight fires on TWA Constellations, resulting in the plane's grounding until the design error was corrected. The Wright engines on the L-049 and L-749 were afflicted with myriad ailments and the whole airplane had so many mechanical difficulties that Lockheed finally assigned about ten mechanics to work with EAL technicians on an eradication program.

The pilots loved the way the Connie flew—it was stable, easy to land, and possessed excellent reserve power—but cockpit visibility was probably the worst of any large transport plane in history. This deficiency was compounded by a cockpit windshield that the crews compared to mirrors in a "crazy house." The glass was collision proof, an admirable feature, but it was so thick that it distorted vision. If you looked through one panel, an airplane might be coming right at you. If you peered through an adjoining pane, the same airplane would appear to be 200 feet higher.

Another bug showed up in the windshield defrosting system, which utilized hot wires embedded in the glass. At full force, the heat distorted the glass so badly that when a pilot landed, the runway would be shimmying up and down or sideways.

The Connie was the first airliner to require the services of a third crew member: the flight engineer. The original concept of this position was that of a jack-of-all-trades—a man who monitored the engine instruments, performed emergency maintenance repairs, and did minor repair jobs. Once the government made the third crew member mandatory on all four-engine transports grossing 80,000 pounds or more (the DC-4 and later the Viscount were exempt even though they were four-engined planes), the industry was faced with two choices: The third crew member should be a mechanic, or a mechanic also qualified as a pilot. Eastern went the first route, Rickenbacker making the decision although both Shannon and John Halliburton favored flight engineers who could take over the controls in a pinch. They argued that there wasn't much a mechanic could do in flight anyway—Eastern wasn't like Pan Am, which had carried mechanics for years because they served stations so remote that maintenance personnel weren't always available. It was Pan Am, in fact, which first called its airborne mechanics flight engineers.

Lockheed was largely responsible for EAL's going with the flight engineer/mechanic; the Burbank company told EVR that the Constellation was so complicated and sophisticated that the third man in the cockpit had to have considerable mechanical knowledge so he could analyze troubles in flight and radio instructions ahead. Rickenbacker bought this argument for two reasons: First, he had a lot of respect for Lockheed, which had cooperated with and contributed toward the promotion campaign accompanying introduction of the Connie; second, he had a soft spot for mechanics, anyway. His vulnerability in this area would cost the airline dearly because it wasn't the first time he was to let sentimentality override the advice of his officers. Eastern was to take three major strikes over the "third man" issue and the last two could have been avoided if Rickenbacker hadn't taken the wrong road in settling the first one.

For the dispute over the third crew member's technical qualifications ended up as a jurisdictional fight between the Air Line Pilots Association (ALPA) and the newer, far smaller Flight Engineers International Association (FEIA) over which union should represent that third man. And as Halliburton points out, "A jurisdictional strike is the worst kind because the settlement you make with one group is unacceptable to the other." The first FEIA walkout, in 1958, would shut down the airline for thirty-three days but not only did it not have to last that long, it would have been possible, given proper handling, to have set a pattern with it that would have prevented subsequent walkouts.

"We had that strike licked," Halliburton recalls. "The majority of our engineers were willing to take pilot training—which would have meant their joining ALPA—and that's the way the crew complement issue eventually was resolved permanently. But Captain Eddie said no and we gave in to the FEIA, which made the next two strikes inevitable."

Cockpit complement problems aside, the Connies were an immediate success and were to serve Eastern faithfully and dependably for more than two decades. But they were assigned to the long-haul routes and EAL still needed a replacement for the venerable DC-3. Rickenbacker gave Froesch the task of picking a short-haul transport with two specifications in mind: It had to have literally the capacity of a bus, forty or fifty passengers, and it had to be economical to operate over the shorter segments.

No one in the industry was any more thorough than Charlie Froesch in analyzing the technical pros and cons of a transport aircraft. The studies he made and the research he compiled in the process of choosing a DC-3 replacement were classic in their objectivity. He had three choices:

1. The Super DC-3, which was eliminated quickly. It was another one of Douglas's "rubber airplanes," being largely a stretched DC-3. A new low-drag engine cowling, a completely housed landing gear, a new-shaped tail, and more powerful engines gave it upwards of twenty miles per hour greater cruising speed than the standard DC-3, but its twenty-eight-passenger capacity was far too small and it still lacked a tricycle gear.

2. The Convair 240, which American had ordered in large numbers. Though it was enormously strong and fast, Froesch considered it deficient in several respects. He wanted a larger wing area with more efficient flaps to provide lower approach and landing speeds. He didn't like the 240's airfoil, which peaked sharply at high angles of attack, giving it—in his opinion—too little warning of an approaching stall. He thought the center-of-gravity travel range was insufficient and would affect critical payload loading. And finally, Eastern's maintenance department dis-

liked the exhaust system as being too noisy and predicted an unsatisfactory service life for wheels and brakes because they were too small.

3. The Martin 202, outwardly almost a twin of the Convair 240 except for the former's exaggerated wing dihedral, so sharply positive (slanting upwards) that even on the ground the 202 resembled a bird in the first stage of flapping its wings. The Martin was about five miles per hour slower than the Convair, but its larger wing area gave it superior approach and landing characteristics—on short flights, the speed disadvantage was insignificant.

Overall, the 202 shaped up in Froesch's view as the best choice and Eastern, on Froesch's recommendation, signed a letter of "intent to purchase" with Martin in late 1945 calling for delivery of twenty-five airplanes. But even though Froesch advised Rickenbacker to buy the 202, he emphasized that no firm commitment should be made unless Eastern reserved the right to demand any necessary design changes. At that stage the 202 was strictly a paper airplane consisting of blueprints, drawings, and tentative promises. And he also knew that Captain Eddie's long friendship with Glenn A. Martin might soften EVR's normally hard-nosed attitude toward any business deal.

The yellow caution signals Froesch hoisted saved Eastern from buying a turkey instead of a falcon. The Martin 202 was a disaster of such proportions that the airplane nearly ruined Northwest, which had built many of its postwar plans around it. But long before Northwest's tragic experiences unmasked the 202's fatal flaw, Froesch already had warned Rickenbacker not to accept Martin's assurances that their proud product was the epitome of safety.

Surprisingly early in the design stages, he had objected to the 202's wing structure as being potentially and dangerously deficient. In a report to EVR he explained his misgivings:

The wing consists of three parts, the center section including the powerplant nacelles and two outer panels. They are joined to the center section by means of bolted step splices. This type of wing joint is

not believed to be good mechanical practice for highly-stressed structures and preference is for a manufactured scarf joint of the Boeing
B-17 type. Unless this can be changed accordingly, no further consideration should be given to this aircraft.

That was laying it right on the line and Froesch could have
gone even further. The wing joint to which he referred was not
only of questionable design, but it was manufactured out of a
new alloy that developed metal fatigue in less than two years of
operational service. The flaw went undetected until August 29,
1948, when a Northwest Martin 202 crashed in a thunderstorm
near Winona, Minnesota, killing all thirty-seven aboard. Investigators were horrified to find the left wing a considerable distance
from the rest of the wreckage, indicating structural failure. Metal-
lurgical tests showed that the joint, also called a flange, had
developed metal fatigue after less than 1,400 hours of flight time.
An immediate inspection of Northwest's remaining seventeen
Martins disclosed that five had developed similiar fatigue cracks
and three of these had cracks in both wings. The government
grounded all 202's until the wings could be modified, two *years*
after Froesch informed Rickenbacker that Eastern should not
accept the airplane unless the wing joint was redesigned. The
official Civil Aeronautics Board verdict on the Winona crash was
a carbon copy of Froesch's early warning: "[the flange] was in-
ducive to high local stress concentration and hence was readily
susceptible to fatigue."

Prior to the Northwest accident Martin had been refusing
to alter the design; now it was mandatory and even the modifica-
tion couldn't save the airplane—the 202 was dead as far as
further airline sales were concerned. Froesch already had complained to EVR about "extremely poor workmanship" when the
first two test 202's were flying. Nor was he happy when Martin
upped the original price per aircraft from $200,000 to $234,000
because of Eastern's demands for design changes in other areas.

Probably any other airline president in the country would
have bailed out of the deal right then and there, but Captain
Eddie was not any other airline president. He didn't disagree with

his vice president of engineering, but he was terribly reluctant to
pull the rug out from under a stricken Glenn Martin. What came
out of this dilemma was Martin's agreement to let Eastern rede-
sign more than fifty percent of the aircraft, adding pressurization
(a feature already designed onto the Convair), the B-17's wing-
joint structure, and numerous other modifications. The changes
were so drastic that the 202 was renamed the 404; Eastern signed
a contract for thirty-five with an option (exercised later) for
twenty-five more and TWA purchased another twenty-five. Eastern was to take delivery of its first 404 in 1950 but Martin, its 202
program destroyed and no orders for the 404 except the EAL
and TWA contracts, was on the verge of bankruptcy—with some
40,000 employees, it was so broke it couldn't meet the next payroll. It already had gone through Eastern's and TWA's 404 de-
posits, plus loans from the Reconstruction Finance Corporation
and the Navy.

Rickenbacker and Laurance Rockefeller went to Stuart
Symington, RFC chairman, asking him to advance Martin additional money. When Symington refused, EVR realized that Eastern would be out its $11 million down payment if Martin folded,
not to mention the airplanes it had ordered. He took up the
cudgels for the ailing manufacturer Charles Wilson, former head
of General Motors and then director of the Office of Defense
Mobilization. Wilson, no admirer of Symington, arranged for the
Navy to loan Martin enough to meet its next payroll while Rickenbacker got William Barclay Harding to work out a reorganization and refinancing plan with the banks. The sacrificial lamb in
this maneuvering was Glenn Martin. He was forced to step down
as president, board chairman, and chief executive officer, but as
Captain Eddie told him privately and most reluctantly, "It was
your neck or your company's survival."

EVR was to assert in his autobiography that if Martin had
folded, Eastern itself would have gone into receivership because
it couldn't have stood the loss of that $11 million down-payment.
This has to be doubted—it is hard to imagine men like Rockefeller allowing the airline to die under those circumstances. As it
was, the 404 vindicated Froesch's judgment: It served EAL over

the next ten years, and became the only transport plane in EAL's history to operate for that long a period without a single passenger fatality or serious injury. There were six Martin accidents, but all minor.

The 404 gained the respect of pilots but seldom their affection; they admired its ruggedness and griped about its idiosyncrasies, such as a poor cockpit layout. The gear handle, for example, was adjacent to the flap controls and one easily could be confused for the other—this actually caused a couple of 404 accidents. The Connie, too, had its share of detractors and, in truth, it was not as easy to fly as TWA's Constellations because Rickenbacker resisted all Lockheed efforts to add various electronic aids.

"Goddammit," he finally told Lockheed's salesmen, "if you can't pull it or push it, don't put it on!"

But Brad Walker did talk him into an expensive advertising campaign based on selling the Connie as "the world's most advanced airliner." A half-million dollars went into Constellation promotion and Lockheed itself chipped in another $200,000. Yet he still skimped on service—the Connie's five-abreast seating being a prime example. Lefty Lethridge once remarked, but not to EVR, "Never have so many paid so much for so little." This most applicable paraphrasing of Churchill's famous line followed Lefty's assignment to find out why EAL was getting so many food complaints. The task was easy but getting Captain Eddie to take corrective measures was not so easy; the Connies had been ordered without booster equipment that would have kept the meals hot.

"Plus the fact that we were paying a supplier only a dollar forty a meal and I couldn't get the Captain to go up as much as ten cents," Lethridge adds.

Yet the irony of his ability to make the buck work was that his image of a tough, lean, hard airline sifted down through the ranks until it became the employees' image of Eastern, too. And this, as much as anything else, made EAL terribly vulnerable to the forthcoming tide of competition.

"Down deep," Lefty points out, "he was a likable, even

lovable guy, but the rank and file didn't often see this side of
him. Most of our people began to ape his image, telling themselves they were tough and mean like the old man. I remember
watching some of our passenger agents working at Newark. It was
a windy day and they were picking up tickets—that's a polite way
of putting it. Actually they'd tear off the top copy and hand it to
the passenger without looking up. Half the time the poor customer would drop it and then go off chasing it in the wind. Yet
these were the days when Delta and National agents were saying
good morning to passengers, and they had boarding shelters so
tickets wouldn't blow away if they were dropped. Sure, Rick was
as good as Woolman or Baker or anyone else when it came to
cost control, but he didn't have their foresight to give passengers
just a little something extra for their dough—like courtesy, for
example. Courtesy didn't cost anything but there were times at
Eastern when you'd think it was part of the budget."

Lethridge's judgment, harsh yet fair, should not lead to the
assumption that Rickenbacker was oblivious or indifferent to
passenger complaints. He wasn't. Because most of the complaining letters were addressed to him, he insisted on answering them
personally and his replies showed understanding, sympathy, and a
sincere desire to correct mistakes. Unfortunately, it was his own
policies that led to many of those mistakes and to the gradual
disintegration of Eastern's reputation. Both EVR and his airline
got away with a cavalier attitude toward passengers longer than
anyone expected for two reasons: lack of major competition, and
the fact that aside from service deficiencies, operationally Eastern
was good. Its very size protected it in many ways, schedule frequency being one of its strong points—National might have been
fifty miles ahead of Eastern in service but it couldn't match the
volume of flights EAL could operate in the bread-and-butter
New York–Miami market.

National itself, not to mention the whole state of Florida,
was the beneficiary of those flashes of Rickenbacker foresight
that were so exasperating to those who couldn't see him as anything but an antediluvian anachronism.

EVR's love affair with the Sunshine State had begun long

before the one he had with the airplane. It went back to 1912 when he was visiting Miami and a car dealer named Carl Fisher rowed him across Biscayne Bay in a small boat, to the mangrove-covered sandbar and swamp that was someday to become Miami Beach.

Rickenbacker shook his head at what could have been a scene from the Jurassic period and muttered something about the oppressive desolation.

"This spot could be a paradise, Eddie," Fisher said. "Millions of people could be sharing these God-given riches of sky, sea, and sun. With the right kind of transportation, Florida's future could be unlimited."

At the time Miami was a sleepy town sixty hours from New York by train and almost four days by automobile. But Rickenbacker never forgot Carl Fisher's vision—a look into the future that became his own. He may have stinted in such areas as in-flight service, but no one can pass full judgment on him without acknowledging his achievements. It was Rickenbacker's Eastern Air Lines that pioneered the New York–Miami route and turned what had been a limited vacation market for the wealthy into a mecca for average Americans.

Captain Eddie went even further. Like all airline chieftains, he deplored any seasonal traffic flows—and Florida was one of the worst examples. As far back as 1940 he had urged Florida officials to stop thinking of the state as solely a winter playground. In a meeting with Sunshine State hotel operators, he urged them to remain open in the summer months, offering reduced rates. In return he promised that Eastern would help sell Florida as a year-around resort area.

"You're being shortsighted," he told them. "You're paying a fortune to close down each spring, turn the hotels back to the jungle for six months, and then go through the expense of re-decorating, cleaning, and reorganizing a trained staff you've disbanded."

The hotels listened politely and did nothing, partly because the war clouds were on the horizon and also because they didn't believe him. In 1948, however, a handful of Miami hotels agreed to stay open during the 1949 summer season provided that Captain Eddie keep his pledge of promotion help. Rickenbacker's answer was a $1.5-million "Visit Florida in the Summer" campaign—in terms of attracting more passengers, the results were meager, but the precedent had been set and a barrier cracked. The few hotels that remained open reported modest but firm profits and the following year their number was doubled. Florida now is exactly what Rickenbacker predicted it should be, a year-around vacationland, and only an airline with Eastern's facilities and a leader with Rickenbacker's drive could have sparked what brought it about. It was no empty honor that the four-mile Rickenbacker Causeway between Miami and Biscayne Keys was named for him.

EVR, in fact, was riding high as the decade of the forties drew to a close. By all odds he was the most newsworthy, visible, and widely known airline president in the world. The fact that he was a long way from being the most popular made absolutely no difference to him—he thrived on controversy, stood unafraid of conflict, and ignored criticism. His attitude toward public relations was one almost of indifference—he relied largely on Bev Griffith's judgment and ingenuity and Griffith, in turn, knew precisely what kind of a PR gimmick would appeal to EVR. Eastern's most successful public relations efforts, in fact, stemmed from Captain Eddie's genuine love of children. Whatever Bev proposed in this area, Rickenbacker approved and never questioned the cost.

Typical was EAL's role in celebrating the opening of Houston's new airport terminal. Griffith upstaged every airline participating in the event by staging special flights for Houston's crippled children—including transporting them to the airport in fire engines.

"It was no contest," another airline PR official conceded sadly. "When Bev pulled off those flights, the rest of us might as well have stayed home."

Griffith also conceived the idea of taking schoolteachers on demonstration flights—he called it "Eastern's Educators' Airlift." He tried it out in Charlotte, North Carolina, and it went over so well that he repeated the "Airlift" in every key city on EAL's system over the next two and a half years—New York and Chicago excepted.

Bill Wooten testifies to the fact that Griffith seemed to come up with these masterpieces as if they were created by spontaneous mental combustion.

"He was in Charlotte that day on what was supposed to be a routine promotion and goodwill visit," Wooten remembers. "No one knows what prompted the idea, but within thirty minutes after he thought it up, he was in the school superintendent's office explaining every detail of the plan."

It was Griffith who put Gideon Bibles on all EAL planes and then arranged to provide Braille editions of the *Reader's Digest* to blind passengers at no cost. Eastern's own advertising might have been hard sell, but Griffith's promotion was soft sell —if it had anything to do with religion, children, education, or the handicapped, EVR was for it. But Griffith, like Lethridge and a few other enlightened executives, quickly learned there was one sure way to turn Rickenbacker against an idea he might normally favor—that was to tell him, "It'll cost *only* such-and-such"; EVR detested the word "only" with the same intensity he bestowed on "socialism," "Democrats," and "liberals."

Eastern was one of the first airlines to advertise on radio, and that was how Captain Eddie first became acquainted with Arthur Godfrey, who delivered some of the early commercials. Their friendship, which grew stronger as time went on, surprised a lot of people because the radio star didn't always see eye to eye with EVR in many areas. There was, for example, Rickenbacker's insistence that every EAL commercial had to begin with the same three words: "Eastern Air Lines," something that bugged this consummate professional who liked occasionally to ad-lib a commercial to give it more of a personal touch. What Godfrey and Rickenbacker did share was an all-abiding faith in aviation; no entertainment personality was more air-minded than Godfrey. He plugged air travel long before it became a mass-transportation vehicle, and also on those occasions when a bad crash prompted black headlines, demands for reform, and threats of congressional investigations.

Godfrey's consistent, even courageous defense of commercial aviation won Rickenbacker's steadfast gratitude—there would come a day when he would present the freckled, red-haired star a DC-3 outfitted as an executive transport. There were some eyebrows raised at this magnanimous gesture but as far as Captain Eddie was concerned, Godfrey had earned the gift. Eastern was one of the airlines benefiting from Godfrey's unsolicited plugs in behalf of air travel, for it was not immune from the plethora of accidents occurring in the mid and late 1940s.

EAL suffered through four tragedies in the last half of that decade, one crash still being listed officially as unsolved and another an accident in which the airline literally was an innocent bystander.

The first involved a DC-4 operating as Flight 605 from Newark to Miami on Memorial Day, 1947. Aboard were forty-eight passengers, an infant, and a crew of four. The accident that took their lives was unique in one respect: It took place in perfect weather before many eyewitnesses and still was recorded as a crash "for reasons unknown." May 30 of that year was bright, warm, and sunny. Flight 605 was cruising at 4,000 feet, made routine position reports over Metuchen, New Jersey and Philadelphia, and during the last report advised Air Route Traffic Control that estimated time of arrival at Baltimore was 5:49 P.M.

Just behind the EAL plane was a government DC-3 flown by two CAB pilots assigned, ironically, to the CAB's Bureau of Safety. The DC-3 was about three miles behind the airliner and five hundred feet higher, its crew idly watching the big transport ahead of them when they saw it suddenly nose toward earth.

The dive became steeper; there was no apparent attempt to pull the plane up. The horrified CAB pilots saw the dive deepen until the DC-4's nose was pointing straight toward the ground. It was almost on its back when it struck in a wooded area near Port Deposit, Maryland. The angle of impact strongly suggested that the plane had gone through the first half of an outside loop. There were no survivors.

The CAB weighed nine major possibilities as to probable cause, ranging from breakage of an elevator hinge to an explosion in the tail surfaces. One by one, they were checked out and eliminated. But four months later something happened to another DC-4 which bore a jolting resemblance to the last moments of Flight 605.

This time it was an American Airlines flight from New York to Los Angles with a scheduled stop at Dallas. A fresh crew boarded at Dallas, along with a DC-3 pilot who rode with them in the cockpit to obtain familiarization with DC-4 equipment. The flight was cruising at 8,000 feet when the captain suggested that the deadheading pilot might like to handle the controls. They switched positions, the captain going to the jump seat. About thirty-five miles west of El Paso the DC-4, for no apparent reason, started to climb. The DC-3 pilot, still flying the ship, rolled the elevator trim forward to bring down the nose, but the plant continued to climb. The puzzled pilot had just started to turn the trim tab to its normal position when the DC-4 pitched forward violently and went into a steep dive.

Down it roared, first vertically and then—in a mirror image of Flight 605—executed the first half of an outside loop until the aircraft was on its back. The pilot flying the plane and the captain, with their belts unfastened, were thrown to the top of the cockpit where their heads accidently struck three of the propeller-feathering buttons. Props one, two, and four feathered and the DC-4 lost power—a freak that saved the lives of all fifty-four persons aboard.

With the power cut, the copilot—the only one in the cockpit with his belt fastened—managed to roll the plane from its inverted position back to level flight, righting it less than 400 feet from the ground. They landed at El Paso and all three pilots told investigators the autopilot must have malfunctioned. But when the device checked out as working perfectly, the CAB continued to question the crew until the captain confessed what really had happened.

It was a bizarre story. Earlier that year a United DC-4 had tried to take off from La Guardia with the gust lock inadvertently engaged—the gust lock being a lever that secured the rudder and elevators while the plane was on the ground, thus furnishing protection against a sudden gust of wind. The UAL plane failed to gain altitude and crashed, killing all aboard. There had been some speculation among pilots as to what would happen if a gust lock was activated in flight instead of on the ground. Speculation leads to curiosity and that's what the American captain succumbed to—while sitting in the jump seat, he had leaned forward and, without telling the other two pilots, had engaged the gust lock.

The DC-3 pilot suspected the gust lock was on. When the nose began to climb and rolling the trim tab had no effect, he had asked the captain, "Is the autopilot on?"

"No," the captain replied.

The other pilot thought immediately of the gust lock and reached out to neutralize it. Before his hands touched the lever, the captain released it himself. It was spring-loaded and snapped back in unlocked position. The effect was like one man releasing a rope held tightly by a second person; the DC-3 pilot had been rolling the trim tab forward trying to bring the nose down and when the captain released the gust lock, the controls were locked in a dive position.

Safety experts immediately noticed that the partial outside loop was a carbon copy of the Eastern incident. The chief difference—and this kept the American flight from disaster—was its altitude, 4,000 feet higher than that of Flight 605, which simply had run out of sky.

Did the Eastern captain also get curious about gust locks in flight? No one will ever know. The CAB, in its final report, emphasized that he had been a former Navy test pilot and was both experienced and reputable.

"He would have been fully aware of the possible results of such speculation," the board added.

Some months later another DC-4 went into the same half-outside-loop near Cleveland, but the captain had sufficient altitude to roll back to level flight after cutting his power. This time there was no question that anyone had been experimenting with a gust lock—because of the Eastern and American experiences, all crews had been warned not to try anything. When the third DC-4 was examined, technicians found a tiny piece of bonding tape on one elevator that had worked loose. Subsequent tests showed that if the slipstream caught the loose tape in a certain position, it created a ballooning effect that caused an inadvertent dive. Air Force DC-4's also began reporting similar incidents and the CAB ordered the location of the tape changed on all DC-4's. Meanwhile, federal investigators went to the warehouse still holding the wreckage of Flight 605 and reexamined the tail. The tape was sealed tightly.

Elimination of the bonding tape as the culprit in Flight 605's death swung the needle of blame back toward the EAL captain. Publicly, and quite rightly, the CAB refused to crucify him on the basis of circumstantial evidence. Privately, however, investigators believed gust lock experimentation was the real cause and, also privately, most Eastern pilots reluctantly agreed.

"There was no way of proving it," says one retired veteran. "You'd have to know the captain and the kind of person he was. He had been in New York when the United crash occurred and he was an inquisitive guy. I suspected he had been fooling around with the gust lock and the minute I heard about American, I knew what happened at Port Deposit."

Port Deposit was the classic example of false leads driving investigators up the proverbial wall. In probing through the wreckage they kept finding engine cylinders which were identified as belonging to Wright engines. The DC-4, however, was equipped with Pratt & Whitneys and this led to an early and admittedly wild theory that Flight 601's power plants were operating with the wrong cylinders. It turned out that about a dozen spare Wright cylinders for Connie engines were being carried in the cargo bin.

Halliburton remembers a nonfatal DC-4 accident around this time which also gave investigators a few puzzling moments. They came across a Braniff stewardess uniform, then one from Delta, a third from TWA, and several more from other airlines. A passenger finally identified himself as a salesman for a uniform manufacturer—his luggage contained a number of samples.

This particular crash was something of a miracle in that everyone walked away. The DC-4 came down with one wing on fire, hit a power line, and ended upside down in a swamp. Among the lucky survivors was a jewelry salesman who informed Eastern's insurance representative that he had lost a briefcase containing hundreds of thousands of dollars' worth of expensive rings and uncut diamonds. Searchers found the briefcase. Inside was a tray of zircon rings with price tags ranging from fifteen to thirty-five dollars, plus an envelope containing uncut zircons with a note reading: "Try to get $.10 apiece for these."

About a year after Port Deposit, Eastern had another DC-4 accident and wound up shouldering all financial responsibility for a tragedy with which it had had nothing to do. The EAL plane had been cleared to land at Washington National Airport when a P-38 flown by a Bolivian pilot violated the control tower's instructions and crunched into the top of the DC-4's fuselage. All aboard were killed and the subsequent probe placed the majority of blame on the Bolivian, with the tower's apparently confusing communications a contributing factor. Lawsuits were filed against the Bolivian, the federal government, and Eastern; a jury ordered the airline to pay all claims.

John Halliburton remembers the legal maneuvering with considerable bitterness. "Our crew followed the tower's directions perfectly but that Bolivian pilot was an accident going someplace to happen. He had been barred from several airports in South America and our own CAA had lifted his ticket for repeated and flagrant violations of rules. I asked the attorney for Eastern's insurance company how the hell any jury could have reached the verdict it did. He told me the jurors felt the families of the victims deserved some compensation, but because collecting from the government involved too much red tape and because they figured it was impossible to get anything from the Bolivian, the jurors decided Eastern was the only party who'd pay."

Rickenbacker, it might be noted, was at his best during any crisis—"the calmest of anybody," one former associate recalls. "Any airline seems to take on the confusion of a Chinese fire drill after a bad crash but he always kept his cool, never stormed around blaming anyone, and tried to calm people down. Any kind of an accident hurt him deeply—you got the feeling it forced him to relive what he had gone through twice himself—but he tried never to show it."

This was not true, however, of his day-to-day relations with top and middle management—his temper was fearsome, if sporadic and short-lived, and nowhere was the fear he generated more pronounced than at his famous system staff meetings. Before the war he had instituted a practice of holding quarterly meetings in different cities, but during the war he abandoned them. When he resumed his monolithic rule, the staff meetings began again. It is starkly indicative of EVR's personality that he was exceptionally proud of a management monitoring procedure that was dreaded by anyone who had to attend one.

Time being a great healer as well as a tranquilizer, present and past EAL executives tend to remember the staff meetings with a kind of wry humor approaching nostalgia. But from their descriptions, the semiannual event prompted all the anticipation the Christians must have felt entering the colosseum. Rickenbacker established three echelons of management: The first was composed of all vice presidents, the second of all department heads, and the third of station managers, city traffic and sales managers, and other field supervisors. The first two echelons formed what he called his "advisory board" and the third his "field board." They met jointly, usually for a full week in Miami or New York, with about 500 persons present—each was expected to deliver a verbal report on his area of responsibility, department, or station. This wouldn't have been so tough except that Rickenbacker saw every report before it was presented—and he'd ask questions before, during, and after the delivery.

"Each meeting," EVR wrote in his autobiography, "was a kind of controlled free-for-all. Questions could be asked and criticisms made at any time."

That was *his* description. One veteran has another.

"You didn't argue with Captain Eddie in front of 500 people," he recounts. "If you did, you were dead. A guy named Gordon Brown, who went with Piedmont, once started to dispute Rick over the type of telephones we were using in reservations. Brown was absolutely right and Rickenbacker was wrong, but the next morning Gordon was no longer an Eastern employee."

Yet he also confirms what has been mentioned previously: Much of Rickenbacker's toughness was a sham, a crusty facade erected for the express purpose of making men stronger and better than they thought they were. He had done it on that raft and he did it constantly at his notorious staff meetings. Says this former officer:

"If he saw a man was extemely nervous—and I've known a couple of them to actually faint—he'd pat him on the ass and whisper, 'Slow down, son—you're doing just fine.' "

It was at these meetings that Eastern's management corps saw Rickenbacker at his best—and at his worst. We shall go into more detail about them in a later chapter because they provide such insight into his mind and his methods. Without a doubt they *were* beneficial in many ways, giving every manager knowledge of problems and policies affecting other departments. They added to both cohesiveness and communications within the management level, and Rickenbacker was to increase the effectiveness of this concept in 1947 when he set up similar meetings involving all assistant city and station managers, chief mechanics, and foremen.

The question was whether the benefits outweighed the harm they could do. Wayne Parrish, one of the few newsmen who ever attended a staff meeting—and he was at several—said he couldn't sit through one from start to finish.

"I couldn't take it," he admits. "There were a lot of arguments for them but I'm sure Eastern lost a lot of good men because they couldn't stand this excruciating examination before so many people."

One major trouble, of course, was that the staff meetings generated plenty of healthy internal criticism but nothing directed toward EVR himself. He was smart, dedicated, and courageous, and more often right than wrong in those days, but

Eastern was growing to the point where it was simply too big for one man to assume not only its rule but its image. A benevolent despot he was, but the virtues of benevolence were not enough to overcome the sins of despotism.

And that was Eastern's chief flaw as it headed into the 1950s—and the first real competition it had ever faced.

CHAPTER NINE

THE FIFTIES—
CLIMB AND DESCENT

In most respects the fifties were the Golden Decade for Eastern —and Captain Eddie, too.

It was a ten-year period marked by expansion, continued profits, massive if not entirely wise fleet modernization, and the biggest merger in the airline's history to date. It also saw the first relaxing of EVR's iron grip, the final years of his presidency (but not his rule), and the worst decision he was to make in the quarter century he ruled Eastern.

As the decade opened, he still was pursuing the same zigzag course which characterized his leadership—liberal one day and reactionary the next. He instigated a stock purchase plan for all employees, putting up an initial 100,000 shares of EAL stock for sale to those with three or more years seniority—at the attractive price of $13.50 a share. Yet he also could nod with chauvinistic satisfaction when a report was placed on his desk indicating that the airline in 1950 had almost completed its reversion to an all-male flight-attendant corps—the culmination of his own edict banning the hiring of any more women as replacements for departing stewardesses.

He was not really antifemale; to the Captain, it simply made no economic sense to permit the high rate of turnover among women flight attendants. This was a cost control item and he set his policy accordingly; the fact that the vast majority of passengers in those days were men who preferred pretty girls was not listed on his bottom line. It may tax one's credulity that an airline president could be that indifferent to customer desires, but it must be remembered that Rickenbacker was in the position of a successful author who can afford to ignore the critics—Eastern might be getting bad reviews, but Rickenbacker was laughing all the way to the bank. Those who did try to argue with him, fight him, or flatly oppose him were invariably stonewalled by EAL's profit figures.

Furthermore, for every recalcitrant officer, he had a couple hundred or more loyal employees who thought he could do no wrong. Two years in a row Captain Eddie staged essay contests which no one above a certain rank could enter. The first was on the subject "My Job and How I Like It." More than ninety percent of some 7,000 eligible employees submitted entries in hopes of winning such prizes as a four-door Buick, Pontiac and Chevrolet sedans, washers, refrigerators, freezers, and radio-phonographs. The next year the contest was on "How I Can Help Make My Company Successful" and the entrants represented more than eighty-two percent of the work force. The three top prizes again were a Buick, Pontiac, and Chevrolet (the Captain was still loyal to General Motors).

It goes without saying that the winning entries stressed virtues close to EVR's heart, such as Diligence, Hard Work, Loyalty, Thrift, and Dedication. Yet behind all this allegiance and homage to the Captain was the average employee's belief in his leadership. Along with Northwest's Don Nyrop, Rickenbacker may have been the most penurious president in airline history, but he also happened to be a battler for the dreams and goals he had for Eastern's future. They knew it, too—two years after the stock purchase plan went into effect, sixty percent of Eastern's employees owned twenty percent of the company's shares. This was more than loyalty; it was faith.

And he tried hard not to let them down. By the start of the

Golden Decade his route-expansion plans—some dating back to the war and earlier—had jelled into four areas: Puerto Rico, Canada, Mexico, and the West Coast via a southern transcontinental route. Puerto Rico already was on the system, with non-stop New York–San Juan service starting in 1951 and supplementing the existing Miami–San Juan route.

Mexico City already should have been part of Eastern's route structure—authorization between New Orleans and Mexico City had been granted in 1946—but service could not be started until a U.S.-Mexico bilateral air agreement was signed, and these negotiations were to drag on for several years. The southern transcontinental route bid turned from a dream into a nightmare. In 1951 the Civil Aeronautics Board, in one of its overly frequent efforts to please everyone without pleasing anybody, diluted the southern transcontinental award into a conglomeration of interchanges and combinations. Eastern wound up with a route it had to share with Braniff and TWA, the CAB granting it Miami–Houston authority. Under the award, EAL would connect with Braniff at Houston, Braniff would operate a Houston–Amarillo leg connecting with TWA at Amarillo, and TWA would fly the Amarillo–California segment.

Braniff had no four-engine equipment at the time, so Rickenbacker made a deal to lease the Houston–Amarillo route while EAL and TWA agreed to interchange Constellations in order to provide one-plane service; Eastern crews would fly between Miami and Amarillo and TWA would furnish pilots and flight attendants the rest of the way. It was a makeshift arrangement at best, but it was the closest Eastern had yet come to transcontinental status, not to mention a major east–west route.

Rickenbacker approved an expensive promotion campaign prior to the scheduled start of service, plus a special preinaugural flight for VIPs, including the press, aboard one of Eastern's new Super-Constellations. The Connie visited all the cities along the new route and ended up in Los Angeles, where Rickenbacker was to speak at a luncheon honoring the occasion. The dessert had just been served and Rickenbacker was about to speak when someone handed him a telegram.

The Captain first turned pale and then red with anger. He

didn't wait to be introduced but rose and read the contents to the surprised audience. National Airlines had obtained a court order staying the effectiveness of the southern transcontinental route award. The infuriated Rickenbacker immediately charged that American was behind the legal maneuvering, but he may well have been firing from the hip—there is absolutely no evidence that American had anything to do with masterminding the road-block; Baker of National largely relied on his airline's brilliant counsel, John Cross, who had found a loophole in the CAB's decision.

Cross had asked for an injunction based on the fact that no interchange arrangement had been mentioned in the CAB hearings on the case; with no evidence of an interchange in the record, he argued, it was impossible for National to oppose it during the hearings themselves. The court's subsequent injunction sent the case back to the CAB for further hearings on a proceeding that dated back to 1946, and it was to drag on for another decade before it was finally settled in 1961. In the interim Eastern received a first-class shafting when the board granted the California leg to TWA again, the Amarillo segment to Braniff once more—and gave EAL absolutely nothing, with the strange explanation that no service was needed between Houston and Miami.

This left TWA and Braniff with a supposed southern transcontinental route that covered only two thirds of the distance between Miami and California. The inevitable happened: TWA and Braniff lost their collective shirts trying to operate an interchange over a truncated route and finally asked the CAB to abandon it. A third round of hearings ended with National getting Miami–New Orleans, Delta New Orleans–Dallas, and American Dallas–Los Angeles via Phoenix; Eastern got nothing. In 1961 the Board came up with its fourth decision—Continental was awarded Los Angeles–Houston, National received Miami–Los Angeles authority via Houston, Delta was awarded Dallas–Los Angeles/San Francisco, and Eastern got the crumbs: Dallas to New Orleans, Tampa, and Miami, putting it in the hopeless position of trying to compete against two rivals operating single-plane service coast-to-coast.

To Captain Eddie it was rank injustice which, naturally, he blamed on "bureaucracy." It *was*, in most respects, an injustice but it is hard to tag "bureaucracy" as the sole culprit in freezing Eastern out of a route Rickenbacker himself had conceived and sought for twenty-five years. Robert Burkhardt, in his fine history of the CAB (Green Hills Publishing Company, 1974), put much of the blame on the Captain for the Board's original decision that was nothing more than an illegal compromise.

"Unfortunately," he wrote, "Captain Rickenbacker, with his usual flamboyant approach, overplayed his part. He literally stumped the South, building up civic support and community pressure so that the CAB would have no choice but to pick Eastern for its long-coveted route. He built up so much pressure, however, that the Board reacted in a contrary way."

That Rickenbacker should have been faulted for trying so hard seems unfair, and it is debatable whether his over zealousness was the real reason for the number done on Eastern. A more plausible explanation may be EVR's own attitude toward what he regarded as regulatory interference and ineptness—an attitude which is not entirely unjustified—although he shared one thing in common with his bitter rival, Baker. National's president was as outspoken as Rickenbacker when it came to unvarnished contempt for politicans. He once publicly called Congress a "den of thieves," going beyond even the Captain's abrasiveness, yet it was National which benefited the most from the CAB's third and fourth decisions in the marathon southern transcontinental case and both were issues while Baker still owned National.

More likely Eastern was jobbed because of a combination of adverse factors, Rickenbacker's unpopularity among government officials certainly being a major one. EAL also was handicapped by the regulatory climate of the 1950s which favored strengthening the smaller trunk carriers to make them more competitive with the so-called "Big Four"—United, American, TWA, and Eastern. This trend was logical and perhaps reasonable, but it affected Eastern more adversely than it did the other three giants because so many of the CAB's route awards went to two of its most bitter competitors: Delta and National.

There are more roads to route expansion than the regulatory path, of course, and Captain Eddie chose the most obvious: merger. Where he had once been adamantly opposed to this course, he now decided that the mushrooming competition of the fifties required a fresh look. And it was to the north that he gazed, in the direction of a faltering small carrier possessing something he wanted badly—access into Canada.

The airline was Colonial, and Rickenbacker wasn't the only one casting covetous eyes. The hard-pressed Montreal-based company also was on George Baker's shopping list and, figuratively speaking, these two paragons of mutual animosity collided in the market aisle.

The Rickenbacker-Baker feud was only slightly less intense than the one which made the Hatfields and McCoys famous. To Captain Eddie, Baker was a crook, liar, and charlatan—he once told a reporter that National's original slogan, "Route of the Buccaneers," merely reflected the reputation of the "damned pirate" who ran it. Baker, in turn, considered the captain a greedy, unprincipled despot whose definition of free enterprise was anything that benefited Eastern. That there was a modicum of proof to confirm both appraisals sums up their unfettered hatred and frequently underhanded strategy.

National's interest in acquiring Colonial first surfaced in 1951 after Baker had been rebuffed in merger talks with both Northwest and Northeast. National and Colonial actually reached a tentative merger agreement which called for the absorption of the smaller carrier in return for slightly over 450,000 shares of National stock to be distributed among Colonial stockholders, or seven shares of NAL stock in exchange for eight shares of CAL.

The merger seemed cut and dried but Baker quickly found out that Rickenbacker never could be underestimated. Shortly after Colonial's board of directors approved the merger proposal, leaving only the stockholders' green light for final consummation, Eastern entered the bidding through a back door. Very quietly a number of Colonial's largest stockholders had sold their shares to some of Eastern's most influential stockholders. To be more specific, subsequent hearings on the proposed EAL-

Colonial merger disclosed that two of Eastern's directors and "persons and firms in the immediate orbit of Eastern's influence" had acquired twenty-one percent, or about 110,000 shares of Colonial's capital stock—sufficient to defeat a merger with National.

Having neatly knifed Baker, Rickenbacker then made his own bid for Colonial—an exceptionally attractive offer amounting to almost 345 percent over the beleaguered airline's book value, which at the time would have been the highest proportional price ever paid by one airline assuming control of another. It was too good an offer for Colonial's aggressive president, Branch T. Dykes, to resist. On March 23, 1952, Dykes recommended to his shareholders that they accept. He pointed out that despite heavy government subsidies, Colonial had accumulated a $1.5 million deficit and that he saw no hope for the future because of a poorly integrated route structure subject to extreme seasonal differences.

He described Eastern as "the soundest of all domestic carriers, one which has never operated in the red and year after year has spurned all offers of government subsidy." Such fulsome praise and telling arguments, however, didn't dissuade either the CAB from holding hearings on the merger or Baker from trying his damndest to block it. Throughout EAL there was considerable concern that the merger might be rejected; Brad Williams, in his history of National (*Anatomy of an Airline*, Doubleday, 1970) writes that everyone got into the act, including the White House and Department of Justice, because Baker "raised so much hell." It was a classic case of the pot calling the kettle black, inasmuch as a few years earlier Baker had tried to take over Caribbean Atlantic Airways, otherwise known as Caribair, only to be shot down by the CAB, which found that National actually had started operating the other carrier without first getting Board approval. It was the same charge Baker was now hurling at Rickenbacker.

"Prior control" was the chief issue in the hearings that opened in October 1952. National introduced evidence that went beyond allegations of purchases of Colonial stock by people "in the immediate orbit of Eastern's influence." It claimed that when National learned EAL had made several changes in the bidding form and requested the same privilege, it was turned down by a Colonial vice president in a telephone call.

"It is now obvious from the record that National's request was not even relayed to the [Colonial] president or its board of directors," the NAL brief stated, "whereas Eastern and Colonial had a meeting among Rickenbacker and several others about the Eastern changes in bidding forms requested earlier. Furthermore, the meeting was held in the offices of Rickenbacker and on Eastern property, and the changes in the bidding form requested by Eastern were made and reported in the corporate minutes of Colonial Airlines."

The CAB's Bureau of Public Affairs counsel, urging the Board to reject the merger, called EAL's tactics a "brazen and willful demonstration of the employment of stock control power to compel a corporation management to accept the offer of a designated bidder, in this case Eastern, by pointedly demanding a meeting for the sole purpose of considering only that one offer. . . . Its coercive effect upon the badgered and bewildered Colonial management, still reeling from the stockholder rejection of the recommendation of approval of a merger with National, needs no amplification."

The CAB, however, initially approved the merger; it conceded that Eastern had not satisfactorily refuted the prior-control charges, but found that the merger would save the taxpayers some $850,000 a year in subsidy payments and this, plus "other advantages of the Eastern-Colonial merger, were considerations for approval of such weight to overbalance the public interest in preserving the integrity of Section 408 [the provision in the Civil Aeronautics Act forbidding prior control]."

The merger still needed White House approval, because Colonial operated a single international route—to Bermuda from New York and Washington. President Eisenhower jolted Eastern by rejecting the Board's decision and sent the case back to the CAB for further consideration. This time the Board reversed itself, found that Eastern had violated Section 408, and recommended that a National-Colonial merger be approved.

Rickenbacker's dejection was matched by Baker's elation—the latter told associates, "We've got Bermuda and Canada in the bag." Williams says what Baker didn't grasp was the resentment he had incurred among Colonial's stockholders, management, and directors—of sufficient proportions to force another round of CAB hearings. By the end of 1954 the ace in the hole Rickenbacker was holding amounted to a simple mathematical matter: Eastern was still willing to pay more than $9.6 million for Colonial's assets, against National's bid of $2.5 million.

Nor was Captain Eddie ignorant of that Section 408 mud Baker had so skillfully tossed. While Baker continued to argue that Eastern already controlled Colonial illegally and should be ousted from the proceedings completely, the EAL stockholders who had bought into Colonial quietly sold their shares and removed prior control as the chief roadblock. This time it made little difference who owned which shares—Colonial's shareholders, directors, and management wanted Eastern and not National and there wasn't anything Baker could do about it; National was not in a financial position to better EAL's offer, which also provided for the exchange of one share of Eastern stock for two shares of Colonial.

This time the CAB, on January 11, 1956, approved the merger and two weeks later President Eisenhower did likewise. The climax of the four-year fight added nearly 3,000 route miles, nineteen new cities, and two countries to Eastern's system. Captain Eddie called the merger "a joining of hands, not dollars," and assured all Colonial employees they would have full job security in all classifications along with the same employee benefits Eastern was giving its own personnel.

By acquiring Colonial, Eastern also inherited its equipment —eight DC-3's and five DC-4's, none of which fitted into EAL's aircraft modernization plans. More important than the planes were the people—Eastern inherited a small but highly skilled and proud group of new employees, and, as is the case with any merger, the majority looked at Eastern with the misgivings of marines suddenly ordered to join the army.

Some had even tried to organize a stock-purchase plan that would have given them control of Colonial, but this effort fell far short; they knew their cause was doomed, anyway, when Colonial lost its bid to become the third carrier in the New York–Miami market—the prize would go to Northeast, in another regulatory donnybrook to be discussed later—but the CAB refused to hear the Miami route case until the Eastern-Colonial merger was settled.

Colonial was as old as Eastern itself—it was incorporated under the name of Canadian Colonial Airways in 1928—and technically was even older. Originally it was a small charter line operating out of Naugatuck, Connecticut, commencing service in 1923 and branching into a regularly scheduled service between Boston and New York two years later. At that stage it acquired the first domestic airmail contract issued after passage of the Kelly Act and its board of directors included none other than Juan Trippe. Trippe pulled out when his fellow directors refused to put up money to buy a fleet of new Fokker trimotors, and went on to found Pan American, while Colonial itself became part of the AVCO empire. By 1928, Colonial actually was two airlines—Canadian Colonial, operating a newly granted route between New York and Montreal, and Colonial Western, which had an airmail contract for the Buffalo–Albany leg; the parent company was Colonial Air Transport.

For a number of years the airline suffered through several corporate reorganizations so convoluted that its ownership couldn't have been determined by anything short of an IBM computer. At one point it actually was three airlines owned in succession by two holding companies and included a number of flying schools. It had won a New York–Montreal route in 1928 but its confused corporate structure was a straitjacket against any real growth until 1939, when a group of investors headed by Sigmund Janas bought control, renamed it Colonial Airlines, and put new life into its operations.

Janas was one of the industry's most colorful characters. He

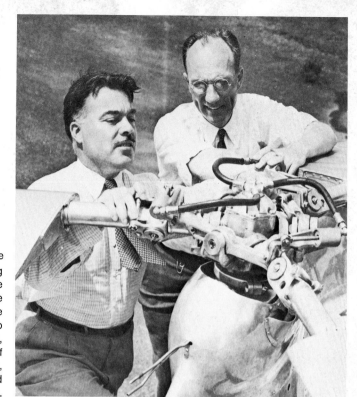

These two men were instrumental in launching what was to become Eastern Air Lines. On the right, Harold Pitcairn, the shy, brooding genius who founded Pitcairn Aviation, shown with his chief designer, Agnew Larsen, who built the famed Mailwing.

The plane that started it all. The original Pitcairn Mailwing eventually evolved into a fleet of some 250 jetliners, but no aircraft in Eastern's history served with greater honor than this tiny biplane.

Curtiss Kingbird at Miami

Eastern's baggage area in Boston, circa 1934. Every piece of baggage had to be weighed in the early airline days.

Eastern's operations office, Atlanta, 1935—not much space was needed in the days when twenty-one-passenger DC-3s ruled the airways.

These twenty-three men and one woman constituted Eastern's entire work force at the airline's major maintenance base in Atlanta in 1930. The current maintenance payroll numbers in the thousands.

A contemporary of the Ford trimotor and the Condor, the Stinson trimotor served in Eastern's fleet only briefly—it flew, according to pilots, like an iron bathtub.

Pulchritude in this case belongs to the women, not the uniforms. These are some of Eastern's earliest stewardesses —before the somewhat chauvinistic Captain Eddie decided that his flight attendants should be men.

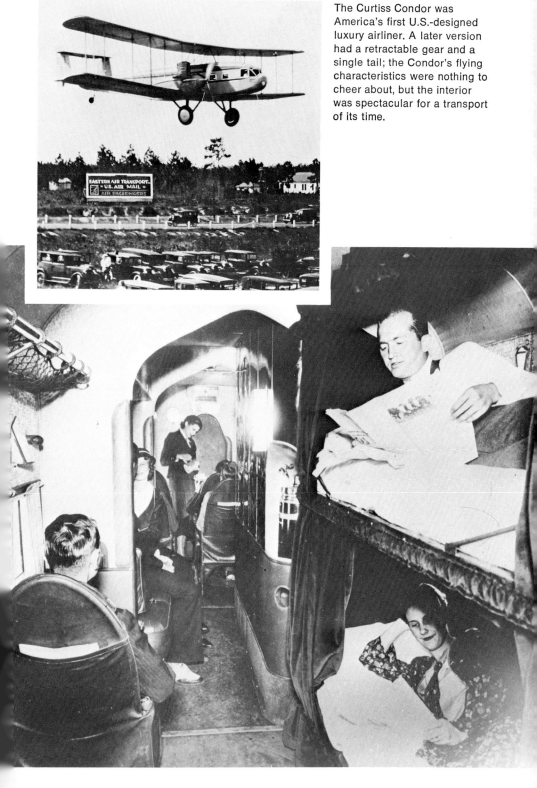

The Curtiss Condor was America's first U.S.-designed luxury airliner. A later version had a retractable gear and a single tail; the Condor's flying characteristics were nothing to cheer about, but the interior was spectacular for a transport of its time.

A dapper EAL flight steward aboard a DC-3. Rickenbacker preferred male cabin attendants because their turnover was far less than that of stewardesses.

This quartet ran Eastern from the mid-thirties to post-World War II. *Clockwise*: Rickenbacker, Sid Shannon, Paul Brattain, and Tom Armstrong—the latter served briefly and reluctantly as a figurehead president.

Frank Sharpe, a man of humor who also had the courage to battle his bosses

Maurice "Lefty" Lethridge, colorful EAL official who served as the airline's president for the shortest span of any chief executive in aviation history— twenty-four hours

Floyd Hall

Edward Vernon Rickenbacker

Eastern goes to war. A C-46 is loaded with military supplies at Miami before taking off for Brazil and Africa—the wartime route EAL served. The DC-3 in the background carries the gaudy lettering Rickenbacker loved on his airplanes.

Heading out on a World War II (1942) Pacific mission, Rickenbacker and his crew crashed into the sea. Here, Captain Eddie (*center*) is helped ashore after being rescued from a rubber raft on which he floated for twenty-four gruesome days and nights. (*Courtesy UPI*)

Two famous captains—Eddie Rickenbacker and Dick Merrill. Note the felt hat on the former—it was a Rickenbacker trademark.

Eastern operated this autogiro briefly between the downtown Philadelphia Post Office and the airport in the late 1930s.

DC-2, The Great Silver Fleet

Martin 404

This shot was taken in the early morning hours of May 1, 1953, as a tractor tows Eastern's ship #344 through the deserted streets of the nation's capital en route to storage. The DC-3, which logged nearly 57,000 hours in the air, is now on display at the National Air and Space Museum.

Art Lewis

Sam Higginbottom

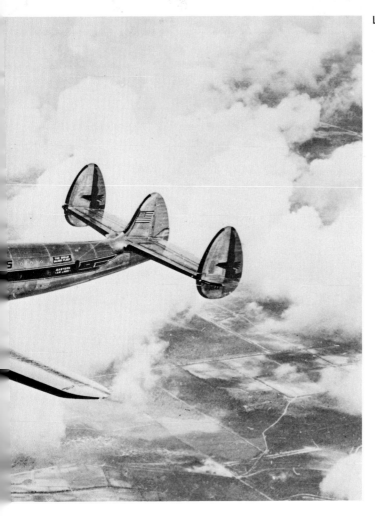

Lockheed Constellation

E. R. "Ernie" Breech

Malcolm A. MacIntyre

These two photographs effectively dramatize the growth of United States air transportation. One depicts Miami airport in 1934, with most of Eastern's DC-2 and DC-3 fleet lined up in front of hangars and what was then the airline's Miami office headquarters. The other picture shows Eastern's current facilities at Miami International Airport. The tallest structure is Building 16, housing EAL's executive offices.

Lockheed Electra

This experimental paint scheme was put on an EAL DC-8 as part of Floyd Hall's new image program. It was abandoned in favor of the "hockey stick" motif.

Frank Borman

Charlie Simons, who survived
years of corporate upheavals
to become Frank Borman's
right-hand man

took over Colonial in 1939 and dominated it much as Rickenbacker did Eastern. Janas was a stocky, cigar-smoking, belligerent man under whose inevitable fedora hat was a mind born to
wheel and deal. His executive turnover required a revolving door
at company headquarters—Janas was tough to work for, extremely demanding, and occasionally devious. Colonial grew
during his rather brief regime, the Bermuda authorization and a
Washington–Montreal–Ottawa route being the chief expansion
moves, but there were those who claimed Colonial stayed alive in
spite of him, not because of him.

Janas was in perpetual hot water with the CAB, which took
a dim view of such activities as charging his personal grocery bill
to the airline; eventually the Board put sufficient pressure on
Colonial's directors to force him out, Dykes replacing him in
1952 as president and chief executive officer. Janas's departure
didn't cause many tears, for his less desirable qualities disenchanted a number of employees and officers alike—a propensity
toward nepotism was an example. Janas named one son chief
pilot at the age of twenty-six and another vice president of traffic
and sales, a post to which he brought a lot of enthusiasm but very
little experience.

Yet Janas also is remembered for keeping the airline glued
together during the war, when the Army took all but two of the
eight planes Colonial was operating at the time. And when
Colonial became part of Eastern, its 800 employees could look
back on one of the unique records of airline history: It was the
only carrier in the U.S. which never had a fatal crash during its
entire existence. Janas, for all his apparent finagling, was prouder
of that accomplishment than of anything else—he is said to have
originated the slogan "Safety Is No Accident."

Colonial was as colorful an airline as the man who guided it
for thirteen turbulent years. Its pilots wore a greenish-blue uniform which, as cynics liked to remind them, closely resembled
the work garments of the New York Sanitation Department.
There were about 120 of them at the time of the merger, and for
many Eastern was a lot easier to work for than Colonial.

Vern Renaud, an ex-Colonial pilot who is now an Eastern

captain, remembers one trip that involved twelve stops between New York and Washington. It started out north from La Guardia and went to Poughkeepsie, Albany, Saranac, Lake Placid, Massena, and Bennington, then turned south and headed for Watertown, Syracuse, Binghamton, Allentown, Harrisburg, and Washington—a flying time one minute short of eight hours.

"The return trip was the same," Renaud chuckles. "Allentown was the favorite stop because there was a nudist colony a little north of the city and we'd fly just off the deck to get a good look. By the end of the trip there'd be so few passengers aboard that we'd invite them up to the cockpit."

Some of the pilots were Canadians and so were a few stewardesses. One of the latter was a French girl named Yvette Fontaine, and her cabin announcements were something no crew member ever forgot because the French accent practically oozed. Renaud particularly loved to hear her on that twelve-stopper marathon after leaving Syracuse for Binghamton.

"Ladeez and Jahntlemon," she would intone, "zis ees Colonial zirty-sree, we fly at ze altitude of sree zounsand feet, and ze next stop is Boomington."

Someone at Colonial sold Janas on the idea of calling the planes "sky cruisers" and once this was adopted, all new stewardesses were warned in training to be careful of the pronunciation. The word of caution went out after several nervous rookie girls turned "Welcome aboard Colonial's sky cruiser" into "Welcome aboard Colonial's sky screwer."

The fleet may have been old but it was well maintained and clean. All thirteen aircraft were war surplus or secondhand—sometimes thirdhand—and one of them had been ferried all the way from China. It had arrived in such a dilapidated state that it took Colonial's mechanics a year to put it in shape to fly airline schedules.

Among those 800 apprehensive men and women coming over to the much larger, uncertain world of Eastern were several Colonial executives. Only one was to remain with EAL—James Reinke, now vice president of government affairs in Washington; at the time of the merger he was Colonial's vice president of traffic and sales, and except for a few pilots is the last link with the gallant little airline. He started with Colonial in 1942 as a meteorologist.

Dykes joined Eastern, too, as vice president of the "Colonial Division of Eastern Air Lines"—Rickenbacker wisely opted to operate the acquired system as a separate airline until it could be integrated into EAL's own route structure. It was a decision W. A. Patterson of United was to wish he had copied when United absorbed Capital in 1960; the integration was attempted virtually overnight and it was chaos for several months.

But Dykes's stay at Eastern was to be of short duration and there is reason to believe Captain Eddie really didn't want another airline president around the premises, not even a former one. Lefty Lethridge is among those subscribing to this theory. Dykes was a solid airline man who had joined the old U.S. Air Mail Service as a mechanic and worked for several airlines before becoming American's superintendent of maintenance. Janas hired him away from American in the same capacity and later promoted him to a vice presidency.

"Eddie really was worried that Dykes might become president of Eastern," Lethridge says.

This may very well have been true. While the merger battle was still being fought at the CAB, Rickenbacker suddenly announced that he was relinquishing the presidency to become chairman of the board and general manager. The choice of what might euphemistically be called his successor was easygoing, popular, and reportedly reluctant Tom Armstrong, EAL's secretary and treasurer.

Captain Eddie's statement, issued August 10, 1953, was more notable for what it didn't say than for what it did.

"The broad economic readjustment taking place in our country, and with our company and the industry facing the transition into a revolutionary new era of jet power," EVR said, "has made it increasingly clear that I must transfer more of the detailed management responsibility to our younger executives. Only in this way can I be free to devote more of my time to the complex problems involved in high-priority policies and long-range planning which means so much to the welfare and future of our company and everyone in the Eastern Air Lines family."

Rickenbacker had been under some pressure by directors to name a successor and no one really quarreled with his choice; Armstrong, a fifty-one-year-old veteran of twenty-five years at EAL, was a competent financial man and well liked. There was, however, considerable speculation as to *why* the Captain picked him over two other candidates, one of whom really wanted to be president. Two men close to EVR are in complete agreement on the reason: Rickenbacker's great dream was to have his son Bill succeed him, and he envisioned Armstrong as purely an interim president until Bill could be trained for the job.

Brad Walker was one of those two intimates. A few minutes after word spread through Rockefeller Plaza that Armstrong would be Eastern's new president, Walker went into EVR's.

"Eddie, for Christ's sake—why?" Brad asked bluntly. "Tom doesn't even want the job."

Rickenbacker looked at him. "Jesus, don't *you* know what I'm trying to do? I just want Tom in there until Bill is ready to take over. Anyway, I got guys behind Armstrong who'll keep pushing him."

Rickenbacker made the same confession to Lefty Lethridge. "Eddie even told me once he wanted Billy to come in and sit by my desk and 'get the benefit of your thinking on the day-to-day running of the airline,' as he put it," Lefty says. "The trouble was that Bill was artistic by nature—he wasn't attuned to corporate life and it took awhile before Rick realized it."

"Everytime Rickenbacker approached Bill about this," Walker adds, "the boy balked. The truth was, he didn't like the airline business and he wasn't temperamentally suited for it. The Captain didn't understand this and he was hurt."

EVR wasn't the only one hurt, for that matter. So was Paul Brattain, who had always expected to be Rickenbacker's successor and was stunned when Armstrong was picked. For five years he had sat on the sidelines while Stan Osborne ran traffic and sales, but in 1950 Osborne resigned—Lethridge says he quit before EVR could fire him—and the Captain asked Brattain to take over those duties again on a temporary basis. He was back to his status as vice-president-without-portfolio at the time of Armstrong's promotion and he had the guts to confront Rickenbacker and ask why he had been passed over. EVR said it was because he was too old—Brattain was approaching fifty-nine. There would come a time only two years hence when EVR would again call on Brattain to help Eastern out of trouble—in 1955 Rickenbacker offered to make him vice president of traffic and sales once more, under the pressure of increasing competition.

"You told me two years ago I was too old to be president," Brattain said firmly. "So now, I'm too old to be vice president of traffic and sales."

The other presidential candidate probably could have had the job if he had wanted it. That was Sid Shannon—no one knows whether EVR actually offered him the job before he settled on Armstrong, but if he did Shannon undoubtedly would have refused. The portly vice president of operations hated New York City and not even Rickenbacker could have enticed him away from the fast-growing Miami base where Shannon had his headquarters.

So it was Tom Armstrong who became Eastern's fourth president—fifth if Harold Pitcairn is counted—and this loyal, dedicated, square-jawed bear of a man knew exactly where he stood: constantly under the ubiquitous shadow of Captain Eddie, whose statement about concentrating on "high-priority policies and long-range planning" was only partially true. There was an oversupply of policies and a plethora of necessary planning to worry about, but EVR's grip on the reins was as viselike as ever and his preoccupation with small problems continued even as he tackled the awesome challenge of the forthcoming jet age.

One of the unsolved mysteries of Rickenbacker's life was his real attitude toward jets. His speeches and statements on the subject are contradictory and his actions even more so. Admittedly he was far ahead of most industry leaders in predicting the inevitability and impact of the jets—an artist's rendition of a future jetliner was in Eastern's 1952 annual report. And the airline came close to becoming the first U.S. domestic carrier to operate jets—two years before Boeing turned out the first American-made jet transport.

The first 707 came off the assembly line in 1954. In 1952 Rickenbacker, Froesch, and other EAL executives flew to England to inspect de Havilland's magnificent new Comet jetliner and it was no pleasure trip for Captain Eddie—he was seriously considering the Comet for Eastern's New York–Miami route. Seriously enough, in fact, to discuss possible delivery dates with de Havilland. There is a dispute as to how close EVR came to actually buying the revolutionary transport. Derek Dempster, in his book *Tale of the Comet* (David McKay, 1958), says Rickenbacker would have ordered no fewer than fifty if de Havilland had been able to meet a schedule that called for delivery of all fifty by 1955—an impossible task, considering what was then the relative slowness of British production lines. Other sources claim the Captain had thirty-five Comets in mind, but Rickenbacker himself—and Charlie Froesch bears him out—said he was never that close to a deal. In his autobiography EVR says he soured on the Comet during a demonstration flight.

"It was an amazingly smooth and comfortable ride," he wrote. "I visited in the cockpit, then strolled back toward the tail. Halfway down the aisle, I suddenly stopped short. I couldn't believe what I was seeing. The sides of the plane seemed to be moving in and out like an accordion. I pushed my finger up against the side. I could feel it.

"It scared the living daylights out of me. Sooner or later that metal would fatigue and crack. At 40,000 feet, the pressurized cabin would explode like a toy balloon. . . .

"On the ground, I talked to de Havilland's engineers, even the directors of the company. They refused to believe me. . . . From my personal experience with the plane, I was able to warn American manufacturers about this accordion weakness, and steps were taken to prevent it."

Froesch, too, says he had the same misgivings about the Comet's structural strength and the jet's tragic record bore out their fears. Three of them did blow up in flight, and in all three cases the first fatigue crack appeared around a navigation window at the top of the fuselage, the rupture spreading instantaneously over the length of the body. U.S. manufacturers, learning quickly from the Comet's fatal flaw, installed metal stoppers along the fuselage strategically placed so no fatigue crack could progress beyond the nearest stopper. Whether this fail-safe concept was prompted by Rickenbacker's warning is questionable—not until the Comet mystery was solved did Boeing and Douglas adopt the stopper principle, although Captain Eddie said his concern was voiced before the first explosive decompression accident.

Froesch remembers one incident from that trip involving humor, not impending tragedy. The Eastern party had been assigned two cars—a rented Daimler limousine and a far more modest Air Force Chevrolet, the latter loaned by the U.S. ambassador who also had assigned his air attaché, a colonel, as the official escort.

They were en route from London to Derby and Rickenbacker was perfectly happy basking in the limousine's luxury—until he noticed that every constable in the small towns through which they were passing saluted the Chevy, not the Daimler. When the group stopped for lunch, EVR approached his escort, who was in the smaller car.

"Colonel, how come you're drawing all the salutes?" he asked darkly.

"We have diplomatic license plates," the colonel explained.

Rickenbacker frowned and walked over to Froesch. "Charlie, from now on you ride in the limo—I'll be in the Chevy."

The Captain's brief flurry of interest in the ahead-of-its-time Comet was not the only time he seemed to be ahead of his contemporaries when it came to recognizing the jet's potential. As far back as 1948 he had told an Atlanta news conference that "within five or six years Eastern will be flying jet-propelled planes from Atlanta to New York in a maximum of an hour and a half." Yet one of those contemporaries, now retired, swears that he heard Rickenbacker make another speech about that time in which he said jets might never be feasible commercially because the flames from the engine exhausts would ignite any aircraft following in their wake. The discrepancy is not too surprising; it was perfectly natural for a man with so much appreciation of technology to welcome the jet age, yet likewise natural for a man with so much fear of financial insecurity to simultaneously dread its coming.

His elevation of Tom Armstrong to the presidency occurred shortly after the airline celebrated its silver anniversary—twenty-five years, during the previous eighteen of which Eastern had earned a profit, and 13 of those without a penny of government subsidy. And Rickenbacker was convinced that he had molded an executive team capable of tackling the challenges of the future, from the forthcoming jet revolution to the equally uncertain problems of mushrooming competition.

As of the twenty-fifth anniversary, the top-level hierarchy included Armstrong, the under-utilized Brattain as first vice president, Shannon as operations vice-president, Les Arnold as vice president in charge of properties and leases, Jack Frost as vice president of traffic and sales, Joseph Brock serving in the newly created post of vice president of personnel and industrial relations, Robert Ramspeck as vice president of federal and state regulatory matters—not the easiest job in the company considering EVR's own jaundiced views toward government—and Froesch as vice president of engineering. Rickenbacker split Armstrong's old job into two positions, naming capable Tom Creighton as the new treasurer and Willard Blackwood as controller.

A new employee with rising influence was Bill Van Dusen, whom the Captain had hired away from Pan Am (he loved to steal executive personnel from Juan Trippe) and assigned the task of handling advertising and public relations. There were some bruised feelings over Van Dusen's appointment—Van Dusen, a big, rumpled man with a good track record at Pan Am, clashed almost immediately with aging Bev Griffith and Brad Walker—the latter was one of the first to hear that Van Dusen had been hired.

Walker was in the Rickenbackers' hotel suite when Captain Eddie broke the news.

"Brad, I've just hired a new guy, Bill Van Dusen from Pan Am," EVR informed him. "I wish you'd get in touch with him and brief him on how we work."

Walker dutifully called Van Dusen, took him for a long drive, and told him what he could about Rickenbacker, the company, and the various officials whom the new public-relations and advertising director would be working with. As Walker recalls it, Van Dusen was rather noncommittal and, as it turned out, he had his own ideas on public relations and advertising matters—tough old Bev clashed with him immediately. Walker's first run-in occurred when EVR approved an ad which Van Dusen saw and wanted to change.

"I think those headlines should be reworded," he told Walker. "And the copy could stand some revisions, too."

Walker smiled tightly. "The Captain's already okayed that ad."

"So?"

"So if you want to change that wording, you take it right to the old man and tell *him*."

Van Dusen backed away from that confrontation with the Captain but from then on there was friction between Van Dusen and Walker that was never really resolved.

The proverbial man in the middle during this time was Lefty Lethridge, ostensibly assistant to Brattain but in reality a kind of troubleshooter, mediator, and jack-of-all-trades throughout the executive echelons. In a sense he also provided liaison between top and middle management, a kind of buffer zone through which two-way communications flowed. He was the perfect man for the job; everyone liked Lefty. He could be tough, sympathetic, funny, loyal, and irreverent depending on the occasion, crisis, or individuals in question.

Infusion of new blood was relatively rare, for Rickenbacker normally disliked going outside the company to fill key positions. Early in the 1950s he had violated that policy by raiding American's reservations department for a quartet of highly respected experts in that field. It didn't start out as a raid; EVR knew Eastern was having trouble with its reservations system, mostly because it was about as modern as an abacus, and he sought outside help from none other than C. R. Smith.

The Captain's unhappiness with EAL's reservations over-rode his reluctance to ask C.R. for anything more significant than the time of day. Rickenbacker, for all his feuding with and sniping at Smith, privately held great respect for American's efficiency and he finally swallowed his pride—with C.R.'s permission, he sent a team over to study American's reservations system. This group eventually reported back to the Captain that American was carrying a third more passengers than Eastern while handling them with only two thirds of EAL's personnel.

That was enough for Captain Eddie. Much to C.R.'s annoyance he promptly hired four of the latter's reservations specialists—Rod King, Harry Battaile, Frank Sharpe, and Bob Winn. King didn't stay with Eastern very long—he took a dim view of Rickenbacker's notorious staff meetings—but Sharpe and Winn were to play major roles at Eastern. Sharpe had a great deal of Lethridge's irreverence in him plus Lefty's natural ability and his refusal to quake at the very mention of the Captain's name. Even so, Sharpe tells a story on himself which pointedly demonstrates the iron grip EVR had on the minds and emotions of even his most independent-minded officers.

"I had been with Eastern for about eighteen months helping to establish a new reservations system," he recounts. "At the time, station operations and dining service were both under flight operations and the Captain decided he wanted to put stations and dining into a separate traffic department—to be called ground operations. So I went down to Miami and set it up. Sid Shannon thought I should stay there and run it, but Jack Frost was raising hell—he wanted me back in marketing. The argument went back and forth between Shannon and Frost until they finally got the Captain into the act.

"I stayed in Miami with my family waiting for somebody to settle the whole thing. One day I was outside in my shorts sunning myself when my son tells me Captain Rickenbacker was calling. I got up, answered the phone—I told the Captain I wanted to stay in traffic—and went back outside. My wife and kids started laughing—so help me, I had put on my pants and a good shirt before I picked up that phone!"

The executive team that served under the Captain in that prejet era was privy to the biggest equipment splurge Eastern had ever undertaken. It began in 1950 with the new Martins gradually replacing the DC-3 and DC-4 fleets—all sixty had been delivered by late 1952, and by the end of the year the last DC-3 had been retired.

Dick Merrill, naturally, flew the final trip, operating as Flight 151 from Chicago to Miami. At its peak the DC-3 fleet had numbered sixty-three aircraft which compiled more than 83.5 million miles—the equivalent of 3,343 trips around the world or 254 years in the air. One Eastern DC-3 which was sold to North Central finished its career in regularly scheduled service having flown more than 83,000 hours since the date of its manufacture, and some 12 million miles, in the course of which it wore out 550 main gear tires, 25,000 spark plugs, and 136 engines. It had burned eight million gallons of gasoline, enough to operate an automobile for eleven thousand years, and someone even figured out the old plane had taxied well over 100,000 miles.

Earlier in 1952 Eastern had ordered thirty Super-C Constellations, officially designated the L-1049C. The outward differences were obvious—square windows replaced the round ones of the older Connies, the fuselage was lengthened by the insertion of two nine-foot sections forward and aft of the wings, the longer nose was more pointed, and the cockpit visibility was markedly improved by a new windshield configuration. More powerful engines, 2700-horsepower Wrights, combined with the larger fuselage, gave the L-1049 a forty percent boost in payload; the L-649's had such limited cargo space that Charlie Froesch had been forced to develop the "Speedpack," an ingenious detachable bin shaped like a fat torpedo, which could be hooked onto the belly.

The combined cost of the Martins and Super Connies totaled some $100 million, but Rickenbacker wasn't finished. In the silver anniversary year of 1953 he ordered twenty-two Super-G Constellations equipped with the new Wright turbo-compound engines—despite the name, they weren't actually turbine power plants but regular piston engines with turbine-driven superchargers that harnessed formerly wasted exhaust, much like the fanjet engines that were to come years later. They also were the first EAL planes to have autopilots, although the installation was solely due to the fact that they originally had been ordered by TWA.

The twenty-fifth anniversary was a sufficiently happy occasion for Rickenbacker to induce him to spend quite a few dollars on a celebration. For the occasion he approved a new design for the famed "Hat-in-the-Ring" emblem first introduced on the twentieth anniversary and awarded to employees with two decades of service. The new pin added a quarter-of-a-carat diamond and Captain Eddie himself made special presentations to four men at a banquet in Miami Beach's Saxony Hotel—Captains Clarence Coleman, Gene Brown, and Walter Shaffer, and Superintendent of Scheduling C. Norman Scully. In his remarks EVR made a point of predicting that the next twenty-five years would witness a complete changeover to jet equipment, the start being "only a few short years away."

The Hat-in-the-Ring pin became something of an unofficial symbol for Eastern. Frank Sharpe once ran into an Aeroflot steward in Moscow and the Russian airline employee needed only one glance at Sharpe's pin.

"Oh, you must be from Eastern," the steward noted.

It was Sharpe who was assigned the job of planning the silver anniversary observance. The Captain had given him permission to rent some old airplanes for an air show that would tour EAL's system, and Sharpe flew to Orange County, California, to see what the Paul Mantz-Frank Tallman air museum had to offer. He lined up a Spad, with its original Hisso engine, and a Mailwing, plus an ancient Curtiss pusher biplane fuselage with no wings. Mantz transplanted the wings off a Jenny and Sharpe headed back east in a newly purchased Dodge truck with all the planes crated up in a special van built by Metro-Goldwyn-Mayer.

The air show lasted thirty-seven weeks and included Air Force jets, the latter presenting something of a problem because the Pentagon informed Eastern that the AF planes could not be used in the show unless all runways had been cleared by a magnetic sweeper.

"This is necessary to prevent engine ingestion," the Air Force advised Sharpe. "Each AF pilot must certify that he saw said magnetic sweeper being used prior to participation of the military aircraft."

The show was supposed to open at Tampa and Sharpe had been unable to find anything remotely resembling the required magnetic sweeper. Furthermore, the AF pilots refused to fly unless one was used. Sharpe hastily departed for two business establishments in downtown Tampa—a hardware store and a liquor store. He showed up at the airport an hour later and walked up to the half-dozen Air Force jockeys idly passing the time. In front of them he placed three bottles of good Scotch. Then he unwrapped a small magnet attached to a broom with a piece of string. Still holding the broom, he walked over to the adjacent runway and ran the magnet up and down the paved surface three times before returning to the mystified pilots.

"Okay, you sonsabitches," Sharpe growled, "now every damned one of you can swear you saw this runway cleared with a magnetic sweeper."

They all signed the necessary document and Sharpe repeated the act at every airport where the show was held. A year and a half later he received a letter from the Pentagon, mentioning that experts had been doing some research into runway metal ingestion and wanting to know what type of magnetic sweeper Eastern had used. Sharpe scratched his head and finally dictated an answer.

"An Armstrong Model 103," he informed the Pentagon.

Another eighteen months went by and Sharpe had forgotten the incident until an EAL lobby receptionist called him. "Mr.

Sharpe, there's a general down here with about nine other officers and they'd like to see you."

They were ushered into Sharpe's office, given coffee, and Sharpe finally asked, "Gentlemen, what can I do for you?"

The general took a thick file out of his briefcase and laid it on Sharpe's desk. "Mr. Sharpe, about eighteen months ago we wrote asking you what kind of a magnetic sweeper Eastern had used at its air show and you replied an Armstrong Model 103. Our procurement department hasn't been able to find this sweeper anywhere and frankly, we'd like to obtain one for testing purposes."

"General," Sharpe asked, "are you a Catholic?"

"No, I'm not."

"Well, neither am I—but it's time for confession."

As of the twenty-fifth anniversary, Eastern was operating over nearly 13,000 route miles and on September 22 of the silver year, the airline carried its twenty-five millionth passenger—by prearrangement, he was Elmer Sperry, who two and a half decades before had bought the first EAL ticket on the Ford trimotor inaugural flight between New York and Richmond. But while the sentimentalist in Captain Eddie was looking back on the past with fond nostalgia, the pragmatist in him was peering ahead. He was the first to admit that Eastern's biggest asset in this pivotal time was its people—still loyal to him and still capable of amazing resilience and ingenuity when faced with adversity. They are qualities shared by virtually all airline personnel but at Eastern they seemed to be needed more frequently than at other carriers.

There was, for example, the day authorities shut down Newark Airport after the third of three fatal crashes that occurred over a span of less than sixty days between December 16, 1951, and February 11, 1952. The trio of accidents killed not only most of the passengers and crew members aboard the aircraft involved but also eleven residents of downtown Elizabeth, New Jersey, located directly on the approach path to the field's busiest runway.

No Eastern planes had been involved, but the airline was

hit hard by the decision to close Newark—sixty-five percent of
EAL's New York operations were handled at Newark Airport
and all of the New York maintenance. Eastern's facilities at La
Guardia, geared to take care of only thirty percent of the carrier's New York arrivals and departures, couldn't absorb the
additional load and EAL had neither a terminal nor hangar at
the brand-new Idlewild Airport (later to be renamed John F.
Kennedy).

Sheppy called the Captain as soon as the news of Newark's
closing broke—he was at his Texas ranch, eighty miles northwest
of San Antonio.

"What's being done?" he wanted to know.

"We're moving everything over to Idlewild," she told him.

"We don't have a damned thing there," Rickenbacker reminded her.

"We do now," Sheppy said calmly. "Tents."

And that was how Eastern operated at Idlewild for almost a
year—in tents. The improvised operation cost a fortune; EVR
himself estimated that Newark's closing cost the airline $1.5 mil-
lion a month in lost revenue. Aircraft fueling cost $25,000 a
month more than at Newark and employee overtime plus additional transportation costs amounted to another $50,000 in extra
expenses.

Flight operations wasn't the only department that could improvise its way out of a crisis. Shortly before midnight, March
24, 1954, a fire and explosion wrecked a five-story building immediately adjacent to Eastern's Atlanta reservations center. The
disaster struck the building at 50 Pryor Street; Eastern's reservations facilities were at 46 Pryor Street and traffic and sales were
next door at number 44. Some thirty EAL employees were evac-
uated immediately, taking with them all reservations records,
control charts, and everything else they could get their hands on.
Once safely out, however, no one could get back in—fire officials
refused entrance to all three buildings.

Employees assembled in a nearby Hertz office a half block
away and set up a command post. At 12:25 A.M. supervisors and
managers met to evaluate the situation and decided to establish

temporary reservations facilities at the airport, in a room behind the ticket counter. This would handle all flights up to 1:50 A.M., by which time a more workable and roomier setup could be installed in the airport's administration building; the latter would take over flights departing after 11:50 A.M. By 1:15 A.M., only an hour and twenty minutes after the explosion, the tiny room in back of the ticket counter was in operation while other employees labored to set up larger facilities in the administration building, using borrowed tables and chairs.

At 1:30 A.M. a message was transmitted to all EAL stations that Atlanta Terminal Control was accepting bookings and an hour later a temporary sales office was in full swing. But it was obvious the temporary quarters were too makeshift and it was equally obvious that fire officials wouldn't let anyone into 46 Pryor Street for at least a week. Even while employees were struggling to keep the operation at the airport going, communications manager Bill Keating had been in contact with Southern Bell. The telephone company offered to let Eastern set up a reservations center in the Hurt Building, owned by AT&T.

Keating made a quick trip to inspect the recommended room and gave Southern Bell a go-ahead. By 6:45 A.M. Southern Bell had twelve telephone lines into the Hurt Building along with three receiving and two transmitting teletypes. At 7:30 A.M. all Eastern stations were advised that Atlanta was back on "sell and report"—full-scale operations—and this was less than eight hours after the original evacuation.

Airport closings and major fires—these were the big moments of crisis. There were small ones, actually petty except to those involved. Airlines, like armies, are run by rules drawn up to cover the majority of circumstances, but there are times when the circumstances make rules seem ridiculous. Eastern had a night aircoach flight operating between Chicago and Miami nonstop, and twenty minutes before departure the captain was notified that instead of the usual load of about twenty passengers, the Connie would have seventy-five aboard.

"Better put on an extra jug of coffee," the captain suggested to a ground agent.

"I can't do that, skipper. This flight isn't authorized for more than one jug."

The captain bristled. "Okay, but until we get that second jug, this airplane can stay at the ramp until grass sprouts under the wheels."

"That's fine with me, captain. I'm just following the rules."

A jug of coffee, worth about two dollars, stood between seventy-five passengers and Florida—that and a manual of rules. Until the captain pulled out his wallet.

"Look, I'll pay for the damned jug myself," he offered.

A few minutes later the plane took off—with enough coffee.

Small but not petty was another incident. A four-year-old boy named Ronald Tisdale of Montreal had swallowed sleeping pills and went into a coma despite the use of a stomach pump and antipoison drugs. His doctor had heard of a powerful new drug and finally reached the Poison Control Center in New York, which had a half ounce available. A fast check of airline schedules disclosed that Eastern had a flight leaving for Montreal in less than five minutes. The Center called the airline—would they hold the flight?

Eastern agents quickly polled the passengers, asking if they'd be willing to delay departure for about an hour, explaining the reason. There were forty-eight aboard and forty-eight affirmative votes—a moot point inasmuch as any dissenters probably would have been thrown out of the plane by the other passengers. A Health Department car with a police escort raced to the airport where the EAL stewardess took personal charge of the precious serum. When the flight landed in Montreal, another police car sped it to the hospital in the time to save Ronald Tisdale's life. The New York *Herald-Tribune* commented in an editorial:

Only one life was at stake, but what great resources of communication, of helpfulness, of cooperation, were called into play to save it. Telephones, autos, airplanes—the willingness to interfere with vital schedules; the singleminded concentration of putting everyone else's plans and purposes secondary to this all-essential one of saving a boy's life.

More than airline employees had been involved, of course, but the story still underlines the esprit de corps existing in every air carrier faced with stress. Rickenbacker certainly had instilled it at Eastern, and despite his penchant for squeezing pennies until Lincoln looked clean-shaven, he was honestly trying to give his employees more effective competitive tools—including pride. True, he was being forced into it by the rising tide of route invasion, particularly New York–Florida, where small but aggressive National continued to give Eastern fits. In 1951 the shadow of a third carrier's proposed entrance into that prime market cast a shadow over 10 Rockefeller Plaza—Northeast Airlines asked the CAB for permission to operate between Boston and Miami via New York, putting the tiny New England regional carrier into head-to-head competition with EAL and National.

To paraphrase that old saying about politics, route cases make strange bedfellows; in this instance, Rickenbacker and George Baker climbed into the same bed with great alacrity, arguing lustily that the market couldn't support three carriers. The New York–Florida Case was to drag on for five years, with both Delta and Pan Am also seeking the same route authority— to Juan Trippe, a New York–Miami route would feed nicely into Pan Am's Latin and South America service and give his airline what it badly needed: domestic authority.

The in-fighting over that five-year period was brutal and bloody. At one point National tried to sneak in the back door by suggesting a merger with Northeast, and at another both Eastern and National proposed absorbing the smaller carrier. As is usual in route cases, some of the claims made by the contestants would have made Ananias envious. Pan Am said it would save the government $8 million in subsidy if it got the route—its arithmetic was suspect inasmuch as Northeast itself was getting only $1.5 million a year for operating its money-losing New England service. And Eastern's lawyers put former Governor Fuller Warren of Florida on the stand to plead for the hundreds of EAL employees who would lose their jobs if a third carrier was added. The day Warren testified, there were two rows of blue-shirted

Eastern employees present to add visual emphasis to the witness's imploring statement—Bill Van Dusen volunteered the information that they had come to Washington "on their own hook" and opposition attorneys quickly denounced their appearance as a staged sideshow.

There were two preliminary rulings issued before the CAB announced its final decision. The Board's counsel recommended that Northeast be given the route, and the CAB examiner in the case subsequently picked Delta. The Board's verdict in favor of Northeast wasn't issued until August of 1956, but the two previous recommendations convinced Rickenbacker that Eastern stood almost no chance of preventing the market invasion. Two years before the CAB announced its decision, EVR announced that Eastern would convert more than fifty percent of its trunk-line flights to coach, providing lower fare service to 1.5 million passengers a year—the entire industry had carried only 3.5 million coach customers the previous year. Cynics remarked that Eastern's regular service was the equivalent of coach but Rickenbacker had had a craw full of such disparaging remarks—in 1955 he ordered twenty new DC-7's at a cost of $40 million, while simultanously ordering the entire Super-Constellation fleet converted into all-coach configuration. The big Douglas transports would be called DC-7B's—a designation which stirred up a brief but heated industry controversy. American and National, which also had ordered the DC-7, claimed Eastern was simply trying to foist off its "B" models as a newer type, and that in actuality the two aircraft were identical.

Douglas wisely kept its corporate mouth closed, for the simple reason that American was right in a technical sense—there was absolutely no difference between the DC-7 and DC-7B in fuselage, engines, electronics, wings, or anything else. Eastern's rebuttal, and the CAB bought it, was that the planes had different interiors—and this was true. For the first time in his regime Captain Eddie had listened to his marketing experts who had pleaded with him to make the DC-7 the most luxurious airliner Eastern had ever operated.

It wasn't really easy to sell the Captain on those interiors, not at first. He wanted the DC-7 itself primarily because National's could make the New York–Miami run fifteen minutes faster than Eastern's Connies—they had the same engines but the Lockheeds were heavier. When it came time to choose the interior decor, his underlings agreed to let Charlie Froesch do most of the selling; they remembered only too well that when Lockheed asked Captain Eddie what he wanted on the Super-C's eighty-eight seats, his reply was a surly "Eighty-eight asses."

Froesch played it smart. He took the DC-7's cabin cross-section drawings to Harley Earl, head of General Motors' styling division and a man whose taste Rickenbacker not only admired but revered. GM constructed a mockup with a blue and gold decor and EVR, knowing that Earl was involved, kept calling Froesch to inquire how it was coming. Earl had suggested that Froesch not tell EVR anything until it was ready, adding, "I'll tell him myself, Charlie—I know what he'll go for."

When the mockup was completed, Earl called Rickenbacker. "Rick, you'll love it—it's what we're putting on our Cadillacs."

That was all EVR needed and when he finally saw the mockup he couldn't hide his pleasure. "Well, Harley," he smiled, "if that's the way it should be, I'll buy it."

The battle wasn't completely over, and it was the team of Frank Sharpe and Brad Walker which supplied the final victory. Sharpe had been arguing bravely with the old man about meal service deficiencies and while the DC-7 interior decorating decision was still in abeyance, Rickenbacker received a letter from a woman passenger complaining about Eastern's food. He showed it to Sharpe, who figured it was time to strike.

"Captain," he said, "she's absolutely right—I agree with her 100 percent. And while we're on the subject, we're buying those DC-7s with the same old thermos jugs and casseroles while everybody else is going for electronic ovens."

Rickenbacker just grunted, but without saying anything to Sharpe, he asked Brad Walker for his opinion. Walker backed up Sharpe. A few days later, while a staff meeting was in progress, Sheppy brought in EVR's mail and the officers sat quietly while

EVR skimmed through it. He came across another letter complaining about meal service and slammed his big fist on the desk after reading it aloud.

"Here we are getting those DC-7's with those goddamned jugs," he roared. "I want electric ovens!"

It was not too long after Eastern increased the DC-7 order to forty planes that Rickenbacker stunned another staff meeting by announcing that he had ordered forty Lockheed propjet Electras at a cost of $2.4 million per aircraft, with an option for thirty more. Including spare parts, it was a $100 million contract, a commitment that some executives privately questioned— Eastern was buying more Electras than any other carrier, with American's order for thirty-five the only one coming close.

The whole equipment program, in fact, had raised some doubts and even fears. There was more than one officer who wondered about the wisdom of buying so many propeller-driven aircraft with the jet age just around the corner—the DC-7, Super-G and Electra orders totaled some $225 million, almost double what Rickenbacker in 1955 had tentatively budgeted for jets.

"If he had put about eighty million dollars more into jets at that time," Lefty Lethridge speculates, "one has to wonder what would have been the history of Eastern today."

It is, perhaps, somewhat unfair to fault Captain Eddie for decisions made long before anyone knew that the jets would revolutionize air travel not merely in terms of speed, but in such areas as operating economy, low maintenance costs, and high utilization. As a matter of fact, despite his own inner doubts about jets, he presented a more optimistic outlook than did some of his peers. Canny, astute C. E. Woolman of Delta, just before Eastern's bitter rival ordered its first jets, commented rather sourly that "we're buying airplanes that haven't been fully designed, with millions of dollars we don't have, and we are going to operate them off airports that are too small, in an air-traffic control system that is too slow, and we must fill them with more passengers than we have ever carried before."

C. R. Smith of American was equally pessimistic. He foresaw a traffic growth rate of less than ten percent for the first five years of the jet age, and pointed out that with this kind of growth, coupled with a greatly expanded capacity, the industry would need load factors of almost sixty-three percent. Rickenbacker, on the other hand, refused to wave any crying towel.

"In my opinion," he told *Business Week*, the trend is now firmly fixed if we can provide the aircraft and the volume service needed to capitalize and profit from the tremendous potential demand for air transportation." He went on to explain that in 1954 only eight million individuals accounted for the thirty-five million tickets sold—the bulk of them took from two to twenty trips that year, enough to reach the thirty-five-million-total-passengers-flown figure. This, EVR said, added up to a huge number of potential customers in the nation's 165-million population.

Young Americans, he pointed out, were "born in the lap of aviation—the airplane is their most natural and preferred means of travel." He said the U.S. population would reach 200 million by 1965, thus providing thirty-five million more potential customers. And with the technical improvements resulting from the shift to jets, he concluded, "air transportation should make more progress in the next ten years than we have been able to accomplish in the past twenty-five."

Yet it was part of his contradictory makeup that he could be so publicly sanguine about the future of jets and so blindly cautious in taking action to make that future a reality. There is little doubt that he over-ordered on both the DC-7 and Electra, not in the sense of piling up an unnecessary debt but because the huge commitment seemed to increase his reluctance to plunge with equal intensity into jet purchases. For all his rosy predictions about the jet age, he honestly believed the Electra would serve Eastern's needs in what he glimpsed as a fairly long interim transition period, during which time the public would gradually get used to jet travel.

The fact is that thanks to Rickenbacker's conservatism, Eastern was better equipped than most carriers to enter the enormously expensive jet purchase program. EVR took a critical view of the industry's heavy debt burden and was correspondingly proud of Eastern's almost total freedom from such debt in those crucial prejet years of the 1950s. This wasn't achieved by the power of prayer, either—it stemmed from the Captain's insistence on conservative accounting methods that wrote off the full value of new aircraft in only four years. Most carriers depreciated equipment over seven years and a few did it in five; Eastern's was the shortest in the industry, and what this practice did was to build up large cash reserves.

Depreciation charges reduce reported earnings but do not involve cash expenditures. Under Rickenbacker's policy the rapid depreciation made cash quickly available in excess of earnings—it literally amounted to enforced savings.

"This short depreciation is necessary," Rickenbacker told Richard Cook of *The Wall Street Journal* in a 1952 interview, "because of the rapid obsolescence of plane design. We don't want to be caught with outmoded planes on our books."

Unfortunately, that's exactly how Eastern *was* caught—not on the books, but in the air, as we shall see shortly. Rickenbacker's heavy reliance on the Electra as the ideal interim transport was a major mistake because the interim proved to be almost nonexistent. It was a superb airplane, beloved by almost every pilot who flew it, and it was to serve Eastern faithfully for almost two decades, but never in the role he intended for the big propjet.

EVR loved the Electra much as its pilots did. Like the DC-7, it was called the "Golden Falcon," and he personally approved—over the futile objections of such advisors as Walker, Lethridge, and Sharpe—an exterior paint job which turned the beautiful ship into a flying billboard. The words "Fly Eastern's Prop-Jet Electra" stretched almost the entire length of the fuselage, above the cabin window line—it would have been very much at home on the side of a circus wagon but on the Electra the design jarred sensibilities. Rickenbacker wanted it, however, and that was that.

When the Electra encountered its structural problems shortly after entering service in 1959, Eastern's fleet underwent the same modifications as the rest of the nearly 180 planes called back to the Burbank factory. In Rickenbacker's autobiography he implied that thanks to his foresight, the EAL Electras didn't have to be strengthened—another of his inexplicable after-the-fact claims to omniscience. He wrote that at American's insistence, the Electra's airframe had been lightened to meet promised performance specifications.

"I was satisfied with it," he recounted, "because I knew that, with more powerful engines, the deficiencies would be eliminated. American, however, threatened to cancel its order.

"The Lockheed people became frightened and lightened the plane by 1,600 pounds in order to meet the specifications. Then it was my turn to become frightened. In my experience, a new plane always requires some strengthening, which means adding weight rather than taking it away. When our planes were delivered, we tested them thoroughly and added reinforcements in certain areas amounting to 600 pounds."

In effect, EVR was blaming American as much as Lockheed for the Electra's misfortunes and this can only be construed as a cheap shot at C. R. Smith. The story of Lockheed's weakening the structure to keep American from canceling its order is simply not true, nor is there any evidence that Eastern added 600 pounds of reinforcements before putting its Electras into service. Charlie Froesch says Eastern's principal contributions were "primarily with respect to the power plants."

"There was not much we could do with the engine except to request a lower idling speed to minimize ramp and taxi noise," he adds.

Other EAL predelivery specifications included increasing the fuel capacity, bigger brakes and wheels, an improved, longer-life propeller instead of Lockheed's original choice, hot-air de-icing of the tail as well as the wings, improved integral fuel tanks, replacement of magnesium sheeting with stainless steel, mechanical disconnects for alternators, stronger baggage-compartment construction, improved corrosion protection, and seats designed to Eastern's own specifications. All this may well have added up to 600 additional pounds, but not one ounce involved the areas which proved to be the Electra's Achilles Heel—the engine nacelles, engine mounts, and the wing structure itself.

In the wake of two Electra crashes—Braniff and Northwest —the Federal Aviation Agency ordered all airlines operating the L-188 to reduce maximum cruising speeds by 100 miles an hour pending solution of the two wing failures. Rickenbacker's autobiography claims Eastern put the reduced speed into effect before the government issued the order and that "the Civil Aeronautics Authority [sic] ordered all airlines to do the same." This, again, does not jibe with the facts and can only be attributed to EVR's combination of pride and ego—he was not the type to admit a mistake. He was not a liar by any stretch of the imagination, but like so many strong men he was prone to rationalize his way into taking unjustified credit. He was firmly convinced, for example, that Boeing widened the 707 fuselage at his suggestion after a demonstration ride in the prototype. All 707 cabins had the identical width of the prototype.

This is not to sully the reputation and memory of a magnificent airline pioneer and a fine American; such incidents are related merely to emphasize what power can do to any man—and Captain Eddie was not the only one—if he holds it for too long. He becomes addicted, as if power were a drug, and among the symptoms is the delusion of omnipotence. Beliefs and prejudices congeal into rigidity. Reasoning becomes inflexible. Decisions are inevitably arbitrary. And the most tragic aspect of this condition is that a strong leader seldom realizes what has happened to him—he deludes himself into believing that the glory of the past is all he needs to meet the present and the future.

Unhappily for Eddie Rickenbacker, someone *did* see what had happened—and he was not among those officers who were either afraid of him, overly fond of him, or helpless to challenge his power.

That was Laurance Rockefeller.

Even while Rickenbacker and Eastern were riding high in the prosperous, explosive growth of the fifties, Rockefeller was beginning to feel concern as to the airline's future and Rickenbacker's ability to face the challenges of that future. Quietly he began monitoring Eastern more closely and in virtually every area from handling of route cases to equipment purchases.

Outwardly there was little to criticize—except that a man

of Rockfeller's business acumen could read between the lines. EVR followed up the mammoth Electra order by signing a $165 million contract with Douglas for DC-8's—sixteen firm orders and an option on eight more. Boeing had made a strong pitch to add Eastern to its list of 707 customers but Rickenbacker's strong friendship with Donald Douglas was the key factor in his decision to buy the DC-8. The agreement was reached after the Captain called Douglas in Santa Monica and asked him to come to New York.

"I don't want to talk to sales teams anymore," he declared. "I want to talk to you."

At the meeting Rickenbacker shot questions at Douglas as if his mouth were a machine gun. The final one was a killer. "Don, I want a noise level no higher or even less than the DC-7—can you guarantee that?"

Douglas was honest. "We can't guarantee it," he said. "All we can do is try."

Rickenbacker laughed. "You've just sold us some airplanes," he declared. "And what we're buying isn't the DC-8—it's integrity."

As the meeting broke up and various Douglas technicians filed out of Rickenbacker's office, the Captain stopped Douglas.

"Just the same, Don," he said, "I hope you'll work hard on keeping that noise down."

"I'll use my integrity," Douglas smiled.

There were other factors involved in the decision to buy the DC-8 beyond EVR's friendship with Donald Douglas and Eastern's long and satisfactory experience with Douglas transports. Eastern's two chief rivals, Delta and National, were also ordering the DC-8 and Rickenbacker had signed before they did. The 707 deliveries were scheduled to start much earlier but EVR wasn't worried so long as Delta and National weren't getting any. For the time being, Eastern's Electras were more than a match for the opposition's DC-7's; Delta had bypassed any prop-jets and National's Electras were far behind Eastern's in delivery dates.

It all looked so great—on paper. Offsetting the blow of the

New York–Florida decision was a happier resolution of the longstanding route-to-Mexico case which dated back eleven years. Service between New York and Washington to the Mexican capital began in the summer of 1957, although Eastern generally was stymied in route development. Interchange agreements were its chief means of entry into new markets—EAL had one with Northwest that provided one-plane service between the Twin Cities and Miami via Chicago, and another with Braniff with an interchange point at Miami for one-plane service to Latin America.

The airline's overall route-development record was one of the items that concerned Rockefeller, and in direct proportion to the increasing competitive pressure from both Delta and National. He felt the opposition's fast-growing route structure had been carved out of Eastern's own system, and to this day he frankly blames Rickenbacker.

"It was all due to his arrogance and his failure to maximize his public relations and service—in fact, he capitalized on it rather than maximized it," Rockefeller says with some regret. "Eastern went through an excessively long period in which lack of support in Washington and a lack of friends resulted in failure whenever we tried to do something positive to improve our route system."

Rockefeller, however, attaches some responsibility to Smythe Gambrell, the courtly Atlanta lawyer who handled so many route cases for Eastern. Says Rockefeller:

"He never grasped what Rickenbacker's attitude had done to Eastern's chances. He thought he could win every case on pure merit, with no politics involved, and his own attitude was one of disdain and a tinge of arrogance toward the CAB. I had and still have great respect for Smythe. With the exception of the Captain himself, no one ever worked harder for the airline. He used to get most of his sleep in planes when he was working on a route case. He was very much like Eddie in many respects—that early American heritage of hard work, frugality, and patriotism. But as far as political Washington was concerned, he was a bull in a china shop."

Lefty Lethridge agrees. "There were times when he'd talk down to the CAB, enough to irritate the members. Only Eddie could get away with it and then not always. I don't say Gambrell was responsible for losing some route cases but it sure as hell helped to make friends. People make a mistake by working for a strong leader and trying to wear his cloak. There was only one Rickenbacker, but I guess when you're with a person like that you begin to make noises like him."

The Florida and Mexico proceedings may well have been what Rockefeller and Lethridge are talking about. In the former, Eastern actually made a strong case against a third carrier. Both Examiner Thomas Wrenn, who recommended Delta, and the CAB itself based their findings largely on the contention that east–west transcontinental traffic developed fewer passengers than New York–Miami and still supported competition among as many as four carriers. The fallacy was that the examiner and full board considered only New York–Los Angeles traffic against New York–Miami. It would have seemed fairer and more logical to consider the number of intermediate cities over the two routes. East–west traffic was strongly supported by such points as Pittsburgh, Chicago, St. Louis, Denver, and Salt Lake City—generating three times more business than the New York–Florida market.

In the Mexico case Eastern simply got a shafting. Mexico was perfectly willing to let EAL serve Mexico City as soon as its own carrier received reciprocal rights. The delays in reaching a bilateral agreement were inexcusable and inexplicable and so were other factors which kept Eastern from implementing a legally granted certificate. One was President Truman's decision to withdraw his 1946 approval of authority granted to Eastern, Braniff, and Western for Mexican service. Truman justified this action on the grounds that the routes hadn't been flown—a curious bit of reasoning inasmuch as procrastination by his own State Department was the only reason they hadn't been flown. The proceeding dragged on for five more years until President Eisenhower, in 1957, reconfirmed Eastern's 1946 certificate after a provisional bilateral agreement was reached with Mexico.

It is impossible to estimate the long-range damage that eleven-year delay inflicted on Eastern, and it is equally impossible to tell whether resolution of the case would have taken so long if Captain Eddie's political views and unconcealed contempt hadn't been anathema to so many politicians and bureaucrats. The temptation is strong to conclude that it didn't help.

It was this intangible liability that bothered Laurance Rockefeller so much, the realization that in making the name Rickenbacker synonymous with Eastern, the airline was as much of a target for criticism as its leader. Gradually the words "Rickenbacker's airline" had come to mean not efficiency and confidence, but poor service and indifference. It was about this time that WHEAL was formed—the initials standing for We Hate Eastern Air Lines. The originators were a pair of Pittsburgh businessmen and exactly how many members they garnered in response to a few newspaper advertisements is uncertain— "several thousand," according to one official at Eastern, who said no one could tell for sure because all the files pertaining to this unique club were thrown away years ago.

WHEAL's very organization, however, went beyond the mere gag stage—it was an honest manifestation of customer resentment against Eastern's attitude toward passengers, and this wasn't lost on Rockefeller, either. What concerned him deeply was precisely what made EVR so strong a leader—the almost fanatical devotion he commanded from thousands of employees, and his equal devotion, however misguided it was becoming, to the airline.

"You were either on his team or against him," Rockefeller muses. "He was the epitome of a monolithic leader. He wanted your support and if you didn't give it to him, he'd get it from someone else. It was very difficult not only to organize a group to oppose him but to do it without breaking him. Let's be realistic about it—as long as Eddie was succeeding, no one could really disagree with him. It was only when he wasn't succeeding that you could challenge his decisions, and that took a long time. Even though the seeds of failure had been planted, they didn't sprout until sometime later. He definitely overbought on Connies and DC-7's, and ordered Electras because down deep he lacked faith in pure jets. In my opinion that huge Electra order really started Eastern downhill."

If that is true, and the evidence supports Rockefeller's beliefs, Rickenbacker compounded this mistake by what was quite possibly the worst decision he ever made. Sometime after the DC-8 contract was signed, he called a meeting of top officers in New York and informed them he had just talked with Donald Douglas. Neither Frank Sharpe nor Lefty Lethridge, both present, will ever forget what followed.

"Don tells me the DC-8 is getting heavier than expected," EVR began. "It'll have to operate wet"—meaning the engines would require water-injection boost on takeoffs—"and basically that means we're getting an underpowered airplane, which Eastern has never bought. Now there is an alternative. We could wait for Pratt and Whitney's new JT-4, which has the power to eliminate any need for wet takeoffs."

"How long a wait?" someone asked.

"At least ten months," Rickenbacker admitted. (It was to take even longer.)

Several officers pointed out that it would be fatal to let National and Delta start jet service ahead of Eastern. The captain conceded this but reminded them that neither rival airline had placed a jet order yet.

"I know it's a crucial decision," he added. "Despite all the talk I've heard about this being a one-man airline, I want whatever we decide to be by majority rule. I'm willing to take a paper ballot."

The subsequent discussion and debate was long and loud, with most of the opposition hammering away on what obviously was the key issue: Would a ten-month delay permit National and Delta to get the jump on jet service? What Rickenbacker was proposing was relinquishing delivery positions for the first six DC-8's Eastern had ordered—those six already had been committed to the smaller engines. He had Charlie Froesch's support—the vice president of engineering was adamantly opposed to buying any underpowered airplane, and to Froesch this was an inviolate rule.

True to his word, Rickenbacker passed out slips of paper for the voting. He counted the ballots himself and announced that the vote was overwhelmingly in favor of giving up the first six jets and waiting for the JT-4.

Later that day several officers got to talking among themselves, expressing surprise that the balloting had been so overwhelmingly in favor of accepting a delay of almost a year—the discussion itself had indicated considerable opposition.

"I give you my word," says Frank Sharpe, "that not one of us who discussed the outcome had voted to wait—and we represented a majority of the executives present."

Hindsight being more accurate than foresight, it is too easy to blame EVR for what turned into a fatal decision.

"It was a major mistake," says John Halliburton, "but I would have done exactly what the Captain did, under the circumstances. He had no way of knowing how Delta and National would capitalize on our delay."

And capitalize they did. Delta's C. E. Woolman found out that Eastern had relinquished its first six DC-8's and promptly grabbed them—water injection and all. About a year before EAL could start its own jet service, Delta began operating its new jets between New York and Houston. Eastern, using Electras on this route, had been averaging a ninety percent load factor—highest on the system. Once Delta started jet schedules, EAL's Electra passengers consisted largely of Delta's overflow business; in only two months Eastern temporarily abandoned the New York–Houston nonstop.

There were the same disastrous results in every market involving Eastern-Delta competition—Chicago–Miami, Atlanta–New York, Atlanta–Chicago, and Detroit–Miami. Yet this wasn't the only karate chop that jolted the suddenly outmoded EAL fleet; George Baker beat both Delta and Eastern into the jet age by signing a jet-leasing agreement with a man he hated almost as much as he did Rickenbacker—Pan Am's Juan Trippe.

Baker had been late in ordering Electras and Eastern's propjets were clobbering the DC-7's of the "Airline of the Stars" in the New York–Miami market. National's president also hadn't made up his mind whether to order the 707 or the DC-8, and equipmentwise he seemed to be in worse shape than Eastern. It was extremely hazardous, however, to underestimate the wily old pirate who ran National. He flew to New York for a meeting with Trippe, offering him an ostensibly attractive and mutually beneficial deal: Pan Am would lease two of its newly delivered 707's to National during the forthcoming winter seasons of 1958 and 1959, and in return Baker would exchange 400,000 shares of National stock for an equal amount of Pan Am stock. In addition, Pan Am would be given an option on another 200,000 National shares—enough to give Trippe control of Baker's airline.

It was strictly a con job but the usually astute Trippe went for the bait. Baker knew that the CAB, which had to approve such deals, moved with elephantine speed. He further suspected, and with admirable logic, that when the CAB did get around to examining the agreement it would toss it into the Potomac. The CAB did exactly that, but by the time it got around to frowning on the leasing-stock exchange deal as illegal acquisition of control, National already had made a mint with the two Boeings in the 1958–59 winter months—leaving both Trippe and Rickenbacker with egg on their faces.

Rickenbacker then made another decision which was to cost the airline dearly, although again, at the time, it was not an illogical one. He canceled his option for the eight additional DC-8's. Considering Eastern's primarily short-haul route structure in those prejet years, the move was understandable—New York–Mexico was the only route EAL was operating that involved a stage length of 2,000 miles and this, plus New York–Miami, constituted the only two routes that really called for four-engine jets. Fear of overcapacity was the principal reason cited for the concellation, yet there is no way of knowing whether EVR's inherent fear of the jets becoming flying white elephants also was a major factor.

United's W. A. Patterson visited him after Eastern cut its DC-8 order and expressed surprise. "Hell, Eddie, you're buying sixteen of these DC-8's when you ought to be buying fifty."

"Listen, Pat," the Captain said soberly, "I've got to get the money, I've got to get the seats filled, and I've got to merchandise them. Sixteen may be too many."

He was a man in the closing years of the decade, and the equipment race was like a deadly treadmill. A year after he ordered jets, he decided he had to replace the obsolete fleet acquired in the Colonial merger, and he bought 12 Convair 440's (a twin-engine piston plane that was an improved version of the 240) for delivery in 1957 at a cost of $10.5 million. Once more it was a move that made sense—the Convairs would go into markets currently served by the Martins, and the latter would be shifted to Colonial's former routes. But it also was an outlay which simply compounded his previous overcommitment to propeller-driven aircraft—the Super-G Connies, DC-7s, and Electras. The Convair purchase would have made a lot more sense if the earlier expenditures had been smaller.

He was trying hard to streamline his executive staff in preparation for the jet age. Paul Brattain, still a presidential bridesmaid, retired. So did Shannon, being replaced as senior vice president of flight operations by John Halliburton. He promoted Jack Frost to the post of vice president and executive assistant to the chairman of the board—giving rise to unfounded rumors that Frost was the new "crown prince"—and named Bill Morrisette the new vice president of traffic and sales. Frost's position as his executive assistant didn't last very long and Lefty Lethridge got that job along with the title of assistant vice president. Bev Griffith, now in his seventies, went into semiretirement, working more as a consultant, and not doing much of that, with Bill Van Dusen running the public-relations show.

Captain Eddie also was trying, in his own way, to improve Eastern's image. He gave Brad Walker a virtual blank check in choosing the DC-8's interior decor, and Walker, working with Harley Earl (who had retired from GM), came up with one of the handsomest layouts in the industry. The main cabin was done in blue carpeting, gold and blue groupings of seats with a silver metallic thread woven into the fabric, and liberal use of plaques, murals, and flags on the walls. The first-class lounge was nothing less than spectacular, utilizing a new shade called Stratosphere Blue for the thick carpeting and the rest of the lounge was done in tasteful golds and sky blues. Shields on the lounge walls were reproductions of the coats of arms of the five countries Eastern served; the disc pattern of the gold ceiling suggested knights' armor and the wall murals were copies of seventeenth-century English playing cards. The overall motif was that of an old English card room.

EVR rescinded his ban against hiring new stewardesses and Lethridge was handed the job of improving their training. Among WHEAL's complaints was the claim that too many EAL girls had the personalities of IRS auditors. Lefty looked into the general situation and found that one problem was the testing procedure. He took a copy of the test given all applicants in to Tom Armstrong, who shook his head and laughed.

"Let's show it to the old man," he suggested.

They put the test in front of Rickenbacker. He took a long look and blew up.

"Good God!" he roared. "I couldn't pass this goddamned test myself!"

"The trouble was," Lefty recalls, "that Personnel had been looking for Rhodes scholars. What we needed was some fairly good looks, personality, and attitude. I did some checking and found that airlines like American, United, and TWA were getting better results by running their own schools—while we were getting our applicants from outside stewardess schools that charged a girl four or five hundred bucks for training she had to go through all over again with Eastern. So I told Eddie we had to start our own school. I went to Miami Springs Villa, rented some bungalows and took Art Bruns out of Accounting to build some training facilities at the Miami base."

Al Goodwin and John Gregg, two of Eastern's senior flight attendants, remember what it was like before Lethridge arranged for the improved facilities. When he was hired, the new class stayed in a hotel on Thirty-sixth Street called the Lawton.

"It wasn't only pre-Villa, it was prehistoric," Gregg says. It had a community john and calling it a dump was giving it more dignity than it deserved.

The first thing the all-male class was told by the then-instructor consisted of a firm warning: "There's two things I don't want to see you guys doing—don't go out of here and tell people you're in training to be pilots, and stay the hell away from the Jungle Club."

Gregg and Goodwin checked in at the Lawton. Next door to Gregg was a Jungle Club waitress. In the room adjoining Goodwin's was a snake charmer and dancer who performed at the Jungle Club.

Lou Devane, a much-beloved character and a former steward himself, was in charge of hiring stewardesses when Rickenbacker caved in and sent Lethridge down to Miami to institute a few reforms. Invariably Devane was hiring girls with big hips because that's the way his wife was built—"I like 'em round," he explained futilely to Lethridge when Lefty told him the appearance standards had to be upgraded.

"The lure of Miami and good surroundings got better applicants," Lefty says, "but as usual we were a little late."

"A little late. . . ."

Those three words carry the essence of what was going wrong in those crucial years preceding the jet revolution. They applied to almost every aspect of Eastern's operations, from stewardess selection and training to jet purchases, and compounding this was the weakness of the route structure itself and the failure to recognize in time that it could not be strengthened measurably given Captain Eddie's lack of influence in political Washington.

The one man with the muscle to do something about the situation did.

Laurance Rockefeller began seeking a more objective appraisal of the company than he was getting either from EVR, his fellow directors, or Eastern executives. He talked Rickenbacker into letting Dick Jackson, a highly regarded official at American, act as a consultant on equipment purchases. Unknown to the Captain, Jackson was under orders to give Rockefeller an honest opinion of what he thought of Rickenbacker's methods.

Subsequently Jackson informed Rockefeller that Eastern had put too many eggs in the DC-8 basket and should have ordered some Boeings to get earlier deliveries. He also was critical of the way EVR was running the company, and he expressed his blunt views to more than just Rockefeller. Captain Eddie's staff meetings jolted him and he once remarked to Lethridge, "You know, Lefty, there hasn't been anything new in this company for four or five years and as you look into the next decade, there will have to be changes made."

Another outsider exposed to the staff meeting ordeal also was sent by Rockefeller to observe—Najeeb Halaby, later to become FAA chief and subsequently head of Pan American. Halaby reported back that "outside of a boy scout rally, I've never seen anything so paternalistic and unreal." Halaby, in his own autobiography (*Crosswinds*, Doubleday, 1978), was even harsher. He said he spent several weeks touring Eastern's facilities in New York, Miami, and elsewhere, and then attended "one of his infamous semiannual management conferences held in the convention hall of a Miami Beach hotel.

"I use the word 'infamous' deliberately," Halaby wrote, "for it was more a cruel fraternity initiation than a business meeting. Rickenbacker and three of his top executives sat like judges and jury on the stage while station managers, supervisors, and vice-presidents marched forward. . . . Some of these very capable young men became so anxious and worried about the allotted five-minute presentation that they got stage fright, nausea, and sometimes a total oral freeze; so choked up they couldn't speak a word.

"There was an aura of phony superpatriotism in the big room. The meeting opened with the playing of the national anthem and the Pledge of Allegiance, and then Captain Eddie dominated the proceeding. He stayed through every session, eight hours a day for four days, asked some very embarrassing questions, and took a number of people to task right in front of their peers. There were some 500 top supervisors in the room, and if it was tedious and exhausting for me, it must have been triple worse for them. I had never seen a more dictatorial example of centralized management nor such public humiliation of employees, to say nothing of the waste of time."

Halaby believes Rockefeller assigned him to the inspection and observation tour with an ulterior motive in mind—namely, to see if Rickenbacker might take to him as a possible successor, and if Halaby would take to Eastern. The answer was a definite no on both counts but Halaby did advise Rockefeller that Eastern needed a strong number two man, one with real authority, to run the airline as president while Rickenbacker stayed as board chairman but with reduced power.

This was the same conclusion Rockefeller already had reached. He was not pleased at EVR's reaction to Dick Jackson when the latter had his first interview with the Captain.

"Who's that stupid young man you sent over to see me?" Rickenbacker inquired. It was a remark Rockefeller was not to forget. When the 1958 flight engineers' strike shut down the airline for more than a month, even some of Captain Eddie's cronies on the board of directors were beginning to have doubts about his leadership.

On October 1, 1959, Malcolm A. MacIntyre, a former American Airlines lawyer and undersecretary of the Air Force, became president of Eastern Air Lines and chief executive officer. Tom Armstrong was named executive vice president for finance. And Captain Eddie remained as chairman of the board but without his title of general manager.

The changing of the guard had begun.

CHAPTER TEN

WILL THE REAL EDDIE RICKENBACKER PLEASE STAND UP ?

When Edward Vernon Rickenbacker ended his one-man rule of Eastern Air Lines, he had compiled the most glittering record of any airline chief in aviation history: twenty-six consecutive years of profit, the last twenty-one without a penny of government subsidy.

He turned over to Malcolm MacIntyre a transportation giant serving 128 cities in 27 states over an area encompassing three fourths of America's population and more than eighty percent of its industry. The 228 great metal Falcons of EAL were flying 1,400 separate trips a day that added up to a half million miles every twenty-four hours—on a route system linking every major city from New England and the Great Lakes to Florida and the Gulf Coast, from the Atlantic Seaboard and Puerto Rico to St. Louis and mid-Texas.

He placed in the hands of this reputable lawyer (but airline neophyte) the destinies of 18,000 men and women, most of whom had never known any other leader except the irascible, sentimental, strong-willed, benevolent tyrant they called—half affectionately and half fearfully—"the Captain." For a quarter of a century he had branded his own image not just on the airline, but on its people—to the point that out of terror or love, or more likely a combination of the two, some had been turned into ineffective imitators or equally ineffective sycophants.

Like the fabled elephant being examined by blind men, Captain Eddie was many things to many people. The older employees, the ones who had been with him through so much adversity and struggle, looked at him with sheer hero worship. The Young Turks—the Lethridges, Halliburtons, Simonses, and Sharpes—admired him without blinding themselves to his faults. And there were some executives so scared of him that they weakened their own judgment and ability.

Jack Frost was one of them. Normally a tough, competent man himself, he assumed all the strength of Jell-O if he thought EVR was going to disagree with him. Frank Sharpe tells of a time when Frost was delivering a plea for fare cuts before a staff meeting. He listed all the compelling reasons for the reduction and the benefits to be gained, then turned expectantly to Rickenbacker, who glared at him from under those bushy awnings.

"I think it's a lousy idea," the Captain said testily.

"That's just what I was saying or about to say," Frost amended hurriedly. "In the end, it wouldn't be a very good idea."

Yet if EVR inspired fear in some, he inspired devotion in others. Any man or woman who worked for him can testify to his countless acts of kindness, most of them performed under pledges of secrecy and dire threats if the recipient let the word get out. To Sheppy he was not only a stern, demanding boss but a considerate friend who treated her like a daughter or younger sister.

Demanding, of course, was the universal adjective everyone applied to the Captain. His refusal to recognize weekends as time for relaxation away from the office was the prime manifestation— if he worked on Saturdays, he expected every executive to work on Saturday's. This edict used to gall someone like Lethridge, who finally conceived the Perfect Crime.

Lefty knew Captain Eddie had the habit of poking his head into various offices, like a football coach making bed check, just to see who was working and who wasn't. So each Friday night before going home, Lethridge would clutter his desk with papers to simulate a work-crowded atmosphere. The final touch was to leave a pair of old reading glasses on top of a pile of papers—the scene he had set was that of a busy man who had just left his office for a few minutes to go to the men's room.

For months he worked this con on the Captain until Rickenbacker got suspicious. He called Lefty in one day.

"What I want to know, Lethridge," he growled, "is why the hell you're always in the john every Saturday morning?"

The contrite Lefty thought momentarily of such explanations as a terminally weak bladder, but decided to confess his dodge. Rickenbacker forgave him but from then on, Lethridge came in on Saturdays.

Lefty became one of EVR's favorites, although it was hard to tell sometimes because the Captain rode his favorites harder than anyone else. In that category went Ambrose Chabot, vice president of maintenance—Rickenbacker loved him, and berated him proportionately. Charlie Simons remembers the days when Captain Eddie would hold court in Sid Shannon's office, deliberating various proposals brought forth by officers.

"Ambrose was a tough ex-Marine," Simons recounts, "and the old man was really fond of him, although you'd never guess it—every time Chabot would try to spend money, the Captain would tear him apart. I was assistant treasurer then and I attended those meetings for six months without opening my mouth.

"Rickenbacker would say, 'Wadda you think of this idea?' but nobody dared say what he really thought unless you knew what *he* thought—and then you'd agree with him. My God, if it was midnight and he'd say the sun was shining, he'd get total unanimity. On this one day I recall so vividly, Chabot wanted to spend a couple of hundred thousand dollars to put in a system of work assignments—how long it would take to do certain maintenance jobs like change a carburetor or put in new plugs. For some reason he didn't berate Chabot with his usual gut reaction —instead he went around the room asking everyone's opinion with that 'wadda you think' and he finally got to me.

"I said, 'If I were you, I'd try it.'

" 'You really think so?' he asked.

" 'Yes, sir.'

"He took out his pen and scrawled on Chabot's memo, 'Approved—EVR.' You just couldn't predict what he'd do."

Simons once wanted to hire additional auditors; he had only three including himself, and they had to visit every station four times a year—"I had a growing family and was away from home more often than a merchant seaman," Charlie explains.

"You don't need more auditors," Rickenbacker decreed after Simons made his pitch. "Tell you what—just go to the stations where you know they're going to steal."

"How would I know that?" Simons asked.

"That's what a *good* auditor would know," EVR assured him.

The semiannual staff meetings referred to in earlier chapters were a perfect reflection of Rickenbacker's management philosophy, which he once told a friend boiled down to "If you grab 'em by the balls, their minds and hearts will follow." Actually, there was much logic to his method—he really was able to spot promising talent from the performances he watched so carefully, with his deliberate goading and feigned (sometimes it *was* feigned) anger.

Bob Winn, who had come over to EAL from American with Sharpe, King, and Battaile, got into an elevator with Rickenbacker after one particularly acrimonious meeting and couldn't resist the temptation of proximity.

"Captain," he said earnestly, "what are we doing wrong? We seem to be bickering and fighting all the time."

EVR looked at him for a moment that seemed like an hour —and he could stare a hole through boiler plate. He poked Winn in the chest with a long, bony forefinger. "Young man, the day I stop fighting with you or anyone else in this company, it's because I've decided you're no damned good and you might as well get the hell out!"

In truth, Rickenbacker seemed to thrive on an atmosphere of feuding. He loved to get a fight going between two departments, and the staff/field meetings were ideal battlegrounds.

Frank Sharpe, as Winn had, asked him one day how he could justify the internal scrapping that erupted at virtually every session.

"Other companies have expensive training programs for young executives," Captain Eddie said with rare equanimity. "I think our way is better. Look, Frank, we put names and even nicknames on those reports I require in advance of our meetings. Where else can officers of a company know every man on the payroll not just by names but by nicknames and in many cases their wives and children? I force people to sit there and listen to the other guy's problems. I make pilots listen to reservations problems. I make marketing personnel understand maintenance problems. This becomes a whole educational process. And another thing, to stand up and talk to 500 peers is something else. I always can find out how a man thinks under pressure. If you're paying attention, you'll find when I get a new man up there, I always have a few questions for him just to see how he thinks on his feet."

At the start of every staff meeting, assistant station managers and supervisors were assured of receiving telegrams from the Captain. The message in every case was identical: "Your boss is now in Miami and you have a chance to prove your ability to take his job." As a pep talk it worked fine, but it also generated a lot of feuds between ambitious young assistants and their suddenly insecure superiors.

Rickenbacker loved stirring up this kind of internal competition. He once opened a meeting by declaring that "the privates are now running this airline.

"They must be running it," he went on, "because I'm not. All the vice presidents are here, so they can't be running it. And you're here—you can't be running it."

A *Newsweek* correspondent was once allowed to sit in on the four-day marathon.

"When each man gets through," he reported, "he looks as if he had emerged from a Georgia convict sweat box, but he is then free to enjoy the torture of his colleagues."

The *Newsweek* account offered excellent testimony to Rickenbacker's ability to undress a man in public. When one minor official proudly reported there were thirty-eight fewer delayed flights in January than in December, EVR demolished him. "There were fewer flights of any kind in January, young man. By your reasoning, you could eliminate all delays by stopping all flying."

Someone reported that pilferage had become a serious problem—college boys and other souvenir hunters were stealing the "seat occupied" cards off planes.

"I don't give a damn," the Captain declared. "If any college boy wants to put an Eastern Air Lines sign in his room, that's goodwill. That's public relations. By the way"—his voice suddenly dripped with sarcasm—"aren't you in public relations?"

If there had been a hole in the floor, the pilferage complainer would have jumped in. "Yes," he almost whispered.

"You should start using your head," Captain Eddie snapped, tapping his own forehead. "That's what it's for."

A maintenance supervisor brought up an incident in which a cargo truck had been pulled up alongside an aircraft. The cargo crew tied the plane's door to the truck so it would stay open, then forgot to untie and drove off taking the door with them. Everyone laughed—except EVR.

"That's no laughing matter, dammit!" he shouted. "I've got four pages here of things just like that—and those four pages will cost this company easily a quarter of a million dollars. What's more, ninety percent of it is just utter stupidity and carelessness."

In the next breath, he beamed when someone reported that a commissary worker had suggested interchangeable curtains for the DC-3's and DC-4's. "That's thinking!" he enthused. "That idea's worth a $250 bond and see that he gets it."

But in the next breath he became infuriated over a report that baggage handlers were stealing chewing gum from the commissary "because we used to get it free and they know it."

"What the hell does it matter whether we pay for it or get it free?" he demanded. "It's not theirs. It doesn't belong to them. They can't walk into a store and take chewing gum or a bar of candy without paying for it. Let's get after this—I want this practice stopped!"

The analogy was typical of the way he framed his arguments. He once got a letter from a dress manufacturer complaining about Eastern's poor meal service. Rickenbacker's answer was a question: "Would you give away a pair of panties and a bra with every dress?

"We're in the transportation business," the letter continued, and we'd rather not get into the restaurant business."

The most widespread story of a staff meeting concerns the time he secretly ordered assistant station managers to deliberately tag about fifty percent of participants' luggage to wrong cities. When the meeting opened, the room was full of unshaven and angry vice presidents, traffic managers, supervisors, department heads, and station managers. EVR got up and addressed the motley assembly.

"I just wanted you s.o.b.'s to know how a passenger feels when we lose his bag!" he roared.

A story not as widespread involves the manager of what was then Eastern's smallest station—Columbus, Georgia. When his turn came to speak, he followed the assigned script: He reported on passenger boardings for the previous six months, his traffic forecasts for the next six months, his general observations on how things were going in Columbus, Georgia, and finally a few items he wanted to get off his chest about Eastern as a whole.

"I have a complaint," he began. "I think one of the biggest problems at my station is that we're getting too much mislabeled baggage that should have gone to Columbus, Ohio."

Rickenbacker jumped to his feet, nodding vigorously.

"Son, you're absolutely right," he announced. "Why, we've got some bastards on this airline who don't know Hartford's in Massachusetts!"

Dick Fisher, now a top assistant to Frank Borman, had just joined Eastern at the time and had been assigned the job of setting up arrangements for the meeting.

"The funny thing," he recalls, "was that no one laughed at his mistake. There wasn't so much as a chuckle in the whole room. All you could hear was the sound of cheeks being sucked in to keep from laughing."

Fisher can verify how tightfisted and cost conscious EVR

could be. He called Dick one day and informed him they would have a guest speaker at the next day's session.

"I'd like to have a reception for him in my suite," he ordered Fisher. "Make sure we have all the necessary items on hand."

Fisher had the hotel outfit the suite while the Captain was elsewhere. The minute Rickenbacker returned, he phoned him.

"Dick, for God's sake what do you think you're doing?" he bellowed. "Are you trying to get 'em all drunk? Now you listen to me, young man—I want credit for everything we don't use and that includes *partial* bottles, and I want to see the credit on my hotel bill."

Fisher is one of many Eastern people who think that the staff meetings, if they could have been stripped of the fear factor, actually amounted to an excellent management device.

"Years after Captain Eddie left," Fisher says, "I was in the office of a management consultant firm and picked up a magazine with an article on what the writer called 'free-mold management.' It was nothing but Rickenbacker's staff-meeting concept. You have to remember he didn't like organization charts which delineated areas of responsibility—he wanted you to speak your piece in any area."

Fisher will never forget his own first report at a staff meeting. It revolved around his idea to operate the Martin 404 fleet as a separate airline, with no food service. EVR praised the proposal, adding that "we've already been thinking of something like that." Fisher learned later this was his reaction to any worthwhile suggestion he hadn't thought of himself.

"You never really brought a new idea to Rick," Fisher says. "He'd invariably thank you but say that it was something he was working on before you brought it up. I've even seen some people convince him he was wrong, which wasn't very often, so he'd switch positions and adopt it as his own idea."

Fisher once submitted a report on the subject of fringe benefits—how they helped employees more than high salaries, and that if you left Eastern for a better-paying job you might wind up worse in the long run. It was a subject close to EVR's heart and before Fisher delivered the report verbally, Captain Eddie told him, "You've got one hell of a good report there, Dick—I want you to get up there and hit it hard."

Fisher was on Cloud Nine, but at this lofty altitude it went to his head and he began ad-libbing and extemporizing. Halfway through the largely improvised report, he felt the telltale tug on his pants leg.

"For Christ's sake," Rickenbacker was whispering, "read it like it's written—it's better that way."

Fisher survived so many staff meetings that like other veterans he began to grasp Rickenbacker's basic softheartedness. He blustered, castigated, scolded, and whiplashed; to outsiders—and there were occasionally non-Eastern people present—the general effect was one of a man publicly humiliating his subordinates. But those who really knew Captain Eddie sensed the subtle difference between stimulation and irritation.

"He knew some of the younger guys were petrified," Fisher says. "He could be very gentle with them, up to a point. He could even be tactful when he had to be and he usually recognized which ones could take a tongue-lashing."

Lethridge agrees—partially. "It's true the higher a man's position, the more likely he was to catch hell at a staff meeting. I've seen him actually go down a row of vice presidents looking for a target to hit, and you knew damned well the whole row wanted to go hide someplace."

In person the Captain was tall and lanky—he never regained all the weight he had lost on the raft. He invariably wore blue shirts and blue suits, plus that crushed felt hat. He drank martinis but there wasn't a man in the airline business who could hold liquor better than Captain Eddie—until he was in his sixties, when his tolerance for alcohol diminished. In his prime, even after a half-dozen martinis, he remained clear-eyed and apparently sober; the only sign of over-imbibing were two little red spots on his cheeks. This was probably just as well, because an alcoholic Rickenbacker would have been unbearable. As it was, he had few if any close friends among his fellow airline chiefs. They generally considered him too boisterous, opinionated, and demanding. If there had been a tape recorder at some of his meetings with his industry peers, the transcripts would have required fireproof paper.

Most of the clashes occurred at sessions of the Air Transport Association, the airline industry's trade organization, where the Captain would have finished quite far back in any popularity contest. And the feelings some airline presidents had toward him were very mutual.

He disliked Tom Braniff and Jack Frye—Wayne Parrish believes he was jealous of Frye. He hated Juan Trippe and George Baker. He feuded eternally with C. R. Smith of American but had a grudging respect for his rival. C. E. Woolman of Delta always could get under his skin, for EVR hated Delta with a passion that stemmed partially from sheer envy. He liked Bob Six of Continental, although they didn't know each other very well—Six, incidentally, never got around to telling him that he had commanded one of the search planes looking for EVR in the Pacific (Six had been in the Air Transport Command).

"I wasn't really close to him," Six says. "I had drinks with him in Kansas City once, and I remember two things—he drank more martinis than I ever saw anyone consume, and I couldn't get a word in edgewise. With Rickenbacker, you didn't do any talking; you just sat and listened while he held court."

Six, no amateur when it comes to cost control, had personal evidence of how far Rickenbacker could carry the policy. His former wife, musical/comedy star Ethel Merman, boarded an Eastern flight in New York many years back and the experience induced her to send an angry letter to the Captain. It was pouring rain and Miss Merman got wet walking to the plane after the ramp agent told her there were no umbrellas.

Rickenbacker's answer was polite enough but didn't help matters much. "Umbrellas are very expensive," he wrote, "and you only get wet a few minutes."

It was C. R. Smith who knew EVR as well as anyone in the industry—he used to infuriate the Captain by calling him "*Mr.* Rickenbacker." C.R. today remembers him as "a very great American and a very sincere patriot," but the stories told about this pair would fill a book of their own. C.R. delighted in needling Captain Eddie. Rickenbacker once told him he was going to stop giving passes to ATA officials—"I don't want them riding around free on Eastern," he groused.

"Don't worry, Eddie," Smith said gently, "they'll only try Eastern once."

They were together at a cocktail reception one night and EVR, in a surprisingly jocular mood, suggested tossing a coin "to see who's the biggest s.o.b. in the industry."

C.R. shook his head. "Eddie, no mere flip of a coin could possibly rob you of that distinction."

Their paths crossed with relative infrequency but when they did, Smith's needle was unsheathed. Jim Verner, a prominent aviation lawyer, tells the story of a dinner attended by both C.R. and the Captain. Rickenbacker launched into his usual harangue about the country going to the dogs at supersonic speed and when he finally ran out of breath, Smith sighed, "Eddie, I love you—I hope you live a year."

Rickenbacker got along best with W. A. Patterson of United, largely because Patterson could get along with anybody, but even Pat fought with him at ATA meetings. On one occasion Patterson had had his fill of EVR's argumentative, sometimes abusive attitude—he had been lambasting his ATA colleagues for spending too much money on food service—and the usually genial head of United exploded.

"Some of us wish you were back on the raft!" he said angrily.

"Guys like you make me wish I was," Rickenbacker retorted.

His conservative attitude toward in-flight service made him something of a pariah in his own industry. He honestly believed that airlines receiving government subsidies shouldn't be spending the money on such frills as filet mignon dinners. When he finally had to match such entrées because Delta and National had gone in for them, he complained it was costing Eastern an extra $15,000 a month. In 1949 he grabbed some big headlines by publicly offering to fly the routes of five competing carriers without subsidy, thereby saving taxpayers almost $10.5 million a year. His targets were National, Delta, Capital, Chicago & Southern (which later merged with Delta), and Colonial, and he made the surprising proposal in a letter to Senator Edwin C. Johnson, chairman of the Senate Commerce Committee.

"Eastern Air Lines, Incorporated, hereby offers to operate the entire domestic system of any one or more of the five above-mentioned air carriers at a non-subsidy rate," he wrote Johnson. "According to my calculations, the five above-named air carriers carried 2,701,000 ton-miles of mail in the above-mentioned areas in 1948 and received an average of $4.45 per ton-mile for doing it, aggregating $12,077,000 received from the government by them in 1948."

His arithmetic was simple. Eastern was making money charging sixty to sixty-five cents a ton-mile; what he was promising was to fly all the mail of his five competitors at Eastern's rate, which would have amounted to less than $1.7 million instead of the $12 million they were getting in subsidies. He professed great disappointment when the five airlines figuratively told him where he could stick what he insisted was a "generous offer."

"Having proved that airlines could be run without subsidy," he wrote in his autobiography, "I was galled by the spendthrift methods of some other airlines, supported through subsidy by the people of the United States. It was infuriating. If we could make a profit for our stockholders, why couldn't other operators at least break even?"

Such sentiments were about as welcome throughout the industry as a case of measles on a wedding night. Perhaps the definitive story of Captain Eddie's unpopularity with his peers involves an airline president—he shall remain nameless—who was invited to join a celebrity foursome at a charity golf tournament. He showed up on schedule and was greeted by the tourney chairman.

"We really appreciate your coming," he chirped. "By the way, Captain Rickenbacker will be in your foursome."

The president's face turned blood-red.

"If I want to play with a prick," he snarled, "I'll play with my own!"

And stalked away.

Rickenbacker, interestingly enough, had a dry sense of humor which didn't pop to the surface too often. Someone asked him, "Do you think aviation will ever take the place of sex?"

EVR sighed before replying, "It has for me, son."

Occasionally he seemed to live in the past, as if nostalgia could erase temporarily the problems and pains of living in the present. Six noticed this about him. "He was a tough old buzzard but in almost every social conversation I had with him, he'd go back to his Spad days, in kind of a wistful way."

Jim Elkins, a prominent Houston banker who went on Eastern's board in 1959 (he later was to be instrumental in Frank Borman's joining EAL) tells a poignant story about the Captain's using the glories of the past almost as a crutch. As Elkins describes it:

"I had asked him, rather idly, about that raft experience. I give you my word of honor—he talked nonstop for an hour in that high-pitched voice of his. It was like a stream of consciousness, starting from the day he went down and ending with a remark that broke me up: 'As you may have noticed, since that time I have never been able to get enough to drink.' He told the story in a very dramatic, emotional way; he had tears in his eyes when he explained how he made everyone on those rafts hate his guts so they'd have a common emotion."

That strange obsession with nostalgia extended even to wearing apparel, the battered felt hat being the best example. He always hated to throw away any item of clothing, but the hat was as much a part of him as the skin on his body. Johnny Ray was with him one day in EVR's Miami office and noticed that the disreputable fedora couldn't have been any worse if it had been run over by a Sherman tank. Ray knew there were no hat-cleaning establishments in Miami and he was flying up to New York that day.

He suggested, "Captain, while I'm there how about my getting your hat cleaned?"

"Don't you ever let any s.o.b. touch this hat!" Rickenbacker shouted.

Adds Ray, "I think it stayed dirty for thirty years."

EVR never really became acclimated to the idea of women working around an airline; during the war he accepted them as a necessary evil but in Eastern's earlier years, females were persona non grata in any position of even minor responsibility. EAL used to have a sales representative named Alice Eckhoff whose territory was the tough New York garment district. In the late 1930s she was carried on the payroll as "A. Eckhoff" so Captain Eddie wouldn't know he had a lady sales rep.

It took a long time for EVR to get used to stewardesses—and vice versa. He took a perverse delight in trying to catch them in some rules violation, and one of his tricks was to charge past the flight attendant standing at the foot of the boarding stairs, seeing if they'd demand to see his pass. He probably tried this about fifty times and never nailed anyone.

One day he boarded a flight manned by a rookie stewardess, Winnie Smith, who didn't recognize him. As he walked by her, he tripped and stepped on one of her $22.50 shoes, tearing a hole in it. Bravely hiding the pain, she asked pleasantly, "May I see your ticket, please?"

"It's a good thing you asked, girlie," he growled, "or I would have fired you on the spot."

(Winnie Smith eventually became Winnie Gilbert—and she also became vice president of in-flight service, EAL's highest ranking woman officer.)

Some of his prejudices were on the ludicrous side, one of them being a distrust of short men. Lefty Lethridge blames this idiosyncrasy on his unhappy relationship with Ernie Breech, who was under five feet four inches—anytime anything went wrong, Lefty recalls, EVR would mumble, "Never hire small men."

"We all smiled," says Lefty, "because about that time he had four vice presidents, none of whom were taller than five foot nine."

Travel agents were another pet Rickenbacker peeve. He took a dim view of this profession, and it was true that in the 1940s and early 1950s a travel agent couldn't do much more for a passenger than an airline agent—particularly in domestic trip planning. For years he fought the growth of travel agencies because he hated to pay the commissions that otherwise would have gone to the airline as part of the normal fare. He never got over this feeling, either, although today more than half of Eastern's tickets are sold through travel agents.

The Captain had a fixation on utilization of equipment—to him, the sight of an airplane sitting on the ground was the epitome of sloppy planning and gross inefficiency. This was true even in the DC-3 days when what became known as "the Jacksonville story" became part of the Rickenbacker legend.

There was a DC-3 in front of the Jacksonville terminal ready to board passengers for a flight to Chicago. They were just heading out to the plane when they were startled to see it take off without them.

"What's going on here?" one shouted at the station manager.

"See that plane coming in for a landing?" the manager said, pointing to a DC-3 on final approach.

The passenger nodded.

"Well, that's flight twenty-one and Captain Eddie's on board. If he saw your plane on the ground, we'd all be out of luck. The Chicago plane will be back in forty minutes, after he's left."

The story may sound unbelievable, but more than one EAL veteran swears it really happened. Even if it was apocryphal, however, there is plenty of other evidence to underline EVR's passion for maximum aircraft utilization. Says Wayne Parrish:

"Keeping planes in the air was one of his most overriding philosophies. If a flight hit Greensboro, North Carolina, at two A.M., that was fine and if passengers didn't want to go out at two A.M., the hell with them—it was a policy that really hurt Eastern but Rick made no apologies. He never made much effort to accommodate cities schedulewise if this meant affecting aircraft utilization. He had the pilots with him—they were devoted to him—but it hurt sales and generated a lot of anti-Eastern feeling throughout the southeast. Literally, he told the cities what they were going to get and he didn't listen to what they wanted, until competition came along. Even today I think there's some resentment and it all sprang from Rickenbacker's attitude—and Brattain's, too, for that matter. He had the guts to argue with the old man on many things but when it came to utilization, they thought alike."

Parrish's word "resentment" is a thick, ugly thread that runs through the saga of Captain Eddie and Eastern. His good deeds and astute decisions were always being balanced against the ill-feeling he could generate out of blind prejudices. Certainly this was true in Washington, where his open contempt of bureaucrats and politicians simply alienated government officials not merely toward Rickenbacker personally, but his airline as well.

When L. Welsh Pogue headed the CAB, Rickenbacker called and asked for an appointment, which Pogue willingly gave him. The Captain charged into the chairman's office and stood in front of his desk.

"Sit down, Captain, sit down," Pogue said with a friendly smile.

EVR wasn't smiling. "What I've got to tell you I'll say right now and I don't have to sit down to do it," Rickenbacker snarled.

As Pogue himself related later, "What he said practically burned a hole in my carpet. But when he walked out, my secretary told me later, he winked at her and chuckled, 'I guess I gave him a piece of my mind.' "

The Captain couldn't resist getting involved in behalf of conservative candidates—Bob Six once commented that "compared to Rickenbacker, a John Bircher was a liberal." The late Senator Robert A. Taft was one of EVR's favorites and he campaigned openly for the Ohioan in 1952 when Taft was battling to win the GOP presidential nomination away from Dwight Eisenhower. Rickenbacker's support led to an incident that almost cost one of Eastern's top pilots his job—Captain Mel French.

French was an avowed "I like Ike" man and he was at Miami International Airport the day Taft flew in for a rally in front of Eastern's hangars. A huge reviewing stand had been erected and Adelaide Rickenbacker was in charge of the whole affair.

French was due to take a flight out shortly, but he had enough time to appropriate an EAL tractor, which he rolled by the packed stands wearing an "I Like Ike" sign on the back of his shirt. This was bad enough, but after he boarded his Constellation, he made a point of taxiing toward the stands where Taft had started speaking.

"Eastern," the tower warned, "your hangar area's closed to all traffic."

French paid no attention at first and came as close to the stands as he dared.

"Eastern, get the hell out of there," the tower insisted.

"Roger," French acknowledged. He turned the Connie's until the triple tail was pointing straight at the speaker's platform. Then he gunned all four engines for several minutes before rolling away. Mrs. Rickenbacker, almost in tears, phoned the Captain, who was in New York, and reported what had happened.

"You couldn't even hear what Senator Taft was saying," she wailed.

At two A.M. a couple of mornings later, the newly elected ALPA council chairman at EAL, Mike Fenello, received a phone call from French.

"Mike, I'm in a little trouble," Mel said in a masterpiece of understatement.

He told Fenello what had happened and pleaded that Mike accompany him to a hearing in Chief Pilot John Gill's office later that morning. Fenello agreed after French swore he hadn't heard the tower's warning. In Gill's office French again stoutly insisted he hadn't heard the tower's initial warning to stay away from the hangar area.

"After all, John," Mel said earnestly, "I'm not some kind of a nut."

At that precise moment a loud alarm clock went off. Gill and Fenello looked around, trying to find the source of the jangling. French took a clock out of his coat pocket and turned off the alarm.

"It's to remind me of an errand I've got to run," he explained. "Now as I was saying, I'm not some kind of a nut. . . ."

Gill had Captain Eddie's orders to "fire the bastard who embarrassed my wife and the next president of the United States," but the chief pilot informed the irate Rickenbacker the pilot involved had been Mel French—an EVR favorite—and explained that Mel simply didn't hear the tower's instructions. Privately, Gill knew that alibi contained about as much truth as a Joseph Goebbels press release but his own white lie took French off the hook.

Whether Captain Eddie would have relented anyway is another matter. He was so fond of his airmen that anyone representing management in contract negotiations with ALPA sometimes found himself battling EVR as well as the pilots. On more than one occasion Rickenbacker stepped in at the last minute and gave them what they wanted. Nor were the pilots the only beneficiaries of his wide streak of sentimentality. Lethridge and a number of other executives who served under him in the forties and fifties believe he was too prone to hang onto deadwood simply because he hated to fire anyone who had exhibited loyalty toward him.

"He hated two things: disloyalty and stupidity," Lefty says. "He had an expression—'He uses poor judgment'—and if he ever said that about you, it was time to check out. Conversely, though, he kept a lot of guys who should have been retired or fired outright—mostly old sales and station managers. And it hurt him in the long run, because he wound up with too many men who wouldn't stand up to him and be counted."

Lethridge told him once that "if you hang onto these guys for another four of five years and then have to fire them out of sheer desperation, they'll be too old to get another job."

"They've been loyal employees," Rickenbacker said softly. "Lefty, I can't do it."

Yet on one occasion he arbitrarily fired a New Orleans station manager who showed up at a cocktail party during working hours.

His was, indeed, the gentle hand under the mailed fist, the marshmallow center covered by a cactus coating. Eastern had an employee named Burt Van Duzer with a leg badly crippled from polio. Every time Rickenbacker went down a corridor with Van Duzer, he would slow down his gait and walk with his arm around him. Maggie Robinson remembers the time when she had just been transferred to New York and was spending her first winter at 10 Rockefeller Plaza. Rickenbacker called her shortly before Christmas.

"Maggie, if you can come up to my office you can get the best view of their lighting the Center's Christmas tree," he suggested.

She used to be the only woman at the staff meetings and she has a somewhat more favorable view of what so many regarded as 500 persons being tortured simultaneously.

"I think they made us the most knowledgeable management group in the industry," she maintains. "I didn't know much about rocker boxes and nozzle pins but I got to understand and appreciate maintenance problems. The staff meeting concept worked in those days because we were so much smaller—more of a large family than a corporation. The first time I had to stand up and give a report, the Captain whispered to me, 'If you're nervous, don't expect me to grab *your* leg to steady you down.'"

When a company is small and dominated by a single person, the "we're just a big family" atmosphere works fine—until major growth exposes hardened attitudes, methods, and policies that may no longer apply. There is unanimity among Rickenbacker's most loyal supporters that this was his fatal weakness: inability to recognize that Eastern was only a part of an industry changing dramatically. In a sense the isolationism he thought best for his country he tried to apply to his airline; the simplistic canons he was taught in boyhood and by which he lived all his life became crusted barnacles in a world and an industry no longer simple.

"He went downhill," says Maggie Robinson, "when Eastern became too big for his sense of a family, of togetherness. He became an anachronism because these ideas were an anachronism in a large corporation."

"The thing that made him most successful in the early

days," says John Halliburton, "was what hurt him in the end. He was in on every minute detail of company operations—even engine overhauls. He'd spend every Sunday going out to first one and eventually all three New York airports, and it was nothing for him to work an eighteen-hour day. But when Eastern grew so big that he couldn't personally oversee and supervise everything, he was reluctant to delegate authority."

"He was an outstanding leader of a small to medium-sized company," says Lefty Lethridge. "He was mentally unequipped to move into an era when air transportation was on the verge of becoming mass transportation. He felt almost every job in the company was his, instead of being more of an executive administrator and passing things onto key people."

"When you have a strong character like Rickenbacker," says Joseph Burke, editor of the *Great Silver Fleet News* in the fifties, "you have to anticipate that any error will be commensurate with the character."

If there is unanimous agreement on what went wrong with Captain Eddie, there also is—significantly—unanimous regret. For every story told of his arbitrary, blind stubbornness, there are ten stories told of his kindness, warmth, and deep feeling for individuals. This was the source of the loyalty so many gave him—Charlie Froesch, for example, was offered three times his Eastern salary to go with Lockheed as a top engineer but refused because he didn't want to leave the Captain.

Generally courtly toward women—except for his habit of calling all stewardesses "girlie"—he had to watch his natural bent toward freewheeling profanity. That was why he preferred male company, where he felt more at ease. When he got together with Bev Griffith, the room needed fumigating—Bev also swore with equal intensity and frequency and was once overheard telling the governor of California to "go screw yourself."

Occasionally Walker and a few other brave souls would violate a Rickenbacker "don't spend a dime on that silly crap" edict—naturally, without ever confessing this unspeakable transgression. Walker did it once when he wanted to move a light over the Constellation's galley service bar so flight attendants could better see what they were doing. It involved a structural change and this meant altering a number of drawings, so Lockheed gave Walker a cost figure of $300 an airplane. Walker took the estimate in to Rickenbacker.

"Go back and tell those bastards to go to hell themselves," he ordered. "I won't pay it."

"We need it," Brad pleaded.

"I don't give a damn. It's extortion."

Walker gave up on the Captain but not on the light change. He quietly told Lockheed to go ahead with the project but added, "For God's sake, don't ever mention it to the old man."

Rickenbacker's work habits played havoc with Walker's need for occasional rest. EVR had the faculty of being able to grab a ten-minute catnap and wake up completely refreshed. He'd tell Walker, "Brad, I'm going to grab a nap—wake me in ten minutes." Walker might be exhausted himself but he didn't dare fall asleep for fear he'd miss arousing the Captain.

A rival advertising agency once made a pitch for Eastern's account, and the elaborate presentation included a market survey depicting the airline's public image.

"That image," intoned the Madison Avenue type, "shows that Eastern has a philosophy of picking them up and taking them some place with the least amount of service and not losing too many on the way."

There was an uncomfortable silence in the room, broken by Captain Eddie's shrill voice.

"You're absolutely right, son!" he said loudly. "That's the only way to make money in this goddamned business!"

Close to EVR's heart were his contacts with the "troops"— the station managers, sales representatives, mechanics, ramp agents, ticket-counter workers, and reservations clerks around Eastern's sprawling system. Quite naturally an expected inspection tour or casual visit by the Captain prompted some nervousness, but he had the knack of making virtually every employee feel the way he wanted them to feel—part of his family. His preparations for a field trip were extensive and thorough; he would memorize not merely names but nicknames, small but touching details about a man's own family life.

He loved to ask a station manager, for example, "How are you people handling this problem?"—he already knew the answer but he wanted the man to have the satisfaction of feeling that the boss was interested in his opinion. Because he knew the answer, of course, it was imperative that the station manager know it, too. No one in the field ever really was sure what subject Rickenbacker might bring up—or when he might turn up, for not all his visits were announced in advance.

Frank Stulgaitis, now EAL's manager in Los Angeles, remembers when he was a young station manager in Birmingham and the Captain walked in one night unannounced.

"It was in 1947," he relates, "and in those days our whole operation was in the terminal. We were working up to twenty hours a day and we were all pretty tired when about ten P.M. in comes Captain Eddie. He said he wanted to tour all our facilities. I showed him around and we came back to reservations, where we had about a dozen people working. He started talking about reservations problems and for over an hour he talked and asked questions. After he left, we spent another hour talking about him. If he had been running for king, he would have had twelve votes right there. He had us bursting with pride and ambition.

"It's only too true that people used to faint at those staff meetings—I was there the time a chief mechanic from one of the smaller stations actually passed out when Rickenbacker asked him to get up and read his report. If you tried to bullshit him, it was lock the door, Charlie—you were dead. I attended a few when I was station manager at La Guardia. I'd get up and read my report and he'd start asking questions. I kept wondering how the hell he knew all this stuff about La Guardia—I found out later that as soon as I left for the meeting, he called my assistant and quizzed him."

Stulgaitis once put in a requisition for additional filing cabinets at La Guardia. The answer he got from EVR was "if you didn't write so much garbage and have so many stupid damned things to file away, you wouldn't need any more cabinets."

At the next staff meeting Rickenbacker closed the first morning session with a long dissertation on filing cabinets, the gist being that excessive purchases of filing cabinets might well bankrupt the airline and were stark proof of just the kind of profligate spending he was trying to stop. It so happened that when Stulgaitis started for his room to wash up before lunch, EVR got into the elevator with him.

Out came that bony forefinger, attached to a hand the size of a ham hock. "And you know damned well what I was talking about, don't you, Frank?"

Rickenbacker had a large ego but very little vanity. The only exception was a reluctance to reveal his real age—he always claimed to be two years younger than he actually was. It took years before his secret got out, and it was his beloved Sheppy who spilled the beans at a birthday party for the Captain. Floyd Hall had asked her how old Captain Eddie was and she told him the truth without thinking. When Hall asked Rickenbacker if Sheppy had the right dope, EVR muttered sourly, "Women talk too damned much."

One of his conceits—perhaps it was more of a personality trait—was his steadfast conviction that he knew something about everything. Wayne Parrish heard someone ask Rickenbacker about steam power.

"My God, he became an immediate expert on steam power," Parrish remembers, "and he didn't know a damned thing about it."

Yet there were times when he displayed a touch of humility. During World War II, when Major Richard Bong broke Rickenbacker's record for enemy aircraft destroyed, EVR sent him a case of Scotch with a brief note of congratulations. And there was one area, one subject, in which he willingly played servant and not master: his religion. His belief in the Almighty was deep and sincere, and religious faith carried him through more than one crisis.

Rickenbacker was as sparse with compliments as with company funds. He apparently was afraid that too much praise would make a man complacent and at staff meetings, when a sales or station manager would report with obvious pride that a quota had been exceeded, EVR would grimace.

"Hell, the damned quota was too low to begin with," he'd declare.

He was schizophrenic about spending money. For a long time he put an absolute $1.25 ceiling on the cost of an in-flight meal; it took John Halliburton only five minutes to sell him on a million-dollar flight simulator for training Constellation crews. "If you could prove an expenditure would enhance safety," Halliburton says, "he'd open the wallet."

He was, in brief, a nineteenth-century American trying hard to cope with the twentieth century—a task in which he achieved both magnificent success and dismal failure. It was a climb and descent of dizzying proportions. For those past and present people of Eastern to whom the memories of Captain Eddie are green, the sentiments of Maggie Robinson are representative:

"I remember his great faith in God, his faith in people, his morals and ethics," she says. "He'd always tell us to do things right. He'd tell us, 'We're not going to cheat, we're not going to pay off somebody. We may not always get what we want but we'll always be able to live with ourselves. We won't take a government subsidy, we'll be honest and fair; we're in business and if we don't make a profit it's because we're not good businessmen.' "

Unfortunately, that is only part of the Rickenbacker legend. A contingency in the legacy he bequeathed to MacIntyre was his reluctance to abdicate completely, to give up all the power he had enjoyed for so long.

CHAPTER ELEVEN

MR. MAC—
"I THINK I MADE
A CONTRIBUTION"

Malcolm MacIntyre was a brilliant lawyer, a close friend and confidant of C. R. Smith, a man of integrity and ability—and he had virtually no experience in the rough and tumble game of running a major airline.

How did he wind up as the sixth president of Eastern? There is a plethora of conflicting evidence and there are no specific records or correspondence to help reach an indisputable conclusion; the story of Malcolm MacIntyre's selection has to be told in the context of individual memories, some clouded by the passage of time and quite possibly by natural subjectivity.

MacIntyre himself says flatly, "I was approached by an emissary from Laurance Rockefeller who asked if I'd be interested in heading Eastern. I said yes, I arranged to meet Rickenbacker, we made a deal, and I became president and chief executive officer—the latter title was at my insistence and the company's bylaws had to be changed to conform with that demand."

Rockefeller denies he was instrumental in the MacIntyre choice and says Rickenbacker himself was primarily responsible

—that EVR simply wanted younger blood, and picked Mac-Intyre as the outstanding candidate.

Lefty Lethridge says there actually was a list of presidential possibilities, drawn up by Dick Jackson acting on Rockefeller's orders.

"There were ten names on that list," Lefty recalls. "Jackson had thoroughly researched every one, and MacIntyre was included among the ten. The list was ready on the day Rockefeller was going to have lunch with Captain Eddie and he took it with him. I know Rickenbacker saw the list and that he told several people he was impressed by MacIntyre's Air Force background. Mac was the only candidate both Rockefeller and Rickenbacker really considered, and it was the Captain who made the final decision."

Sheppy, certainly privy to at least some of EVR's inner thoughts, is convinced that the Captain advised Rockefeller against hiring MacIntyre because "he didn't think he had the airline background necessary to run Eastern."

Charlie Simons is of the opinion that EAL's directors forced MacIntyre on Rickenbacker. Harper Woodward, Rockefeller's close friend and business associate, says he never heard of any ten-man list but tends to agree with Rockfeller that Mac-Intyre was largely the Captain's own choice. Woodward, who went on the Board shortly after Mr. Mac became president, adds:

"Apparently Eddie felt the airline had grown too much for his original teammates to handle—Mac was a different kind of executive. The others were from the vineyards, all totally self-made, right out of the grass roots, a dedicated group who never looked at a clock and worked seven days a week."

Rickenbacker himself left the question unresolved in his autobiography. There is only one mention of MacIntyre in the entire book, and that lone reference is subject to two interpretations. The Captain prefaced the topic of his successor by denouncing "the trend toward more and more bureaucracy, more and more governmental control," which he said had reached the stage where the CAB by 1961 had allowed nine airlines to operate between New York and Washington. Where he got that figure of nine is unknown—only Eastern, American, Northeast, and National had nonstop rights and the latter two had to operate under certain restrictions—but EVR likened the situation to having nine separate telephone companies, nine water companies, and nine utility companies serving New York and Washington.

"As I neared the age of seventy," he went on, "I became so disgusted with this trend toward socialism that I felt like stepping out of the airline business completely, provided that we could find the right type of executive to take over from me. Some of our directors felt that Eastern should have a younger chief executive officer, to which I agreed. Malcolm A. MacIntyre, a brilliant lawyer but a man inexperienced in airline operation, took over. . . ."

Does that mean EVR agreed merely to the idea of a younger president or to MacIntyre specifically? The reference to Mr. Mac's inexperience would seem to indicate the former, but in light of what was to happen under the MacIntyre regime— namely near disaster—the Captain may well have been trying to create the impression that MacIntyre was not his choice; it would have been totally unlike Rickenbacker to admit that he picked the wrong man.

The best guess of what really occurred is that the directors, Rockefeller in particular, did want younger leadership and that MacIntyre, if not EVR's actual choice, didn't arouse any strong objections from the Captain.

In any event the question of how and why MacIntyre was picked is rather moot, for it didn't make much difference who became Eastern's new president and chief executive officer—not while Captain Eddie was around to peer over his successor's shoulder. Quite justifiably Mr. Mac feared interference, and quite naively he expected that his title as chief executive officer protected him from it—EVR, with MacIntyre's hiring, became strictly chairman of the board with no specific definition of authority.

No more intelligent man ever headed an airline than Malcolm MacIntyre. A Yale graduate and Rhodes Scholar, he had served in the Air Transport Command during World War II, rising to the rank of colonel, and had a distinguished law career that included serving as American's general counsel for almost a decade. C. R. Smith thought enough of him to consider him as a possible successor; MacIntyre says Smith actually offered him the job in 1958 while Mr. Mac was undersecretary of the Air Force, but MacIntyre had promised Dwight Eisenhower he would stay at the Pentagon for at least two years; in 1958 he had served only one.

Handsome, dynamic, and forceful, MacIntyre was the direct antithesis of Rickenbacker in one key respect: He was not afraid to experiment, to try new ideas and methods. This more than anything else brought him into almost immediate conflict with the Captain. They both manfully tried to coexist peacefully, and for a while even the volatile Rickenbacker made an honest effort to stay out of the new leader's hair. He even stopped going out to La Guardia and Idlewild Airports on Sundays, according to Sheppy, which for him was nothing short of abdication. But the end of the honeymoon was as inevitable as the sun rising in the east; EVR still was regarded as the boss by too many EAL officials, not to mention the majority of employees, and MacIntyre was only too well aware of that impossible situation.

Harper Woodward got one early indication that their relationship was going to fall well short of a Damon-Pythias friendship. The first time he saw them together, Rickenbacker started to talk, MacIntyre did likewise, and both kept talking simultaneously.

"They had a duet for five minutes," Woodward remembers.

In one of Mr. Mac's first meetings with Lethridge, Lefty suddenly blurted, "Are you really chief executive officer?"

"You're damned right," MacIntyre snapped, annoyed at the question. Four years later, while Lefty was in the president's office discussing some problem, Lethridge happened to remark that a similar difficulty had arisen under Rickenbacker. MacIntyre shook his head. "Lefty, do you remember asking me when I came here if I was really the chief executive officer?"

"Sure I do."

"You know, that was quite a question. I think at the time I gave you the wrong answer."

That the predecessor and successor had to clash came as no surprise to officers like Lethridge. "As long as a man with Rickenbacker's dynamism was in the same building," Lefty says, "no one could be chief executive officer except in title."

MacIntyre and the Captain started off on friendly terms, meeting frequently for talks about Eastern's problems and prospects. It was at one of the very first of these sessions that the new president got a disturbing insight into EVR's philosophy. They were discussing the airline's tardiness in starting jet service and MacIntyre expressed concern about Rickenbacker's obvious pessimism about and even prejudice toward jets.

"They'll revolutionize commerical aviation," Mr. Mac argued. "I honestly can't understand your attitude."

"Because of the Rickenbacker car."

"What's that got to do with jets?"

"Well, that was the first car with four-wheel brakes and I went broke. I'd much prefer having someone else be first."

There was no single item or event which shattered their uneasy live-and-let-live relationship; rather, a series of small disagreements leading to major ones, and overall an accumulation of conflicts that crushed the resolve of both men to be friends. There is no doubt that Rickenbacker took a dim view of one of MacIntyre's earliest decisions—he hired back as executive vice president Robert "Bob" Turner, whom Rickenbacker had fired just before Mr. Mac took over. Sheppy says Rickenbacker resented the move but it was not the only source of friction.

It didn't take long for MacIntyre to realize the airline of which he had assumed command was suffering from a multitude of ailments. Profitwise it seemed in good shape, but it was more a feverish flush than a healthy glow.

"It was primarily a north–south carrier," MacIntyre reminisces. "It served a lot of business cities but it didn't connect many. It was far too heavily oriented to and dependent on Florida, the South, and vacation travel. In those days sixty percent of its traffic was generated from December through February and the other forty percent was spread throughout the rest of the year. When I came on, Eastern was trying to compete with Electras against National and Delta's jets—our own jet-acquisition program was in a shambles. I tried to turn it all around but the problems were immense."

Try he did. He began by launching a campaign to get rid of all unprofitable points and eventually about seventy percent of them were turned over to local-service carriers. But this particular reform movement came too late. "We were the last major airline to dump all these money losers," Lethridge points out, "And as with the jets we just missed the boat. By the time we did get them off our system, they had cost us millions."

Many of the smaller points had been added after the war as part of Rickenbacker's strategy to keep the local-service airlines from ever becoming a competitive threat.

"If we can short-circuit these feeder lines," he had once explained to Lethridge, "the smaller cities will come to us. If we don't, the feeders will merge one by one and we'll have a whole new airline competing against us."

His strategy worked in the sense that the cities much preferred to be served by a big airline like Eastern than by a small regional carrier still operating DC-3's. Where it didn't work is that such stations didn't develop enough traffic to make service profitable without subsidy—which EVR steadfastly refused to even consider. The Martins and Convairs serving these points were still too large for the markets, and this added up to overcapacity simultaneously compounded by the obsolescence of the four-engine fleet. When Mr. Mac became president, Eastern still didn't have a single jet flying and of the fifteen DC-8s ordered, only eight had been placed in service by December 1960, when the second full year of the jet age was ending.

If Rickenbacker resented certain MacIntyre moves, the feeling was mutual—Mr. Mac felt, with justification, that he had inherited a can of worms when it came to equipment and overall employee morale. The latter were intertwining problems; EVR's aircraft decisions had resulted in an oddball fleet that tried to compensate for its inadequacies by frequent scheduling. This led to overutilization which begot mechanical delays, angry passengers, and frustrated EAL personnel. Lethridge, a firsthand observer of on-the-line problems, recalls them only too vividly.

"A guy would report for the start of his shift and see nothing but a line of irate passengers. I don't care what kind of person you are—this atmosphere didn't generate courtesy and sympathetic understanding. Our people got tired and irritable themselves and it became nothing but a vicious circle."

One of MacIntyre's biggest headaches was trying to figure out how to use the huge number of Constellations Eastern possessed. There were ten Super-G's, twelve Super-C's, and eighteen even older 749 models—a total of forty airplanes for which there was virtually no heed. They were too big for the short-haul routes already served by the Martins and Convairs; there were forty DC-7's already available for the larger markets, and the forty Electras had been assigned to the prime routes. A few Super-G's were converted into all-cargo aircraft and most of the Super-C's were put on an experimental "Air-Bus" service between Miami and the cities of Pittsburgh, Cleveland and St. Louis. It was the oversupply of the 749 Connies which led to creation of the famed shuttle service—as MacIntyre puts it, "There was no other place to fly them so we put them on the shuttle." (The complete story of the Air-Bus experiment and the subsequent development of the shuttle will be told in the next chapter.)

Mr. Mac was an innovator and his chief aide, Bob Turner, was the creative type—a combination which at least took Eastern out of the stodgy mold EVR had cast even though it was not exactly successful. Lethridge a few years later was to remark to a group of directors that "it was too bad both MacIntyre and Turner came to Eastern simultaneously; separately they came up with some great ideas but working as a team, they tended to go too far."

One of MacIntyre's handicaps, of course, was the residue of one-man loyalty that had marked the Rickenbacker regime. It took a long while for him to be accepted by his fellow officers as a legitimate leader, and a few never did accept him. One reason was the natural inclination to question the selection of an outsider; the general feeling was that EVR could have picked his successor from within Eastern's own family—men like Halliburton and Sharpe each had their supporters and so did Lethridge. Another potential successor was a popular associate of Smythe Gambrell, George Smith, who eventually wound up with Frontier Airlines, as was Charlie Simons, coming up fast as a responsible, capable finance man.

"The Captain could have sold any of us to Rockefeller," Lefty remarks, "but to Eddie we were like sons and to a strong father, a son never really grows up."

There wasn't much doubt that MacIntyre intended to lead, not pay mere lip service to his two titles, and there were no sacred cows to be coddled or protected. One of his most controversial moves was to wipe out all city ticket offices along with the entire corps of field sales representatives. He had absorbed C. R. Smith's feeling that the representatives didn't really sell many tickets, being used mostly for retrieving lost baggage or handling passenger complaints, and that their duties could be more efficiently covered by city managers and through advertising. His action caused a bitter feud with Bill Morrisette, vice president of traffic and sales, who objected strongly and vainly. There also was dissension between Morrisette and Turner leading eventually to the former's resignation. But such internal strife never came close to matching the intensity of the MacIntyre-Rickenbacker wrangling.

Brad Walker, so close to Eastern's policies and problems yet not an officer himself, was caught right in the middle of their mutual dislike. It was Rickenbacker who had broken the news to him about MacIntyre.

"He's going to be Eastern's new president, Brad," EVR had told him. "He's a fine man—very intelligent and I think he'll do a great job."

Walker hesitated, but laid his cards on the table, face up. "Well, Eddie, then my job is to work with him."

"That's exactly what you have to do," the Captain assured him.

From that brief conversation, Walker gained the natural

impression that Captain Eddie had every intention of letting the new regime run its own ship. It took very little time for him to realize there was no love lost between the two men. One of the early signs was open resentment on MacIntyre's part toward Lethridge for spending what Mr. Mac considered an exorbitant amount of time with the Captain. It was Walker who reminded the new president that "Lefty has to maintain contact with the old man, Mac—hell, he's chairman of the board."

What Walker didn't add was that Lethridge had suddenly found himself the unofficial vice president of keeping-peace-in-the-family—he had become a kind of mediator between the chairman and the president, and things got so bad that even the normally cheerful, perennially optimistic Lefty despaired of ever getting the two belligerents to agree on any subject remotely tinged with controversy. Rickenbacker simply was congenitally unable to keep from riding MacIntyre; after a quarter century of total power, interference came as naturally as breathing.

Walker remembers Mr. Mac coming out of the Captain's office after what obviously had been a heated argument, his face white with rage. He looked at Walker and then said, slowly and with deadly emphasis as if he were enunciating each word with a fist pounding on a desk: "I'm president of this airline and that's the way it's going to be, no matter what *he* says!"

Like Lethridge, Walker was on a tightrope strung precariously between these two strong men, both possessing hair-trigger tempers. Inevitably, the better Brad got along with MacIntyre, the angrier Rickenbacker became. At one point Mr. Mac suggested that Walker end the airline–ad-agency relationship and come into Eastern as a senior vice president; the idea appealed to Walker but it infuriated the Captain. When MacIntyre suggested it to EVR, the answer began with a terse "No, goddammit!" and ended with a question—"Why add his salary to our payroll?"

Some of the interference was subtle, some of it open opposition. Walker, who liked and respected both men, won't make excuses for the Captain but he does offer a believable explanation.

"It's only too true Rickenbacker was a sideline critic," he says. "He'd sit back and snipe at Mac and in his own forceful way, he'd try to control him. Eddie just had to keep running that airline, even through Mac, because he was that kind of person. I think Rockefeller wanted him to stay out of MacIntyre's hair but even Laurance couldn't do it no matter how hard he tried to get Eddie to calm down."

Yet Walker still is convinced that Rickenbacker had good intentions. During MacIntyre's early days in office, EVR used to express great pride in his successor's background, especially his Pentagon stint.

"He's exceptionally bright," the Captain once remarked to Walker. "I think he'll do a hell of a job as an airline manager—we need brains around here."

But those good intentions were overwhelmed by his refusal to let go. Walker admits today that everyone, himself included, should have seen it coming—Rickenbacker had made the same remarks about Tom Armstrong and then refused to give him one iota of authority. It reached the point where Armstrong told Walker one day, "Damn it, Brad, I don't have anything to do—I'd rather go back and just be the treasurer again."

The difference between Armstrong and MacIntyre, of course, was that the latter *did* have authority. And the trouble was that the directors, in providing him with power, never really took much away from Captain Eddie; it was a perfect environment in which to mature the seeds of friction and not even Rockefeller could prevent it—one does not tamper with an institution, which is precisely what Captain Eddie was, unless one also is willing to risk destroying it.

MacIntyre was smart enough to recognize Eastern's weaknesses and gutsy enough to do something about them. With Brad Walker's aid he mapped out a new advertising campaign pegged to the theme "New Things Are Happening at Eastern Air Lines" and emphasizing improved ground services instead of Rickenbacker's beloved dependability-and-experience pitch. More efficient handling of baggage and reservations, self-ticketing, faster check-ins, simpler timetables, and more realistic scheduling to achieve better on-time departures—these were all measures instituted in 1960. Admittedly they were stopgaps designed to maintain the airline's competitive status until the fleet could be modernized.

The first equipment decision MacIntyre made also was of the stopgap variety—he ordered fifteen Boeing 720 jetliners, a slightly smaller version of the 707, twelve to be delivered before the end of 1961 and the remainder of early 1963. Of the fifteen, however, ten would be owned by the Prudential Insurance Company and leased to Eastern. Charlie Foresch didn't really like the 720; he considered it underpowered and not really designed for EAL's route structure, but he agreed with Mr. Mac that the Boeing had one major advantage: It was available for quick delivery and could serve as an interim jet until Douglas could fill the rest of Eastern's DC-8 orders. The 720 literally was an "off-the-shelf" airplane.

Froesch's heart and soul were wrapped up in another Boeing design—the three-engine 727, whose design carried considerable Froesch input. The 727 concept dated back to 1956 when Boeing, immersed in the 707 program, still found time for some preliminary design work on a smaller, short-to-medium range jet transport. In June of 1959 Froesch told a top Boeing engineer that Eastern would be interested in such an airplane; he mentioned that it might be something like the French Caravelle, whose twin engines were aft-mounted on the fuselage, except that he preferred three engines—thus leading Boeing to ask the obvious question: "Where the hell do we put the third engine?"

Boeing from the start envisioned the two-engine design but Froesch, with support from TWA, was adamant on rejecting this plan. He pointed out that Eastern would never operate two-engine equipment on an overwater route such as New York–Puerto Rico and would have to have four engines or preferably three. United, incidentally, was insisting on four and American wanted two. The argument was going on heatedly when Britain suddenly announced plans to build a three-engine jet called the Trident and Froesch didn't let Boeing forget that if the British could do it (the third engine was buried in, and was fed air via a duct hooked to an inlet on top of the rear fuselage), so could Boeing.

Froesch kept pouring ideas, suggestions, and demands into the Seattle hatchery. He wanted the original cabin design lengthened by forty inches, and he proposed a "T" tail that would raise the surfaces clear of jet-stream vibration. He insisted on over-sized wheel brakes and above all on performance characteristics that would let the plane utilize La Guardia with its relatively short runways. There would be no compromise on this demand, he informed Boeing. To meet that specification, Boeing redesigned the wing, installing triple-slotted rear flaps which achieved the near-impossible task of turning a wing swept back thirty-two degrees for high-speed cruise into a wing with a twenty-five percent greater area for low-speed approaches. To this design Boeing added forward-edge flaps as well, leading one pilot to comment after his first 727 flight, "On this airplane you don't lower the flaps—you disassemble the whole damned wing."

When United and American finally gave in on the three-engine concept, the 727 was set for production and an honored place in aviation history—today it is the best-selling jet transport ever built and by any standard of measurement can be called legitimately the DC-3 of the jet age. Eastern ordered forty, but only after MacIntyre went to the mat with Captain Eddie in one of the worst arguments they were to have during Mr. Mac's tenure.

The recommendation for the forty-aircraft purchase came from Lethridge, who at the time was executive vice president in charge of schedules, planning, properties, and community relations. In addition, he proposed taking an option on ten more planes and MacIntyre bought the entire plan.

"I guess we'd better go see the Captain on this," MacIntyre suggested.

Lethridge will never forget the meeting. Rickenbacker listened for a few minutes, then shook his head.

"You don't need more than twenty," he decreed positively.

Lethridge was stunned but MacIntyre became angry. The session degenerated into acrimonious name-calling and became so heated that at one point MacIntyre was threatening to resign if the Captain didn't accept the plan. It was Lethridge who finally calmed both of them down by employing a little strategy he had learned from Paul Brattain.

"If things are going wrong with the Captain and he gets irritable," Brattain had advised, "just close your briefcase and tell him, 'That's it, sir.' Nine times out of ten he'll back off."

While Mr. Mac and EVR were yelling at each other, Lethridge suddenly started gathering his papers on the 727 and putting them into his briefcase.

"What the hell do you think you're doing?" EVR demanded.

"I guess I've lost the argument, Captain. My people have been working on this for months and I think we're right but you think we're wrong and that's that."

"Let me have those papers, Lefty," Rickenbacker growled.

MacIntyre, sensing the wind shift, nodded. "Give him the papers."

Lethridge complied. This was on a Friday, and Monday morning Captain Eddie summoned them to his office. "Go ahead on your forty airplanes," he announced. "I don't know about those ten options—let's wait awhile."

MacIntyre wasn't bluffing when he threatened to resign. He knew Boeing would not go into 727 production unless it received orders for at least 100 airplanes, and Pat Patterson had told him United wanted only twenty with an option for another twenty. A firm Eastern order for forty plus ten options would bring the conditional total up to ninety and Boeing was willing to accept that. Mr. Mac knew that if Eastern reduced its order, the whole 727 program probably would go out the window and he also knew that EAL badly needed the airplane. Under those circumstances he was very ready to challenge Rickenbacker, even to the extent of a "him or me" ultimatum to the directors.

It never came to that, of course, but the MacIntyre-Rickenbacker feud erupted over other issues—Lethridge, like a man plugging a leak that would reopen instantly through an unsuspected break, would help resolve one dispute only to have another burst out. It got so bad that even their secretaries became involved. MacIntyre had brought his own secretary over to Eastern and Captain Eddie, of course, had his Sheppy.

"If you got a call from one," Frank Sharpe says, "the other would call wanting to know what the other one wanted."

Yet some of the more serious friction resulted not from open disputes but from Rickenbacker's over-confidence in his own grasp of strategy and policy.

Something of this kind seems to have occurred when the CAB was considering the Southern Transcontinental Route Case, a proceeding to award new authority between the west coast and Atlanta and Miami—briefly, one-carrier coast-to-coast service for the South. It was vital for Eastern to win this one; it already had been shafted in the original southern transcontinental case and its route development had stagnated in direct proportion to the rapid growth of such rivals as Delta and National.

Public hearings had been concluded shortly before MacIntyre joined Eastern and he made it a point to be briefed thoroughly on the case and what it meant to the airline. He had been president for only a few months when Rickenbacker suggested they fly down to Atlanta.

"I'm going to introduce you to the leading lights there," he promised. "We need their support if we're going to win that case."

According to MacIntyre they went to a swank luncheon club where the Captain, fortified by a few martinis, got up and made an impromptu speech.

"John Kennedy had just been elected," MacIntyre recalls. "When Rickenbacker got up he forgot I was along and launched into a big speech about the whole Kennedy family being a bunch of traitors. I came home and told my wife we weren't going to win anything in the Southern Transcontinental Case and I was right—in a regulated world, one injudicious remark can kill you."

Every time he asked EVR about the case and whether Eastern should be doing more to help win it, MacIntyre adds, Captain Eddie would airily dismiss the matter.

"I know the right people," he assured Mr. Mac. "Just leave everything to me."

"So I left everything to him," MacIntyre says with some bitterness. "Delta and National got everything. We got nothing."

Defeat in the Southern Transcontinental Case—the CAB decision came in 1961—wasn't the only blow Eastern absorbed under MacIntyre. In 1960 three adverse events hit the airline in relatively quick succession, although none could be remotely associated with his administration. The first involved the structural difficulties of the Electra, resulting in speed restrictions and a general black eye in the public's mind. Passengers actually boycotted Electra flights in alarming numbers; on Eastern alone, Electra load factors dropped from a normal seventy-five percent to below fifty percent.

The Electra mystery had been solved and corrective measures were well underway when death slipped through a sliver of a loophole and demolished Eastern's own perfect safety record with the propjet. The date was October 4, 1960, and the aircraft involved was operating as Flight 375 from Boston's Logan International Airport to New York and points south. The captain was Curtis Fitts, a veteran from the Mailwing days, but not even his thousands of hours logged could prevent what happened. Exactly 47.5 seconds after Fitts told the tower "Three seventy-five, rolling," the Electra was under the waters of Boston Harbor and of the seventy-two aboard, only ten survived.

The takeoff had been normal but just as the plane broke ground, it faltered and yawed. It continued to climb, but only for a few seconds. The left wing dropped, the Electra fell into a half-roll, and plunged into the bay. Unlike the other Electra accidents this one was solved quickly: bird ingestion, of sufficient proportions to cause a momentary but critical loss of power in three of the four engines. The power loss had occurred at the most critical stage—Flight 375 was too high to abort the takeoff and too low to climb out of trouble. If the birds had hit the engines five seconds earlier or five seconds later, there would have been no crash—as it was, only a few more feet of altitude would have given Fitts enough room to put the nose down, pick up a little speed, and then climb out of danger. It is interesting to note that government investigators, in the course of determining the cause of the Boston accident, put sixteen senior Electra captains into an L-188 simulator and recreated the circumstances that had befallen Flight 375.

First, impact with the birds fifty-six feet off the ground. Number-one engine loses power and autofeathers. Numbers two and four lose all power for about six seconds. Number three falters just long enough for the electrical system to quit, and this was the key to 375's fate.

The Electra's hydraulic system is activated electrically and will operate so long as at least one engine is functioning normally. In this instance, however, there probably was a multiple power loss in all four engines, the equivalent of turning off the ignition in an automobile and losing all power steering. True, number three faltered for not more than a second, and the hydraulic boost system was reactivated as soon as the power surged back to normal. But at this particular moment Fitts was trying to correct the left bank into which the aircraft had been thrown when the two engines on the left side flamed out. He would have been on hard right rudder and full right aileron just when the boost system was restored—and the result would have been an uncontrolled roll and stall at an altitude too low to permit recovery.

This was the deadly chain of circumstances fed into the Electra simulator, to see how the sixteen exceptionally skilled Electra pilots could handle the situation without any warning of what was going to happen.

All sixteen "crashed" on their first try.

The investigators then tried another experiment. It was possible, they thought, that number three engine never did quit because a surviving stewardess had testified that the cabin lights never went out. In that case there would have been no interruption of hydraulic boost. So they fed into the simulator, again without warning, the same Boston accident data, but this time with full power on number three. It made little difference; a handful of pilots managed to avoid a crash but the majority still couldn't keep the simulator under control. A total sixty-six simulated takeoffs were made and while most pilots did better as they gained experience with the reproduced conditions, it was strictly because they had some warning of what was going to happen. Fitts had had no such warning—and paid the price.

While the Boston tragedy in no way resembled the other Electra crashes, it still added darker hues to the plane's damaged public image and for Eastern, operating the world's largest Electra fleet, this was disastrous. And so was another calamity occurring in 1960—a twelve-day wildcat strike by EAL's pilots that cost the airline $8 million in lost revenue and the pilots their precious rapport with Eastern's management.

The walkout was ill-advised; even the Air Line Pilots Association declined to support it and for a very logical reason—the dispute which ignited it was of a rather petty nature and reflected not a quarrel with EAL but with the then new Federal Aviation Agency and its tough administrator, Elwood R. "Pete" Quesada. The former Air Force general was running his powerful, independent agency like a no-nonsense police chief and had started cracking down on flight crews almost as soon as he took office. One of his edicts was an increase in check rides by FAA inspectors, on jets especially and including Eastern's DC-8 cockpits. There was one small problem: The inspectors insisted on occupying the seat normally used by the third pilot—and the fur flew.

Eastern's DC-8's were manned by a four-man crew, a policy directly traceable to Rickenbacker's anxiety to placate the flight engineers without alienating the pilots; that was how the 1958 dispute had been settled. Thus every EAL DC-8 had three pilots and a flight engineer, although the third pilot had virtually no duties other than to be present if one of his cohorts had a coronary. He occupied a seat just behind the captain, and when the FAA inspectors said they had to sit there because it was easier to monitor crew activities from that position, the pilots objected. It was their contention that an inspector could see just as well from a jump seat located opposite the flight engineer's station, behind the third pilot, as they did on other transport planes.

It was this game of cockpit musical chairs that caused the illegal strike—when the FAA refused to give in, Eastern's pilots walked out claiming that safety was involved. The strike lasted less than two weeks, but coupled as it was with Eastern's overall problems and the third unfavorable event—the 1960 recession —its results were harmful enough to spoil MacIntyre's first full year on the job. For the first time in twenty-six years the airline failed to make a profit, losing more than $3.6 million despite the second highest revenues in the company's history. Were it not for the pilot's strike EAL would have finished in the black, and MacIntyre was understandably embittered.

He had never been a patient man and he lacked Ricken-backer's charisma with the rank and file, not to mention the majority of his officers. To a man they not only respected his intelligence but marveled at it. "I pride myself on handling figures," Charlie Simons comments, "but I couldn't match Mac-Intyre."

"He had many fine qualities," John Halliburton says, "such as the most brilliant mind I've ever known. With that agile brain of his, he thought so much farther ahead of the average person that sometimes you'd come out of his office with a misunderstanding of what actually had been agreed. I got burned on this a couple of times and always went over it with him."

Mr. Mac could be tough and cutting. A few weeks after he came to the airline, he called Halliburton in Miami. "I'm coming down there tomorrow, John, and I want you to get your department heads together and set up a luncheon at some hotel."

The lunch was duly scheduled, the dishes had been cleared, and MacIntyre opened fire, aiming right at Halliburton.

"There's one thing I want you to get straight right now," he said. "Operations is no longer running this company."

Halliburton, suspecting that somebody had been feeding Mr. Mac a line of propaganda, replied, "Well, Mr. MacIntyre, in the first place I never knew that operations *was* running this company."

MacIntyre once got into an argument with Halliburton over some issue, so minor that Halliburton now doesn't remember what it was. But Mr. Mac became angry and finally snapped, "You don't have enough sense to come out of the rain." The next day Bob Turner called Halliburton to relay MacIntyre's apology.

"Mr. Mac doesn't have to apologize," Halliburton said, "but if he thinks he should, I'd appreciate his calling me himself."

He didn't, but six months later MacIntyre asked Halliburton's opinion on some matter foreign to the operations department. "I'm surprised you're asking me," Halliburton commented. "Not too long ago you told me I didn't have enough sense to come out of the rain."

MacIntyre laughed. "John, I don't always mean what I say."

After a few early misgivings some of the veterans, like Halliburton, Lethridge, and Sharpe, began to like him as a person. He was almost as bad as Captain Eddie when it came to reaming somebody out, but like EVR his anger seldom lasted and he was not one to hold a grudge. He jumped all over Lethridge one day and then apparently figured he might have been too rough.

"Lefty, you've got to be a son-of-a-bitch at least once a week," he smiled in half-apology.

"Yeah," Lethridge sighed, "but I wish you'd pick any day but Friday—you've ruined my whole weekend."

They all admired him for constantly trying, for his willingness to attempt new ideas and methods, his open-mindedness to fresh approaches. Not that they agreed with many of them. Sharpe, for example, thought he invited ill-feeling and a certain amount of dissension by openly stressing the lack of college graduates in Eastern's management corps. There wasn't any doubt that a need existed—when MacIntyre asked the personnel department to give him company records on college graduates, the answer was ten out of some twenty thousand employees, excluding pilots. Word of this survey got out, accompanied by a rumor that he was going to replace, with college-trained youngsters, a horde of old-timers who had come up from the ranks. No such mass turnover took place, but morale was affected nevertheless. MacIntyre's reasoning was that the airline had no real management training system, with too many lower-echelon promotions based on seniority rather than ability.

Gradually he did away with the never-to-be-forgotten mass staff meetings, although he enjoyed the first one he held—everyone sang the current song hit, "Mack the Knife." But he didn't think they were very productive and he phased them out; his policy was to move deliberately away from Rickenbacker's more personal style of management toward a system in which more decisions were left to individuals. While the staff meetings lasted, however, they uncovered in full view of everyone the festering Rickenbacker-MacIntyre feud—it became quickly apparent that their dislike was mutual and they didn't bother to hide it.

Dick Fisher was a witness to the bad blood between the two. Staff meetings had always been EVR's business, but when MacIntyre took over, he told Fisher exactly how he wanted the head table arranged. Fisher knew the Captain was vitally interested in such matters as where to place certain officers and he noticed that MacIntyre's list was not the way Captain Eddie would have done it. Playing it safe, he gave the list to Sheppy, adding, "Run this by the Captain."

He heard nothing from Rickenbacker and figured he had approved—not knowing that Sheppy had forgotten to give him the list or had misplaced it. Fisher came into the banquet room, took one look at EVR's thundercloud-hued face, and knew he was in for trouble.

Rickenbacker waved his arm in the direction of the seating cards at the head table. "Whose idea was this?"

Fisher saw Sheppy standing behind the Captain and didn't want to involve her.

"Captain, didn't you know about the head-table arrangements?" he hedged.

"Whose idea was this?" Rickenbacker repeated.

"But Captain, I thought you knew about this well in advance."

"Who told you to do it this way?" Captain Eddie said, his voice trembling.

Fisher surrendered. "Mr. MacIntyre."

Rickenbacker glared and pointed a finger at him as if he were pointing an assassin's gun. In a loud and deliberate voice, he said, "Let the chips fall where they may!"

EVR was, after all, chairman of the board, and Fisher figured he was going to be fired. He turned away sadly and was walking out of the room when MacIntyre stopped him.

"Well, Dick, how are things going?" he asked pleasantly.

"I don't think very well," Fisher said. "The chairman of the board is going to fire me."

"What?"

"Mr. MacIntyre, he's very upset about the head-table seating arrangements."

MacIntyre laughed. "Don't worry about that, son. Now, what's the program for the evening?"

Encouraged by MacIntyre's casual reaction, Fisher told him it was Rickenbacker's birthday. "We have a large cake for the occasion," he added.

Now it was MacIntyre who turned livid.

"What do you mean, a big cake?" he shouted. "Don't you know the problems I'm having trying to manage this airline without the Rickenbacker image over everything? And now you've got a big cake for him and . . . !"

To this day Fisher believes Sheppy did show the Captain the seating chart, and that he just wanted to find out in his own way who had done it. Admittedly, a head-table arrangement and a birthday cake are petty argumentative points, but they also were symbolic of the MacIntyre-Rickenbacker relationship. MacIntyre himself says EVR's interference was more subtle than direct.

"The problem was that a great many people at Eastern were beholden to him," Mr. Mac says. "He had his own intelligence network and he'd feed stuff back to the opposition. As I look back on those years, I realize I should have insisted that the board of directors be changed. Second, I should have written off through depreciation all our prop planes—taken a blood bath and blamed it on the previous management, which deserved the blame. Instead I tried to make money depreciating just aircraft that were already obsolete; in effect, I tried to make money with Connies in a jet world."

That wasn't all he tried. He began a full-scale campaign to "make first class something more than just a wide seat," as he put it. He improved meal service in first class and installed special ground lounges at such major traffic points as New York, Atlanta, and Miami where no one could enter unless he or she possessed a first-class ticket on an Eastern flight. These were the forerunners of what were to become the Falcon Lounges—they are now Ionosphere Rooms.

Throughout his tenure he labored under two handicaps he could not control—Rickenbacker, and the general economic climate which wreaked havoc with virtually the entire industry during his first two years. That Eastern, with its short route structure and reliance on seasonal markets, was particularly vulnerable, was not his fault—he recognized the airline's weaknesses and did his best to correct them, as the massive 727 purchase demonstrated. Yet the very pressure under which he was forced to operate led to some bad decisions, not to mention a personal failing which is painful to relate but essential in any objective account of the men responsible for Eastern's destinies.

He had, to put it as bluntly as possible, a drinking problem in those tense days. It must be added quickly that he didn't have one when he came to Eastern. Virtually every former associate of his who was interviewed in the course of the research for this history is convinced that Rickenbacker's persistent second-guessing, interference, and sniping literally drove MacIntyre to drink.

He began consuming several martinis at lunch and would come back to his office raising hell and making impulsive decisions that defied common sense. Lefty Lethridge, when he accompanied Mr. Mac to lunch, used to sneak away to a phone just before they returned to the office and report on how many martinis MacIntyre had downed. He was quick-tempered anyway, and intoxication made him worse. The strange thing is that while his subordinates disapproved of his drinking and feared its consequences, they understood why he drank, and managed to live with it. There was even sympathy toward him.

Harper Woodward, who came on the EAL board in 1961 as Rockefeller's replacement, was a firsthand observer of the tortures MacIntryre was going through. He had known Mr. Mac when he was a top lawyer in New York and when he was at the Pentagon.

"He was a very good lawyer," Woodward says, "exceptionally bright. Pete Quesada once told me, 'If you're the chief executive of a company and one of your directors gets your goat, you're dead.' Well, Eddie got Mac's goat and it damned near killed the poor guy. He was terribly frustrated because he couldn't do a lot of things, and he made some mistakes.

"He went to lunch one day, for example, had a few martinis, and got to wondering what he could do for employees. So he thought up the idea of giving them unlimited pass privileges. Once you've done this, you can only move in one direction—my God, we spent years trying to get out from under this. There were times when we didn't have enough room for paying passengers. Mac had a lot of ideas, but most of them were impractical. The shuttle was his baby but it was also his mistake thinking that the appeal was its low fare. All our surveys showed the fare had nothing to do with its popularity and we lost money flying full loads. Today the shuttle yield is sixteen cents a mile, and when Mac started it, the yield was only six cents."

Woodward took Rockefeller's place on the board, incidentally, at the latter's own request. Rockefeller felt his presence was a handicap, not an asset. As he told Woodward, "These route decisions going against us are all political—if I'm there as a Rockefeller, I'm sort of a negative influence, so why don't you go on as my replacement?"

They sounded Rickenbacker out on the idea while lunching at the Louis XIV Restaurant, the Captain's favorite dining spot —they always had a table reserved for him and even when he was missing in the Pacific, the owners refused to let anyone else sit there.

"That's the greatest idea I've ever heard," Captain Eddie declared. "Laurance, you're a real handicap to me—you're in the wrong politics and everything else. Now Harper will be wonderful—nobody's ever heard of him."

He was wrong if he thought Rockefeller was going to stay

out of his way. In the sense of wielding tremendous influence on the airline's fortunes, the Woodward-for-Rockefeller substitution changed nothing; Rockefeller had complete trust and confidence in his associate, and Woodward made sure he was advised of everything that was happening at Eastern.

While many of MacIntyre's—and Eastern's—problems were legacies from previous policies and decisions, not all were inherited. Lethridge tells of a call he got from Mr. Mac one day.

"I want to start a morning, noon, and night schedule between New York and Charlotte using Electras," he informed his vice president of scheduling.

"Mac," Lefty warned, "it'll take five or six airplanes and they won't run half-full."

According to Lethridge, MacIntyre just "blew his stack" at the opposition. Lethridge told his scheduling supervisor, "This is it, man—assume the position."

"So we ripped a couple of airplanes out of the schedule pattern," Lefty continues, "and inside of six weeks it fell flat on its ass—there simply weren't enough passengers. All these experimentations were disruptive and helped create confusion and turmoil among employees, which in turn resulted in a poor service. I'll have to admit that Mac made tremendous improvements in food service, and the same with stewardess appearance and attitude. But there were times when he had everyone running in four different directions—I remember John Halliburton telling him once, 'Mac, you can't run sixteen hundred pilots up the hill in one direction and then order them to turn to the left and go another three hundred feet.'

"Yet it wasn't all Mac's fault. One of the major reasons for Eastern's decline starting with the 1960s was the Captain's failure to have continuity in management. MacIntyre had to go through a learning period just at a critical time—Eastern couldn't afford the luxury of treading water while he learned. Hell, he was a lawyer, not an operations man nor a salesman. Some of the things he did were out of sheer desperation because he didn't have the experience to judge whether they were worth a damn."

. Lethridge was not afraid to challenge MacIntyre, and neither was Tom Creighton, who had replaced Armstrong as treasurer and vice president of finance after Armstrong's retirement in 1960. Mr. Mac quarreled with both frequently, and at one point he put Lefty on probation. Yet just before he left Eastern, when Lethridge and Creighton went into his office to say good-bye, MacIntyre told them, "I'd be better off if I had listened to you two guys instead of those I did listen to."

For all his penchant for innovating, MacIntyre could be the epitome of conservatism on occasion. That side of him may have cost Eastern dearly in 1960—a chance to grab some of failing Capital Airline's routes when they were up for grabs. He was conferring with Lethridge and their conversation was interrupted by a telephone call from C. E. Woolman of Delta. Woolman had an interesting reason for calling—Delta's Bill Costello (who once worked for Eastern as a pilot trainee and would join the airline later as a vice president) had put together a plan to split up Capital's routes among three carriers—Delta, Northwest, and Eastern.

"Capital's going under," Woolman informed MacIntyre. "Northwest's interested and if we can get Eastern in on the plan, I think we can get the CAB to approve it. They wouldn't go for one or two carriers taking over but splitting Capital's system among three is a different matter—there'd still be some competition and the three of us could absorb most of Capital's people."

Woolman's analysis made a lot of sense. Capital was in hock to Vickers, the British aircraft manufacturer, for $34 million still owed on the airline's Viscount fleet, and Vickers was threatening to foreclose. Bankruptcy appeared to be the only alternative to the canny Woolman's Delta-Eastern-Northwest acquisition plan. But MacIntyre, according to Lethridge, was in a sour, irritable, unreceptive mood and he first reacted with disinterest.

He apparently had some second thoughts, because Costello says an agreement actually was worked out, only to fall apart when MacIntyre realized Eastern's 1960 balance sheet was being printed in red ink. He regretfully informed Delta and Northwest that Eastern couldn't take on the expansion involved in acquisition, nor raise the cash required to pay off EAL's share of Capital's huge debt. These were trying times for MacIntyre and he had even worse ones coming up.

On February 18, 1961, the Flight Engineers International Association struck seven carriers—Eastern, along with American, Flying Tiger, National, Pan American, TWA, and Western. The walkout erupted after the National Mediation Board ruled that all jet cockpit crews should be represented by a single collective bargaining unit. It was a solar plexus blow to FEIA, which stood no chance of winning any representation contest with the much larger ALPA, but the strike itself was an equally damaging blow at Eastern, still hamstrung by its short-haul, predominantly north–south route structure, its lack of modern jet equipment, its top-level internecine feuding. The strike lasted only six days and ended when President Kennedy named a special fact-finding commission, headed by Professor Nathan Feinsinger of the University of Wisconsin, to investigate and recommend a final solution to the crew complement issue. A six-day strike to a prosperous carrier like American was serious but far from crippling; on beleagured Eastern, it had an economic impact equivalent to a six-week shutdown.

The FEIA mess was followed by Delta and National winning awards in the Southern Transcontinental Case, which EVR really expected to win. Some of his misplaced confidence may have stemmed from what he regarded as Smythe Gambrell's finest performance, at the conclusion of the Board's public hearings. Bob Six still remembers that day with mingled admiration and amusement:

"Eddie sat in the front row, holding the old, battered felt hat in his hands, while Gambrell went into an impassioned plea about the Captain being in the twilight of his career—'ready for his last flight,' I think was the way Gambrell phrased it. It would have drawn tears from a statue, although what the hell it had to do with the merits of Eastern's case was something else."

There were pitifully few bright spots in the year, the chief one being the somewhat surprising achievement of Eastern leading all major airlines in on-time performance, almost a miracle considering EAL's route system. Another was the birth of the Air-Shuttle and the beginning of the phase-out of the Connie and DC-7 fleet. But in general Eastern continued its downhill slide. It would wind up 1961 with a net loss of $9.6 million—the six-day flight-engineers' strike cost the airline $5.5 million in lost revenue. It was no wonder that Mr. Mac couldn't stir up much more than a ceremonial expression of regret when a man who had played such a colorful role in the company's past walked away from the left seat in an Eastern cockpit for the last time—that was Dick Merrill.

He didn't want to retire; he was forced to by FAA Administrator Quesada's mandatory retirement rule for all airline pilots reaching the age of sixty. When he signed off his final EAL log, it showed 36,650 hours of flying time, but no logbook can be a pilot's true biography. Merrill lived the kind of life that a movie scriptwriter would have rejected as too unbelievable. He had flown mail planes. He had crossed the Atlantic twice in single-engine aircraft, the first a 1936 New York–Wales hop with entertainer Harry Richman in a plane whose wings and rear fuselage were packed with three thousand ping pong balls to provide buoyancy in the event that they were forced down; the second a crossing with fellow EAL pilot Jack Lambie to England, where they picked up pictures of King George VI's coronation and flew them back for delivery to the U.S. press—a feat which earned them the 1937 Harmon trophy.

His final Eastern flight was a New York–Miami DC-8 trip —a long way from the Pitcairn Mailwing. He was to tell interviewers later that his favorite airplane in all his years of flying was the Electra; the choice was not surprising, for Merrill had defended the embattled propjet when it was the subject of congressional hearings as to its safety. The latter occasion was merely one of many in which Captain Eddie had utilized Merrill's charisma with the news media, his bent for good public relations, and his so very likeable—and believable—personality. Merrill flew virtually every Eastern inaugural trip that came along, and also special VIP flights, all on Rickenbacker's orders.

The pilot asked EVR one day, "Dammit, Eddie, am I the only airline pilot around here?"

"No," Rickenbacker replied, "and I don't even think you're the best. But I know one thing—you're the luckiest."

Lucky he was—but also skilled. He worshiped the Captain and the deep affection was mutual. No one was happier than Captain Eddie when the swinging, gambling pilot finally abandoned bachelorhood and married a movie actress—who else?—named Toby Wing, who was to bear him a son and give up her own promising career.

Twenty years after his retirement he still was as peppery a figure as ever, spiffy in the rather loud sport coats he loved to wear. At eighty he passed the tough FAA first-class physical and had already logged an additional eight thousand hours since he'd left the airline, flying everything from supersonic fighters to Eastern's new A-300 Airbus. The airline used him frequently as a kind of unofficial ambassador; for several years he stayed on the payroll, although not on a captain's salary, on Rickenbacker's orders. Unlike later retirees, he did not have a generous pension and wound up taking a job as curator at the Shannon Air Museum in Fredericksburg, Virginia, owned by Sid Shannon's son. In his career was the story of commercial aviation—and beyond that he came close to being a symbol for an airline pilot's ideal.

If safety came first to Dick Merrill, consideration for his passengers ran a not-too-distant second. It was ironic that he worked for a man and for an airline who both acquired a reputation of indifference toward the customer. He had a regular clientele of passengers who went out of their way to book his flights; he knew many of them by their first names. To Merrill, inconveniencing a passenger was a cardinal sin. More than once, in the more informal DC-3 days, he falsified fuel loads on his dispatch clearances so he wouldn't have to offload anyone because of extra fuel requirements. He would come into Charleston late at night, for example, and Dispatch would tell him some passengers en route to New York would have to get off because the weather in New York was bad and he would need a full fuel load for safety reasons.

"Go ahead and top [fill up] the tanks," he'd tell Dispatch, "but show me carrying four hundred gallons." That figure was below the DC-3's capacity but it made the takeoff legal with a full complement of passengers—and Merrill was one of the few pilots who could get the usually hard-nosed dispatchers to go along with this chicanery.

If Rickenbacker mourned his departure as the passing of a glorious era, MacIntyre didn't have the time. Late in 1961 he managed to get away for a few days of vacation with his wife, Clara—it was mostly at her urging because she could see what the constant stress was doing to him. This was the side of airline life she hated; the rest she enjoyed, for Clara MacIntyre was proud of her husband's position and almost from the start of his regime she was determined to involve herself in the company's affairs. For example, she became interested in communicating with the wives of EAL officials and started the "Eastern Officers' Wives Association"—one of many projects she dreamed up as a means of getting employees to know her and her husband better.

Mrs. Mac's most ambitious endeavor was a cookbook, for which she solicited recipes from around the system. John de Rose, a thirty-year veteran with EAL, was sales promotion manager in New York at the time of the cookbook project—he remembers nobody liked the title, *Jet-Set Cookbook*. It sold for around two dollars, was printed as a paperback on good stock, and de Rose was named head of a committee to cull recipe submissions. They had to engage a cookbook firm with kitchen facilities to test them and the final product contained about 100 pages.

"It didn't sell very well even though guys were being pushed by their wives to buy several copies," de Rose says. "The most awful recipe sent in was something with shark meat as the main ingredient and so help me, I think it would have poisoned a shark. But Mrs. MacIntyre insisted on including it because we served Bermuda and she thought the recipe would be good promotion. Believe me, when she got involved in something, she got involved—the damned cookbook had top priority and she was on our backs constantly during the production process. We had to cooperate—my God, she was the president's wife!"

Clara MacIntyre was fiercely protective of her husband and terribly anxious for him to succeed. There were those at Eastern who thought she carried her zeal too far, but they admired her spunk.

"She was especially interested in the Shuttle," Frank Stulgaitis recollects. "She became its official monitor—she'd ride the flights, turn in reports on service, and even check the restrooms in the terminals."

The Shuttle.

It became almost an obsession with MacIntyre, as we shall see in the next chapter. He seemed to feel his success or failure as Eastern's president hinged on this massive experiment. And he had good reason for betting so heavily on the outcome, because in virtually every other area the airline was in a nose dive. So great a dive that, without his knowing it, the maneuvering began for the most drastic action of all—a merger with American Airlines.

Officially the merger was proposed toward the end of 1961—preliminary negotiations and exploratory talks had been going on behind the scenes, apparently, for some time, but the first MacIntyre heard about it was when he returned from the previously mentioned vacation. His initial reaction was almost totally negative—because, he told associates, the CAB would never permit a marriage between two of the nation's largest carriers. But he had to go through the motions of supporting it because it was only too apparent that EAL's directors, and Rockefeller, too, thought it was Eastern's only course.

The impetus seems to have come from American. One longtime Eastern official, who prefers to go unnamed, says he was sitting in a restaurant one day and overheard C. R. Smith and a top American vice president discussing plans to merge with Eastern—"and this was at least three years before any merger proposal was made public," he adds.

Rockefeller readily admits he spearheaded negotiations with C.R. and that neither Rickenbacker nor MacIntyre was brought in on the earliest talks. There were reasons for this: Rockefeller knew there was no love lost between Smith and the Captain, and he also suspected that MacIntyre wouldn't be happy with the merger unless he wound up as chief executive of the merged company, something C.R. might not have allowed.

"C.R. actually told Mac," Rockefeller says, that 'I know you're one of the best airline lawyers in the business but I don't know if you're a good airline president and I'd have to find out.' "

Rockefeller was optimistic that the merger, opposed by virtually the entire airline industry, would be approved, simply because he had in his figurative hip pocket the tacit approval of President Kennedy. The catch was that JFK attached one large condition—he'd okay a merger agreement, assuming the CAB would send it to him approved, if his brother Bobby also bought it.

"His dear brother," Rockefeller adds, "said no." But by that time the merger attempt was on an irrevocable course. When the bulk of the merger debate was in progress, Eastern was in even worse shape in 1962 than ever before. And as it struggled for survival on its own, the desperate thrashings generated some moves that would come back to help defeat the merger.

One of them was a deliberate policy to overschedule, so as to drown the opposition under a flood of flight frequencies. It was justified in the sense that it compensated for the lack of modern equipment, but it also was self-defeating—tremendously expensive, with insufficient load factors to make up for the huge operating costs.

Smack in the middle of the merger fight came the biggest disaster of all—another flight engineers' strike, this one a horrendous, bloodletting thirty-day affair that brought the airline to its knees with merger, indeed, appearing to be the only alternative to bankruptcy. It was ignited when, in accordance with the final decision of the Feinsinger Commission, Eastern reduced the jet crew complement from four to three men and laid down the requirement that the third man had to be pilot-trained even though his duties were that of a flight engineer. The net loss in

1962 would be $15 million and it made little difference that President Kennedy himself characterized the walkout as "the height of irresponsiblility" on the FEIA's part.

There was little disagreement with JFK's harsh criticism, but within Eastern itself the strike merely emphasized the mistake Rickenbacker had made when he went for a four-man crew against the advice of men like Halliburton and others. EVR's policy was in contrast to the way airlines like United and Delta had handled the touchy crew complement issue. Delta, for example, had decided to insist on pilot-trained flight engineers as far back as the piston days; Woolman had been the architect of that policy, with the argument that "you must never put a board on a man's head." He meant that a mechanic-engineer stood no chance of further promotion, whereas pilot-engineers could always achieve captaincies. Delta acquired the first four-engine transports requiring a three-man crew after merging with Chicago & Southern; Woolman gave the thirty flight engineers who had been working C & S Constellations the choice of transitioning to pilot training, reverting to the status of regular mechanics with no loss of seniority, or receiving a full year's severance pay if they didn't want either.

The major flaws in Rickenbacker's decision to go with a four-man crew were twofold: It added millions in extra operating costs that amounted to nothing more than paying for featherbedding, and it was a shaky compromise that merely delayed a final solution to the jurisdictional dispute. The unnecessary strike was its almost inevitable result.

The merger hearings themselves were a disaster of sorts. Six airlines formed the phalanx of the opposition, Delta leading the way and calling most of the antimerger strategy shots. It called so many shots, in fact, that at times it appeared that Delta was waging a one-airline fight against the merger, and at one point during the oral arguments Woolman became worried.

"Maybe you'd better let some of the other airlines ask a few questions," he told Dick Maurer, Delta's legal vice president.

"But Mr. Woolman," Maurer explained patiently, "we can't count on anybody asking the right questions."

"Just give 'em the questions," Woolman suggested.

The questions were built around Eastern's contention that it probably couldn't survive without a merger; the EAL case was aimed at repeating the strategy employed in the United-Capital merger proceeding, in which both those carriers hit hard on the argument that Capital was going to fail anyway. The trouble was that neither Eastern's nor American's witnesses could prove that Captain Eddie's airline was finished; both MacIntyre and Smith wound up admitting that the "failing business" concept didn't really apply to this merger.

Delta, with Maurer and attorney Frank Rox conducting the cross-examinations, hammered away with the argument that Eastern's troubles were largely of its own making and were not uncorrectable. They cited "Eastern's intentional delay in ordering jets," its policy of deliberate overscheduling, and its expensive efforts to improve its public image.

Much of the antimerger testimony appeared to be an indictment of both Rickenbacker and MacIntyre. A National exhibit, for example, showed that Mr. Mac's various image-improving moves had added up to a total cost of $57 million in additional expenses over a three-year period, causing unit costs and break-even load factors to rise sharply even as load factors declined sharply.

Ironically, two of Delta's key witnesses—finance vice president Todd Cole and Bill Costello, director of economic research—were to join Eastern's executive ranks in a few years as vice president. But during the merger hearings they were Eastern's relentless enemies. Cole was on the witness stand longer than any other opposition witness, explaining the voluminous exhibits he had prepared to emphasize the competitive impact of an American-Eastern combination and the source of Eastern's obvious economic difficulties; the latter, Cole kept repeating, were not so much due to the national economy or to EAL's posture in the industry, but rather were the result of certain management decisions, the Electra situation, the airline's tendency to fall behind in crucial equipment programs, and labor problems. If Eastern had not suffered an admittedly serious loss of markets because of equipment decisions and labor troubles, Cole said, it would be in much better shape and still could be if the merger were rejected.

Some of the backstage maneuvering would have made James Bond envious. Certain Eastern employees (or officers, perhaps) kept leaking confidential documents which somehow found their way into the hands of Delta's legal staff. One of Eastern's chief points, for example, was the claim that it didn't have the financial strength to spend so much as a dime toward improving the shuttle. Delta introduced a purchase order for hundreds of new seats for shuttle aircraft—an order which American didn't even know existed. The document apparently came from someone in Eastern.

"We'd get such stuff mailed or delivered to us by second persons in unmarked envelopes," Costello says. "They weren't really solid evidence and we had no way of knowing whether they were legitimate, but by using carefully framed questions it was possible to bring out their contents. In the case of the shuttle seats, it became obvious that American and Eastern weren't leveling with each other."

This, of course, was not only obvious but a vital indication of the merger proposal's principal weakness: It quickly became apparent that Eastern was the reluctant bride in this corporate marriage, the leaking of confidential material with antimerger implications by EAL personnel being just one manifestation of internal resistance. One Eastern employee somehow got his hands on engineering drawings showing how Eastern planned to shift all Electras over to the shuttle, using smaller seats. He gave them to someone at National who, in turn, passed them on to a Delta employee so the latter wouldn't know who at EAL had supplied them. Bob Winn of Eastern was on the stand denying that the Electras would be reconfigured for shuttle operations and persisted in the denial until Rox mentioned the name of the company which had supplied the drawings.

Another stolen document which found its way into Delta's clutches was a confidential letter Halliburton had sent to all EAL pilots. It was strictly an internal communication to the effect that

Eastern was going to smother the competition by stepping up schedule frequency so much that pilot vacations would have to be postponed. Delta leaped on this as evidence of EAL's predatory overscheduling practices and as a refutation of Eastern's and American's claim that overcertification of competitors on EAL's routes—in other words, excessive competition—was responsible for Eastern's financial crisis. The effectiveness of the leaked Halliburton letter as antimerger ammunition was demonstrated when CAB hearing examiner Ralph Wiser, in recommending merger rejection, listed overcapacity as a prime reason for Eastern's troubles and cited the Halliburton letter as specific proof.

Delta wisely split the cross-examination chores between Maurer and Rox; the former was a rather deceptively polite interrogator, while Rox could attack like an avenging prosecutor. The theory was that Maurer could use a rather gentle, statesmanlike approach while C.R. was testifying—after all, he was one of the nation's great airline pioneers—with Rox handling someone like MacIntyre who had a low boiling point and presumably would be easy to rile. Actually, MacIntyre held his temper better than anyone expected, even when Rox got him to list Eastern's twenty-six consecutive years of profit before he became president, then asked him whether there was any correlation between the first red-ink year of 1960 and "the fact that you became president that year." MacIntyre merely smiled and shook his head, but his wife became furious and according to one person present at the hearing that day had to be restrained from attacking the Delta lawyer.

Maurer treated C.R. with respect but still was tough when the occasion demanded. He spent a great deal of time trying to get Smith to admit that merger negotiations had been conducted secretly much longer than either Eastern or American was willing to say, and Smith's denials were not entirely convincing. Maurer had him on the stand virtually all of one day and Rox did likewise with MacIntyre. Surprisingly, Mr. Mac kept his cool but C.R. occasionally became irritated—Maurer believed he had expected to be questioned only briefly and wasn't really prepared for a polite but extensive grilling.

Some of Smith and MacIntyre's testimony showed that neither of their airlines had done all its homework. The proposed merger announcement had projected a savings of over $50 million in annual expenses and more than $100 million in capital investment. When Maurer questioned C.R. closely on this point, he was unable to produce any study which supported such estimates and Rox drew the same admission from MacIntyre. Maurer brought up Eastern's claim that the merger would result in a $15 million savings resulting from retirement of the Connies from the shuttle service, and asked C.R. whether the claim was valid. Smith conceded that he understood Eastern eventually would replace the Connies with Electras regardless of the merger. The cross-examination of the EAL and AA chiefs created a picture of alleged savings that could not be substantiated.

Many factors were responsible for the merger's ultimate defeat, not the least of which was Eastern and American's inability to refute the main argument raised against it: that it would create a giant controlling one third of the U.S. air transportation system. This single point brought the Department of Justice into solid opposition—Maurer heard reports that word was going around DOJ to "take a close look at this one—it's a dilly."

Eastern's chief thrust, that as a result of competitive awards invading its route structure it could not survive, fell apart when MacIntyre admitted it could. And far more telling was Delta's argument that poor management, not excessive competition, was at the root of EAL's dilemma.

Examiner Wiser's initial decision against merger cast a shadow of final defeat, but C.R. still had hopes. He came into American's Washington office one day after the hearings had ended and asked Dwight Taylor, one of his top route-development officers, how he thought the CAB would vote.

"It hasn't got a chance," Taylor said bluntly.

C.R. jammed his hat back on his bald head and stomped out. Taylor was the last man he should have asked for an optimistic appraisal, because months before Taylor had spent almost an hour telling him the merger was dead—Kennedy liberals were running Washington and to them the whole deal looked like the kind of power grab that would have been involved in a General Motors-Ford merger. It wouldn't be too long before Taylor would join Cole and Costello at Eastern.

Part of C.R.'s optimism was based on his long friendship with then Vice President Lyndon Johnson, but LBJ couldn't help him much. American made one last-ditch attempt to win approval by hiring attorney Lloyd Cutler to work out a special supplimentary proposal: a promise that if the merger was approved, American and Eastern would turn over fifteen cities to local-service airlines, and with CAB permission would also remove route restrictions at the junction points of the EAL-AA systems, thereby opening up nonstop authority. American's George Spater, who became president a few years later, was to comment that "if we could have gotten started on this earlier, I almost think we could have pulled it off. It proved a very basic lesson, though—it's pretty damned hard to put through a merger with an unwilling partner."

But the Cutler plan came too late and it's doubtful whether even its earlier introduction would have been enough to tip the scales. Wiser's decision, issued July 31, 1962, was not only negative but scathing. It was not until 1963 that the merger was finally put in the grave, although there was never an official CAB vote; American and Eastern simply withdrew the proposal before the CAB issued a verdict. According to Maurer, however, a vote was taken and it was unanimously against the merger—the two airlines were tipped off and withdrew their application before any public announcement could be made.

It cannot be said that MacIntyre was unhappy at the way it turned out. What he failed to realize was that the merger defeat was a prelude to his own Waterloo. Thwarted in the attempt to consolidate Eastern and American, EAL's directors looked for a scapegoat amid the company's declining fortunes. It was easy to find not just one but two—MacIntyre and Captain Eddie. Rockefeller, still off the board but still very much a power behind the throne, became convinced that they both had to go, and in that he had the support of the overwhelming majority of directors.

The execution was no quick or easy job—almost the entire year of 1963 was spent in searching for Mr. Mac's successor.

And while the search was going on, Eastern, saved from the corporate oblivion it would have suffered with American as the merger's surviving carrier, headed pell-mell toward financial oblivion. The 1963 net operating loss would hit almost $38 million, and there were only two bright spots—introduction of the Boeing 727, and the surprising acceptance of the Shuttle.

On both counts MacIntyre was to say, with shy pride, "I think I made a contribution."

He did. The Shuttle became his legacy and his monument—for what he contributed was not merely to Eastern but to the entire air transportation system.

CHAPTER TWELVE

THE SHUTTLE

It is doubtful whether any air transport innovation had more proclaimed (and self-proclaimed) fathers, mothers, godparents, and obstetricians than Eastern's Air-Shuttle.

By all standards of measurement the Shuttle has been the most successful marketing experiment in airline history—as well as the most daring and risky. At times it was the difference between red ink and black ink on the airline's ledgers. EAL is coy about disclosing specific profitability, explaining that exact cost allocation is difficult to pin down because some of its ground equipment, aircraft, and personnel are also utilized for regular schedules, but without question it *is* a money maker.

More important, the Shuttle has become an institution, totally unique in its original concept and still adhering to the basic ingredients of that concept: no reservations, on-board ticketing, and guaranteed space even if it requires one multi-million-dollar airplane to carry a single person. That was, and still is, the formula for its success. The Shuttle, quite literally, became a transportation way of life in the heavily traveled Washington–New York–Boston corridor; the very phrase "I'll catch the

Shuttle" implies acceptance and approval of its taken-for-granted convenience. In 1978, the Shuttle carried 2.7 million passengers, more than Eastern flew in the entire decade of 1930–1940.

Yet like that of Eastern itself, the Shuttle's history has been turbulent and controversial. It was almost abolished on three separate occasions, the first two times because it was losing money and the third during the 1974–1975 fuel crisis. Its very origin is a matter of heated debate—as one EAL official wryly puts it, "The number of people who say they were on Rickenbacker's raft in the Pacific or who were supposed to have been Frank Borman's roommates at West Point is exceeded only by those who claim to have thought up the Shuttle."

Actually, no single individual can claim credit. Like so many good ideas, the Shuttle was the product of several minds and its beginnings can be traced back not to Eastern itself, but to arch-rival American Airlines. Admittedly, such a flat statement could cause Captain Eddie to revolve in his grave like a propeller, but the truth is that Rickenbacker's old foe, C. R. Smith, in the late forties asked some of his planning experts to study the possibility of a shuttle-type operation, primarily between New York and Boston.

As C.R. conceived it, the principal feature would be a no-reservations service, and the chief motivation was the elimination of the "no-show" problem that plagued all airlines serving the corridor. A passenger would fly from New York to Boston in the morning, booking space on a four P.M. return flight. But often he would finish earlier than expected, grabbing a mid-afternoon flight back to New York and never bothering to cancel space on the four P.M.

There were so many no-shows, in fact, that American, Eastern, and Northeast at one time established joint ticket counters so they could control space more efficiently; if, say, an American flight was full, a customer merely had to request space on the next available Eastern or Northeast flight. But the cost of operating a reservations system for this short-haul, low-yield, and rather hectic market galled C.R. into suggesting a first-come, first-serve operation.

Among the staff members Smith had studying a no-reservations service were two men who later became instrumental in organizing Eastern's Shuttle. One was Frank Sharpe, American's assistant director of reservations and ticket offices; the other was his assistant, Warren Robbins Winn, known to all as Bob. Working with other planners, they developed a no-reservations blueprint which C.R. liked. Tentatively it was decided to assign three DC-6's and four DC-3's to the operation, but enough American brass had second thoughts to convince Smith he was opening a Pandora's box. One of the dissenters was vice president Art Lewis, later to become Eastern's president, who was vehemently opposed.

"It'll be impossible to handle peak-hour traffic with a no-reservations system," he told C.R. "It would make a lot more sense to have reservations switch traffic over to earlier or later flights if peak-hour business gives us trouble."

Even today Lewis insists that he was right in talking C.R. out of a shuttle service, but he readily concedes it wouldn't have been the kind of operation Eastern finally inaugurated.

"C.R. was strongly committed to it," Lewis recalls. "He felt it could be a low-cost operation by saving money through elimination of reservations in a short-haul route. But when my department analyzed the original plan, we showed him that utilization of equipment and manpower would drive up costs much higher than what could be saved through no-reservations. The principal problem, as I explained it to C.R., was that overall load factors would be too low—high during peak-hour periods, yes, but uneconomically low during off-peak hours. At least reservations were controlled; you could balance your schedule in accordance with demand."

What neither Lewis nor anyone else at American foresaw, of course, was the gimmick of using backup aircraft and crews to handle peak-hour traffic—which made the eventual guaranteed-space feature possible. Lewis admits that even if these elements had been part of the proposed American shuttle, he probably would have recommended against it.

"They would have made the shuttle even more costly to

operate, and impossibly expensive for any low-fare service," he adds. "This is why the Eastern shuttle at first was an artistic success but a financial flop—the fares were set too low."

So the whole scheme lay dormant until 1950, the year that Rickenbacker himself unwittingly sowed the seeds for what would become the Air-Shuttle. When he raided American for the four reservations specialists, the quartet included Sharpe and Winn— and both, of course, were particularly well versed in what would have been American's version of a shuttle; Sharpe, in fact, had made the oral presentation at American when the idea of a New York–Boston shuttle-type service was first proposed, and the presentation was based largely on Winn's notes.

Winn brought his data over to Eastern; immersed with his overall duties as assistant superintendent of reservations under Sharpe, he was willing to let his files gather dust for nearly eight years until William L. Morrisette, Eastern's vice president for traffic, sales, and advertising, suggested that Winn dust off the plan and head a group to study a no-reservations service between New York and Washington. In that respect, not only Winn and Sharpe but also Morrisette deserve inclusion in the lengthy "who thought up the Shuttle" list.

It was Morrisette who on April 23, 1958—a full three years before the Air-Shuttle actually began—submitted a memo to Rickenbacker on what he termed "a No Advance Telephone Reservations plan applicable to commuter service." He informed EVR that "Bob Winn and some of the other boys have been working on this project for quite some time" and attached a copy of Winn's outline, along with a memo he (Morrisette) had sent Winn asking him to explore "certain other angles."

The memo to EVR continued:

Frankly, we are of the opinion that such a plan is entirely feasible and if we could make it work between New York and Washington it is entirely possible that with added experience we could also make it work between other high density points regardless of the length of haul.

As you know, this has been the dream of many air carriers for a long time and whether or not it will be accepted by the public probably cannot be determined until we actually try it. I do believe, however, that we have a fairly good approach to the problem and that the various departments that would be involved would benefit much by a round-table discussion.

Naturally I am anxious to get your reaction and comments, together with any instructions you might have.

Morrisette is dead now and there is no record of how long it took Rickenbacker to reply. But there is a record of *how* he replied. Captain Eddie, who on occasion could be verbose, also was capable of a brevity that had all the staccato impact of a lightning bolt. He had the habit of drawing a squiggly vertical line, resembling a child's impression of a small snake, through whatever paragraphs he didn't agree with or like; in the case of the Morrisette memo, there was such a line scrawled through the three paragraphs cited above—and it meant, simply, "no action."

That killed the idea of a no-reservations shuttle service for another two years. Significantly, Winn's detailed suggestions did not include any recommendations for backup planes or guaranteed seats. Yet Winn did urge using part of Eastern's Constellation fleet for the proposed service, increasing the seating capacity from sixty to sixty-seven by removing the forward galley, forward coat rack, one stewardess seat, the rear galley, and one washroom.

The Winn plan also called for elimination of all meal and snack service; along with the no reservations feature, he estimated that the savings would allow Eastern to make money with a ten-dollar, one-way fare—which was only a few cents higher than the coach rail-fare.

At the time Morrisette sought Rickenbacker's approval, American was carrying the bulk of New York–Washington air traffic. Much of the business was of the "standby" nature—passengers who didn't bother trying for reserved space but who went out to the airport and grabbed the earliest available flight. This was particularly true in Washington and Winn felt "the pattern . . . has set a precedent in passenger habit which would be attracted by the service."

While the plan lacked the guaranteed-space factor that would make the future Air-Shuttle so popular, it did contain a provision that came close. Winn and his fellow planners proposed that passengers unable to board one of the hourly departures would be protected on the next flight, in effect giving them guaranteed seats by making them wait no longer than sixty minutes. Winn thought this advantage should be advertised heavily and his own report to Morrisette noted that "this was the point that American forgot and as a result gave up the project."

Morrisette bought the whole plan with one exception—he thought the Connies could be configured to carry eighty persons instead of sixty-seven.

"The Baltimore & Ohio is discontinuing New York–Washington passenger service in five days," he informed Winn on April 22—the day before he put his own memo on EVR's desk. "We should thoroughly analyze this market as to total air traffic, as well as rail traffic."

He already had discussed with Winn and others the advantages and disadvantages of a commuter service. To passengers the plan offered reduced fares, gate check-ins, frequent departures, and carry-on baggage—the latter was an integral part of the project. They seemed to outweigh the two chief disadvantages: no firm reservations and no in-flight service. Likewise, the project would involve such attractions to EAL as no oversales, reduced baggage handling, no baggage tagging, a smaller reservations workload—and, of course, the rather intangible yet potentially beneficial improved public image.

No one knows why Rickenbacker's reaction was so abruptly negative; an EVR "squiggle" was the last word on any given proposal, and even the outspoken Morrisette wasn't about to argue with the Captain. Admittedly, there were legitimate arguments against the commuter plan; the expense of modifying the aircraft plus their low utilization during off-peak periods, the possibility that the low-fare operation would simply divert traffic from Eastern's regular flights—all these were disadvantages Rickenbacker presumably considered in his typically cavalier rejection.

This is not to suggest that EVR had to be wrong. For all his curmudgeon personality and mercurial temper, the Captain was an astute, albeit close-to-the-vest businessman and it is entirely possible that in 1958 the timing wasn't right for a shuttle service —not in the form which had been proposed. Yet the idea was far from dead, for Eastern was going through a crucial and trying period thanks to its lack of long-haul routes and the increased competition; more than one official at EAL, the Captain included, knew the airline needed some marketing innovations.

Malcolm MacIntyre's selection as Eastern's new president created an atmosphere conducive to experimentation. The first manifestation was the rather daring "Air-Bus" service from Cleveland, Pittsburgh, and St. Louis to Miami, inaugurated October 13, 1960. Using fully depreciated Constellations and offering a minimum of in-flight service, EAL was able to offer a forty-dollar fare from the three northern cities—twenty-six percent less than day tourist, fifteen percent under night tourist, and actually equal to what Greyhound was charging for a trip that took twenty-five hours. The rail fare was six dollars higher and Eastern's promotion emphasized that the per capita cost of driving one's own car would be at least forty-five dollars, including meals and motels over a three-day span.

MacIntyre, whose stormy tenure at Eastern was marked by his willingness to experiment, had early high hopes for the Air-Bus. A survey taken after its first year of operation revealed that seventeen percent of its passengers were flying for the first time, and more than thirty percent would have gone by surface means if it were not for the low air fare. But traffic, while promising, was never particularly lucrative and it would be stretching the truth to say that the Air-Bus spawned the Air-Shuttle.* Yet EAL still had an inkling of a low-fare potential on other routes—literally swapping frills for convenience—and another carrier's marketing test already had supplied further ammunition.

In 1959 Allegheny Airlines had introduced a no-reservations service between Pittsburgh and Philadelphia with the added

* Air-Bus service was extended in 1962 to other city pairs in the Great Lakes–Florida market but the public response was lukewarm.

feature of in-flight ticketing. It was moderately successful, its chief weakness being the lack of guaranteed space (although only five percent of the passengers were turned away without seats) —an item which did not escape MacIntyre's attention.

It is at this point that nostalgia and understandable pride befogs historical accuracy. It is generally agreed that sometime later in the spring of 1960 Eastern's officialdom began thinking seriously about a shuttle operation. The source of the initial impetus is in dispute, and the fairest conclusion is that it came— almost spontaneously—from several directions.

One instigator was an EAL pilot, First Officer Fred Epson, who was ferrying a Constellation from Washington National Airport to Louisville, Kentucky, where the aging but still service- able airliner was to be put in storage at Standiford Field. The man in the left seat that day in May 1960 was Captain Paul Slayden and Epson remarked what a shame it was to mothball so many fine Connies.

"They're fully amortized, too," Epson added sorrowfully.

Slayden nodded. "I agree, but what the hell would the company do with 'em?"

"Run 'em between New York and Washington at special fares," Epson said.

Slayden looked interested and Epson, encouraged, ver- balized an idea he had been mulling over for some time: a no- reservations service, using enough Connies to provide extra sec- tions if the regular flight was full. As he unfolded his "Air-Bus" plan, which basically fitted what was to become the Air-Shuttle, Slayden became enthusiastic himself and when the two pilots returned from the ferry assignment, they talked to their chief pilot, Capt. F. E. Davis.

The latter was impressed enough to call Rickenbacker. EVR made no comment but, according to Epson, promised to have Lefty Lethridge contact Epson. There were some discus- sions between Lethridge and Epson, but meanwhile others at Eastern seem to have simultaneously come up with the same plan as the young pilot. And one of them was Malcolm MacIntyre.

To this day MacIntyre says he knew nothing of the Epson-

Slayden proposal—which may be the truth, because by that time he was feuding bitterly with EVR, who might not have even mentioned it.

"I got the idea mainly from the headaches of commuting between Washington and New York when I was a practicing lawyer," he recalls.

The first official discussion of a shuttle service actually took place at an EAL staff meeting, and it was MacIntyre who brought it up. He announced he wanted a study made of a no-reservations service between New York and Washington.

"You may not need much of a study," Frank Sharpe remarked. "American had the whole thing worked out several years ago—Bob Winn did most of the planning. As a matter of fact, Captain Eddie looked at Winn's file on it back in '58 and decided against it at the time."

"So he did," Morrisette confirmed.

"I'd like to see it," MacIntyre snapped.

That was the first of many meetings on the proposed shuttle —and most of them, it must be reported, were on the negative side. MacIntyre found himself marching to the beat of a lonely drum; only a few of his fellow executives were sold on the shuttle. MacIntyre says, "There were just two who agreed with me and they shall remain nameless."

Sharpe was not one of them. Despite his role in shaping the original American project, he was pessimistic about such a plan working at Eastern. Not to the idea of a no-reservations service, but to MacIntyre's insistence on the one feature that eventually made it work: guaranteed space by use of backup crews and aircraft, positioned to meet peak-hour traffic demands. If the Air-Shuttle was not entirely Malcolm MacIntyre's idea, he was largely responsible for its principal ingredient; he literally rammed it down the collective throats of Eastern's upper echelons—including Edward Vernon Rickenbacker.

Inevitably MacIntyre had to "bell the cat," marching into the Captain's office one day to explain—or rather defend—the Air-Shuttle.

"It's nothing but a damned bus service," Rickenbacker snorted.

"Well, you've been running a bus service to Florida for years," MacIntyre retorted. "What's the difference?"

Publicly, however, EVR did not oppose the Shuttle, and there is conflicting evidence as to the extent of his support. Bob Winn believes he was against it but went along because he figured it was doomed to failure and would thus discredit MacIntyre. Yet Lefty Lethridge was present at a meeting between MacIntyre and Captain Eddie late in the fall of 1960, an occasion on which EVR gave the project his official blessing.

Only a few days before that meeting the opposition was still open and vociferous. About a week before MacIntyre finally demanded that EVR say yes or no, the president called a final staff meeting on the subject—it was a Friday afternoon. Lethridge led the attack, backed up by Sharpe.

"Nobody is going out to an airport and wait an hour if they can't get on the shuttle flight they wanted," Lefty argued. "You can't get passengers on an if-and-when basis."

"Here we go again with that goddamned Lethridge speech!" MacIntyre growled. "I've told you a hundred times—they won't have to wait an hour if we use backup equipment and backup crews."

"You can't get a crew out to La Guardia or Washington National in less than an hour," Lefty protested. "What'll you do—have 'em sit around the airport waiting to see if they're gonna fly?"

Which, of course, was precisely what MacIntyre had in mind—even though his colleagues almost unanimously agreed that this would spiral operating costs up to the point where the Shuttle could not possibly fly in black ink. But Mr. Mac was adamant. On the following Monday he poked his head into Lethridge's office, standing in the doorway with a slight smile on his lips. "Lefty, my mind's made up—we'll go with backup crews and airplanes."

"When will you break the news to the Captain?" Lethridge asked quietly.

"In a day or so."

Lethridge will never forget that meeting. Rickenbacker, for several minutes, studied the voluminous reports, traffic projections, and logistics MacIntyre had handed him to read. Then he looked up at the ceiling.

"Mac," he said, "there's only one thing I ask. You're planning to start this thing December fifth when our winter schedules go into effect. Take my advice and wait for next spring. This won't succeed unless it's almost foolproof. If you try to get it going when we have a lot of fog and heavy snow, you're gonna stub your toe."

"Okay, Eddie," MacIntyre agreed. "We'll start in the spring."

It was the following May when the Air-Shuttle was launched officially, and Eastern really had needed the extra months Rickenbacker had urged. Long before the final green light was flashed, it had been decided that if there was to be an Air-Shuttle, it would be extended to the New York–Boston market as well as that of New York–Washington. The upper-echelon planning group included Sharpe, executive vice-president Bob Turner, Lethridge, and MacIntyre, but the "man in the pit"—to use a pro football expression—was Paul Quigley of Flight Operations, who was assigned the Augean Stable task of working out aircraft positioning, flight patterns, crew scheduling, and all the other elements involved in a shuttle service based on guaranteed seating. It cannot be stressed too often that this was the pivotal factor, and by the same token it is extremely frustrating not to be able to pinpoint the credit. The most objective appraisal is that the two pilots, Epson and Slayden, first proposed it, but that without MacIntyre it never would have been made such an integral part of the project.

And not even Mr. Mac really expected the Air-Shuttle to become an immediate financial success. He was only too well aware of the enormous operating-cost penalty of providing the planes and crews for extra sections, without ever being positively sure to what extent they'd be needed at any given time. The market surveys he had ordered in the early planning stages were not the epitome of optimism—a fact which Sharpe frequently brought up.

"I don't think it means very much," MacIntyre said doggedly. "And I'll bet traffic will be fifty percent greater with guaranteed space."

He made that prediction at a time, he remembers, "when we didn't know how many people we'd need, how many planes we'd have to use, how to schedule the crews, or how much to charge."

Pricing was in fact a major problem. "We couldn't decide whether to set fares as cheaply as possible to attract passengers or make them higher because convenience was our prime selling point," MacIntyre adds. "We finally had to admit we didn't know how convenience would rate as a means of attracting customers, so the fares were pegged low."

Too low, as it turned out. This, combined with the high operating costs of standby crews, made it inevitable that the Air-Shuttle would be unprofitable for a time—Mr. Mac said it would take six months before the red ink shaded into black and he wasn't far off in his estimate. As far as can be determined, it began showing a small profit before its first year was up—just about as long as it took Eastern to eradicate a few bugs and acquire some experience in the art of positioning aircraft.

The Air-Shuttle made its debut April 30, 1961, operating thirty-two flights that day between Washington, New York, and Boston and carrying 640 passengers—about the same number Eastern carries today in a single hour in the same market. The service began with only sixteen Constellations, configured for ninety-five passengers, which on a Connie was wall-to-wall people, but it quickly became apparent that not even the higher-density seating could keep up with the demand. The original schedule called for flights every two hours, but within four months Boston–New York frequency was increased to hourly and Washington–New York was stepped up to hourly a month later, while the fleet itself mushroomed to thirty-three Connies and a half-dozen Martin 404's used for backup.

To Malcolm MacIntyre the Shuttle became almost an obsession—he regarded it as his baby, and he didn't believe in absentee parenthood. He spent almost as much time in the Shuttle terminal at La Guardia as in his downtown Manhattan office —and was nearly as proud of that terminal as he was of the

Shuttle itself. About half of it had been part of a hangar and it cost Eastern only $350,000 to convert it into a terminal building —"the most effective, efficient, and cheapest ever built," MacIntyre says.

It was MacIntyre who thought up the very title "Air-Shuttle" and he used to bristle everytime he'd hear it shortened to "Shuttle." He was so touchy about this that he made it an official order: No employee was ever to refer to the operation as anything but "Air-Shuttle." With the natural propensity of Americans in general and airline people in particular to abbreviate, the order enjoyed little compliance unless Mr. Mac was within earshot, but it emphasizes his deep personal interest.

Walter J. "Mickey" Dane, EAL's vice president–eastern region, was station manager at Washington National Airport when the Shuttle began. He ruefully admits that no one, including himself, thought it was workable and that he was among those who tried to talk MacIntyre out of the whole scheme.

"While it was still under consideration," he recounts, "Mr. Mac flew down to Washington one day and sounded me out on the concept. I told him it was impossible—hell, we had 125 daily flights operating essentially out of only four gates at National, and I couldn't see how we could handle the kind of operation he was plugging.

"He insisted that I fly back to Newark with him and he kept talking. A limousine met him and I went into Manhattan with him. I think we must have driven around Central Park six times before he finally convinced me it could be done. I became project coordinator with Frank Sharpe."

Sharpe, incidentally, never let his misgivings toward the Shuttle affect his efforts in its behalf. He was an airline pro—he could fight like a wildcat against some idea he considered wrong, but once the decision was made, no one worked harder to make it succeed. He wasn't an innovator himself, but he had the knack of convincing others to do things differently. Frank Stulgaitis worked for him in the early Shuttle days and affectionately refers to Sharpe as "one of the best dancers in the industry—he could bounce off projects quicker than anyone I knew, getting people to start things and then being smart enough to know what to pick out that would work."

Sharpe, along with everyone else, waited impatiently for the inevitable day when Eastern's promise of a guaranteed seat would be put to its severest test—flying a single passenger in a ninety-five-passenger airplane. McIntyre talked about it at several staff meetings.

"We'd better have photographers standing by at all three airports until it happens," Mr. Mac said just before the Air-Shuttle was launched. "There's no telling when it will happen but when it does, it'll be a publicity gold mine."

So cameramen were assigned to the three airports, staying discreetly out of sight, until it finally happened—at La Guardia within a month after Shuttle started. An older man was the ninety-sixth passenger trying to board a ninety-five-passenger Connie and the figurative alarm bells began ringing. Cameramen, EAL publicity personnel, agents, and supervisors came out of the woodwork and descended on the startled customer.

"The second section's ready, sir," an agent informed him.

The passenger looked around. Obviously he was the only one boarding. "You mean I'm going alone? You have a plane just for me?"

"That's right, sir. We promised you a guaranteed seat and you've got it."

"I won't do it!"

All EAL smiles suddenly vanished.

"Not on your life," the man repeated. "You people must be crazy—using a whole crew and plane to take one guy to Washington!"

They pleaded with him but he wouldn't relent. Not until June 12—the day the Air-Shuttle terminal officially opened at La Guardia—did Eastern finally operate an extra section carrying a single passenger. The publicity was spectacular and probably did as much to establish the service in the public's mind as all the Shuttle advertising combined. A "Mr. 96" was boarded about fifty times in the Shuttle's history, almost entirely in the Connie days, and eventually the occurrence not only ceased to be newsworthy but also ceased per se; in fact, as of mid-1979, Eastern hadn't had a one-passenger extra section for almost a decade.

Assignment of extra sections was part careful logistics, part Kentucky windage, and part luck—good and bad. When the Air-Shuttle was approaching its first Thanksgiving weekend crush, Sharpe figured they'd use a scientific approach. He had his staff survey scores of schools and military bases in advance, so that aircraft could be positioned in accordance with such factors as when classes ended, how many military leaves were being granted and at what starting times, the number of student and military personnel whose families were in the three-city Shuttle area, and so on. Based on all this data it was concluded that the big rush would start at two P.M. Wednesday, the day before Thanksgiving, and the planes were positioned accordingly.

At noon, a full two hours before the rush was supposed to start, Sharpe got an anguished call from the station manager at Boston's Logan Airport.

"All hell's busted loose," he wailed. "The terminal is jammed with kids and we've got only one Connie at the gate."

Fast equipment reshuffling and improvising finally eased matters, but Sharpe was determined that this wouldn't happen again during the Christmas avalanche. What apparently had happened at Thanksgiving was the unexpected decision of students to cut a few late-morning classes and get out of Boston before noon. Eastern ran the same survey in December and was all set to handle an unexpected mob around noon. There was no mob—either at noon or throughout the afternoon.

"We found out that most kids had arranged car pools at the last minute," Sharpe remembers, "and our traffic just didn't materialize. For the Shuttle's second Thanksgiving, we knew what had gone wrong the year before and made our plans accordingly —we were all set for the rush to begin late Wednesday morning and we had the equipment and crews ready by eight A.M. just to make sure. The roof fell in. Early Tuesday afternoon all three Shuttle terminals notified us they were swamped. It seems this time the kids had been hearing radio reports that the weather might be bad Wednesday so they cut Tuesday classes in droves and showed up."

As the Air-Shuttle gained operating experience, however, equipment and personnel positioning became a fine science—to the point where Eastern actually could forecast loads at any given hour, at any terminal, and achieve reasonable accuracy. Not always, of course: There was the horrendous night at La Guardia when the entire Boston Symphony showed up at the last minute for the final Shuttle of the day to Boston—more than 100 musicians, *with* instruments. What with the regular flight almost full, EAL needed another plane for most of the orchestra and a third aircraft to carry the instruments.

On another occasion some 500 European travel agents arrived at La Guardia bound for Washington via the Shuttle and flew back to New York the same day, with almost no advance warning. Such incidents provide the principal reason why the Shuttle must operate on a relatively slim profit margin—to position aircraft for peak hour or unexpectedly heavy traffic demands, it requires an unusual amount of empty, nonrevenue ferry flights. Admittedly there is less of this than there used to be but the one thing certain about the airline business is its uncertainty.

For example, southbound traffic out of La Guardia for Washington is heavier in the morning and lighter in the late afternoon. Yet for no explainable reason this flow can be reversed at any time and the positioning rat-race starts all over again. A three o'clock Washington–New York Shuttle, which normally would employ one extra section at the most, has been known to operate six extra sections.

By June of 1962—less than fourteen months after it started—the Shuttle had passed the one million mark in passengers carried. The exact date was June 11 and then Civil Aeronautics Board Chairman Alan Boyd took the trouble to issue a statement on the occasion.

"The Air-Shuttle is the greatest thing that has happened in air transportation in years," Boyd enthused. "I would like to see a lot more of this kind of thinking in air transportation."

It is axiomatic in the publishing industry that rave reviews don't necessarily sell books, and the same thing applies to the airline industry—for all the praise heaped on the Shuttle by men like Boyd, and the overwhelmingly favorable response of the flying public, Eastern's noble experiment took a shellacking where it counted the most—on the ledgers. The fourteen-dollar New York–Washington and the twelve-dollar New York–Boston fares were pegged too low to offset the predicted high operating costs.

It was precisely the low fare structure that appealed to Boyd, who had been telling the airlines for a long time that they could make more money if they charged less and thus got more people to fly. Unquestionably the bargain rates, combined with unheard-of convenience, also was the Shuttle's big selling point with passengers. But from the very start of the Shuttle, MacIntyre was plagued by its financial troubles. Yes, it began turning a profit after the first few months but not in the proportions Mr. Mac had hoped and, in truth, the black ink was more of a pale gray. Any adverse external pressure, such as employee contractual pay boosts, higher fuel costs, or even increased landing fees, was sufficient to turn the gray into pink and even bright red. Financially speaking, the Air-Shuttle was a financial roller-coaster—at times encouragingly profitable and at others a sieve that seemed to exist only to enhance the airline's public service image.

MacIntyre did more than play an obstetrician's role in bringing the shuttle to life; he also raised it, from its fumbling beginnings to a toughened maturity. It was at Mr. Mac's insistence that it operated literally as a separate airline, utilizing its own aircraft, crews, and—in most cases—even its own ground personnel. That key decision encountered strong resistance from many of MacIntyre's subordinates, particularly in Flight Operations, who on more than one occasion pleaded for permission to blend the Shuttle into regular schedules. Their reasoning was logical: The Shuttle fleet was averaging only four hours utilization daily, compared to EAL's system average of ten hours. It made a lot of sense to Eastern's operations officials to integrate at least some of the line aircraft into the Shuttle. This was talked about informally but MacIntyre finally put his foot down when he specifically was asked why a Constellation being operated on a trip from Charlotte, North Carolina, to Washington couldn't be used as the three o'clock Shuttle out of Washington.

"It arrives in Washington at 2:30 P.M.," MacIntyre was told. "That's plenty of time to load it with Shuttle passengers, fly it up to New York, and then use it as equipment for an early-evening nonstop to Montreal."

"No," Mr. Mac ruled firmly. "You run the Air-Shuttle as a separate airline and if you don't do it that way, you're sunk. Any kind of delay on that Charlotte–Washington leg, weather or mechanical, and it ruins the Air-Shuttle schedule."

Throughout his tenure at Eastern, MacIntyre fought off every attempt to modify or even abolish the Shuttle. Mr. Mac himself believes if the proposed merger of Eastern and American Airlines in 1962 had been consummated, American—the surviving carrier—would have terminated the shuttle service.

"When the negotiations were going on with American, C. R. Smith [American's president] told me it would be dropped if the merger went through," MacIntyre says. This would explain, at least partially, why MacIntyre's support of the merger, while publicly dutiful, was never really strong privately. When he asked Smith why American would scrap the Shuttle, C.R. argued that in the merged carrier, it would merely divert business from full-fare flights.

MacIntyre never wavered in his conviction that the Shuttle would be not only a success but a monument to his own embattled regime. For one thing, he recognized very early in the game that rail passenger traffic in the Boston–New York–Washington corridor was going to disappear as a major competitive factor. Shortly after the Shuttle started operating, he had lunch with James Symes, president of the Pennsylvania Railroad. Symes got to the point quickly, asking MacIntyre several questions about the Shuttle.

"Mac," he said finally, "are you really in this for keeps?"

"Sure. Why?"

"Because we'd like to stop carrying passengers. We're losing money on every passenger train we operate."

MacIntyre knew then that the experiment no longer was

just an experiment. Eastern's Washington–New York traffic went up fifty percent immediately after the Shuttle began and was seventy-five percent higher by the Shuttle's second year. Profits have fluctuated, but volume has never slackened perceptibly. Today EAL carries three out of every four persons who travel by air between New York and Washington, and two out of three between New York and Boston. Before the Air-Shuttle began, Eastern's share of those two markets was only forty and thirty-five percent. In fact, the Shuttle now carries more passengers annually—close to three million—than Eastern's total traffic in 1960, the year before it was launched.

These statistics merely underline the significance of MacIntyre's unwavering faith in the project. At the time the Shuttle started, it was hard even to get crews willing to fly its schedules, particularly flight attendants. The average stewardess considered working a Shuttle trip a kind of airborne Siberia; the result was that Eastern had to assign virtually all junior girls to the operation because no one would bid for the Shuttle. Pilots were low in seniority, too; like the stewardesses, many considered the Air-Shuttle somewhat degrading, boring, and unchallenging—"You had the feeling you were driving a damned Greyhound," one captain recalls.

Now the Shuttle's DC-9 jetliners are manned mostly by senior captains who like the absence of layovers. And the same is true of flight attendants.

"The girls bid Shuttle trips because they can get home every night," says Pat Kelly, base manager of In-Flight Services at Washington National. "Now and then they'll bid a system trip for a change of scenery, but the average seniority for a flight attendant working the Shuttle out of Washington is twelve and a half years. And let's face it—with no meal or beverage service, the job's fairly easy. All they have to do is wheel the ticket cart up the aisle."

In-flight ticketing, of course, was one of the Air-Shuttle's most popular features. In the Shuttle's initial years passengers usually paid cash—that was when the UATP (Universal Air Travel Plan) was the only credit card honored by the airline industry. Most passengers today use general credit cards or those issued by the airlines themselves, but when cash business was heavy, stewardesses were tested frequently by customers presenting $100 bills and claiming, "It's the smallest I've got with me."

The girls circumvented this dodge with a simple solution: They'd have the captain radio ahead, and the flight would be met by an agent with a fistful of bills. Even so, there were moments when EAL officials at least pondered—and once actually tried—doing away with in-flight ticketing. The attempt was made years after the Shuttle had become well established, and followed a survey by a new marketing officer which showed that eighty-seven percent of the Shuttle passengers polled would like snacks and drinks.

"It didn't mean a goddamned thing," Frank Sharpe scoffs. "If you ran a survey asking how many people would like to have three silver dollars handed them at the end of every flight, what kind of a response would you get? If we had asked for a choice between convenience and in-flight service, the survey would have been turned around."

Sharpe opposed the trial snack-and-beverage service but its proponents figured the revenue from drinks would cover the cost of ground ticketing—there was no possibility of having in-flight service *and* in-flight ticketing because there wasn't time for both on a fifty-five-minute flight. So Eastern took the plunge; the experiment lasted only five months, with the complaints on ground ticketing far outnumbering the original gripes received on the lack of snack and drink service.

Another short-lived experiment involved specially prepared newscasts on Electra Shuttle flights—the Electra being the only plane in Eastern's fleet at the time with a decent cabin PA system. Brief news bulletins, stocks, and weather were aired just before landing, and the idea seemed to be popular but not quite popular enough. A few complaints about "invasion of privacy" prompted a general survey of passenger reaction. Less than five percent of the respondents were opposed to the newscasts but that was sufficient to cause their abandonment.

Another flop was the introduction of ten-ticket commuter

books at a discount, although Dane remembers that everyone had high hopes for this idea. Why it never went over, considering the high repeat business the Shuttle enjoys, nobody can figure out and Dane, for one, believes a discounted commuter book may be tried again.

"Sure we've tried some innovations at various times," he comments, "but we always have to keep in mind that the public has made it vividly clear it's satisfied with the basics."

When MacIntyre resigned in 1963, there was some sentiment for letting the Air-Shuttle leave with the man so instrumental in its inception. A number of EAL officials honestly felt that the Shuttle contributed to Eastern's poor image, with its aging, rather shabby Constellations and one-dimensional service. Thus it was only too natural for the anti-Shuttle voices to argue lustily that Eastern's new image under MacIntyre's successor, Floyd Hall, would be tarnished if the Shuttle continued. Hall instead chose a sensible alternative—he upgraded the Shuttle fleet with Electras, as fast as the Electras could be replaced on prime routes by pure jets; the Connies then were relegated to extrasection backup duties, and eventually (in February 1968) were phased out entirely. At the time Hall assumed Eastern's presidency, the Air-Shuttle was contributing an incredible twenty percent of the airline's total passenger traffic—which meant that one out of every five passengers had been boarding a dilapidated Constellation. The decision to use the Electra as the Shuttle's primary aircraft was made after a survey of passengers disclosed that the Shuttle, while ranking high in convenience, ranked at the bottom of the page in equipment.

The other major change to occur during Hall's administration was a fare raise—a chancy move that really tested the "people will pay for convenience" theory of so many EAL executives—Hall and Art Lewis in particular. The increase was modest at first but subsequently kept climbing steadily until at this writing it is forty-seven dollars for the regular one-way Shuttle fare between New York and Washington. Despite the higher fares, however, Eastern successfully fought off every competitive challenge in the corridor market.

One such challenge came from American in 1967, when C.R.'s aggressive, businessman-oriented airline inaugurated "Jet Express" service over the Boston–New York route, using British-made BAC-111 jets with hourly departures. Northeast countered with even more frequent schedules but Eastern held onto its share of the bitterly contested market and today continues to dominate it, as it does on the New York–Washington route.

The most severe test of the Shuttle's popularity came in 1966 when a machinists' strike shut down Eastern and four other carriers for forty-three days. American was not affected and scheduled unprecedented extra sections to handle traffic in the Corridor market. Much to everyone's surprise, American's business in that market went up less than ten percent and train traffic increased at about the same ratio. Unexpectedly, the traffic had just dried up. Yet when Eastern resumed service, anticipating that it would take at least three days for Shuttle passenger volume to build up again, business on the first day was eighty-five percent of normal and completely normal within another twenty-four hours. It was only too apparent that the Air-Shuttle had become a transportation way of life, no matter what the competition offered in conventional service, and this was an eye-opener at Eastern as well as to the entire industry—even then, there still were some EAL brass who felt that the Shuttle damaged the airline's new image.

Imitation being the sincerest form of flattery, it is interesting to note in 1976 British Airways took the Air-Shuttle blueprints and virtually duplicated the entire concept in its London–Glasgow service. It was by no means a form of aerial plagiarism —marketing and operations experts from the British carrier came to Eastern for advice, suggestions, and training, and wound up with a strikingly similar version. Tridents reconfigured to 100-seat capacity were used in sufficient numbers to provide backup capability.

In a pressure cooker that has generated as many as seventy-two extra sections per day, the Air-Shuttle's safety record has been impressive. In the first nineteen years of its existence, with nearly sixty million passengers flown, there has been only one fatal accident—a midair collision between a TWA 707 and an Eastern Constellation operation as a Newark–Boston Shuttle flight December 5, 1965. The EAL captain, Charles White, crash-landed the Connie on a hillside after the impact severed his controls—a miraculous job of airmanship in which White maneuvered solely with his throttles. A single passenger died— along with White himself, who reentered the burning plane in a vain effort to save him.

Equally impressive is the Shuttle's on-time performance, among the best in the industry, consistently running between ninety-two and ninety-four percent. In the Corridor's combat zone, such on-time performance is close to a miracle; it is achieved by the simple process of dispatching first sections as soon as they are filled—usually twenty minutes ahead of scheduled departure. The second section usually leaves the gate right on schedule and the policy is to dispatch the final section no later than twenty minutes after scheduled departure.

The Shuttle also rates high grades in baggage handling, a constant industry headache but almost foolproof in the Air-Shuttle operation. When it first started, there was a long and loud debate over whether to put the usual claim checks on luggage. MacIntyre argued against it, insisting that passengers could simply leave their bags in a special preboarding area and claim it in a similar area at destination. It's still done that way, and the Air-Shuttle has the fewest complaints and the lowest lost-bag percentage in the industry. (One of the few bags reported lost belonged to an EAL vice president who was raising hell until someone discovered he had left it in the men's room at National Airport.)

Naturally the Shuttle is plagued by the usual delays applicable to any carrier, but on one occasion fell victim to Eastern's admirable practice of dispatching each flight as soon as it's loaded—a procedure which comes close to being perpetual motion. It was a busy Friday afternoon and the Shuttle boardings at La Guardia that day looked like an assembly line—pull up, fill up, and pull out.

One extra section was completely full, the stewardesses had

welcomed everyone aboard, the cabin PA safety message had been delivered—and the plane just sat there. After ten minutes of waiting, the senior flight attendant went up to the cockpit to inquire about the delay. She got the answer quickly: Nobody was in the cockpit.

They had run out of standby crews.

Then there is the ultimate Air-Shuttle story, generated by the debacle of the 1968 air traffic controllers' slowdown that almost brought the U.S. air transportation system to a halt. At the height of the snarled mess, a passenger boarded a Shuttle flight in Washington shortly before five P.M., landed in New York less than fifty minutes later, and was so impressed that he lagged behind to praise the deplaning pilot.

"Captain," he said pleasantly, "I just want to compliment you and Eastern. I was expecting all kinds of inconvenience—I figured the five o'clock Shuttle would be lucky to land at La Guardia by eight, yet here I am and it's only a few minutes after six."

"Thanks," the captain said dryly, "but you were on the two o'clock Shuttle."

On November 1, 1977, Eastern retired the last of its Electras—probably the Shuttle's best all-around airplane—and went all-jet with the DC-9 as the primary aircraft and Boeing 727-100's as backup. On more than one occasion an Electra beat a DC-9 to destination by as much as thirty minutes, even though it was operating as an extra section; the propjet's ability to operate more efficiently at lower altitudes made the difference. But the Electra's maintenance costs had soared to the point where its versatility was no longer a major factor. It was costing Eastern $8,000 to replace a propeller that had cost only $2,700 when the plane was brand new. Prop overhaul alone for Eastern's last three Electras required a ten-man shop crew in Miami, and some replacement parts were being built to order for an aircraft that was averaging only two hours daily utilization.

Boeing 727-200s, carrying 177 passengers in an all-coach configuration, are gradually replacing the DC-9 as the Shuttle's primary airplane. As of mid-1979 the Shuttle fleet included seven of the stretched Boeings and nine DC-9-30's seating 118 people, and as more Boeings are converted to all-coach, the DC-9's will be shifted to other routes. It is imperative for Eastern to operate the Shuttle with as few aircraft as possible without affecting the guaranteed-space attraction, for the Shuttle is a classic example of a high-cost, short-haul operation.

Eastern's break-even load factor between New York and Boston was a whopping seventy percent in 1977 and soared to more than eighty percent in 1978. On the Washington–New York segment, the 1977 break-even point was sixty percent and this rose to seventy percent the following year. During the 1974–75 fuel crisis, when the Air-Shuttle actually faced extinction because of the double impact of fuel allocations and higher fuel prices, it was saved partially by the decision to drop Newark as a Shuttle terminal and let regular flights serve the New Jersey airport in the Corridor. (Newark became a Shuttle point in 1962, with a flight every two hours; another factor in its elimination was a survey showing that some eighty percent of Newark's Shuttle flights were averaging only five passengers.)

The Air-Shuttle's very success makes it an inviting target for competition, notwithstanding the fact that it has beaten every attempt to dislodge its dominance. Not even American could do it, despite all its marketing acumen and its reputation as a businessman's airline. During CAB hearings on the proposed merger of Pan Am and National, Pan Am announced it would start a Washington–New York shuttle if the merger was approved, charging only thirty-seven dollars for a one-way trip. But nothing was said about guaranteed space and backup flights—after nineteen years, still the key to the Shuttle's cemented hold on the market.

Today Eastern carries seventy-one percent of Boston–New York traffic, competing against American, Delta, and TWA, and sixty-eight percent on the New York–Washington route where the competition consists of American, Braniff, National, TWA, Southern, Piedmont, and Allegheny. There is some grumbling that EAL charges too much for the no-frills service—the current charge of nineteen cents a mile is one of the highest per-mile costs in the U.S. Yet while Eastern doesn't deny that Shuttle fares are high, it also emphasizes what MacIntyre learned the hard way—the passenger is paying for incredible convenience, not frills. And even at that, the per-mile tariff might be compared to the forty-three cents a mile prevalent in most European markets.

One of Malcolm MacIntyre's greatest sources of pride when he remembers his years at Eastern is the Air-Shuttle. "I get on the Air-Shuttle today and I have yet to meet a crew member who remembers me," he says rather wistfully. "I guess people forget."

Maybe. But when Eastern dedicates its new $25-million Air-Shuttle Terminal at La Guardia in 1982, Mr. Mac will be specially honored. Frank Borman, who was a young airman administering projects for the Air Force Aerospace Pilots School the year the Shuttle began, will see to that.

The concept was so skillfully planned and brilliantly executed that it has remained unchanged for almost two decades, yet, in the U.S. at least, no airline has ever dared to duplicate it. Harper Woodward for years tried to get C. R. Smith to start a New York–Chicago shuttle patterned after Eastern's.

"The density was there," Woodward says, "but it was impossible to convince him. We never published a separate accounting statement for the Shuttle, and C.R. couldn't believe we made money."

Both Rockefeller and Woodward still express warm admiration for MacIntyre, conceding that he was beaten by many factors beyond his control and granting him the major share of credit for the Shuttle.

Unfortunately for Mr. Mac, its success came too late to save him.

CHAPTER THIRTEEN

EXIT MACINTYRE– ENTER HALL

As so often happens when a top executive is in the process of being ousted, Malcolm MacIntyre was the last to know.

He was isolated from the harsh facts of life by the natural ego and pride that go with the lofty position of a corporation president. He knew things were going badly, but the crisis facing Eastern in 1963 monopolized his thinking and affected his judgment of his own leadership. The solution others had arrived at for Eastern's problems was his own dismissal.

He was, in that year of unrelenting setbacks, a somewhat embittered man. The third strike to hit the airline in the three years he had served as president soured him not only on labor but on Captain Eddie's image of Eastern as a big family. After the 1962 flight engineers' walkout, he angrily told Lethridge, "I don't want to hear that family reference ever used again—what kind of a family do you have when you have strikes every year?"

One aftermath of that strike was the permanent grounding of all sixty Martins; they would never fly another trip for Eastern and were put up for sale as part of MacIntyre's almost panicky panacea: Save money by slashing schedules. He wasn't the first airline president to resort to this drastic measure, nor was he the first to find out that it seldom if ever worked—the end result was a loss of competitive stature that wiped out operational savings.

The Shuttle's successful debut gave Mr. Mac the idea that he could duplicate it in another high-density market—New York–Miami. When he proposed it at a staff meeting, eleven out of the twelve persons present voted to approve the plan—Captain Eddie was among them. The only dissenting voice was that of Lethridge, and MacIntyre came close to firing him for his vociferous opposition. Lefty argued that it wouldn't work because the market was a one-way proposition—"You'll need God knows how many extra sections going down to Miami in the wintertime and you'll have to fly 'em back empty," he warned.

The Miami shuttle was exactly the fiasco Lethridge had predicted. It began February 15, 1963, and there were days when eight extra sections weren't enough to handle the demand; on one occasion some 400 angry passengers were left behind because there were no more airplanes available. But unlike the original Shuttle, whose traffic flow was in both directions, the Miami operation needed a 100 percent load factor just to break even because there was little or no demand for return flights.

"We never could figure how we could make it work with the aircraft we had without ripping our whole schedule apart," Lethridge says. "It was impossible to position aircraft like we did with the Shuttle—hell, New York was only 200 miles from Washington but 1,200 miles from Miami. We simply didn't have enough airplanes to make it work and by the end of March, when people were complaining to the CAB about being left behind, the Board made us take out newspaper ads apologizing for the whole business. It lasted only that one winter."

After its demise Lethridge asked the Captain why he voted for it in the first place.

"I thought they were talking about an air-bus kind of thing," EVR said. "I didn't know they were talking about a shuttle type of operation."

Among MacIntyre's problems was overall morale. There is no doubt whatsoever that the merger fight had demoralized the entire company. Lefty understood why. "Employees couldn't understand how we could go from industry leadership to near oblivion," he explains, "and the effects of that letdown lasted a long time." It didn't help, for example, when some EAL official ordered Eastern's hangar in Atlanta painted over in American's colors—this happened while the merger still was being debated, and as of the spring of 1979 it was still wearing those colors.

MacIntyre himself was unfairly blamed for instigating the merger. The rumors spread through Eastern that he had been "planted" in EAL's top spot by American, solely to implement the merger. There was absolutely no truth to this—MacIntyre privately opposed merger and publicly just went through the motions of supporting it. Yet like all rumors, it persisted and is believed by some EAL people to this day.

There was another merger possibility around this time, however—one involving Northwest. MacIntyre's attitude toward it is in question; according to Mr. Mac, he proposed a merger with Northwest "to certain people" and was told "we're tired of living through merger fights—we don't want to try it." Adds MacIntyre:

"I did talk to Don Nyrop [president of Northwest] and I know I could have gotten that one through. A certain chairman of the CAB told me informally it would fly. Nyrop was a friend of mine—he was in favor of it. We never did get to the point of deciding who would be the surviving carrier."

Harper Woodward tells a somewhat different story. "While Mac was still president, I saw an overlay of route charts putting various airline combinations together. One of them depicted Eastern's and Northwest's routes if they merged. I went and saw Mac, who scoffed at the idea—'All we'd have is a long string from Tokyo to Miami,' he told me. 'It doesn't make any sense.' Some years later Roz Gilpatrick [another EAL director] and I talked to Nyrop, who said the merger never would have been acceptable to Northwest because it couldn't have afforded to take on Eastern's debts. The only thing that would have been bad about a merger with Northwest would have been the equipment —it was completely incompatible."

The discrepancies seem a bit hard to explain unless one accepts the inevitable weaknesses of human memory. A third unnamed EAL official says he believes the first overtures made to Northwest came while Rickenbacker headed Eastern and when Croil Hunter was president of Northwest—sometime in the early 1950s. He is of the opinion that it was EVR who rejected the plan and that MacIntyre resurrected it after the American merger went down the drain.

It doesn't make much difference which account is more accurate; given the shape Eastern was in, the airline was dealing from weakness, not strength, a poor posture in any merger negotiations. Actually Eastern came relatively close to another merger in 1963 as part of the directors' efforts to find a replacement for MacIntyre. The search had been going on for about six months, conducted by a special directors' committee consisting of Fred Turner, retired board chairman of Southern Bell, Smythe Gambrell, and Woodward. They picked the man they wanted: Harding Lawrence, now Braniff's chief but at the time executive vice president of Continental and Bob Six's right-hand man.

Lawrence was too loyal to Six to conduct any talks with Eastern behind his back. He not only informed Six that overtures had been made, but suggested that if Eastern wanted him as badly as it seemed to, maybe they'd also consider a Continental-EAL merger. Lawrence was unhappy with Continental's then limited route structure and figured this was an ideal way to expand. Nothing came of the negotiations, however. Woodward says, "It fell through because of a misunderstanding—Bob thought we were going to get Harding Lawrence only if a merger was consummated, while we thought we were going to get Harding first and then continue to discuss a merger."

MacIntyre was not aware of the Continental-Lawrence talks, although he was no fool—he knew he was in trouble with the directors, some of whom were hinting to him that it might be a good idea if both he and Captain Eddie left. At this point in time he was fed up anyway. The two-year merger battle had sapped his strength, and he was particularly disillusioned about his inability to shore up Eastern's executive echelons with fresh, younger blood. This was an impossible task while there was a chance of the merger going through; every promising airline executive he talked to would say, "It sounds fine, but where will I stand if Eastern merges?" Mr. Mac had no answer. Not until the merger was dead did he finally hit paydirt in his search for new executive talent—he hired Todd Cole away from Delta, naming him senior vice-president of finance and administration and giving Tom Creighton the title of vice-president and secretary.

Mr. Mac landed a person of Cole's caliber for one reason: Todd Cole felt he had gone as far as he could go at Delta and he wanted to progress one more step up the ladder—to succeed Woolman. There were many at Delta who thought him eminently qualified, too, but Woolman apparently didn't see it that way. Cole theorizes that Woolman instinctively resented the prospect of being succeeded by someone he remembered as a young greenhorn—Cole had been with Delta since 1940. When Woolman finally decided it was time to name a so-called "crown prince," he shocked his airline by going outside for Earl Johnson of General Dynamics. It was never revealed exactly what commitments C.E. made to Johnson, but he did give him the only long-term contract he ever awarded to a Delta executive.

The contract, not to mention the hiring, turned out to be a mistake. Woolman never did see eye to eye with his supposed successor and eventually made a severance pay arrangement— one of the classic stories told around Delta concerns the time the accounting department was supposed to send Johnson his first severance check.

"By the way, Mr. Woolman, how do you want us to send this?" accounting inquired.

"Surface mail," C.E. glowered.

By this time, however, Cole already had departed Delta. He'd been interested in Eastern before MacIntyre hired him, having gotten a thorough look at the airline's problems during the merger fight, and expressed his interest to George Moore of the City National Bank in New York. It was Moore who put him in touch with Mr. Mac.

Cole had no idea MacIntyre's own position at Eastern was about as secure as a two-ton girder suspended from a frayed cable. "I was naive on that score," he admits, "having grown up in Delta's solidly structured, stable organization." He knew Mr. Mac was having his troubles, of course, and that Rickenbacker was one of them. Curiously, Cole is one of the few who doesn't think Captain Eddie's interference and second-guessing were deliberate or malicious.

"Interference, yes," Cole says, "but not deliberate. Rickenbacker's having an office in the same building, plus his strong personal ties among the people of Eastern, made interference inevitable. He had a much stronger personality than Mac. People would come to him with problems and ask for advice and he'd give it. A forceful man like the Captain simply generates strong emotions."

It is generally believed that when Cole joined Eastern, MacIntyre had promised him the presidency. Cole denies any such specific promise was made, for the obvious reason that directors, not outgoing presidents, choose presidential successors. But MacIntyre did give Cole the impression that he had no intention of staying at Eastern very long, and apparently hinted that he would recommend Cole as his replacement. In any case, Cole himself was aware that the directors were looking for a new president—relations between Mr. Mac and the board were becoming openly strained—and while he hoped it would be him, he was not surprised when a different choice was made.

The choice was Floyd Hall, senior vice president and system general manager of TWA, whom the selection committee wooed for almost six months before he agreed to take the job. Erudite, articulate, and personable, Hall had MacIntyre's intelligence plus the priceless asset of airline experience, not merely as an executive but as a line pilot—he had started with TWA as a young copilot and after making captain had climbed rapidly up the management ladder. His reputation in the industry was that of a highly competent executive whose outer suaveness was draped over a tough, decisive mind. His well-groomed appearance, complete with a dapper mustache, fooled people.

"You look at Floyd," a friend said of him, "and you think you're seeing a William Powell type of guy, very fastidious, nonchalant, and easygoing. But when you got to know him, he was more a John Wayne or even, on occasion, a Wallace Beery—he could talk about opera one minute and ream you out like a Marine drill instructor the next."

Hall's cool, logical mind made him that much harder to woo. He was extremely secure at TWA, where president Charles Tillinghast considered him not only one of the industry's brightest young men (he was forty-seven) but a definite possibility to head TWA sometime in the future. One of his greatest assets was versatility—he knew virtually every facet of the airline business from flight operations to cabin service. In the latter field his innate sense of good taste came as somewhat of a surprise to those who considered him just a capable pilot with a flair for operations management. Given authority in areas other than flight operations, he revitalized TWA's service on its transcontinental and international routes to such an extent that it successfully competed against United and American domestically, destroyed Pan Am's long dominance in the North Atlantic market, and even challenged foreign carriers whose forte was providing airborne luxury. Todd Cole's remark, when he was asked his opinion of Hall by an EAL director, was an apt if inconclusive summary of his modus operandi.

"All I know about him," the blunt Cole replied, "is that he has the reputation of creating a passenger service that uses eleven napkins between New York and Los Angeles."

Under Hall, TWA had put together what was then probably the finest marketing organization in the industry—an area in which Eastern was sadly deficient. It was this weakness that sent the "search team" troika to Hall in the first place, asking Tillinghast's permission to talk to him about Eastern's marketing problems. At the time Tillinghast as president and TWA Board Chairman Ernie Breech were embroiled in a legal clash with Howard Hughes over control of the airline and for all practical purposes, Hall was running TWA.

The first EAL-Hall talks ostensibly concerned marketing,

Hall bringing along his new marketing vice president, Tom Mc-
Fadden, who had been head of sales at the National Broadcasting Company before Floyd hired him. This was early in 1963 but
by midsummer the wooing of Hall began to intensify. The selection committee invited him to a meeting at the Hampshire House
in New York, where Turner had a suite, and asked him directly
if he would have any interest in taking over at Eastern. Recalls
Hall:

"I told them I really didn't have much interest. I had an
excellent position at TWA. We were having difficulties with a
new financial man who was giving me a lot of trouble—I found
one of his guys going through my desk at night and I raised
bloody hell. Yet there was something about Eastern that intrigued me. Over the years I had evolved certain philosophies of
management that I wanted to try out. I can't say TWA didn't
encourage me—they did; they gave me a very free hand. But it
wasn't quite the way it would be at Eastern because here was an
airline flat on its ass and here was a place you could really test
your theories of management."

So his first answer to Eastern, in effect, was a "Not really—
but . . ." Subsequent contracts between Hall and the committee
sent him finally into a conference with Tillinghast and Breech, in
which he disclosed his talks with the EAL directors. Tillinghast
reminded him that he was heading for the presidency of TWA—
if Hall would stay, he promised, in two years at the most Breech
would retire, Tillinghast would move up to chairman, and Hall
would take over the airline.

It sounded great, but Hall wanted to know if they were
prepared to muzzle the finance officer who was giving him fits.
They could give him no such assurance and Hall understood
why—"If they gave in to me," he says, "they'd be captive to me."
There was more discussion concerning Hall's future at TWA but
Breech suddenly ended the debate.

"Floyd, you know what's the matter with you?" he observed. "You've arrived! Goddammit, nothing is going to satisfy
you until you get a chance to take some downtrodden company
and put it on its feet. As badly as we'd hate to see you go, and

believe me, we don't want you to leave, take Eastern up on their offer."

Enthused as he was about the idea of rebuilding the crippled, debt-wracked airline, Hall still wouldn't give Eastern an unequivocal answer. He was not being coyly reluctant—he knew, and the three directors knew, that the Rickenbacker situation was the biggest stumbling block. Aside from agreement on financial considerations, Hall wanted to make sure he was not going to be plunging into the same morass that had virtually destroyed MacIntyre.

"I knew Mac and Eddie had been feuding badly," Hall says. "And I knew Malcolm never really had a chance to run Eastern. Nobody to this day can tell whether Mac was a good, bad, or nothing president. It didn't take me long to realize, even before I accepted the job, that Eastern was divided into two camps—one Eddie's and the other Mac's. Things were so bad that people used to leave their offices at noon because they were afraid what would happen some afternoon when Eddie with a few belts of Early Times in him and Mac with a few martinis might actually come to blows. They were that uptight."

Hall got no arguments from any director about the seriousness of the feud. Even while the committee was negotiating with Hall, an embarrassing incident had taken place at a board meeting when Captain Eddie unexpectedly announced that he had sold his Eastern stock—100,000 shares, disposed of gradually and secretly. The stunned directors stared at him, and EVR gruffly explained, "I have all my eggs in one basket and I can see too many damned holes in the basket."

MacIntyre, his face the color of freshly spilled blood, said nothing at first but as the meeting adjourned, he asked the Captain, "I'd like to know at what price you sold."

"None of your goddamned business!" Captain Eddie answered. Several board members, overhearing the exchange, shook their heads.

So when Hall demanded total autonomy, the directors agreed—and that included not only the Captain's retirement as board chairman but his actual physical exile from Eastern's executive offices. He told Laurance Rockefeller, "Look, I'm not even going to sit down in my office until Rickenbacker is out of his."

That stipulation may have seemed harsh, but there wasn't a director—and this included those who were close friends of the Captain—who didn't agree that it had to be done. Harper Woodward says of MacIntyre's downfall:

"We came to the conclusion that both he and Eddie had to go, for you couldn't dismiss one without the other. I'll tell you how things stood with them: Someone once told me that if you asked Rickenbacker to jump out of the window, he'd say, 'Sure if I can take MacIntyre with me.' "

It was a painful decision and an even more painful task to break the news to the man whose name had become synonymous with that of the airline itself. The directors assigned this unpleasant chore were Jim Elkins, Paul Reinhold (a Jacksonville, Florida, dairy-firm owner), Turner, and Woodward. As gently as possible they told Rickenbacker that the board, in deciding to replace MacIntyre with Floyd Hall, also felt it was time for Captain Eddie to retire as chairman.

"He didn't take it very well," Elkins recalls in a masterpiece of understatement. "All we could do was sit back, bite the bullet, and wait for the explosion."

It came. One by one, Rickenbacker blasted each man in the room, pointing that bony forefinger and accusing him of disloyalty. He was a wounded, angry lion, backed into a corner, still snarling defiance. But he also was a man of courage, possessing amazing resilience and, in his own way, a sense of humility. A few days later Rockefeller and Woodward went to his office, believing it was time to persuade Rickenbacker to exit gracefully. They asked him to join them in Turner's suite that evening.

"I'm having an early dinner with Warren Lee Pierson [by coincidence, former TWA board chairman]," EVR told them, "but I'll come by as soon as we finish."

"Eddie, we've got some important matters to discuss so take it easy on the cocktails," Woodward suggested gently. Fred Turner had a rule there could be no drinking until all business matters had been completed, and EVR knew it.

"I won't have anything to drink," the Captain promised.

He showed up at the Hampshire House an hour and a half late, "really rolling," to quote Woodward. Before anyone had a chance to say a word, he began talking about the past, mostly retelling the story of how Alfred Sloan had given him a chance to buy control of Eastern. It was a story both Rockefeller and Woodward had heard at least a dozen times but they let him ramble. "With Eddie," Woodward says, "you either waited for him to get sober or just get angry and leave."

The long discourse finally ended. Captain Eddie looked around the room. Now his voice was razor sharp—no more aimless nostalgia, fueled by alcohol.

"If any of you people tell anyone what I'm about to say, I'll kill you," he declared.

There wasn't a sound.

"Okay. I'm willing to leave the whole damned thing to Floyd Hall. I'll move out of my office like you guys want. No more arguing, no more fighting. I'll do what you want me to do."

In that surrender, there was dignity worthy of a Captain Eddie.

And he lived up to his word. His bitterness was replaced by resignation, and he even made every effort to welcome Floyd Hall not as the man who had caused his ouster but as the bright new, young executive who had come to rescue the airline. Rickenbacker personally composed the official teletyped announcement that was sent throughout the airline's sprawling system.

ALL OFFICES   ALL OFFICERS
TO ALL MEMBERS OF THE EASTERN AIR LINES FAMILY
   TODAY FLOYD HALL TAKES OVER AS PRESIDENT AND CHIEF EXECUTIVE OFFICER OF EASTERN AIRLINES.
   WE ARE FORTUNATE TO HAVE THE SERVICES OF ONE OF THE INDUSTRY'S OUTSTANDING YOUNG LEADERS. MAKING AIRLINE MANAGEMENT HIS CAREER, HE BEGAN AS A PILOT AND, THROUGH STUDY AND APPLICATION, WORKED HIS WAY UP THROUGH THE RANKS. HE THUS COMBINES VISION WITH PRACTICAL "SHIRT-SLEEVES" EXPERIENCE IN EVERY PHASE OF MODERN AIRLINE OPERATION, MARKETING AND MANAGEMENT, AND IS STILL NOT AFRAID OF GETTING A LITTLE GREASE ON HIS HANDS.

I ASK ALL OF YOU—YOU YOUNGSTERS WHO HAVE MORE RECENTLY
JOINED OUR RANKS AS WELL AS YOU VETERANS WHO HELPED ME BUILD
EASTERN AIRLINES THROUGH THE YEARS—I ASK ALL OF YOU TO GIVE
FLOYD HALL THE SAME FULL MEASURE OF LOYALTY AND COOPERATION
YOU ALWAYS GAVE ME IN THE PAST.
CAPTAIN EDDIE RICKENBACKER
CHAIRMAN OF THE BOARD OF DIRECTORS

That communication, of course, contained no mention of Rickenbacker's own impending retirement, which the Board had agreed would take effect as of January 1, 1964. It was transmitted over EAL's teletype network November 20, 1963, immediately after Hall accepted the job, and simultaneously Eastern's vice president of public relations, Bill Van Dusen, issued to the media the news release on Hall's appointment; the announcement said Hall would take over his new post December 16, but Floyd asked for brief delay.

Long before it was made official, of course, the word was out within Eastern itself. And while MacIntyre years later was to insist that it came as no surprise, people who know him say it still was a stunning, bitter blow. Both Rockefeller and Woodward had been warning him for five months that the directors were losing confidence in him—they had even gone to the point, shortly before Hall was named, of sending Rockefeller a letter detailing their unhappiness with EAL's current management. MacIntyre received a copy and immediately asked Rockefeller to lunch, where he blurted, "My God, why didn't you tell me all this before?"

Rockefeller shook his head in disbelief. "Harper and I have been trying to tell you this for five months, Mac. You just weren't listening."

But while he had plenty of indications he was going to be fired, the name of his replacement was kept from him. He was one of the few EAL executives who didn't know. Frank Sharpe knew and went through the tortures of the damned trying to decide whether to tip off Mr. Mac, whom he liked and admired. Sharpe got a call from Smythe Gambrell at six A.M. one day.

"Are you alone?" Gambrell asked.

Sharpe glanced at his wife, still asleep beside him. "Well, yes."

"Good. Do you know Floyd Hall?"

"I've heard of him but I never met him."

"Well, completely off the record, and MacIntyre doesn't know this yet, Floyd Hall will be our new president. I want you to take him around to those ad agencies we've been talking to and let him hear their pitches so he'll be tuned in."

The latter was a reference to a decision quite a few Eastern veterans deeply resented—ending the airline's long relationship with Brad Walker's agency. Walker still won't comment on the unexpected rupture but others say it was pressure from Gambrell, aided and abetted by Van Dusen, neither of whom had gotten along with Walker. Sharpe didn't mind doing what Gambrell had ordered, but remarks that "he was putting me in one hell of a position—my relations with Mac were pretty good."

In the end he decided not to say anything to MacIntyre. By this time the airline gossip-and-rumor factory was in full production but Mr. Mac went about his business as if he were deaf in both ears. He flew to Miami in November to speak before the Miami Bar Association and was in John Halliburton's office, waiting for the vice president of operations to drive him to the dinner; Clara was with him. Halliburton's secretary came in and said, "Mr. Fred Turner is trying to get you, Mr. MacIntyre."

"Take the call in here, Mac," Halliburton offered. "We'll wait for you outside."

They left MacIntyre alone for about five minutes. When the president of Eastern emerged, his face was the color of chalk, but he said nothing except, "I have to go back to New York tonight, right after the dinner."

His wife asked why. MacIntyre took her back into Halliburton's office and closed the door. A few minutes later, when they were in Halliburton's car en route to the predinner cocktail party, Clara MacIntyre began to sob. Mr. Mac patted her hand.

"I'm out, John," he said. "I thought I had gotten our financing straightened out but . . ." His voice trailed off.

Like Rickenbacker, he went out with dignity. There was a brief flap over termination arrangements—Woodward suggested he get a lawyer to represent him but Mr. Mac said he could do it himself—and an amicable settlement of sorts was finally reached.

"I felt and still feel no bitterness," he says today. "I enjoyed it. But I'm equally glad I'm the hell out of it."

He sold all his Eastern stock, philosophizing that "when you get out of an industry, it's best to get the hell all the way out." He went with Martin-Marietta briefly on Brad Walker's recommendation, and after going through major heart surgery returned to private law practice in New York. He remains very active and in the best health he has enjoyed for years. "I have a motto," he chuckles, "that it's better to wear out than rust out."

He has seen virtually nothing of his old comrades at Eastern, most of whom remember him with great affection—including a number of older captains. Mr. Mac, thanks mostly to his labor headaches, didn't get along with the flight crews too well and once called the pilots "a bunch of bus drivers." But they still considered him a square-shooter, a man of integrity who tried his damndest. He did write John Halliburton a letter just before the latter retired; Mr. Mac had been elected mayor of Scarsdale, New York, and wanted to know if Eastern's meteorology department could furnish the town with advance snow warnings.

Exit Malcolm MacIntyre. Enter Floyd Hall.

He was cleaning out his desk in TWA's executive offices in New York when one of his public relations men, rotund, sardonic, but immensely popular Ken Fletcher, stopped in to say good-bye.

"Floyd, I just want you to know I'm sorry to see you leave," Fletcher told him. He meant it; Ken was an iconoclast when it came to most brass hats, but Hall he respected as the man largely responsible for TWA's comeback after years of management turmoil under Hughes.

Hall smiled. "Ken, once in a lifetime a man gets a chance to save a company. I'm getting two chances. I can't turn it down."

He was supposed to start with Eastern January 1, the day Rickenbacker's retirement became effective, and at Rockefeller's own suggestion he took his wife to Puerto Rico and other Caribbean spots for a vacation early in December. It was cut short by a telephone call from Smythe Gambrell who told him, "Things are deteriorating rapidly—we feel you should come back right away."

The earliest he could return was December 15 and MacIntyre cleaned out his office and left on the thirteenth—leaving Eastern minus a president, contrary to the corporation's bylaws for one day. So to conform with that legality, the board elected Lefty Lethridge president of Eastern Air Lines to serve for just twenty-four hours—the shortest tenure in the history of commercial aviation.

And on December 15, 1963, Floyd Hall became Eastern's seventh president—eighth counting Lethridge—and there were those who likened this event to assuming the captaincy of the *Titanic* after it hit the iceberg. It wasn't really that bad, for Hall quickly realized he had a few things going for him. One was employee loyalty and determination to make Eastern come back —all the rank and file asked for was good leadership. A second asset was a cadre of management veterans who weren't afraid to tell Hall how they felt about the airline's past mistakes. When he asked men like Sharpe, Lethridge, Halliburton, and Froesch for advice or opinions, they were willing to give voice to their views. They expected that a new administration was going to use one mammoth broom on the management staff, and that many an executive neck would be going under the guillotine, but they told him what they thought he should know, not what they figured he wanted to hear.

Frank Sharpe was one. He was among the first officers Hall talked to, asking him about Eastern's weaknesses and strengths.

"The greatest asset you have," Sharpe told him, "is Eastern's people. You've got a bunch of managers out there who'll do the job, no matter how many hours they have to work. And I'll tell you something else, Floyd—no matter what you do, don't get rid of the Hat-in-the-Ring pin. I know you'll hear a lot about all the mistakes Captain Eddie made, but never forget he has a hard core of sentiment and loyalty among people who've given their lives to this airline. You put a picture of Rickenbacker on the wall of a twenty-year dinner and the place goes wild. The same goes for a picture of that twenty-year pin."

Hall took that advice to heart. He had a pretty good idea that Rickenbacker was hurt by his forced retirement, although he had tried to hide it; Sheppy could tell from his very quietness as he prepared to move from the office on the sixteenth floor of the Rockefeller Plaza building he had occupied for a quarter century. It was a corner room, pleasantly though not luxuriously furnished, with six chairs and a fairly large desk, nondescript drapes, and carpeting—rugs *were* the exception in EAL executive offices in those days. Eastern today has vice presidents with more attractive quarters than Rickenbacker had, but he always seemed to feel that too much swank in his working space was out of focus with his spartan spending policies. He loved that office, however, and it was a sad day for him when he moved.

Space had been found for him in a much smaller office at 45 Rockefeller Plaza, just across the street. He asked Bev Griffith and Sheppy to make sure the new room looked as much like the old one as possible; Bev actually took photographs of the pictures and plaques on the latter's walls so they could be rehung in exactly the same places. The moving began on a Friday afternoon and was completed by noon the next day. He never went back to 10 Rockefeller Plaza to the day he died, but Floyd Hall made a point to drop in on him from time to time, telling him how things were going at the airline and asking his opinion of certain moves—something the old man appreciated, even though he knew his opinion didn't make much difference anymore.

The young president—he was a year younger than Captain Eddie had been when the latter became Eastern's chief executive officer—always treated him with great respect and consideration. EVR, in turn, openly liked Hall. He kept telling everyone he knew Floyd very well; in truth, they had never met, but the Captain didn't let that bother him because he was honestly anxious to have Floyd succeed and his little self-deception was a means of letting people know he approved of the board's choice. Actually, they first met right after Hall was named president and Rockefeller had to tell the old man Floyd wanted to move into EVR's office as soon as possible.

"Hell, that's no problem," Captain Eddie allowed. "Tell the young man I'd like to see him."

When Hall came in, accompanied by Woodward, to pay his respects, Rickenbacker was exceptionally friendly. "There are a few things I want you to do, son. First, I want you to occupy this office and you can move in anytime that's convenient for you. Second, if you'd like to have my furniture, that's fine with me. Sit right here where I do." His voice dropped a little and Hall could almost swear there were tears in the old man's eyes. "That'll mean something to the boys and girls of Eastern, Floyd."

"That'll mean something to the boys and girls of Eastern." In that one brief sentence, Floyd Hall, disciple of modern management, got a glimpse of what had made Eastern great. The hell with all the past mistakes, he thought—this airline is worth saving.

But he also decided this was the time to bring up the touchiest point of all: interference.

"Captain, you have the largest pair of shoes in the industry," he told Rickenbacker. "I can't possibly step into them"—and as EVR nodded, Hall added meaningfully, "nor into your shadow."

Captain Eddie turned to Woodward. "The young man is absolutely right!" he exclaimed.

Hall did put his own desk and chair exactly where the Captain's had been, after insisting that the old man take his furniture with him. He also had air-conditioning installed—Rickenbacker hated artificial cooling systems. As long as Captain Eddie lived, Hall treated him with kindness and skillful deference; on EVR's seventy-seventh birthday he would dedicate a fountain erected in his honor in front of the new General Offices (Building 16) in Miami. When the Air Force Academy hung Rickenbacker's portrait, Hall took all of the Captain's surviving squadron mates out to the ceremony in an Eastern plane. Floyd's parents lived in southern Colorado, so after the dedication he personally took the old man back to his hotel room, put him to bed at ten P.M., and drove to his parents' home. When he returned the next day, he found that Rickenbacker, Reed Chambers, and the rest of the old pilots had gone downtown to a bar where they drank and raised hell until four A.M.

EVR never saw Brad Walker again, but he kept up a close relationship with Lefty Lethridge. The day Rickenbacker moved out of his office, Lethridge walked in to say good-bye. The room was full of boxes and packing cartons and the Captain seemed a little harrassed. But he walked over to Lethridge and put his arm around him.

"Lefty, you remember a few years ago when you sold me on ordering those forty 727s?"

"I remember, Eddie," Lethridge said softly.

EVR chuckled. "I know why, you bastard. You only wanted to do it because you wanted to match United's order."

Such moments of happiness were rare for the retired monarch, however. His major activity after the move was to write his autobiography; he had taken Sheppy with him to the new office and the book occupied most of their time. He would dictate on records, Sheppy sending them to Booten Herndon, a free-lance writer of highest repute, who transcribed them and then edited the voluminous output. Several publishers had approached him for the autobiography and he almost chose Doubleday because they had published his previous *Flying Circus* and *Seven Came Back*. He finally signed with Prentice-Hall, solely for the reason that they did a lot of school books and EVR wanted his autobiography to be in as many school libraries as possible; when it was finished, he sent a copy to almost every high school and college in the United States, the funds coming from friends whom he had asked to contribute for this purpose. He didn't feel up to autographing books for the thousands of employees who wanted personalized copies, but he did paste a short message with his signature in each volume, and he did autograph some 5,000 copies for friends and associates.

The Captain worked on the autobiography for about a

year, plus a few months longer cutting and revising it with Herndon's help. In a way he regretted its completion because there wasn't enough to keep him busy once it was published. He still insisted on coming into his office at eight A.M., just as he had done when he was running the airline, but he took a brief nap around nine. Those daily naps had become part of his routine in his old office during the later years, but he considered them a sign of old age and ordered Sheppy never to tell anyone. She didn't, but most of his officers knew about them anyway.

His principal activity once the book was finished was reading reports and answering correspondence—much of it from youngsters. Sheppy remembers that he was a sucker for young people; Boys' Clubs were his favorite charity and all the honorariums he received for speeches during World War II and later were turned over to various Boys' Clubs. He even called in special problem children he had heard about and would talk to them in his office. Sheppy remembers one youth emerging from a session with EVR, shaking his head.

"Something wrong?" she asked.

"Well, I asked him what I should do to become successful."

"What did he tell you?" Sheppy inquired.

"He told me to cut my damned hair."

His visitors at 45 Rockefeller Plaza were few, and there were times when he seemed a little despondent. Those who did take the time to see him thought he had mellowed, but Sheppy saw something else: an old man who had been hurt, who hated feeling unneeded. Rockefeller and Woodward would lunch with him occasionally and so did Lefty Lethridge and some of his other old associates at Eastern. Rockefeller, knowing EVR was restless, suggested he get involved in some kind of public service, like scouting.

"It didn't quite work out the way Laurance expected," Woodward laughs. "All Eddie did was tell the scouts off-color jokes. We had a lot of trouble with his book. He bought God knows how many copies and distributed them free to employees. But that was the Captain—you'd hate him one minute and love him the next."

But more was changing around Eastern than Captain Eddie's status. Floyd Hall took command of a demoralized airline army, so battered that when an outside firm made a complete financial analysis at Hall's request, it reported that unless drastic measures were taken, America's fourth largest air carrier could not meet its payroll by August. Hall was stunned; he knew things were bad but he hadn't expected Eastern to be a literal shambles. It had compiled five years of deficits totalling $70 million. Employee morale could be compared to that of a football team with a twenty-five-game losing streak. Most of its fleet was obsolete and there was no money for modernization. Its route structure was a hodgepodge of uneconomical short-haul segments and the only two new route awards for the past three years—Twin Cities to Miami, and Toronto to points south via Buffalo—were both loaded with so many restrictions that they were liabilities.

The airline's proud on-time performance had deteriorated from first in the industry to next to last. The WHEAL Club was in full swing, marketing and promotion were almost nonexistent, and like Custer surrounded by angry Indians, Eastern was being clobbered in every direction with competition from aggressive, smartly run rivals possessing better routes, equipment, and service. The slogan Mr. Mac loved so much—"The Nation's Most Progressive Airline"—sounded hollow and almost presumptuous.

Hall had a few meetings with MacIntyre just before the latter departed, going over management personnel and other problems—Floyd had always liked him. "He was a good friend," Hall relates. "Sure he was a little bitter—he was made to look like the guy who failed. But he was a big man during the difficult transition, always willing to discuss a problem with me."

What appraisals Mr. Mac gave him about individual officers will never be known, but the subsequent shakeup was of cataclysmic proportions. Among the heads sent rolling were Walton Cutshall, vice president of sales and advertising; Jerald Jarrard, vice president of industrial relations; Robert Lipp, vice president of market and economic research; and Ambrose Chabot, vice president of maintenance. Significantly, all these positions were in the areas Hall considered as major weaknesses.

Many of those who survived the Hall version of the French Revolution suffered demotions in the sense that they lost their status as executive vice presidents or had their jobs as well as their titles changed—Hall disliked the word "executive" preceding a VP designation, and preferred to use "senior." Under MacIntyre only one man was a senior vice president and that was Bob Turner; in the Hall regime, he became simply a vice president and no pre-Hall officer was made a senior VP. Lefty Lethridge went from executive vice president of staff services to vice president of civic affairs, Tom Creighton lost his jurisdiction over finance and became VP and corporation secretary, and Frank Sharpe, executive vice president of sales and services under Mr. Mac, became vice president of customer services.

The title changes went deeper than mere semantics. For Hall in effect shoved virtually all the former top brass down a few notches and brought in a whole new platoon of upper-echelon officers from other carriers. American and TWA were the chief sources of his recruiting efforts, and the only holdover from the MacIntyre era to not only retain his status but improve it was Todd Cole, who had come from Delta. Hall named him one of the two senior vice presidents in the new establishment—Art Lewis, enticed away from American, was the other. Cole remained in charge of finance and administration and Lewis was designated senior vice-president and general manager—the new "crown prince," as it were.

One by one they came aboard the apparently sinking ship —men of outstanding talent and with a universal belief that Eastern could be saved. Among their attributes was ambition—it was to be said much later that Hall formed one of the most brilliant teams in aviation history, so superb that eventually he couldn't control it, as the "togetherness" of the 1964 crisis degenerated into squabbling and jockeying for internal supremacy. This was far in the future, however; the atmosphere in 1964 was of dedication to a common cause, a common desire to see the gallant old airline survive and prosper even though the industry cynics were already writing its obituary.

In addition to Lewis, there was Bill Crilly of TWA, the new

vice president of planning . . . Sam Higginbottom, TWA's crack maintenance expert who succeeded a tired, dispirited Chabot . . . Ralph Skinner, named the new vice president of industrial and personnel relations, whose main job was to repair Eastern's tattered labor situation . . . George Gordon, taking over as vice president of marketing . . . Dwight Taylor, handed the herculean task of shoring up Eastern's route-development efforts in Washington under the title of vice president of public affairs.

But equally important were the "little people"—the 18,000 men and women of Eastern who had seen their airline buffeted by labor strife, management mistakes, and a quandary of bad breaks, not the least of which had been the devastating succession of adverse decisions in route cases. To them, as well as to all officers, Hall sent a personal message.

"We don't have any money," he told them. "Our airplanes are obsolete, we can't spend a dime on our ground facilities except what we can do with soap, water, and elbow grease. Our company is either going to go down the drain or it's going to make it—it's up to all of us."

He translated those words into a course of action that became known as Operation Bootstrap—quite literally, the well-nigh impossible task of an airline trying to grab its ankles and lift itself off the floor. But before he could put it into operation, he first had to determine exactly what had to be done—"in one hell of a hurry," to use his own words. A few days after he became president, he got a symbolic, firsthand look at how shabby the airline had become—he was in a Shuttle Connie when a metal strip on the overhead baggage rack came loose and almost hit him on the head. He got another when he showed up at a pilots' meeting to discuss the airline's current status and plans for the future—the captain running the session remarked that he had just heard some good news and bad news.

"The good news is that Pan Am and Eastern are going to merge," he said with a straight face. "The bad news is that the new airline will be run by Eastern's management."

Hall laughed but his second thought was how far Eastern's hierarchy had sunk in the eyes of employees. He had to restore more than pride in their company; they also needed to have more confidence in their leaders. To implement Operation Bootstrap, in essence an employee-motivation plan, it was necessary to demonstrate that management, too, meant business.

Equipment, for example; when Hall took over, jets constituted less than fifty per cent of Eastern's fleet—the lowest percentage in the trunkline industry. Less than one fourth of the seats being offered the public were in jets, again the worst jet-capacity figure among the major airlines. The Electras were superb airplanes, but they weren't jets and they had been bought in such numbers that Eastern was paying some $65 million a year *in interest alone* on the propjets. The leased 720's equipped with water-injection engines were so underpowered that they couldn't fly nonstop between New York and Houston without weight restrictions. And Eastern's DC-8's, even with the bigger engines for which Rickenbacker had insisted on waiting, had the highest operating costs of any jet flying.

Knowing that the airline's most pressing need was short-range jets, Hall fixed his sights on the Douglas DC-9, a twin-engine jetliner ideally suited for EAL's myriad short-haul routes. He turned the financing and contractual arrangements over to Todd Cole; given Eastern's financial posture in the fall of 1964, when negotiations with Douglas were in full swing, the assignment was slightly easier than digging for diamonds with a dull butter knife. Cole's ace-in-the-hole was his long rapport with Douglas, dating back to his Delta days, plus the fact that Douglas badly needed an Eastern order to get the DC-9 program off dead center; when Cole began his parleys with the manufacturer, only TWA and Delta had ordered the new jet.

No contract would be signed officially until February 1965, but before the end of '64 Hall knew he had solved at least part of the airline's equipment headaches. The DC-9's would replace the Electra on most of the latter's routes and the propjet, in turn, could be assigned to the Shuttle. This would allow the bulk of the dilapidated Constellation fleet to finally be retired.

For MacIntyre's pride and joy, the Shuttle, Hall did what Mr. Mac had fought against for so many years—he listened to the pleas of Art Lewis, Frank Sharpe, Lefty Lethridge, and a few others and raised fares by four dollars. At the time of Floyd's takeover, the one-way fare between New York and Washington was only eleven dollars and this was raised to fifteen. Pending delivery of the DC-9's and the release of Electras for Shuttle duty, the Connie fleet was refurbished.

Operation Bootstrap itself was aimed at achieving specific goals in four areas: (1) generating more revenue, (2) improving on-time performance, (3) decreasing passengers complaints, and (4) increasing passenger compliments. Every employee visibly contributing to meeting any of these goals was awarded one hundred dollars' worth of Green Stamps—this incentive program was the brainchild of George Gordon, the new vice president of marketing.

Even today Floyd Hall is prouder of Bootstrap than of anything else he achieved at Eastern.

"I knew what I wanted to do," he says. "It was part of this grand scheme of mine. I think a corporation has to do more than just exist and create profits. It has to relate to the community it's in, to serve that community, and this is especially true in the airline industry. It has to build confidence in that organization. So I wanted to set up an organization that made every employee sensitive to the fact that the customer is the only one keeping us in business. It was almost the antithesis of what we had been before. If you build a really dynamic company, you light a fire in all employees to such an extent that it'll glow outside and your image will actually show outside. Our objective was that everything the customer sees, hears, touches, and comes in contact with, from the first phone call for a reservation to when we put him in a taxi at his destination, has got to show. I like to call it 'inventive considerateness.'

"What we did with Bootstrap, instead of calling it something like Operating Plan Five, was to give it a name employees could relate to. The whole purpose was to put some excitement in one's daily job. And secondly, we wanted everything outside the airline to reflect the image of what was happening on the inside."

There was more to Eastern's comeback than Bootstrap.

New route awards were given the highest priority, and Hall had to make one of those tough decisions that come with the presidential territory—he took the major job of handling Eastern's route cases away from Smythe Gambrell and gave this responsibility to Dwight Taylor, who had learned the way into Washington back doors while he was with American. Gambrell's law firm, however, was retained as the airline's outside legal counsel and Hall thus prevented any hard feelings. For Gambrell, however, it meant the lessening of influence he had wielded from the earliest days of Captain Eddie, and in a way it was just as well that it coincided with EVR's own departure. Gambrell and Rickenbacker were devoted to each other; the lawyer was much like the old war-horse in philosophy and methods. They were both totally honest, blunt, and hardworking.

Before putting Bootstrap into effect, Hall leaned heavily on the experience and observations of Art Lewis, a young "old hand" in the airline game. Lewis had gotten into the business via a college thesis he wrote on air transportation. It was good enough to be published in the *Harvard Business Review*, and one chapter appeared in the *Journal of Air Commerce*; Lewis sent reprints to several airlines and received an offer from American to join its staff as a research analyst just before the U.S. entered World War II. Lewis rejoined American after eighteen months on military duty and rose swiftly through the executive ranks to become an assistant vice president for planning. He worked with both operations and marketing and was largely responsible for American's buying the DC-7 because of its nonstop transcontinental capability—a decision some of his colleagues challenged with the argument that there wasn't enough coast-to-coast travel to justify a sixty-passenger airplane.

Lewis left American in 1955 to become president of Hawaiian, a carrier close to bankruptcy; he turned it around and then had the airline sold out from under him. American wanted him back and TWA made some overtures, but by coincidence he met Floyd Hall for the first time on the same day Hall took over EAL—a mutual banker friend had suggested they talk.

"I haven't had time to organize anything yet," Hall told

him, "but I'd like to keep you in mind," It sounded like a don't-call-us—we'll-call-you kissoff, but in February Lewis got a call from an executive talent "headhunting" firm.

"There's a rumor you're going back with American," he was told.

"Well, I guess that's right. I've pretty much made up my mind."

"How firm?"

"I've told C.R. I'd take the job."

"Eastern's looking for a top man, Art. Is there anything we can do to change your mind?"

Lewis is a pragmatist. "If I received an offer from Eastern that was so much better than American's, I'd be willing to go back and talk to C.R.—I'd want his okay because I've already accepted his offer."

"What Eastern has in mind, Art, is senior vice president and general manager in charge of all line operations on a day-to-day basis. How does that sound?"

"Good enough for me to see C.R.," Lewis admitted.

He saw C.R. and also Marion Sadler, Smith's immediate predecessor after the latter moved up to board chairman. C. R., who had mellowed somewhat himself, refrained from telling Lewis what he had told MacIntyre sarcastically six years earlier —that "ninety percent of Eastern's people couldn't get a job with American"—and released him to accept Hall's offer.

On the way back to Hawaii to clean up his affairs prior to joining Eastern, Lewis took along a simple document to study: EAL's schedule.

"I analyzed it," he recalls, "and came away with the conclusion that the company could be turned around a lot faster than anyone supposed. Having been an old hand with schedules, it was easy to see why Eastern was in such terrible shape—its schedule pattern was a mess, totally inefficient from the standpoint of equipment utilization and business travel patterns. When I got back, I told Floyd if we could just clean up the schedule, we'd get significant and fast improvement."

Hall asked him to tour the airline's facilities. He laid a report on the president's desk that was nothing short of an indictment. "Generally disreputable conditions," he informed Hall. "Everything is just plain bad, from the dirty, actually filthy terminals to the executive offices and the appearance of people on the line."

"It looks like an airline run down at the heels and that's exactly what we have," he added.

Lewis also found what he termed "shocking disorganization of day-to-day operations." In the spring of 1964 Eastern was canceling up to three percent of its flights daily because of maintenance problems. Nor was equipment being routed or organized in such a way as to reinforce itself—cost cutting and penny pinching had left the airline almost completely bereft of spare parts. There was no backup protection for canceled flights, for the bulk of the cancellations were on an ad hoc basis, contrary to the industry's general practice of trying to plan some percentage of cancellations in advance so alternate arrangements can be made for the affected flights.

One out of every three flights was late. For every one thousand passengers carried there were four pieces of mishandled baggage—an industry high—and errors in reservations were at an all-time high. Passenger service was, to put it charitably, desultory. "In trying to save money," Lewis observes, "they had begun treating people like digits. The Eastern reservations system had been designed to cut costs, with no capability of following through on a passenger. There was no control of connecting flights, which simply compounded the problems of missed connections, lost luggage, no-shows, and mishandled passengers." One of Hall's first reforms was to beef up reservations with skilled personnel who set up improved control procedures— Eastern's record for oversales was grist for the WHEAL complaint mill.

No matter where Lewis, Higginbottom, or any of the new team turned, they saw chaos. Marketing had been decimated, again as an economy measure, with field sales offices wiped out and capable people fired throughout the system and in the general offices, too. All this had accomplished was a reduction in revenues canceling out the money saved. The Hall administration restored the district sales offices and created an overall marketing structure.

Higginbottom, a man who had made TWA's maintenance department one of the finest in the world, was appalled at what he found at Eastern. He first talked to Hall about an EAL job in January of 1964 and was supposed to start work March first, but Floyd asked him to come down to Miami a week ahead of time and look things over. He arrived the same day that Lewis started work in New York—February twenty-fifth—and that happened to be the day that an Eastern DC-8, operating as Flight 304, crashed shortly after taking off from New Orleans. It was the final leg of a Mexico City–New York trip but the big jet went out of control at a relatively low altitude and plunged into Lake Pontchartrain, killing all fifty-one passengers and the crew of seven.

It was a rude beginning for the new officers, and the subsequent investigation offered stark and tragic evidence of how badly Eastern's once-proud maintenance record had deteriorated. It disclosed the flight had been operating with a faulty Pitch Trim Compensator (PTC)—a unit that had been removed no fewer than fifteen times from various aircraft before it was installed in the DC-8 that crashed. The PTC is a device that offsets a jet's tendency to "tuck under"—assume a nose-down attitude—at high speed even when flying level. Mechanically it consists of a tiny computer which senses the critical airspeed at which tuck-under occurs and automatically sends compensating signals to an actuator. The latter, in turn, trims the controls for level flight.

Pilots had been complaining about this particular PTC on several occasions, reporting that it was producing unwanted extension—in other words, it was activating trim when it wasn't needed. Eastern's mechanics kept removing the unit, could find no discrepancy, and continued to put it back into service. Later it was found that Eastern's PTC tests were not capable of detecting certain computer malfunctions.

Captain William Zeng, commanding Flight 304, had noticed in the aircraft log book turned over to him by the crew of the southbound flight that the PTC had failed a ground check in New York just before takeoff and was inoperative. Zeng, because of that, filed a flight plan calling for reduced airspeed all the way back to New York. As it turned out, this precaution proved futile. Less than six minutes after the plane left New Orleans, the PTC activated without warning, literally locking the stabilizers in down trim, creating an abnormally heavy force on the controls. The crew reduced airspeed to relieve the yoke pressure but just at the moment the airspeed reduction lessened the control forces, the DC-8 was hit by turbulence. Unprepared for the released pressure Zeng apparently overcontrolled the DC-8 while trying to combat the turbulence. The DC-8 went into a dive with no room to recover.

It would be patently unfair to blame the crash solely on Eastern's maintenance practices—the investigation showed that other DC-8 operators were following the same inadequate PTC-test procedures. But to Higginbottom, it was part of the pattern he found throughout the airline's maintenance department—poor morale, understaffing, below-par training, and overall discouragement that had led to indifference or carelessness. Higginbottom's own words offer the best recollection of what the situation was in the spring of 1964:

"I walked into the damndest boar's nest I had ever seen. The three percent of the flights Eastern was canceling added up to eight percent of its mileage, all for mechanical reasons, and there were a hell of a lot more delays. It was a demoralized airline at that point. They were in a negative position on spare engines and other parts. They had a long policy of not operating with spare aircraft. They were working an excessive amount of overtime. There was a lack of communication between the mechanics and their union leaders, and almost none between both these groups and management.

"In fairness, there were some problems beyond their control. Eastern's fleet was the most polyglot in the industry—seven or eight airframe types, at least as many engine variances with spares for some and absolutely none for others, and worst of all they didn't have people well trained on all this hodgepodge of complex equipment. It was impossible to run an efficient maintenance organization when every job assigned to a mechanic was almost a new experience to him. Nor was there enough repetition for them to become really proficient in any single job."

Sam Higginbottom was an indefatigable, demanding, tough, but fair boss and he turned Eastern's maintenance department around in an amazingly short span of time. Working with scheduling, he managed to scrape up enough reserve aircraft to provide some backup. Three hundred new mechanics were hired and assigned to engine overhaul—the most undermanned area of all. A supply of spare engines was leased from other carriers and most important, Higginbottom established the beginnings of what Eastern now calls "system control"—placing competent technical men in key spots on a twenty-four-hour basis, and centralizing control of all maintenance work. By the end of the summer, flights were being run with reasonable reliability, a spare-parts inventory was being built up, and with the most pressing immediate problems just about licked, Higginbottom went to work developing a long-range maintenance system that featured inventory control with a minimum of waste and a maximum of efficiency to achieve fast corrective action at the lowest cost. And he wasn't averse to doing what Floyd Hall was doing in other areas: raiding rival airlines for key personnel.

Men like Lewis and Higginbottom were the hard-nosed, practical types; Hall, even though he had been teethed in the cockpit and educated in the realistic, factual world of flight operations, was a dreamer—the "big idea" man whose thinking was on a grandiose scale. Bootstrap appealed to him because it was dramatic, it challenged human emotions, it involved motivation—a magic ingredient in every modern management system. But part of motivation consisted of pride in whatever product a company was trying to sell and this, in turn, had to involve the intangible yet vital factor of image. Change Eastern's image for the better, Hall reasoned, and this image could become an all-important element of Bootstrap.

That the image was generally abysmal was only too obvious. Art Lewis says the thing that struck him about Eastern early in '64 "was that service was impersonal, uncaring, self-oriented."

"It didn't have special people at airports to make sure lines were moving efficiently. There were no ground hostesses to handle people with special problems. The average employee viewed the average passenger as a digit, not as an individual. But if Eastern's people were indifferent, it was because they had lost pride in their company and in themselves. They were battered and defenseless; there was no close identity with the company even though many of the older employees had a great and deep sense of loyalty—the senior pilots, for example. But it wasn't cohesive, and at least some of the loyalty was directed more toward Rickenbacker than the company. Yet many of our service weaknesses weren't even employee related—they stemmed from some unbelievably shortsighted management decisions. Such as Rickenbacker's refusal to buy baggage loaders for the DC-8's. My God, you couldn't put enough men on a DC-8 to load baggage by hand at places like Miami and San Juan in less than forty minutes.

"I remember right after I joined Eastern I asked why we didn't have jetways at Kennedy. One of the old timers—it may have been Lefty or Frank Sharpe—told me the Captain had issued orders against their installation because he thought they were an unnecessary luxury. Somehow the signals got mixed up and they were installed anyway. When Rickenbacker came out to the airport and saw them, he blew up and ordered them pulled out. It cost Eastern a million bucks to tear them down and we had to board passengers in rain, snow, slush, all in a dirty ramp area, for almost three years. That's how long it took us to get the Port of New York Authority to give us permission to put them back. We didn't have jetways at most of our airports, for that matter, and we still don't at the La Guardia Shuttle terminal. We did finally get 'em into Washington National."

Bootstrap was launched officially at a meeting in Houston in June of 1964, but for Hall it was only part of what had to be done. He went to a small but imaginative firm of creative consultants, Lippincott and Margulies. Hall and Walter Margulies were kindred souls; it was the latter who cautioned Floyd that before changing a corporation image, it was best to find out what was wrong or right about the old one. The firm did a survey among passengers and found the public split right down the middle in its attitude toward Eastern—about half had strong loyalties toward the airline and an equal number hated it with the intensity that had spawned WHEAL. Those who liked EAL cited its experience and safety record—they had a sense of security about the company. Another curious fact emerged from the survey, however; it showed that in the key New York–Miami market, Eastern was carrying almost sixty percent of the traffic during the winter months and most of it consisted of older, wealthier persons. But in the off-peak months, when younger people were flying, Eastern's market share dropped to less than half.

Hall was advised to retain that part of the otherwise damaged image—keep emphasizing stability, substance, and security, he was told, but at the same time present the picture of an airline that's also aggressive and innovative. The final recommendation was to change Eastern's visual image.

Hall wanted to drop the falcon symbol; he favored one proposed design that had a kind of bullseye on the aircraft tail with "EAL" in the center, but he was the only one who liked this approach. Margulies suggested a modernized version of the falcon—it was stylized, streamlined, and very clean, and this was the design chosen. The visual-image committee also decided on a new color scheme for aircraft window lines, finally picking a light shade called "Caribbean blue," as well as "ionosphere blue," an unusual, very deep shade that was almost purple. "Ionosphere blue" inspired a decision to change the name of Eastern's special airport "Falcon Lounges" to "Ionosphere Clubs." Hall loved the evocation of soaring flight far above the earth. It had almost an ethereal sound to it, and from "ionosphere" it was an easy step to what would become Eastern's new slogan: "The Wings of Man."

The new image, however, required some reforms on the ground as well as in the upper atmosphere. There was even a special program to train EAL's skycaps. A veteran from JFK,

P. T. Heinz, traveled all over the system teaching skycaps how to greet passengers. The stewardesses got new uniforms, aircraft interiors were refurbished, and when Eastern purchased a fleet of limousines for VIPs, the drivers were equipped with sales kits and received training for handling any unusual problems. One driver landed a $3.5 million travel account by going out of his way to help a limo passenger.

All in all the new image was acquired at a bargain: The Lippincott and Margulies fee was a little over $200,000. It cost a lot more to redo aircraft exteriors and interiors but this was accomplished during regular major overhaul periods. More important, it was all beginning to pay off; by the winter of 1964, traffic was soaring.

Admittedly, Hall could get a mite overzealous in his burning desire to create what amounted to a new airline—one with style and class. As part of a campaign to upgrade food service, for example, he ordered expensive Rosenthal china for use in first class, along with Reed and Barton silverware; this was what he had put on TWA's jets. Frank Sharpe, as vice president of customer services, argued against it.

"A Rosenthal china glass will last about three trips," he warned. "The lip is round and too easy to chip."

Hall wouldn't budge, but Sharpe decided to try an end run. He bought some cheaper but still attractive glasses resembling Rosenthal and took them on a flight to Bermuda for an officers' meeting. Wives were invited and Sharpe gave each a nicely wrapped package of two dozen ersatz Rosenthal glasses. Only one spouse spotted the difference, and this got back to Hall, who called in Sharpe.

"What were you trying to pull with those glasses?" he said angrily.

"I don't know what you mean, Floyd."

"You know damned well those weren't Rosenthal glasses."

Sharpe sighed. "Floyd, I was trying to make a point. Those wives are pretty sophisticated people and if they can't tell the difference, how the hell can the public? The glasses I handed out cost twenty-three cents each and I got about twenty trips out of them. The Rosenthal glass runs more than a buck plus what it costs for special protective handling. I can't get the lips reground without sending them to Germany and we can't afford that. If you want to put them on the hotshot flights like New York–San Juan or New York–Mexico, that's fine, but to put 'em on a New York–Miami flight where we're in a price war, I don't see how you can justify it."

Eventually the Rosenthal china disappeared from Eastern's planes, but the Reed and Barton silverware caused another clash. When Hall announced he wanted it, Sharpe objected again. "You don't want those," he said firmly.

"Why not? We used them on TWA."

"They've got too much silver content, Floyd. They just won't stand up."

Hall relented to the point of suggesting that they try testing several silverware samples for durability. Sharpe went to Reed and Barton, which gave him four different types, including the kind TWA had used. They were put through a hundred washing cycles. The less expensive type Reed and Barton had recommended stood up well, but the TWA silverware was all scratched after only ten washings. Sharpe took the samples to a directors' meeting; this, he acknowledged later, was a mistake. "I should have done it with Floyd on a one-on-one basis," he says.

He put the samples on a piece of black velvet for the directors to inspect; a small sign explaining how many washing cycles each had gone through was placed above each sample, and it was only too easy to deduce that the TWA-type silverware was totally impractical. Hall blew his stack.

"Why do you object to me trying to build a quality airline?" he demanded.

"Floyd, I'm not objecting. I'm trying to build you a quality airline we can afford."

Hall's taste, indeed, was superbly aesthetic but his promotion-oriented mind occasionally inspired some projects of questionable merit. He went to a Miami Dolphins football game and was fascinated by the fans' custom of waving white handkerchiefs when the team scored. Hall ordered $25,000 worth of handkerchiefs carrying the new EAL logo to hand out at the next home game; it wasn't a bad gimmick but there were some who doubted whether it was worth $25,000.

Over the objections of practically everyone involved, he once insisted on installing white floor-tile in the aircraft galley area. Sharpe led the assault on this plan, warning that in rain and wet weather it would be a disaster. It took about eighteen months before maintenance finally convinced Hall it was impossible to keep white tile clean. These disagreements caused some friction between Hall and Sharpe, who was finally shifted out of customer services and to put to work on Eastern's bid for a Pacific route.

"Floyd's trouble was that he had champagne taste and a beer pocketbook," Sharpe says. "But there never was any really hard feeling between us. I learned a long time ago that if you don't disagree with your boss, you've got a problem—but if you disagree with him more than ten percent of the time you'd better go elsewhere."

In light of later events Sharpe's criticism seems justified, but this does not take anything away from what Hall accomplished while Eastern was on the ropes. By the end of 1964 revenues had jumped by $11 million over the disaster year of 1963—gross income hit $414 million, which was $59 million higher than what the "survival plan" had called for. Instead of the projected loss of $40 million, the net deficit was cut to less than $6 million.

The comeback continued in 1965 at an event faster pace, with revenues climbing to a record of more than a half billion dollars; black ink was back on the ledgers for the first time in six years with a net profit of almost $30 million.

"Nothing brings people together like adversity," Hall muses today. "They had been kicked around and stomped on for so many years that they were just ripe for someone to come along and tell 'em they weren't licked."

Perhaps the best demonstration of Eastern's return from the dead was an incident that occurred in Hall's office midway through 1965. His secretary informed him there were "two businessmen from Pittsburgh" outside who wanted to see him.

EXIT MACINTYRE—ENTER HALL

"They give their names?"

"Yes, sir. The names didn't mean anything but"—she hesitated—"but they say they started the WHEAL Club."

Hall can't remember those names and there is no mention of them in any Eastern files, but he does remember that they walked in and announced, "You don't know us; but did you ever hear of the WHEAL Club?"

"I've heard of it," Hall assured them.

"Well, Mr. Hall," one said, "we run the club and we just came in to tell you we're willing to burn the charter."

Hall was so surprised he didn't think of telling them to wait until he rounded up a photographer—something he still regrets. So there is no photographic record of the historic event that followed—they lit a match, burned the charter, and dropped the ashes in the wastebasket. Hall took them to lunch and WHEAL went out of business.

In his first two years as president, Hall made a practice of having every passenger complaint letter placed on his desk—he read them all and answered each one. "Jesus, it was a lot of work," he adds. But one gripe was brought to his attention when he was trying to recruit a new board member. He had read an article about the new head of the Pet Milk Company, Ted Gamble, a "shirttail" relative of one of the founders and a bright, modern young businessman. Hall impulsively phoned him and asked if he could see him.

"Why?"

"Well, I was thinking you'd make a fine director of Eastern. That's why I'd like to come talk to you."

"You don't have to come here," Gamble said. "I'll be in New York in a couple of days and I'll drop in to see you."

He kept his word and sat on a couch smoking a pipe while Hall gave him a sales pitch about joining Eastern's board. "We've got a company that's flat on its ass and I'm trying to recruit not only good management but good board members."

Gamble shook his head.

"Mr. Hall, I think I'd better tell you a story. About three years ago I was in Memphis on business. I got up in the morning of a beautiful day, called my wife in St. Louis, commented on how gorgeous the weather was in Memphis, and told her I'd be home that afternoon. She said the weather in St. Louis was fine, too. So I went out to the airport, walked over to the Eastern ticket counter, and was informed the flight was canceled. I asked why and the agent said it was because of bad weather in St. Louis. I said, 'Look, don't give me that crap—I just talked to my wife in St. Louis and she said the sun was shining just the way it is here.' The agent tells me, 'Mister, if you don't like the way we run this airline, why don't you go out and get yourself your own airplane?' So, by God, I did—I bought three Sabreliners and I haven't been on your goddamned airline since!"

Hall put out his hand. "Ted, you're exactly the kind of man we want on our board."

Gamble became a director and served ably until his untimely death from a heart attack a few years go.

There were executive casualties, of course, on the way back to recovery. At various times during Hall's tenure, many veterans retired—Creighton, Halliburton, and Froesch, for instance —or were shifted to less demanding posts, or were quietly asked to leave. Bill Van Dusen became a kind of vice president emeritus when Jonathan Rinehart of *Newsweek* was hired as the new public relations director; Van Dusen was to wind up his career starting a history of Eastern that was in the early stages of preparation when he died.

Bob Winn, one of the Shuttle's midwives and vice president of schedules, was subjected to what could have been a humiliating demotion—Hall replaced him with Wes Kahldahl of American and shipped Winn down to Orlando, Florida, as a district sales manager whose territory embraced five small counties with virtually no major traffic potential. But Winn, a balding, pleasant, unflappable man with a smile that could light up a room, didn't sulk or complain, even though most men in his spot would have considered Orlando a Siberia with orange trees. He intended to do his job quietly and efficiently, but almost as soon as he arrived in Orlando he began hearing rumors of something big stirring in central Florida.

There had been some tract of land purchases by unknown parties, and speculation was rife that a huge corporation was going to locate a new plant in the Orlando area—among the companies mentioned were Ford, Burlington Mills, and Hercules Powder.

"Nobody guessed," Winn smiles, "that it was a little rat named Miguel."

Mickey Mouse.

On November 15, 1965, Walt Disney announced plans to build a $750 million "Disneyland of the East" to be called Disney World, located a few miles from Orlando. When Disney officials eventually let it be known they would like to choose one carrier to be Disney World's official airline, Winn immediately contacted Floyd Hall.

"If we get it," he promised Hall, "I'll give you a four-point premium"—meaning that he was pledging to carry at least four percentage points above the share of the Orlando market Delta was then carrying. There were three carriers serving Orlando before the Disney World announcement—Eastern, Delta, and National. By the time the park was opened in 1968, Southern had joined the competition and later Air Florida, then an intrastate airline, wedged into the market. The Orlando area was booming even before Disney World was launched, thanks first to the nearby space program and later by the Navy's opening a training base nearby with a total personnel of some 12,000 and nearly 700 recruits and graduates moving in and out every week.

Prior to Disney World, Delta dominated the market, carrying thirty-two percent of the traffic; Eastern's share was around twenty-five percent. There were those who told Winn he was sticking his neck out by promising Hall EAL could pass Delta if it became the "official airline of Disney World." Today Eastern has fifty percent of the Orlando market competing against six airlines. And to Bob Winn, now retired, goes a large share of the credit—he became Eastern's liason man with the Disney organization, with the help of Jim Cammisa of EAL's advertising department. The two of them put together the package that won the official airline designation.

The price was not cheap; Eastern agreed to pay a total of $10 million at the rate of $1 million annually for a ten-year period, and sign a one-time marketing agreement for $100,000. The $10 million was for designing, constructing, and operating an Eastern Air Lines attraction at the park, and not a few EAL officials were against that kind of financial commitment. But Winn had been smart enough to get Floyd Hall's ear right from the start; the press conference announcing construction of the mammoth park was hardly over when Winn was on the phone to New York, suggesting that Hall fly immediately to Los Angeles and meet with Walt Disney himself.

Hall took the advice, saw Disney, and got along well with him; it was Hall's enthusiasm for Eastern's participation, more than any other single factor, that was responsible for what turned out to be a happy and profitable association. The objectors raised their voices louder than ever when Disney insisted that Eastern's $10 million exhibit charge no admission; it was bad enough putting that much money into a still-to-be-created attraction at a park that could well wind up as history's biggest white elephant. Foregoing any revenue from the exhibit, they argued, was flushing $10 million down the toilet.

Winn's rebuttal was that Disney World would generate enough new traffic to justify spending twice that amount—that's where the revenue will come from, he predicted, and never mind our exhibit, which will simply be good public relations and excellent exposure to the traveling public.

The figures speak for themselves. Disney himself predicted the park would draw eight million visitors the first year. It drew ten million. Eastern was boarding 10,000 passengers a month at Orlando before Disney World opened. It now boards 145,000. At the start of Disney World, EAL was serving Orlando with ten flights a day. It now has more than fifty. Between June of 1972, the year Disney World began operating, and September 1978 more than forty million people had gone through Eastern's *If You Had Wings* attraction. And the $750 million spent to build Disney World was paid back in three years.

Winn remembers that one of his chief opponents in the

project was an ex-TWA man who had gone through some trying experiences with Disneyland in southern California. He kept trying to tell Winn that Disneyland as an air travel stimulant was vastly overrated, because only ten percent of its visitors came from east of the Rockies, and he couldn't see how Disney World would be any different. Winn's counterargument was a Disney survey showing that eighty percent of the Florida park's potential customers would come from out of state. This meant the huge complex would be tourist oriented and tourist dominated, and it all added up to a huge air travel market.

There also were objections raised against the EAL exhibit on the grounds that most persons going through it would be children, quite a few years away from becoming paying passengers. Actually, Disney World sells four adult tickets for every child admission, and this ratio of visitors to the Eastern pavilion is identical.

What they see has to be experienced to be believed. Basically a "ride," it was worked up by Winn and Cammisa, who wanted to achieve three things: the illusion of great speed, a lot of simulated action, and a diorama to add realism. It starts with a brief ride depicting scenes from cities on EAL's routes. The car then passes through a large porthole and the riders find themselves in a "mirror room" where in rapid succession they ski down a mountain in the Rockies and race over the desert in a dune buggy. From the mirror room the cars pass into the "speed room"—chairs tilt automatically to create the illusion of climbing fast. There are ninety-seven synchronized projectors providing all the make-believe in the exhilarating ten-minute ride.

There was no actual bidding on the "official airline" designation. Eastern and Disney officials reached an agreement on the general concept and Disney's contacts with the other carriers ended. Winn says the basic reason behind selection of Eastern was its status as the dominant carrier in Florida. The $10.1-million price tag was agreed on later; as it turned out, it was a bargain and one of Floyd Hall's best decisions in all the years he spent at the airline.

He didn't seem to be making many bad decisions in the first

few years of his regime. Under his leadership the airline staged a comeback on a scale most of the industry had thought impossible. There still were problems ahead—Eastern's long starvation diet when it came to new route awards, to cite one major item. But Hall firmly believed this could be overcome, too, and that he had the management muscle to achieve it.

It was quite a team he had formed—able, tough, and dedicated. Yet it had one great weakness that not even this man of intelligence and personal integrity could foresee, particularly in the heady, deceptive euphoria of his initial successes.

Yes, it *was* a team—at first. But it was composed largely of men roughly his own age, his own experience, and his own ambition and drive. In forming it he had unwittingly invited conflicts and feuds among strong-willed individualists. As Eastern turned around, the team became more a collection of all-stars—men of great talent and ability, but also men seeking their own destinies, each jealous of his prerogatives, each firm in the conviction that his programs and policies were right.

Most of the crew he enlisted had the potential to become airline presidents in their own right; three of them did, and several would have jumped at the chance.

In that kind of atmosphere there had to be trouble ahead.

CHAPTER FOURTEEN

RISE AND FALL– HERE WE GO AGAIN

The first feud started early and stayed late.

It involved Todd Cole and Art Lewis and it had begun when Lewis joined Eastern and was named senior vice president and general manager, second only to Floyd Hall in rank. Cole had swallowed his disappointment when Hall took over and told Hall, "If you're going to run the airline, fine—I'm just content to be here and I'll help you all I can." But after MacIntyre's implied promise to make him president, Cole considered himself still the number two man at EAL and bristled when Lewis was moved ahead of him—not even Todd's own title as the only other senior vice president could soften his resentment.

Both these antagonists have long since mellowed and tend to deny they were really bitter enemies. Cole says, "I fought with Art, yes, but I felt out of step not just with him but with management in general."

From Lewis: "I suppose Todd always resented me for coming into the number two spot. It did lead to an undercurrent of problems between us, but nothing of any great consequence. Ninety percent of my work with Todd's office was through Charlie Simons, the controller, who had the strength to function independently of Cole. If it hadn't been for that, I suspect I would have had a much more difficult time with Todd. I honestly don't remember any policy differences between us being of major significance. His line of communication went straight to Floyd. His personality was such that I never took anything to him I didn't have to take but from the standpoint of corporate policy development there wasn't any real feud—people thought there was but this wasn't true."

From a third former Eastern officer, anonymous because he admires both men: "No feud? They've got to be kidding. It was so bad, I remember Floyd telling them one day he'd have to fire both of them if they didn't quit fighting. They wouldn't even stay in the same room together unless Hall was there, too."

This much can be said without contradiction, however: Cole, basically conservative (he even looks like a man Central Casting would pick to play a bank president), was not enamored of Eastern's overall policies, even though he conceded Hall had pulled off a near miracle of resuscitation. But he also questioned what he considered overemphasis on the "image-making" so prevalent in Hall's recovery plan. Image carried so high a priority that at one point Hall and others were considering changing the airline's name.

"I was and still am of the belief that a corporation should be a profit-making entity," Cole declares. "I agree that improving Eastern's image was necessary but a poor image was only part of the airline's problems. The majority of officers paid lip service to profits. They were more interested in market share, in the exact shade of blue for the new corporate identity program, in new stewardess uniforms, in the ratings the new advertising program received. I was very much in the minority when I argued that Eastern was more image-oriented than profit-oriented."

Hall felt, of course, that without a good image there wouldn't be much profit but Cole's somewhat negative attitude was the first sign of a schism in the executive ranks. It was just a tiny crack at first, a whisper of caution amid the din of pride and confidence generated by the recovery. Ironically, Hall was starting to paint himself into the same corner in which Rickenbacker eventually had found himself—the triumphs of the present were obscuring all the potential dangers of the future. Just as Captain Eddie had brushed away every criticism simply by pointing to the bottom line, so did Hall respond to warnings from men like Cole simply by pointing to Eastern's comeback—he had even given it a name: "Sunrise at Eastern," the title of a well-crafted documentary film he had ordered for distribution throughout the system. The sound track included the theme music used in the airline's radio and television commercials—sweeping, soaring notes that managed to convey not only the very feeling of flight, but the new spirit within the company.

It is hard to blame Hall for not recognizing danger signals until it was too late. He had the enthusiasm of youth, the brash confidence that comes with unexpectedly quick achievement, and both enthusiasm and confidence can be traps. Certainly he had the whole airline behind him; not even the disastrous 1966 machinists' strike that shut down five major carriers, Eastern included, for forty-three days in the summer of 1966, could dent employee morale. Eastern's mechanics had to follow the dictates of the national IAM when it shut down National, United, Northwest, and TWA; it was Art Lewis who sold Hall on joining the other carriers in joint bargaining with IAM—a step he admits was a sad mistake. Lewis thought that if negotiations failed and all five airlines were struck, there would be a national emergency and the Johnson administration would apply pressure to settle quickly.

What Lewis didn't anticipate was the IAM's strategy to pick the joint airline negotiations as a test case in an effort to break Johnson's wage-increase guidelines—the president had put a 3.5 percent ceiling on any wage boosts. The IAM, determined to demolish the guidelines, as was its parent AFL-CIO, rightly figured that a strike by five major airlines would create a national issue—which is exactly what happened. Eastern's members had had no desire to walk out—in fact, the final settlement granting increases of a little less than five percent was something the company had been ready to give before the strike occurred.

Instead of applying pressure for settlement, LBJ applied

pressure in the opposite direction: He urged the airlines to hold out and they were forced to accede—they were a regulated industry and the president of the United States wouldn't let them negotiate for anything higher than his 3.5 percent limit, until it became apparent that the union wouldn't break.

Eastern still netted $14.7 million in 1966, but the figure would have been much higher were it not for the long strike. Considering Eastern's enormous commitments for new aircraft —in 1966 alone the airline put sixty-five new DC-9s and 727s into service, more than Delta had in its entire fleet—the modest profit might as well have been a deficit. The additional planes meant increased crew-training costs and other heavy expenses associated with the introduction of new equipment, including high interest rates.

The pilots, of course, were in hog heaven. They were finally getting rid of their antiquated piston aircraft and the 727 quickly became their true love. Eastern had been the first airline to put the trijet into service and it was an EAL captain—rumor has it that his name was Slim Cockes—who on one of the earliest 727 trips hoodwinked a control tower into letting him land ahead of other traffic by radioing, "We're coming in on three engines."

Never having seen a 727 before, the tower gave him emergency clearance.

If Cockes was the captain involved, nobody would have been surprised. Slim was one of the legendary figures around Eastern—somewhat of a successor to Merrill, in selling air travel as well as flying his plane. He was a big, crusty, outwardly bad-tempered kind of guy whom passengers loved, chief pilots deplored, and air traffic controllers prayed would retire. His running feud with controllers was an aviation classic, for Slim was only too happy to share his low opinion of them with his passengers.

He was coming into Atlanta one clear night and ATC gave him an indefinite approach delay because of runway congestion. The airport had just opened a new $23-million terminal but this didn't impress Slim quite as much as the fact that at the time, there was only one runway in use. Having been advised of the delay, Cockes picked up the handiest weapon—his cabin PA mike—and fired.

"Folks," he drawled. "I've just been told there'll be a delay in landing on account of the runway's a bit crowded." He paused, for dramatic effect. "Now I wanna congratulate all you folks on this here airplane who are from Atlanta. That new terminal of yours is really something. In all the years I've been flying, I've never seen anything so beautiful—all those hanging mobiles and stuff. That building is worth the twenty-three million bucks it cost. There's only one thing wrong with it"—he paused again—"I can't land this damned thing in the lobby!"

Slim fitted in well with the new competitive spirit. His PAs were often sales pitches, although their accuracy was in question. He used to pretend officials of other carriers were aboard so he could tell his passengers that even the opposition chose Eastern. "I'd like to thank all you folks for flying Eastern," he'd say, "and that includes Mr. Maytag who, as you know, is president of National and always flies with us if he wants to get to Miami on time."

In normal conversation Cockes could sound as erudite as Floyd Hall himself, but over the cabin PA he affected an Andy Griffith drawl which used to make his copilots wince. "Howdy, folks, this is your captain, ole Slim. In a few minutes those li'l girls back there are gonna start rattling those pots and pans and whip us up some vittles. You folks jes relax, take off your shoes, and lean back, while ole Slim heah takes you all flyin'. . . ."

John Halliburton swears he actually has seen four or five people take off their shoes "like it was a computer-programmed response.

"When Slim would go into that country-boy act of his," Halliburton laughs, "it used to embarrass me. But we used to get more complimentary letters about Slim than any other captain we had."

He wasn't always funny. When Southern Airways pilots went on strike and the airline hired nonunion crews to fly its trips, Cockes swore "I'll get those g-d scabs." He spotted a Southern DC-3 manned by non-ALPA pilots at Atlanta one day and taxied his Electra around it so that the Eastern plane's tail was just ahead of the DC-3's nose. Then he gave all four Allison engines full throttle while stomping hard on the brakes. The blast blew dirt and gravel right through the DC-3's windshield and dented the nose and leading edges of the wings. Southern had to cancel its trip and Slim got two weeks off without pay.

The stewardesses were scared to death of him—until they found out there was Jell-O under all the barnacles. Winnie Gilbert, when she was Stewardess Winnie Smith in her pre-vice presidential days, had a run-in with Cockes on one of her first trips. For some reason he took a violent dislike to a scarf she was wearing and ordered an agent to "tell her to take that damned rag off." Throughout the flight he never spoke to her except through the copilot or flight engineer—they'd inform her, "Captain wants his dinner" or "Captain says to bring him some coffee." It was a night-coach trip and when all the passengers were asleep, she sat down to rest a minute. Cockes chose that minute to wander back through the cabin and spotted her.

"Nobody sleeps on a Slim Cockes trip!" he growled. She was so startled that he had to stop her from waking up the passengers.

On her last trip of the month she bumped into him around midnight at a layover hotel and he invited her to have some coffee.

"I think I will," Winnie agreed. "Just to tell you you're a mean, cruel, miserable, autocratic, pompous son of a bitch." He laughed and the two talked in the coffee shop for an hour before Winnie went back to her room for some sleep. She forgot to set her alarm and the hotel failed to make its wake-up call; Cockes woke her with a phone call from the airport wanting to know where the hell she was. She dressed and was in a cab in five minutes but the flight had left without her. Heartbroken and positive she was going to get fired, she caught a later flight back to Miami and finally walked into crew schedule.

"I'm Winnie Smith. I . . . uh . . . I missed my trip."

"Oh, so *you're* Winnie Smith. Captain Cockes told us if we reported you, he'd have us fired."

Slim is retired now, but there is scarcely a controller in the air-traffic control system who doesn't remember him. When Eastern began flying contract flights to the Viet Nam theater, Captain Frank Kern was commanding a westbound trip one night and had just given ATC in Honolulu a position report.

"By the way, Eastern," the controller asked, "is Slim Cockes coming out here by any chance?"

"Negative," Kerns told him. "I don't think he's senior enough to bid these trips."

There was an audible if metallic sigh. "Thank God," the controller said. "I left the States to get away from the bastard."

When Winnie made vice president, Slim was one of the first to congratulate her—for a man with such positive opinions, he was surprisingly free from prejudices. Eastern did have a captain, however, who hated blacks and was furious when the airline began hiring black stewardesses. He once refused to move his airplane away from the gate because one of the flight attendants had an Afro hairstyle. Called on the carpet for his demonstration of bigotry, he claimed, "She was a fire hazard."

With Eastern's shift to jets, the rapport between the cockpit and cabin crews so prevalent in the prejet days rapidly diminished—the jets were too demanding for the old closeness and informality. Yet there were still vestiges left. Still the comradeships, and quips, the repartee. Like the time a captain who was something of a martinet asked Sandy Logan if she had read her manual lately.

"I'm waiting till they make it into a movie," she said placidly.

The intense rivalry between Eastern and Delta spilled over among the flight attendants. Delta had and still has a very effective slogan—"Delta's Ready When You Are"—which occasionally EAL employees could use as a boomerang. Ann Rucco was working a flight that had boarded twenty-five passengers from a canceled Delta trip. Advised of their presence by an agent, she beefed up her usual pretakeoff announcement. "I'd like to welcome all our Eastern passengers and those people from the airline that's ready when you are but this time wasn't."

This recalls what went down in Eastern's annals as The Perfect Retort. An Eastern reservations agent received an obscene phone call late one night. After the usual graphic description of what he would like to do to her, the caller concluded, amid heavy breathing, "And you've got me so turned on that I'm about to explode—what would you say to that?"

"I'd suggest you try Delta," she answered. "They're ready when you are."

The veteran flight attendants who flew when Rickenbacker ran the airline still remember him with affection. They don't yearn for the old days, but they concede they may have been more fun. John Gregg, for example, recalls the 749 Connies, which had a forward compartment originally intended for the use of ambulatory passengers—it was called the Skyroom and it had four large seats and room for a bed. The flight attendants used to sell the Skyroom seats to amorous passengers on late-night flights. If one questions the ethics of this practice, it must be emphasized that Eastern's pay scale at the time called for ingenuity if one was to eat regularly and pay rent on time. Occasionally a caterer would board extra sandwiches—a great source of additional income; Gregg would sell the sandwiches for fifty cents each, an arrangement he considered perfectly fair because the airline wasn't paying for the excess food.

Nobody really missed the piston era—except that as the mammoth jet equipment program began dominating everything from schedules to training, there was a tendency to prefer the simpler days. That included the pilots, many of whom remembered the training sessions when one man would lecture on the subject with which he was most familiar. A pilot named Eddie Harrington was the resident expert on wheels, tires, and brakes. A sample of his learned, highly technical discourse follows:

"Well, now, I'll demonstrate how you stop a Connie. You grab both hands around the goddamned yoke, you rear back in the seat, and you stomp the hell outa the goddamned brake pedals, and that's how you stop a Connie. But now you take a goddamned DC-7. You take off your shoes, grab the wheel with your thumbs, and you touch the brakes with your toes, and that's how you stop a goddamned DC-7."

Nor could the jets, for all their slick efficiency and gleaming newness, completely eliminate the occasional unplanned crisis which put flight attendants to their greatest test. Phyllis Ash was working a flight where the smooth routine was suddenly interrupted by a ten-year-old boy who went to the "blue room" (toilet) and proceeded to get his penis stuck in his zipper. Solving this type of emergency hadn't been included in the stewardess training curriculum and Phyllis was at a loss to cope with it. The youngster, a cute kid with red hair and freckles, was taking it more calmly than his parents, who were on the verge of panic—especially when the first ministrations caused the organ to swell, making matters even worse.

Phyllis reported the crisis to the captain. He didn't believe it at first but agreed to send the flight engineer back. The flight engineer tried everything. An ice bag to reduce the swelling. Scissors to cut away the cloth around the zipper. Pliers. Butter. Oil from the first-aid kit. When nothing worked, the captain messaged ahead for a paramedic to meet the flight at the next stop. While the boy was being taken off the plane, Phyllis went to the cockpit with the forms she had to fill out for reporting the incident. She was having trouble with the line that said: "State nature of emergency."

"How should I phrase it?" she asked the captain.

"Just put down 'penis stuck in zipper,' " he suggested.

Eastern retained a fair number of male flight attendants even after the girls predominated, in sufficient ratio to infrequently have a flight manned entirely by men. A passenger got on one such flight, looked disapprovingly at the all-male cabin crew, and walked over to the galley where Pete Bishop was checking supplies.

"Hey, where the hell are all the tomatoes?"

"In the salad," Bishop said politely.

In the years immediately preceding Hall's myriad reforms, Eastern's flight attendants were especially vulnerable—no one is more exposed to passenger ire than the people in the aircraft cabin, even if the cause of anger is due to somebody else's mistake. Some of the airline's worst morale problems involved the flight attendants, and it took an exceptional employee to keep poise and pride intact in a situation where it was not unusual to have ten or twelve unhappy or irate passengers on one flight.

Susan Smith was one such person. When she found her mood so bad that she could hardly face a trip, she began wearing a special name tag with the words "Human Being" replacing the usual "Miss Smith." One passenger asked her flying partner, "Is that really her name?"

"Yep."

"Are you serious?"

"Sure. We call her Hume for short."

After the flight the passenger came up to her. "Miss Being," he said, "I just want you to know you have a lovely name—and it was a fine flight."

A flight attendant named Carol Roberson once drew an unwanted flight to San Juan—a full airplane, with half the passengers children. She worked the trip on a foul mood and was considering the desirability of resigning in the near future when a little Puerto Rican girl, about six or seven, left her seat and came up to her. She took Carol's hand, put something in it, closed it, smiled shyly, and returned to her seat. The stewardess opened her hand. In the palm was a dime. The little girl's spending money.

Carol Roberson didn't resign.

Nor, in effect, did the whole airline—that was what "Sunrise at Eastern" and Operation Bootstrap were all about. And fortunately for this airline army, surviving as only airline troops can in the face of setback after setback, crushing adversity, and often with no weapons other than a sense of humor and patience, it had no way of knowing that in a few short years it was going to have to live through the same nightmare all over again.

There was no pivotal point at which the airline's magnificent climb became an irrevocable descent, no single, overriding reason why the comeback course was reversed; it has been said many times that no air crash ever has a single cause, and the same applies to an airline's economic decline. Events, circumstances, coincidences, mistakes, and bad luck all are piled one on top of the other until the edifice being built with these faulty bricks suddenly falls apart.

And so it was with Eastern as the brave, bold years of 1964–1966 gave way to the disaster years of 1967–1973—a six-year period in which past gains were wiped out, morale crumbled once more, and the falcon again hovered perilously close to extinction. There never was a single villain, scapegoat, or fall guy to blame, but a remark made by Todd Cole a long time after it all happened comes close to pinpointing perhaps the most significant causal factor.

"There was a tendency at Eastern," Cole commented without rancor, "to spend money as soon as you saw a little black ink."

There had to be spending, of course—on new planes, on the new image, and on the dilapidated ground facilities. But as with most reform movements, the pendulum swung too far—from years of penny-pinching and a corporate wallet that creaked when it was opened, Eastern gradually and steadily became immersed in various expansion programs that were not only costly but beyond the airline's financial capability. Management itself was expanded—by the early 1970s Eastern was to have nearly seventy vice presidents, and aside from what this policy did to the payroll, seventy vice-presidents added up to about thirty-five potential feuds.

A second key factor was the personality of Floyd Hall. Basically he was a troubleshooter who welcomed challenge, but having met that challenge, he tended to climb into a corporate ivory tower and concentrate on problems and projects somewhat removed from the more prosaic, day-to-day operations of an airline. This may be oversimplifying it somewhat, for Floyd never abdicated leadership entirely; he retained a gut feeling for employees (he would go out to the three New York-area airports on Christmas and New Year's Eves, for example, and personally thank whoever was working those holiday shifts—he was an exceptionally thoughtful, considerate person), and while he delegated a tremendous amount of authority and responsibility, he never passed the buck.

But the directors, starting in 1967, began to question some of his involvements, and so did many of his associates. One could feel the breeze from the raised eyebrows that followed his insistence on spending almost a half million dollars of EAL funds cosponsoring the Metropolitan Opera. Hall considered this part of the image-rebuilding process, but Harper Woodward openly questioned it.

"You keep saying it relates to our business," he told Hall, "but it seems to me that's getting pretty remote."

"New York is a big city," Hall argued, "and to have Eastern identified with something like the Met is a definite plus."

Woodward and other directors also wondered about such esoteric terminology as "Wings of Man" and "Ionosphere Lounges"—Woodward once remarked that Eastern apparently was acquiring an intergalactic look. Hall could be very persuasive, because he was so articulate and earnest; yet some directors, while they could accept high-flying slogans and highbrow opera sponsorship, eventually began to express concern over a far more vital direction into which Hall was steering the airline. Floyd loved a carefully-structured management, complete with organizational charts, job descriptions, performance ratings, and definitive lines of authority. Board members like Woodward, while they didn't interfere, believed a company could be run just as successfully and perhaps more efficiently just by "putting people in the right job and the hell with the organizational charts," as Woodward put it.

Hall's philosophy of modern management was not a fatal mistake in itself, but in combination with so many other external and internal pressures, it made his carefully structured world top-heavy—to phrase it in the simplest terms, there were too many chiefs and not enough Indians. His greatest single weakness, anyway, was his inability to control the conglomeration of ambitious talent he had gathered under Eastern's roof.

And as the decade of the seventies drew closer, Floyd himself changed. His health was not good (he was to have major surgery), he was having serious marital problems that would culminate in a divorce, and he seemed to lose much of his priceless ability to objectively analyze and advise.

In 1968, he phoned Harper Woodward and said he wanted to name Art Lewis president, leaving himself as chief executive officer.

"I think you're making a mistake," Woodward said frankly. "Art's had no experience running a company the size of Eastern. He's the kind of guy who thinks he can tell everyone at ten A.M. they have to start driving on the left side of the road by noon and doesn't expect to have any accidents. It may have worked with a small airline like Hawaiian, but not at Eastern."

Hall said he didn't agree, that he thought Lewis would make an ideal president.

"Well," Woodward said, "I still think you're wrong but I'll vote for him because I think you should pick your own team."

So Art Lewis became Eastern's eighth president, not realizing that the cards were stacked against him. The entire industry was heading for a troubled period with a recession just over the horizon and a new menace suddenly parked right on the doorstep.

Hijacking.

Eastern suffered its first one in September of 1968 and over the next six years was to experience twenty-nine more—as a carrier based in Miami, with such close proximity to Cuba, it was particularly vulnerable. One hijacking attempt resulted in a crew fatality. The victim was James Hartley, Jr., a copilot murdered by a gunman who got into the cockpit of a DC-9. The captain, Robert Wilbur, managed to land safely even though he had been wounded in both arms. Eastern's training center in Miami is named for Hartley, who left a wife and two small children.

In another 1968 hijacking there were two groups of hijackers aboard—nine in all—and neither group knew the other was on the plane; by coincidence, both wanted to go to Cuba.

Eastern today is spending more than $32 million on security per year, the bulk of it going for armed guards and screening personnel—more than seventy million persons were screened in 1978 and even more in '79. The airline launched what probably was the industry's most extensive security program in 1969 after experiencing seventeen hijackings in that and the previous year; Mike Fenello, vice president of safety, assigned John Shields to be manager of operational security, partly to work with the FAA on the problem and also to set up EAL's own security measures.

Shields, a retired Marine Corps fighter pilot who once headed security for Varig Airlines in Brazil, was a member of the government-industry team that worked out the "profile" scheme —spotting potential hijackers by means of preestablished behavioral and physical characteristics. On Shields's recommendations, however, Eastern at first refused to accept the FAA-sponsored program of federal sky marshals. He did go through the FAA's first sky-marshal school, but when he returned, he told Fenello, "We don't want 'em, Mike—first I think they're probably very unsafe, and second it's a total waste."

Shields agued that if Eastern had to use marshals, they would be more valuable on the ground, where they could participate in screening; but the FAA called a news conference to announce the sky-marshal program and the 100 percent cooperation of the industry.

"I hope I won't have to announce that Eastern is the only exception," an FAA official told Shields and Fenello meaningfully. So Eastern had to accept them, although it used only twelve compared with the 200 assigned to TWA—and as Shields had predicted, the marshal program was a flop.

"They were eating the airlines out of house and home," Shields recalls. "There were instances of them falling asleep on duty and in a couple of cases they dropped their guns on the cabin floor when they dozed off."

Profile screening and improved detection devices did far more to curb hijacking than did the widely publicized sky marshals. Before all the airports EAL served got efficient detectors, however, the airline was hit by a hijacking in the unlikely city of Allentown, Pennsylvania; this was in May of 1972 and at the time Eastern was giving detector-installation priorities, for its nine hundred gates, to the bigger airports.

This was an extortion attempt, the hijacker demanding $303,000 in denominations of fifty- and one-hundred-dollar bills. After the money was raised, he forced the crew to fly to New Orleans and then to Honduras, where he got off the plane and went into hiding. Eventually Shields learned where he was holed up and when the FBI announced that his whereabouts were known, he panicked and turned himself in—at the U.S. Embassy. He was afraid the Honduras police would murder him for the money.

A U.S. Marine sentry at first refused to let him in. "Come back tomorrow morning," he was told.

"Tomorrow morning I'll be dead," he pleaded. "You gotta let me in."

Eastern flew a DC-9 to Honduras and the hijacker actually was smuggled out of the country—before he boarded, they hid him under the hoses of an airport fire truck because the FBI feared that people might try to free a man they considered something of a folk hero for twisting the tail of the giant from the North. He was sent to prison, and there he confided to a cellmate the location of the money. The FBI sent two informants to Honduras. The first picked up $100,000 and the second the rest of the loot.

The success of the U.S. antihijacking program is well known, but when the crime wave began in 1968 it was one of the biggest headaches Art Lewis faced. Not the biggest, though—he found himself in almost immediate conflict with the man at whose insistence he had been given the job. Lewis believed his main task was to retain and even improve the quality of service but at the same time start getting operating costs down, a concept with which Hall expressed agreement but one which his own actions and decisions belied.

Their differences actually began in 1967 when Lewis became concerned over Eastern's mushrooming operating costs. It was easy to spot the biggest problem: the oversupply of short-haul routes, with an exhorbitant proportion of total operations concentrated between Boston and Washington. This became particularly bad in the summer of '67 when congestion in the Boston–New York–Washington corridor reached an epidemic stage. Contributing to the mess was the FAA's failure to have backup equipment for ATC outages—aircraft would be kept on the ground for two or three hours awaiting takeoff clearances. This in turn affected crew time, and on one occasion Eastern had three DC-8's grounded at Tampa because the pilots had run out of duty time while waiting for congestion to lessen in the New York area.

On the 1,200-mile segment between Miami and New York, Eastern's northbound flights were entering holding patterns over Norfolk, Virginia. Flights from Washington to La Guardia were being held over Hartford. What must be understood is the effect such delays have on an airline with Eastern's route structure. Eastern, for example, cannot have the same profit potential on a New York–Miami flight as, say, United does on a Washington–Denver flight, even though the mileage is almost identical; the difference is the greater probability of serious delays for the carrier with New York as a key hub. A New York–Washington flight that normally involved a 200-mile trip often became a 500-mile flight.

Both Hall and Lewis thought they saw relief in the form of a long-haul route award in 1967—the first in years. Dwight Taylor's Washington team, one including Bill Costello and Bill Crilly, had won a route from St. Louis to Seattle that gave the airline a limited but welcome transcontinental status, for it permitted through service all the way from Cape Kennedy.

It had been a long, tough fight for the route-development team. Taylor, a colorful, rather controversial figure in Eastern history, says nobody expected EAL to win—not even the CAB's own staff. Jack Rosenthal, a CAB staff officer, commented, when Taylor informed him the airline was going to put up a battle for the route, "Eastern to Seattle?—you're smoking opium."

The heart of the Seattle case was the buildup of space traffic from Florida to the Pacific Northwest, home of the giant Boeing Company. Planning was not even in the preliminary stage; yet when Taylor had dinner one night in Seattle with Stanley Brewer, professor of transportation at the University of Washington and a consultant for the Seattle Chamber of Commerce, Brewer had with him a red-ink pen with which, over dinner, he was drawing up various route combinations that might be involved in the forthcoming Pacific Northwest–Southwest Case, as the CAB had designated it. At that stage neither Taylor nor anyone else at Eastern was quite sure what route EAL would apply for—the general goal was simply to get into the Pacific Northwest somehow.

Brewer drew the rough outlines of a map on a paper cocktail napkin and handed it to Taylor. "Dwight, do you know what's missing?"

Taylor shook his head. Brewer drew a red line between St. Louis and Seattle.

"Why the hell can't you guys operate that service?" he asked. "You're already into St. Louis."

Taylor still has that napkin.

L. Welsh Pogue, whose law firm had replaced Gambrell's as Eastern's outside legal counsel in route cases, handled the oral argument. It helped that then-CAB chairman Charles Murphy liked Eastern and that one of his top staff members, Irv Roth (now a vice president of United), had great admiration for Crilly.

Crilly and Costello were the main authors of Eastern's bid for a transpacific route, a case that dated back to 1959 and by all standards of objective, impartial judgment can be termed the most botched, mishandled, politics-ridden proceeding in the history of the Civil Aeronautics Board. When it was over, the board had succeeded only in giving everyone something in such a manner that it pleased nobody—and the sole carrier which came out with absolutely empty hands was Eastern.

Eastern's proposal made sense to the CAB examiner hearing the case, to the CAB staff, and to a number of influential congressmen, including "Mr. Aviation" of the Senate: Mike Monroney. The plan would have provided direct nonstop service between Hawaii and such mainland cities as Atlanta, Houston, Dallas, St. Louis, Chicago, Boston, New York, Philadelphia, and Washington. While most other airlines were scrapping for West Coast–Hawaii authority, Eastern proposed to overfly the West Coast using stretched DC-8's capable of flying nonstop from the East Coast to Honolulu.

As far as Eastern was concerned, the villain was CAB Chairman John Crooker, appointed to the board by President Johnson to succeed Murphy. To this day, no one connected with

Eastern's fight for a transpacific route can speak of Crooker without turning purple.

"Crooker wouldn't go to the bathroom without LBJ's permission," one of them comments. "American was in solid at the White House, because of C.R.'s friendship with Johnson, and American had Crooker in its hip pocket."

The Pacific defeat was a deep, scarring disappointment to EAL, from Hall right on down through the ranks. It was especially painful because under Crilly, Taylor, and Costello, the airline had gained a friendlier status in the nation's capital. At first their reception had been on the cool side. "The climate was as close to being anti-Eastern as you can get," Taylor recalls. "It was a Democratic town then, and there was still a residue of ill-will from Rickenbacker's right-wing speeches. It was in an era when past sins, political ridiculousness, and every faux pas in the book came back to haunt us. Alan Boyd [former CAB chairman] once told me that 'Eastern's lawyers were the best allies American had.' "

Taylor knew the Pacific decision was going to go against them. Hall didn't believe him; Floyd had been talking to friends in Washington and they kept reassuring him that it was in the bag. Finally Taylor called an old friend who wasn't with the CAB but had extremely close connections.

"I think you know the decision," Taylor said. "Will you tell me?"

There was what is known as a pregnant pause. "Eastern won't get a damned thing," he finally said. When Taylor reported this conversation to Hall, Floyd still wouldn't believe it.

Dwight Taylor looks back on his years at Eastern with pride. He himself was not the easiest man to work with—Charlie Simons remembers him as "an intellectual giant so dedicated that he'd work around the clock." Taylor was a bachelor when he was with Eastern and had no conception of what family responsibility meant to someone like Simons. Taylor was in New York one week to confer with Simons, who had come up from Miami for their sessions. Charlie would call his wife every night, be asked what he was doing that evening, and he'd tell her "I'm having dinner with Dwight." This went on for five consecutive nights and at the end of the week, when Simons informed his wife "I gotta hang up—here's Dwight," she sighed, "You know, I've reached the point where I'd just as soon you went out with girls."

The Taylor-Crilly-Costello-Pogue team gradually acquired a reputation for able handling of route cases. "Eastern did as good a job as any airline and better than most," Taylor says. "We put together exhibits that were absolutely honest and totally supportable. We wrote briefs that were straightforward, reliable, and with a minimum of bullshit. Hall wouldn't tolerate any crap, Pogue wouldn't, Crilly wouldn't, and neither would I. We really tried to put cases together purely on merit, and that's where it got so frustrating. Trying to do a truly better job on the merits than the other guys, only to see yourself slaughtered by politics. Take the Toronto–Miami case, for example. We got a Toronto–Miami route but it was loaded with restrictions—we had to stop at four intermediate points although we had asked for nonstop authority. Northeast wound up with a Montreal–Miami nonstop —they had hired LBJ's chief fund-raiser, some lawyer from New York, as a consultant, and we didn't know about it until we saw his $30,000 fee listed in a trade press summary of consultant fees. In 1969 we did get Atlanta–Dallas and Atlanta–Los Angeles, but the Atlanta–San Francisco route award went to National, which wasn't even in Atlanta at the time. That was thanks to Mr. Crooker."

Despite the setbacks, however, Eastern's route awards from 1964 through 1967 added more than $32 million worth of new revenue. And there is reason to believe that in the end the Pacific defeat probably was just as well.

"It would have worked only if Eastern had gotten a monopoly," Costello theorizes. "There wasn't enough traffic for two carriers out of all the points Eastern wanted to serve."

The decision still hurt, however, coming as it did at a time when the airline was starting to struggle again. From that modest 1966 profit, Eastern slumped to just about breaking even in '67, lost $12 million the following year, and another $2.3 million in

'69. In an atmosphere that was now thick with bickering, name-calling and disagreements, the upper-level frictions became tension and tension turned into open warfare between Hall and Lewis.

Lewis kept urging spending cutbacks as early as 1967. Late that year he had suggested a freeze on new pilot hiring and told Hall, "We're operating too much mileage." But when Lewis saw the budget for 1968, he learned that Crilly had budgeted for a thirty-three percent mileage increase by the fourth quarter, although Eastern's 1968 traffic forecast estimated a modest nine percent increase.

"There's no way you can increase scheduled mileage by over thirty percent with that kind of a traffic forecast and achieve a reasonable load factor," he warned Hall. Floyd did agree to drop the planned thirty-three-percent boost down to twenty-seven percent, but Lewis still argued that this was foolhardy when weighed against only a nine percent increase in traffic. The nine-percent estimate turned out to be right on the button, and coupled with the whopping twenty-seven percent jump in capacity, it was a disaster.

In the spring of '68, while Hall was vacationing in Europe, Lewis put the pilot hiring freeze into effect. "We're going to operate in the fall with whatever pilots we have," he told his fellow executives. But when Hall returned, he rescinded the freeze and the conflict between the two was deepening. Up to May, Eastern's load factors had climbed to sixty percent but then, as the increased scheduling began to take effect, it dropped three points—and to an airline like EAL, a one percent load factor decline can mean an annual revenue loss of up to $60 million.

"We just couldn't penetrate our markets enough to handle the increase in capacity," Lewis explains. "And we were selling in too damned many markets, of which only a few were really profitable."

The quarreling continued. Lewis wanted to start disposing of the 720's; Hall's answer was an angry, "Goddammit, we've got these airplanes and we ought to fly them."

"We've always known we were going to phase out the 720's and the Electras, and this is as good a time as any to start," Lewis retorted.

An unsatisfactory compromise was reached—they began using the 720 fleet in charter service, but this was about the only semiagreement they achieved. Northeast, now reinforced by a financial transfusion from its new owner, the Storer Broadcasting Company, started to increase schedules in the New York–Miami market, using brand-new 727's. Up to then they had never garnered more than eighteen percent of the market while Eastern had never gone below fifty percent; by early 1968 Northeast's market share had climbed to as high as forty percent. Lewis changed Eastern's then-current schedule pattern, which at the time amounted to almost hourly service, to departures that would concentrate available seats in accordance with traffic demands. When Hall heard about it, he ordered the schedules returned to their former pattern.

Lewis recommended pulling out of the St. Louis–New York market, which had been losing about $1.3 million a year for the past three years.

"We don't have any backup traffic out of St. Louis," he pointed out. "We've made our play and it didn't work, so let's get the hell out."

Floyd refused.

There were times when Lewis simply put economy measures into effect "while Floyd was looking the other way." These cuts involved the operating divisions which reported directly to Lewis, but staff divisions—which reported only to Hall—refused to follow suit.

"Something happened to Floyd the last two years I was there," Lewis says. "He came damned close to a nervous breakdown just before I left. He was under great emotional strain—he had health and marital problems. In the first few years we were like twins in advertising goals, service ideas, in almost every area. Later there was nothing I'd propose to which he didn't take exception. Floyd was my big problem, not Todd Cole."

They collided again when Hall came up with the idea of

converting a number of DC-9's into an all-first-class configuration of fifty-six seats. He wanted to try them in such markets as New York–Houston, New York–Palm Beach, and Atlanta–St. Louis. As far as Lewis was concerned, Floyd might as well have proposed installing benches. EAL at the time was down to load factors of between forty and fifty percent in first class, compared to coach load factors as high as sixty percent. Charlie Simons did an analysis showing that first class actually was losing money while coach was making it. Hall refused to accept these figures as valid, ordered the all-first-class experiment which he called "Eastern I," and it laid an egg.

The final confrontation came in November of 1968 when budget planning for '69 got underway. It was more of the same: Hall wanted a seventeen percent increase in capacity in the face of industry estimates that traffic wouldn't go up more than eight percent the following year. Lewis spent two days arguing futilely against the scheduled mileage hike and at the end of the two days, walked into Hall's office and resigned.

Hall says today that he didn't want Art to leave—"He was a hell of a lot better president than some of the ones we've got today"—and that the Lewis-Cole feud was the prime reason for his departure. The directors, Hall adds, were down on both Lewis and Cole and more or less forced him into letting them go. Todd resigned from EAL early in 1969.

Lewis insists he had a good relationship with the board of directors. "Like all boards, you have stronger ties to some directors than to others. There's no doubt the board was worried and concerned about what was happening to the company. When we lost money in '68, I think there was a lot of playback about conflict between Todd and me to the extent that it was hurting profitability. When I did resign, Floyd didn't try very hard to talk me out of it and I couldn't blame him—by that time our differences were deep. But I never tried to undercut him. I never went bitching to the board or anyone else. And I never knew what he told the board about why I quit."

Ironically, to a certain extent Lewis and Cole were on the same side when it came to believing that Hall eventually went too far in his zeal to improve Eastern's image. Lewis, for example, agreed with Frank Sharpe when the latter fought against such gimmicks as Reed and Barton silverware and crystal glasses. And he had another bout with Floyd over a plan to improve first-class service. For two years Eastern had been promoting "famous restaurant flights" which featured entrées from some of the better metropolitan dining places over EAL's system. It was fairly successful but after it seemed to have run its course, Lewis proposed taking the money they were spending on this promotion and using it to upgrade first-class service on a broad scale. Hall turned him down.

Yet Lewis was one of the few executives who didn't criticize spending a half-million dollars on the Metropolitan Opera.

"If you look at our advertising expenditures for a period of five years, 100,000 a year out of a total budget of twenty-five million wasn't a great deal," he says. "I thought Eastern stood to gain credit by projecting our corporate image as a patron of the arts. The disagreement I had with Floyd concerned having silver when we could have had stainless steel, and those cloth napkins, tablecloths, and towels and crystal glasses—that stuff cost tens of thousands of dollars a year."

In general there seemed to be more of a clash of personality between Lewis and Cole than a conflict over policy—to a somewhat lesser degree, Art was as convinced as Todd that there was a limit to image making. And both were equally worried about the decline in revenues and the corresponding dip in profits. One of the major disputes between Lewis and Hall came in 1968 when Floyd intervened in a labor dispute involving the pilots. In February of that year, and again in March, the pilots staged slowdowns in an effort to pressure the company into signing a new and fatter contract. Lewis and Ralph Skinner, vice president of industrial and personnel relations, decided to get an injunction that would halt the slowdowns. When they told Hall, however, he stepped into the negotiations and in a few weeks settled by giving the pilots the best contract they had ever had—including a thirty-nine percent wage increase over a thirty-nine month period, plus a number of fringe benefits, not the least of which were new duty rigs that in effect cut their working hours to the point of adversely affecting pilot productivity. The slowdowns alone had cost Eastern some $5 million in over-the-budget operating expenses, and Cole was just as disturbed as Lewis.

Todd Cole left Eastern shortly after Lewis resigned—whether because of board pressure on Hall or because Cole just got fed up is debatable. Hall says his departure was triggered at a board meeting—Cole was present as a member—when a director introduced a resolution to make Hall board chairman *and* president. After the meeting, Floyd recalls, Todd came into his office.

"If I understand this correctly," he said, "I guess I'd better start looking for another job."

Hall, knowing that Cole felt he had been passed over again for the presidency largely because there was considerable opposition to him among the directors, did not argue with him or make much effort to talk him into staying.

Yet the departures of both his chief lieutenants saddened Floyd Hall. Even today he believes Eastern's future would have taken a different course if he had been able to hang onto them—Cole in particular. "I could replace Art, but Cole's loss was a severe blow to Eastern—I didn't have anyone to replace him. Charlie Simons is top-notch, but at that point in time he was no Todd Cole yet. Todd was absolutely the smartest financial man I ever met."

Hall's choice to replace Lewis was Sam Higginbottom, although he wasn't elevated to the presidency until early in 1970; the delay reportedly stemmed from pressure by some directors on Hall to move cautiously, reminding him that he had been advised to wait awhile before making Art Lewis president. Higginbottom was first promoted to executive vice president and general manager, which meant he actually was assuming most of the duties of a president, and there was no real opposition to him; his record at both TWA and Eastern had been exemplary, and his reputation throughout the industry was that of a solid, thoroughly competent and experienced airline man, although his forte was engineering and operations, not marketing.

Higginbottom's want of marketing experience worried directors like Harper Woodward somewhat. He had always felt that Hall brought too many officers into Eastern who didn't really understand that the airline had problems peculiar to EAL, especially its route structure, which led to high operating costs and marketing difficulties. Passengers who criticized Eastern too often contrasted its short-haul service to what they got on American's and United's long-haul flights. Eastern carried more passengers than any U.S. carrier except United, but its costs on a passenger-per-mile basis were far higher, so much higher that its fare structure was incapable of following any cost curve. Yet virtually every top man Hall had recruited came from carriers with long-haul route structures and possibly were psychologically unacclimated to what they found at Eastern. Like Floyd himself, they had big ideas, big dreams, and big plans, but when the 1964–66 honeymoon was over, they had to start learning the facts of life as Eastern lived them. And while they were learning, the airline went downhill. To Harper Woodward, vice president of marketing Tom McFadden was a prime example—Woodward once commented to Hall, "You know, Tom's one of the nicest fellows I ever met, but I have no idea at all whether he's effective in his job."

So Sam Higginbottom was president number nine—holding as well the title of chief operating officer, which in itself was a mistake. It put him on an immediate collision course with Hall, chairman of the board and chief executive officer, and their lines of authority and power became hopelessly tangled. They each had a different notion of a chief operating officer's responsibilities, and in a way it was the old Rickenbacker-MacIntyre situation all over again. Two able, well-meaning men struggling for supremacy in a corporation ripped apart by their disagreements.

They started out with every good intention of cooperating for the airline's good. For one thing, Higginbottom took over after six years at Eastern and was well acquainted with its problems. To use his own words, "I knew it was—and still is—a very difficult airline to operate; it has so damned many passengers, it has such a short average segment length, it operates in many markets where customers are both demanding and unforgiving, and the very nature of the company with its high debt structure means an eternal shortage of cash for accomplishing things you have to do."

Knowing all this, he became president determined not to repeat the mistakes of his predecessors. Art Lewis, for instance, he regarded as a "bright, energetic guy whose strong points were marketing and planning, but somewhat overenthusiastic and overly optimistic." He wanted to avoid the kind of situation that had Hall and Lewis at each other's throats; while he shared Art's belief that something had happened to Floyd, that he wasn't the same man who had come to Eastern's rescue like the U.S. Cavalry, he insists he accepted Hall as the company's chief executive officer with the right to organize management as he wished. Yet he did not cotton to the idea of having corporate headquarters in New York, more than a thousand miles from operating headquarters in Miami, and he felt that the corporate staff was not only too large but not fully supportive of the operating side.

"Rather than make an issue of it," Sam says, "I concentrated on running the operating side."

Unfortunately, while he may not have wanted to make an issue out of it, it became one—so hot an issue that eventually it was to destroy them both. For the very distance separating New York from Miami was a 1,200-mile moat dividing Hall and Higginbottom in every phase from policy to philosophy. The first minor conflict between them involved Higginbottom's decision to move the entire operating staff to Miami—plus some people from marketing and other departments—an action he felt was justified after a cost analysis showed that the shift would save money in the long run. Hall wasn't very enthused about it; from his standpoint, it meant he would have to spend more time in Miami (he finally did set up an office there) although he preferred New York.

The physical separation of the two headquarters staffs actually created a two-headed airline and the result was inevitable diffusion of goals, methods, and authority. It didn't happen overnight, for in the early stages Higginbottom and Hall saw eye-to-eye on several matters. Both, for example, were lukewarm over Eastern's diversification efforts—something Crilly had pushed hard to the point of getting the airline to invest in some hotel properties and an ill-fated project involving computerized warehouses, with Eastern handling the shipping via truck and plane. Crilly's concept had looked promising and even the conservative Cole didn't oppose it, but the execution was poor and it was a financial disaster. Higginbottom thought such ventures diverted too much of the airline's rather limited managerial talent, a view which Hall shared, and while diversification never did get very far, such projects consumed effort, time, and money they felt could have been better spent on the airline.

The question of spending, however, became a major issue between them. In the end Hall would accuse Higginbottom of needless extravagance, and vice versa; the evidence supplied by those who worked with them suggests both were guilty to an extent. These serious differences, however, did not arise during Higginbottom's initial year in office, which actually was moderately successful—Eastern wound up that year with a $5.5 million profit. During this period, they worked reasonably well together and their disputes, while occurring too frequently for the board's pleasure, at least were not of a violent nature. Hall had tremendous respect for Sam's admitted skill in running the operations side, and for all Eastern's admitted financial and service problems, it still enjoyed a good reputation within the aviation industry for its technical know-how.

Higginbottom and Hall were both instrumental in hiring Scott Crossfield, a veteran test pilot and aeronautical research expert, as a vice president and technical adviser. Crossfield's biggest contribution was the development of a unique area-navigation system designed to ease congestion problems in the infamous Corridor. In 1968 Eastern equipped an experimental STOL aircraft (Short Takeoff or Landing) with a Decca area nav system and shot more than 160 simulated low-visibility landings at Boston, La Guardia, and Washington National.

The test flights demonstrated that using a STOL aircraft with this type of navigation could double airport capacity with virtually no additional investment in runway expansion or navigation facilities. Furthermore, the 188, with a cruising speed of less than 300 miles an hour, consistently beat Eastern's DC-9's and Electras from gate to gate during peak traffic hours.

The experiments were so successful that a joint committee composed of Air Force brass airframe manufacturers and the airlines was established to set up commonality of military and civil STOL requirements. It was well on the way to an agreement when the U.S. Senate blasted the Air Force for trying to justify its own STOL development program by demonstrating its civil application. The Air Force had to pull out of the project and its STOL development program continued without civilian input.

Hall thought he could still salvage something out of Crossfield's impressive test program; if the airlines weren't going to get any STOL aircraft, he figured, Eastern still might be able to use area navigation on its conventional planes. Alan Boyd, just before he left his post as secretary of transportation to become a railroad president, told Hall and Higginbottom that DOT still had about $25 million available for STOL/area navigation experimentation. Hall went to see John Volpe, Boyd's successor, and asked him about releasing the funds.

"If there ever was any $25 million around, it's gone now," Volpe said. "I don't know what the hell ever happened to it."

So nothing ever came of Crossfield's project, something Hall still regrets. "It could have worked through a data link providing automatic traffic-control separation, hooked to the autopilot so if you got on a collision course the computer would have changed course automatically."

Hall's last effort to move ahead with area navigation was to set up a symposium on the subject headed by former Air Force General Bernard "Benny" Schriever, an EAL director and chairman of the airline's technical committee.

"He couldn't get anyone to really listen," Hall mourns. "I think the problem was that we were about twenty years ahead of our times—and we aren't even ready for it now."

On matters like this Hall truly shone, with his flair for innovations and his courage to plunge into areas that the more cautious avoided. The Shuttle alone could have benefited hugely from a perfected area-navigation system; the one Crossfield developed was part Decca, part Doppler, enabling a pilot to fly any of a dozen tracks, and while it had its bugs, they were not serious enough to discourage further development. To Hall, it added to Eastern's image as a progressive, modern airline willing to experiment and improve. He always was a great admirer of men with technical skills, and this may have been one of the reasons why, in 1969, he hired as a technical consultant one of the nation's astronaut heroes.

The astronaut was forty-one (he was born the same year as the airline) and was best known as the commander of the *Apollo 8* space flight, the first manned lunar orbital mission in December 1968. Hall first thought of him as a potential EAL executive while he was trying to get James Webb, then director of the National Aeronautics and Space Administration, to become a director. Webb declined for reasons of health but added:

"If you're looking for talent, Floyd, I know a young man I feel has more ability than any of the other astronauts. Before he gets committed to some other company, you ought to take a look at him. His name is Frank Borman."

Hall called director Jim Elkins in Houston and asked him if he knew Colonel Borman.

"Ever since he became an astronaut," Elkins replied. "Matter of fact, he and Susan, his wife, have been guests in my home. I think very highly of him."

By coincidence Eastern's board was about to hold a meeting in Houston and Elkins invited Borman to a party he was throwing for the directors. Hall was impressed to the extent of offering him a job, which Borman tentatively declined, explaining that while he was ready to leave the Air Force and the space program, he wanted to look around a little. But Hall did get him to join Eastern's technical advisory committee as a consultant—the fee was nominal, about $5,000, as Borman remembers it.

Hall and Higginbottom watched his work on the committee with interest—he was sharp, incisive, capable. Floyd, who could be as persuasive as Captain Eddie when it came to courting talent, kept up the pressure for a full year and, late in 1970, specifically offered him the post of vice president of maintenance.

Borman had a few other irons in the fire, although none burned as hotly as the one he had placed on Eastern's grill. He did know he wanted out of the space program, having already informed NASA that *Apollo 8* was his last mission, and he was tired of working for the Air Force's research and development program, which seemed to offer nothing new or challenging. Several corporations had approached him but Eastern's major competition came from none other than the White House.

Every president, from Kennedy on, had courted the astronauts, and Borman was rather close to Richard Nixon, a relationship dating back to NASA's assignment of Borman as its liaison man with the White House in connection with the *Apollo 11* mission: the first lunar landing. There was considerable concern about public reaction if this, the riskiest mission of them all to date, should not only fail but culminate in tragedy. Borman was instructed to call Bill Safire, a trusted Nixon advisor and chief presidential speech writer, and suggest that the White House be thinking "of some alternate posture for the President in the event of mishaps on *Apollo 11*." Borman relayed the message in this stilted phraseology and then ad-libbed, "You know—like what to do for the widows."

Safire, in his well-received account of those pre-Watergate years (*Before the Fall*, Doubleday, 1975), wrote this impression of the young astronaut:

Borman was the kind of well-organized, highly motivated, intelligent serviceman Nixon admired, the product of a mission the President identified with.

The President, through Bob Haldeman, eventually offered Borman a job.

"What would I be doing?" Borman naturally wanted to know.

"It would be a position of responsibility at the White House," Haldeman informed him vaguely—too vaguely, Borman thought. When he pressed for more details, he was told it would involve "input into policy" but Borman never could get Haldeman or anyone else to spell this out. Susan Borman was absolutely opposed, anyway—she loved the Nixons but like Frank she didn't think much of an offer that didn't define the job specifically.

Borman also became friends with Ross Perot, a billionaire computer manufacturer close to Nixon, and discussed with him a project to set up "town meeting of the air" TV programs presenting both sides of controversial issues. They progressed far enough to propose it to the networks, who weren't interested, and by that time Borman had been smitten by the airline bug. "I wanted to sink my teeth into something to do with airplanes, which I knew something about. I considered a lot of offers and some would have made me far better off financially, but when Hall gave me a chance to be an Eastern vice president, that was it. It looked exciting and that's all I needed."

He had no regrets about turning away from the heady prospects of becoming a White House official; no one was more disillusioned than Frank Borman when the Watergate scandal broke —he had sincerely admired Nixon and still remembers with pride his brief stint at the White House—one of his jobs there had been helping with the wording of the plaque to be placed on the moon.

He became senior vice president of operations after only six months—obviously a man on his way up. But the promotion came in spite of, not because of, Sam Higginbottom; Sam reportedly came close to firing him and actually turned in an unfavorable evaluation report to Hall based on Borman's handling of pilot contract negotiations, and the subsequent scheduling of the pilot work-force based on the agreement Borman had reached with ALPA.

The new contract came just at the time Eastern was receiving additional new jets, bigger DC-9's and the stretched 727-200's; the deliveries put many pilots back in training and this, coupled with the new duty rigs the contract had granted, left the airline so short of crews that Eastern had to cancel trips right in the middle of the peak winter season.

Higginbottom denies he wanted to fire Borman but admits

he was angry enough to propose a reduction in the vice president's incentive compensation (a type of bonus system Borman was to abolish a few years later). The suggested reduction, along with Higginbottom's "below-average" evaluation of performance, didn't sit well with Hall. He pointed out it hadn't been Borman's fault that new planes were delivered at a particularly inopportune time insofar as pilot availability was concerned, and that Borman had been put on the spot when labor negotiations, an area with which he was totally unfamiliar, were dumped in his lap.

Sam had second thoughts, gave Borman a satisfactory evaluation grade, and restored the incentive pay. There never was any animosity between the two; Higginbottom, to use his own words, thought Borman "very much above average in intelligence, energy, and leadership qualities."

"In the early days," he says, "Frank had a tendency to be impulsive. He didn't have any airline background and in the area of complex labor contracts, he simply walked into a situation he wasn't prepared to handle and made decisions that weren't well thought out."

But while Borman liked Hall and Higginbottom as people, it took very little time for him to start wondering what he had gotten into—his first impressions of Eastern were dismal.

"Being from the military and NASA, I was expecting a more austere operation but instead I found it pretty plush and very structured, full of committees and policy groups which met only once a mouth. It was a long way from the management style I was used to at NASA, where the guy who had all the information and knowledge was directly involved in staff meetings— his information wasn't sifted through three levels of management. When we had a review of Gemini, the engineer who designed an individual system was sitting in the room with his boss, and we asked them whatever questions we wanted answered. As soon as I became vice president, I told everybody under me that was the way I was going to operate at Eastern. Sure, I was shaking the management structure and there wasn't a hell of a lot I really could do about it until I became president. I can understand how some of the older vice presidents felt—here I was, a new guy with no previous airline experience telling them to run the show differently.

"I found Eastern's stratified structure absolutely repugnant. I had no way of knowing whether it was symptomatic of the whole industry or just peculiar to Eastern. But I already knew and greatly admired Bob Six, and I couldn't believe he or anyone else would run an airline this way. Frankly, I wasn't aware of the financial problems at Eastern—I didn't pay any attention to them at first.

"I got along well with Sam for a while, although we had different management styles. I had to admit he was having a difficult time with Floyd. Something would be decided at one of these committee meetings, then Sam would report the decision to Hall, who'd decide something else. All I knew, with all my inexperience, was that we were doing a hell of a lot of things that were totally without cost justification."

Borman, incidentally, defends that disputed contract he signed with the pilots. He hadn't been at Eastern very long when Hall insisted that he take a thirteen-week course at Harvard Business School. While he was gone, the pilots repeated their 1968 slowdown tactics, and when Borman returned from Cambridge, the contract negotiations were deadlocked with a great deal of rancor on both sides. It was nothing but a can of worms and Borman's only guidance was the so-called "Gold Book" contract signed in 1968, which had left Eastern with the lowest utilization of pilots in the industry. What Borman agreed to was an extension of that agreement, with slight improvements; he knew Higginbottom regarded it as a "sweetheart deal" and was furious, but he felt he had no other choice. But Frank Borman was not to make a mistake twice; since that 1970 contract, Eastern's pilot productivity has gradually improved to the point where it has matched Delta's.

The friction between Higginbottom and Hall that Borman observed began rising in temperature in direct correlation with falling profits. It was kept reasonably in check during 1971 and 1972, when Higginbottom was able to report net profits of $5.6

million and \$19.7 million respectively. In '72 Eastern became the first airline to fly the new Lockheed 1011, a wide-bodied trijet the airline had ordered in 1968 when Art Lewis was president. It had been the largest aircraft purchase in Eastern's history in terms of monetary value—\$800 million for thirty-seven firm orders and options for thirteen more which were later exercised —and it also was the most controversial.

The L-1011 commitment was to take much of the blame for Eastern's subsequent financial crisis. Like all new transports it had its share of bugs, and the chief target for criticism was its Rolls-Royce engines; Lockheed, competing not too successfully against the McDonnell Douglas DC-10, had worked out a deal by which British Airways would buy the 1011 provided it was equipped with the British engines, and Eastern's engineers— impressed with the past Rolls-Royce reputation for superb products—were happy to accept the same airframe-engine combination.

There were several reasons for choosing the L-1011 over the DC-10. Price was vital: The L-1011 ran as much as \$3.5 million per unit less than the DC-10 for the first twenty-five ordered, and Charlie Simons—who had succeeded Cole— worked out a deal by which Eastern paid \$1 million for a guarantee that the price on the remainder would not rise beyond an agreed-on level. The second factor was Eastern's poor relations with McDonnell Douglas at the time; both the DC-9's and larger DC-8's had been subjected to long delivery delays—up to seven months in some cases—which had put the hard-pressed airline into a terrible competitive bind just when it was trying to modernize its fleet. Schedules, drawn up as much as two years in advance, had to be reshaped. EAL, in fact, estimated it had lost \$45 million because of McDonnell Douglas's production line problems and sued the manufacturer for damages—the lawsuit was settled later when McDonnell Douglas agreed to cut the price of new stretched DC-9's that Eastern wanted.

McDonnell Douglas made a strong pitch to sell Hall the DC-10, but the price quoted amounted to \$125 million more than Lockheed was willing to accept for the same number of aircraft.

Nor were either Hall or Higginbottom convinced that McDonnell Douglas had solved its production difficulties. The two airplanes looked almost identical on paper—about the same payload, speed, fuel consumption, power, handling characteristics, and operating costs; if anything, the 1011 seemed slightly superior in the latter category.

When the L-1011 went into service, of course, its reliability record was a nightmare of canceled and delayed flights, becoming epidemic early in 1973. Both Hall and Higginbottom were criticized sharply for choosing Lockheed, but some of the criticism was pure hindsight. Most of the L-1011's troubles stemmed from its Rolls-Royce engines and this had to be a major shocker —Rolls-Royce's reputation was incredibly solid. The R-R engines on such transports as the F-27, Viscount, VC-10, BAC-111 and some models of the 707 had compiled the finest reliability record in the industry. But the RB-211 engine designed for the big Lockheed trijet came along just when Rolls-Royce was on the verge of bankruptcy and in no shape to pay the kind of attention to technical problems that should have been paid.

The RB-211's weakness lay in its fan-disc design, which contained a flaw built into the disc during the manufacturing process. It caused premature failure from metal fatigue, culminating in a ruptured disc, and the engine shutdown rate on Eastern's L-1011 fleet was astronomical. The situation was serious enough for Rolls to seek help from its American competitors— General Electric and Pratt & Whitney; their cooperation in aiding the British firm to solve the problem was typical in commercial aviation where a technical crisis suspends normal competition.

Eastern considered the GE engine for the L-1011, but when Hall met with GE engineers just before the final power-plant decision was made, they could not promise a means of increasing thrust without radical modifications and Eastern at that time was looking ahead to a possible Pacific route award. Rolls did promise that the RB-211 had easy growth potential, and six months later GE managed to come up with a way to increase thrust so it could get its engine on the DC-10.

The L-1011's troubles couldn't have come at a worse time, what with the Hall-Higginbottom relations reaching a breaking point, the New York–Miami rivalry approaching the status of two armed camps, traffic growth still sluggish, and prosperous Delta with the best labor relations in the industry (it has no unions other than ALPA) giving Eastern competitive fits. Interestingly enough, Delta had ordered the L-1011, too, but the L-1011 was not Eastern's first wide-body. EAL operated a pair of leased Boeing 747's briefly because National was flying the giant plane between New York and Miami. Hall actually had ordered four 747's but never took delivery, turning them over to TWA instead. So the L-1011 became EAL's big hope for 1973— a superb competitive weapon and technical achievement. The airplane of the future was in the fleet today.

It was, but it stayed mostly on the ground for weeks. The engine troubles were serious enough to force cancellation of scores of L-1011 schedules during most of the 1972–73 winter season. And the trijet's reputation was further blackened when it became involved in the first crash of any wide-body transport. On December 29, 1972, an Eastern L-1011 operating as Flight 401 from New York to Miami crashed into the Everglades eighteen miles from the Miami International Airport. Of the 163 passengers and 13 crew aboard, 93 passengers and five crew members were fatally injured.

The aircraft was on final approach when the flight crew noticed the nose gear indicator showed the wheels were not down and locked. They suspected that the indicator light was faulty and were trying to check the gear visually, the flight engineer climbing down into the forward electronics bay from where the gear could be seen. Flight 401 was on autopilot, in level flight, but as the pilots peered down into the bay to see how the flight engineer was progressing, one of them apparently pressed against the control yoke, dislodging the autopilot. They never realized that the giant jet had gone into a gentle descent and while their attention was still distracted, the L-1011 landed in the swamp.

A crash triggered by failure of an inexpensive bulb, an accidental dislodging of an autopilot, and a distracted crew could not be construed as an indictment of the airplane itself, but the L-1011 still bore part of the blame as far as the public and the press was concerned. And by the time the tragedy was off the front pages and the engine gremlins eradicated, summer traffic was running far below estimates, and recovery in the fall, traditionally Eastern's poorest period, was impossible. There was a standard joke that Eastern's formula was to make all the dough possible from January through August, knowing you'd lose everything you've made by the middle of November, and then pray for good weather the last two weeks in December.

And in 1973 Eastern didn't make money at all. It lost a staggering $51 million and the wolves were howling. In this climate of disaster Hall and Higginbottom stepped up their mutual sniping, although the strange thing about their feud was that their respect for each other never wavered—it was as if the pressures of the financial debacle made them say things and do things which simply made matters worse. A present EAL official who was close to both men in those unhappy days sums it up as objectively as it can be phrased:

"When Sam became chief operating officer, part of the terms he demanded was that fundamentally he'd have his own staff. And he got his own group—he even had his own public relations department. He did spend a reasonable time in New York but being primarily a nuts and bolts man, he eventually had to set himself up in Miami and the polarization was underway. As the power base shifted south, the competition increased between Floyd and Sam. New York kept trying to push the idea that Hall was still running the airline. Those in Miami, who finally acquired some power of their own when Higginbottom moved to Miami, would say, 'Yeah, we know who's running Eastern—and he's down here.' The friction was so bad that loyalty became a matter of allegiance to the Hall faction or the Higginbottom faction, not to the airline. It wasn't disloyalty to Eastern as such, but rather that each side felt his man was best for the company's welfare and so loyalty became more and more personalized toward individuals—Sam on one side, Floyd on the other. Then it got completely out of control. Orders were countermanded. Projects were wiped out. God, you could feel and see the friction. And to climax all this polarization, along came the L-1011 catastrophe—that really pushed us over the cliff.

"Frankly, we came damned close to bankruptcy. The directors had been watching developments closely and it became obvious Sam had to go. In many ways Sam was the fall guy—he tried like hell to pull things together but I think he was afflicted with the same disease that marked Eastern's management policies during the entire decade of the sixties—remember, this was the era of the jet revolution. The philosophy was that you could spend your way to prosperity. Eastern had a semblance of economic controls but it didn't really mean that much. We went on a buying binge—airplanes, people, computers, a new General Offices building in Miami—Christ, we spent a fortune building the damned thing and another fortune remodeling it. Some of all this had to be done and everyone thought it's what Eastern needed. Floyd Hall had his faults, but he took a shoddy, dirty airline and made it respectable, and Sam made his own contributions in that area. We had gotten so bad that to this day, every time we slip someone says, 'Same old Eastern.'

"But after Hall turned us around, that's when competition began to develop within management. Floyd wasn't every good at controlling it; he wasn't the kind of guy who could keep a tight rein on people. He had a bunch of Young Turks, ambitious and smart, and they needed a strong hand to keep them in line. It began to be a situation in which people were pitted against one another—it became a game to see who was going to survive. The company was being torn in two. It was operating headquarters in Miami against financial headquarters in New York. Since the seat of ultimate authority was in New York, the polarization produced another bad side-effect: It became apparent that executive promotions were going to those in New York while people in Miami were being generally ignored.

"Why did the split develop? I think largely because those in New York rationalized that the main power-base had to be there —in their minds, New York was the center of the universe, the communications, financial, and cultural capital of the world. The truth was that executives in New York didn't really like the operating side of the airline, they didn't want to be associated with nuts-and-bolts types. The attitude was that the operating side was okay, but it was mostly hired help doing what they were paid to do. New York was supposed to be the bastion of higher thinking—let Miami do the mundane work. All this had a psychological effect on people in Miami. Number 10 Rockefeller Center was castle keep and everyone else was a serf laboring in the fields, hoping for an occasional favor so long as you stayed in your place. I remember there was talk of consolidating the two headquarters but it got nowhere because the only logical location was Miami and the New York crowd wouldn't buy it.

"When Sam became president, the polarization gradually became concentrated into a Higginbottom faction versus a Hall faction. Their own personalities symbolized the gap already existing between the two power bases and from then on, everything just degenerated."

This "Tale of Two Cities" crystalized into charges and countercharges of extravagance. Higginbottom was bitterly critical not only of Hall but of some of the executives who were closely tied to the Hall faction. Tom McFadden, vice president of marketing, for example: Higginbottom once remarked that "Tom's way out of a problem is to hire more people." It was only too true that McFadden, with Hall's blessing, was hiring additional reservationists, ramp agents, and ticket agents just when Higginbottom was trying to economize, and this policy was a chief factor in the eventual blowup.

Hall, in turn, thought Sam's economizing was out of focus with such spending habits as having Cadillacs available for officers and VIPs. Higginbottom said they were no worse than the fleet of limousines EAL had in New York for the same purpose—they used to drive right up to the planes until ordinary passengers complained. Floyd actually didn't object to alleged extravagances as much as he questioned Higginbottom's timing. The previously mentioned refurbishing of Building 16 was a case in point; it was prompted by the move of so many management people from New York to Miami, requiring changes in office space and the shifting of entire departments to different floors. "When you tear down the interior walls of an office structure," Hall concedes, "you have to put things back in shape and that means redecorating." But it didn't sit very well with employees threatened with mass furloughing when they saw the extent of the refurbishing in a building that was only four years old, including expensive new furniture, drapes, and other trappings of executive luxury.

Hall, so sensitive to the image-making process, felt some of Higginbottom's actions were inadvertently creating an image problem—the image employees had of Eastern's management. The Taj Mahal interior at 16 was one example and another was a Lockheed JetStar which various officials used for business trips —and, it was claimed, for occasional trips that seemed to be more pleasure than business. Hall winced when he heard one mechanic sarcastically refer to the JetStar as "the Wings of Sam."

Lefty Lethridge, still with Eastern as vice president of civic affairs and somewhat of a respected elder statesman by then, looked askance on that JetStar. "Throughout the system they'd see it coming in with company officials on board and they knew the damned thing cost us three hundred thousand bucks a year to run."

Frank Borman, the first time he saw the sleek executive jet, remarked, "We've got 250 jets—what the hell do we need a private airplane for?"

Lethridge adds, "Sam was as bad as Floyd when it came to spending dough—almost as if he were trying to match him."

Charlie Simons, who was trying hard not to associate himself too closely with either faction, agrees. "When they accused each other of spending Eastern into bankruptcy, they were both right. They spent for different purposes and it was for different things, but it was spending."

Employee resentment of visual manifestations of management privileges is to be expected as part of the perpetual capital-versus-labor game. But at Eastern the vein of resentment ran much deeper—remember, this was a company whose ranks still included many employees raised in the old Rickenbacker "count mills, not pennies" tradition and still worshiping the far simpler, almost spartan image of the Captain with his old felt hat, his easy rapport, his natural charisma, and his "we're all just one big family" philosophy. Few employees got to know Sam Higginbottom very well. He was a reasonable man but he was tough— very tough, and the impression he gave to many of Eastern's rank and file was that he was exactly that and more—a tough, unfeeling, s.o.b.

There were hundreds, perhaps even thousands of Eastern people who could not help comparing the togetherness of the Rickenbacker era with the computerized aloofness of modern management. And on July 23, 1973, the man who symbolized those glory days of the past died in Zurich, Switzerland, at the age of eighty-two.

Captain Eddie's last years were filled with emptiness and his last months with pain.

After he finished his book and a subsequent promotion tour, he did what most retired, once-powerful individuals did— he tried to keep busy and found that most of his activities were built around nostalgia, memories, and yearnings for the past. His office was crammed with mementos and if any visitor commented on a particular item, he would be treated to the complete story of its origin and significance. One of his favorites was a plaque on which had been mounted the gear of a Constellation engine, and he relished the story behind that plaque.

He had been visiting the engine shop in Miami, checking into a persistent maintenance problem involving one particular gear. EVR asked to see the part that had been causing all the trouble, examined it briefly, and frowned.

"Did you count the teeth in this damned thing?" he asked the supervisor.

They hadn't, but now they did—and discovered it had one too many. The mechanics had the guilty gear mounted and presented it to him at a party for his retirement.

Some of his most treasured possessions he kept locked in

the bottom drawer of his desk, and Sheppy would open it for no one without his permission. Frank Sharpe saw the contents one day and almost lost his eyeballs.

"The old man had original photographs of Spads in there," he recounts, "and there were letters from people like Pershing and the Canadian ace, Billy Bishop—they must be worth a fortune now."

Lunches with old cronies and associates at Louis XIV furnished the happiest moments of his waning life. Lefty Lethridge, with whom he had fought about as bitterly as anyone else, was one of his most frequent luncheon companions. Lefty, in fact, was with him the last time he dined at that restaurant, a week before EVR had to undergo emergency surgery to remove an obstruction in an artery.

They had just been seated when the head waiter whispered to Captain Eddie, "We've got a good-looking girl coming in." They looked up and saw Joan Crawford, accompanied by three young men with long hair and a rather effeminate appearance. Lefty thought they looked like ad-agency types. Miss Crawford spotted them and called out, "Hello Eddie, you old rascal, how are you?"

Rickenbacker beamed. "Just fine, Joannie, just fine." Lethridge commented that she was still a beautiful woman.

"Yeah," Rickenbacker growled, "but where the hell did she pick up those three fags?"

The aneurism operation occurred two days after he celebrated his eighty-second birthday at his villa in Miami—Lefty had seen him on one of his increasingly rare trips to New York. EVR had dined on stone crabs, his favorite food, and the next day suffered what was diagnosed as a stroke; the blood clot was discovered at the hospital and his doctors decided only surgery could save his life.

The man he saw most often in Florida was Ed Yarnell, who had known the Captain since 1941 when Yarnell was an EAL baggage handler and ticket agent in Indianapolis. They became extremely close friends, and Rickenbacker let him handle some successful business deals for him. Yet he never got around to making Yarnell a vice president—Ed believes it was because "he knew I wouldn't want to be a vice president unless I made it on my own—and I respected him for it."

Yarnell was district sales and traffic manager in Miami during the last months of Rickenbacker's life. He would go out to the villa and chat with the old man for hours, sitting on the veranda overlooking the ocean, watching the seagulls and pelicans. On some days the Captain's memory would be incredibly sharp. He would talk about World War I as if it had happened yesterday, about his old racing cars, Eastern's formative years. The next day he would seem to remember nothing at all. Adds Yarnell:

"He told me his biggest mistake at Eastern was making Malcolm MacIntyre president, that Rockefeller had lunched with him one day and recommended MacIntyre. He said he didn't even know the man but trusted Laurance. But he really liked Floyd Hall, who was wonderful to him—used to call and ask him to lunch, or he'd tell him about some new program at Eastern and would say, 'What do you think of it, Eddie?' Hall tried to make him feel he still belonged. After the stroke his interest in the airline lessened. He cared, but not like in the old days."

As ill as Rickenbacker was, Adelaide apparently was in even worse condition, afflicted with low blood pressure and painful arthritis, and, on top of all this, was going blind from glaucoma. It was his wife's health that sent EVR on his final trip. He told Sheppy they had heard of an eye specialist in Zurich who might help her regain her vision; accompanied by Sheppy and a chauffeur/aide, the Rickenbackers left for Switzerland aboard Swissair July 9, 1973. Sheppy didn't want to go—she thought the trip was too much of an ordeal for both EVR and his wife, and she didn't buy the explanation about the eye doctor, knowing that advanced glaucoma was considered virtually incurable. She suspected they merely wanted to take one last trip to Europe together; another reason, she learned later, was EVR's desire to visit the graves of his Swiss grandparents one final time.

The flight was tiring; Adelaide went right to bed as soon as they got to the hotel. EVR retired early, too—he had caught a cold. On Friday, July 13, Sheppy and the Captain had been out to lunch and Sheppy noticed his breathing seemed labored. When she mentioned it to Mrs. Rickenbacker and the aide, both said they had been aware of it, too. The next day, when a doctor came to visit Adelaide, Sheppy asked him to also take a look at Captain Eddie. He finished his examination and drew the two women off to one side.

"I think he should go to the hospital for some chest X-rays," he told them. "He is a very sick man."

Adelaide said, "I can't tell him that—he'll scream his head off."

"We won't tell him tonight," Sheppy suggested. "We'll tell him tomorrow at breakfast after he's had a good night's sleep."

The next morning EVR asked them rather casually, "By the way, what did the doctor have to say about my chest?"

Sheppy, also trying to be casual, replied, "Well, he wants you to go into the hospital for some X-rays."

Instead of blowing up as expected, Rickenbacker merely said, "All right—I suppose it's best." Adelaide was pleased but Sheppy thought his reaction ominous; she even mentioned to the aide, while EVR was dressing, "I think he's taking this too calmly."

Later that Sunday morning they drove him to the hospital the doctor had suggested. The Captain climbed into bed dutifully, put his head back on the pillow, and seemed so content that Sheppy was even more worried—this wasn't natural. Around three that afternoon the doctor talked to Sheppy alone.

"He has pneumonia," he told her. "I don't think that would be serious by itself, but you didn't tell me he had a heart condition."

Sheppy was shocked, and said, "He's never had a heart condition."

"He has one now," the doctor said grimly.

On Tuesday the hospital informed Mrs. Rickenbacker that EVR's heart wasn't responding and his condition was serious. It became critical Thursday, when he almost died, and Adelaide stayed by his bedside from then on. Sheppy doesn't remember exactly when she saw him for the last time; she only recalls that his bed was covered with flowers, and that the last time he spoke to her it was to comment on the beautiful view from his window.

He was in constant pain but death came quietly, in his sleep, the following Monday. Swissair officials cabled the news to Floyd Hall, and he immediately called in Lethridge.

"Who was closest to him, Lefty—I mean at Eastern?" Hall asked.

"Ed Yarnell in Miami," Lethridge replied.

"Okay, I'll call Ed. We're sending a DC-8 to Zurich to pick up his body and bring the family back. You make all the necessary arrangements at this end, and I'll tell Ed to go over there with the airplane."

Lethridge knew that Captain Eddie had desired cremation, and called the president of Swissair to ask him to handle it. When Hall got in touch with Yarnell—he found him already acquainted with the sad news—Adelaide had phoned his wife, Jane, from Zurich.

Yarnell boarded a stretched DC-8-61 manned by a full crew, including stewardesses, in Miami the next day and the aircraft was flown first to New York, where Lethridge inspected it and briefed the crew. Lefty remembers thinking at the time how considerate Hall was being.

"The guy had class," he says. "Here we were up to our armpits in debt and Floyd thought enough of Eddie and his family to pull a jet right out of service and ship it 4,000 miles away. It was his own tribute to the old man."

Swissair officials met the DC-8 when it landed and furnished Yarnell with a chauffeured car, which was at his and the family's disposal until they boarded the plane for the sad trip home; the airline also supplied the necessary food and beverages and both Yarnell and Lethridge still speak gratefully of Swissair's unfailing courtesy and kindness.

The stewardesses made up a berth for Mrs. Rickenbacker; she was demonstrating great bravery but was terribly weak. Yarnell remembers that the flight back to Miami took some ten hours and that it seemed like a million years.

"I don't think there were three words spoken the entire

trip," he says. "The stewardesses were magnificent—they served drinks and meals and never tried to intrude on our thoughts."

Captain Eddie's ashes were in a metal box, wrapped in brown paper, and sealed with wax. A color guard and some 1,500 employees met the plane at Miami International Airport and Yarnell decided to stay aboard with the ashes, in accordance with the wishes of Mrs. Rickenbacker, who also didn't want them photographed.

"I just didn't want to carry them out anyway," he also explains. "I didn't want to expose that part of his death to the public."

While Adelaide was being helped down the loading stairs, Yarnell was close enough to the open cabin door to hear some radio or television announcer intone, "Well, this is the end of Captain Rickenbacker." Yarnell, clutching the metal box, remained aboard until the DC-8 was towed to a hangar. He drove to the Rickenbacker villa and put the ashes in a closet.

Memorial services were held at the Key Biscayne Presbyterian Church July 27. Jimmy Doolittle delivered the eulogy and Eastern captains formed an honor guard; both sons were there (David had come back on the DC-8 with his mother) but doctors ordered the widow to stay in bed—by now she was exhausted and almost in a daze. The church was filled with flowers, including a spray from President and Mrs. Nixon.

The final episode took place a few days later in Columbus, Ohio; Captain Eddie had expressed a desire to be laid to rest there, by his mother's side, in the family plot. He also had left instructions that his ashes were to be buried in advance of the funeral ceremony and Ed Yarnell took care of that detail—he and Lefty and four members of the immediate family were the only ones present, standing silently in a drizzly rain. For the funeral services themselves, held the next day, Lefty had arranged for the 94th Fighter Squadron based in Tampa to fly four jets to Columbus, coming over the cemetery at a prearranged time. The day before the funeral he told the minister, "When you get to a certain point, I'm walking out of this chapel and I'll be signaling to a colonel who'll radio those planes circling Columbus—so you'd better stay on schedule or nobody'll hear what you're saying."

A few minutes before the services began, the rain was coming down in buckets. Lefty said he wasn't worried. "If Eddie's luck holds out," he insisted, "you're gonna see sunshine." The rain stopped and the sun came out just when everyone emerged from the chapel to see the last salute—four jet fighters approaching slowly and then turning on their afterburners just as they screamed their own requiem over the cemetery. Someone said to Lefty, "Boy, wouldn't Eddie have loved that!"

On the Rickenbacker Fountain outside the huge building 16, there is a marker with this inscription:

Edward Vernon Rickenbacker
"Captain Eddie"
1935—Eastern Airlines—1963
Dedicated to his inspired leadership
of Eastern Air Lines and the aviation industry.

These were words inscribed in stone. He inscribed more than mere words in the hearts and minds of those who followed him; whether out of duty or love, fear or respect, made little difference. Whatever the motive for responding to his leadership, the common denominator was loyalty to the Captain and his dreams for the airline he loved above all else.

Ed Yarnell still wears his wristwatch, given to him by Adelaide, who passed away in 1977; she committed suicide after an operation failed to restore her sight.

To Floyd Hall he willed his old felt hat. But this symbolic gesture of affection and trust contained no magic for the young man he admired so much. The real inheritor of Captain Eddie's leadership mantle was a colonel named Frank Borman.

CHAPTER FIFTEEN

FROM THE CAPTAIN
TO THE COLONEL

By mid-1973 Sam Higginbottom was ready to jump without the necessity of being pushed.

His faith in himself had never diminished—this was not conceit but honest conviction. After all, in 1970 he had turned down an attractive offer to become president of Pan American and the wooing had been intense. Najeeb Halaby, who headed Pan Am then, tried for six months to talk Higginbottom into leaving Eastern and his bid was $175,000 in annual salary plus stock options. Sam said no for two reasons: (1) he was concerned about the influence Juan Trippe still wielded within Pan Am and he didn't want another EVR-Mac situation, and (2) he was enjoying himself at Eastern where he still felt there were some goals he could accomplish.

But three years later the picture at Eastern had changed. He even told Borman one day that Eastern was an almost impossible company to manage. He figured he had done what any capable airline president could accomplish under the circumstances: He had put in at least some budget restraints, made all departments justify expenditures, installed a modern inventory-management system, recruited good technical personnel, and modernized the fleet. Despite all these achievements Eastern was drowning in deficits, staggering under its debt burden (because of its poor financial condition, EAL financed the L-1011 program only by paying some of the highest interest rates in the industry), and coming apart at the seams moralewise as the result of the New York–Miami power struggle. And what convinced Higginbottom he had taken enough was an offshoot of that struggle—what he interpreted as a deliberate attempt to blame him for Eastern's dilemma.

It began in the spring of '74 when the directors themselves began moving into the battle zone. An informal committee was formed, consisting of Woodward and Elkins with Laurance Rockefeller as a kind of ex-officio member, and its purpose was to convince Floyd Hall that something had to be done. The "something" was a suggestion that was more of an order—spend more time in Miami and work things out with Higginbottom. Hall says one director told him, "Sam's running roughshod over people," and another said, "You've got to go down there and actively take over the running of this airline."

Hall was reluctant; for all his quarreling with Higginbottom, he liked Sam and he suspected that what the directors were demanding would be regarded by Higginbottom as blatant interference and lack of confidence. This is exactly what happened, of course; Higginbottom threatened to resign right then and there. When Hall urged him to stay, Sam said, "I'll give it until October."

But there was no improvement in their relationship, nor in the airline's fortunes. The lid blew off in early fall when *Business Week*, the *Miami Herald*, and *The Wall Street Journal* all published articles on the Eastern situation, each story implying that Higginbottom was on the way out. Sam accused Eastern's vice president of public relations, Jonathan Rinehart, of planting the damaging stories, and when he accused Rinehart, he was accusing Hall; it was Higginbottom's belief, one held by other EAL officials in Miami, that Rinehart was more loyal to Floyd than to the airline—that in effect, he was Hall's personal PR man. Rinehart denied that he had anything to do with the bad press, but by this time a denial had the same effect as patching a blown tire with a piece of paper.

Almost simultaneously with this fresh donnybrook came a decision by Hall and McFadden to hire hundreds of additional people to improve the airline's marketing position—reservationists, ticket agents, and ramp personnel, mostly. On October 1, 1973, Samuel L. Higginbottom sent a letter to the board of directors tendering his resignation as president, chief operating officer, and director.

In it he defended his administration as one that had earned profits up until 1973. He sharply criticized "the hiring and spending policies practiced in recent months and still being practiced," declaring that taking on additional manpower would "not significantly contribute to a higher quality product."

"Nor will it," he added tartly, "overcome the historic handicaps of Eastern: (a) a high break-even load factor, (b) many years of low to median profit performance compared to the industry, (c) high indebtedness, (d) a highly competitive, essentially short-haul route system."

He noted that Hall had advised him he was going to become "very much more active in the day-to-day operating affairs of the company." In doing so, Higginbottom declared, "he made the position of president superfluous." He said no one person should be blamed for the 1973 debacle, which he ascribed to such factors as a sluggish economy that stymied anticipated traffic growth, inflationary pressures, abnormally severe winter weather during the peak traffic season, major new competition, and what he termed a "one-two punch on the L-1011—a crash and phase-in problems."

He reminded the board that he had predicted a disastrous year as early as May when he warned that spending had to be brought into line with anticipated revenues. The warning, he added, went unheeded.

He emphasized that he had no intention of taking the rap for the L-1011, pointing out that its selection, "while shared by many, ultimately was made by the chairman and endorsed by the board." And Higginbottom concluded by saying that his differences with Hall were not personal but philosophical.

His resignation was accepted. Today Sam Higginbottom is in charge of Rolls-Royce's North American operations and is particularly proud of the fact that Pan Am chose the L-1011, equipped with R-R engines, as the replacement for its obsolete 707 fleet; to Higginbottom, his defense of the Lockheed purchase has been vindicated.

With Sam's departure Hall resumed full command—in Miami, not New York, it must be added: The power base already had shifted, but not in the way Higginbottom had intended. What Hall did was simply move the majority of his New York corporate staff to Florida and the friction, if anything, got worse. Those who were around at the time still refer to it as "the carpetbagger era," an invasion of northerners who took over Miami like an army of occupation. Jim Ashlock, now Eastern's news bureau director, remembers a public relations staff meeting when Jonathan Rinehart told his underlings, "the only criterion is loyalty."

Hall, who purchased a condominium in Miami, was willing to make some economy moves, such as chopping off about 600 heads in the marketing division. He even asked Frank Sharpe to return to his old job as vice president of sales and services, making the offer through Russ Ray, a former Lockheed engineer who had joined Eastern as vice president of consumer affairs with rather loosely defined duties. Ray's position at EAL then was as something of an officer-without-portfolio and his duties were rather vague, but he was well liked and Hall respected his judgment.

When Ray relayed Hall's invitation, Sharpe told him, "I want it so bad I can taste it, but my wife has cancer, Russ, and the doctors don't give her much time—I want to be with her as much as I can." Hall tried to persuade him personally, but Sharpe shook his head. "Aside from my wife's needing me, Floyd, I have to ask you one question: If I was so stupid four years ago that you took me out of my job, what has happened in the meantime that makes me such a genius that Eastern needs me right now?"

"I made a mistake," Hall said. "One of my biggest."

One unexpected departure was that of Jonathan Rinehart. He lasted in Miami only long enough to revise the "pecking order" in public relations—his New York staff members generally were put in positions outranking the Florida staff. But Rinehart had incurred the enmity of an influential director who happened to hold great respect for Higginbottom; the board member couldn't save Higginbottom's job but he didn't like the way Rinehart had handled the resignation story and he convinced Hall that the vice president of public relations had to go.

In February 1974, Lefty Lethridge, whose personal popularity among both factions made up for his lack of public relations experience, succeeded Rinehart. Lethridge proved to be a bit tougher than anyone had expected—he cut his staff from forty-four down to twenty-seven. Lefty's biggest problem was Hall's belief that public relations belonged under the jurisdiction of the marketing division, headed by McFadden—an organizational setup that simply fanned the flames of discord.

Yet there was sympathy for Hall even among the simmering Miami contingent. Floyd obviously was emotionally exhausted and distraught. He did get Sharpe to agree to serve as Eastern's representative to the International Air Transport Association (IATA) until he retired in 1977—Hall himself was president of IATA, a post he loved but one which the directors had questioned because it absorbed time and energy he could have expended on Eastern's affairs.

The airline managed a modest comeback in 1974, showing a $10.3 million net profit that year. But the black ink was deceptive; it was achieved largely because of the fuel crisis, which forced Eastern to cut schedules to such an extent that the cost savings were enormous. In the end it added up to artificial respiration because when the fuel shortage ended, Eastern's slump not only continued but accelerated like a runaway juggernaut. Losses were so heavy in 1975—at year's end they would amount to an unbelievable $88.7 million—that the directors stepped in again.

There was no immediate desire to lower the boom on Hall. For one thing, Rockefeller was extremely close to him and had utmost sympathy for what he had been going through. The boom *was* lowered, but it was a gradual thing and done as diplomatically, even delicately, as possible. Rockefeller's term for Hall in the catastrophic year of 1975 was "disoriented"—not in the sense of being mentally ill, but rather of having lost touch with the realities of a terrible situation.

Rockefeller's first suggestion was to send a new board member to Miami with instructions to report back exactly what was happening to the crumbling airline. The new director was Walter Hitesman, president of *Reader's Digest* who had left the *Digest* after a difference of opinion with publisher DeWitt Wallace. Hall made him a senior vice president in the marketing division for a brief time, but in that role Hitesman was a bass trying to sing tenor and that wasn't his real assignment, anyway. He was there to observe and it took little time for him to inform Rockefeller and the board that Eastern was being flown right into the ground, and that mismanagement was at the controls.

Hitesman spent far more time probing, looking, and talking to various EAL officials than in trying to learn about marketing, in which he had little real interest. He kept digging for the reasons behind the airline's crisis and one day asked Lethridge why Delta was coining money.

Lefty pointed out that Delta didn't have Eastern's debt— "We're paying out sixty million bucks a year in interest charges," he said defensively.

"You forget that debt reflects the poor management decisions you've made in the last fifteen years," Hitesman remarked.

Hitesman stayed with Eastern just long enough to gather facts, figures, views, complaints, alibis, and explanations from virtually every EAL officer; he had made it a point to sit with each of the various executives from one to three hours at a time, digesting whatever information and background they were willing to impart. What he turned over to the directors was never made public, but the aftermath of his continued reports was a corporate convulsion that shook the airline. He never did report directly to Rockefeller, but Woodward kept the latter advised of what Hitesman was sending back and even Laurance finally had to agree with Hitesman's major conclusion: Hall was no longer an effective leader.

In that respect Floyd Hall was in at least partial agreement —he was tired and he thought it was time to turn Eastern over to new blood. He still insists he was never fired, and refers to his leaving the airline as "a kind of accelerated departure." In truth, the directors didn't want to fire him; they had in mind letting him stay on for a while as board chairman, with a new president actually running EAL. It worked out that way but not for the length of time Hall expected, because the man chosen to be Eastern's tenth president was absolutely determined to have total, complete control.

For too many years he had seen a great air carrier torn apart by divided authority, and for better or for worse, Colonel Frank Borman was perfectly willing to accept full responsibility for whatever happened.

When Higginbottom left, Borman served as executive vice president; he was running the airline operationally and learning more every day. He made no bones about what he was aiming for: He wanted to be president. As a matter of fact, that's what Hall wanted for him, too. The day he hired the ex-astronaut, he had told him, "Look, if you make a success of this, your age is just about right—I'll be stepping down and then Sam will."

"I figured right then and there," Borman recalls, "that if I didn't blow it, I'd be president."

The learning process forged what would become his own policies and methods, and it must be admitted that most of what he learned was in the "I won't ever do it this way" category. For example, he was surprised to find that hardly anyone at Eastern or at other carriers, for that matter, had any awareness of the cost of carrying around extra weight on an airplane. "We had seats attractive from a marketing standpoint but which weighed about forty pounds per seat more than necessary. Nobody thought about that vital, last percentage of cost that can make so much difference. I guess it was because fuel was so cheap that airlines didn't worry about carrying around heavy seats and air-stairs and containers. But I had just come out of a field where weight meant everything, where even the saving of a single ounce was important."

He regarded with distaste the rancor he found in the executive ranks. The competitive situation between different departments—maintenance fighting with sales, for example. To him, trained from early youth to revere teamwork and cooperation, it was as if management's style was to pit people against each other to see who survived. Eastern reminded him of a company being run with all the latest Harvard Business School techniques that may have worked well for an ITT, but not for an airline. He was not against scientific management per se, but he got the feeling that Eastern was being managed by people who had opened a business school textbook and were following its pedantic rules page by page. He also saw the inevitable residue of a decaying corporate body—executive deadwood, kept on because the men involved tended to protect one another.

He knew five years hadn't made him an airline expert, and he tried to avoid any friction with Hall, toward whom he felt gratitude and a great deal of sympathy. Only when he deemed it essential did he oppose Floyd—he remembers one instance when Hall wanted to install high-fidelity electronic headsets on all aircraft and put them on a DC-8 as a test model; Borman talked him out of it. And he talked Floyd into selling the JetStar, originally acquired at a bargain price because the first twelve L-1011's delivered were far over Lockheed's promised weight specifications; Borman sold it for about a million dollars.

He learned the hard way, firsthand, about the worst nightmare any airline employee can have, from president down to ship cleaner: the anguish, terror, suffering, anger, and bewilderment that are handmaidens to a fatal crash. He was at home the night Flight 401 crashed, reading in bed, when a phone call told him an Eastern L-1011 had disappeared off the radar scope. Before the terrible night ended, he was wading through the murky swamp, with no boots, helping to rescue victims and load survivors into helicopters; at one point he threw his own coat around a stewardess he had found in shock. Thirty months later he had to go to the scene of another crash—an EAL 727 which was caught in a violent wind shear just as it was about to land at Kennedy. Death was no stranger to Frank Borman—he had faced it as an astronaut (Susan Borman didn't expect him to return from *Apollo 8*) and he had been on the team that investigated the spacecraft launching-pad fire in which three fellow astronauts had died. But personal risk in a job one is trained and paid to perform is one thing; the innocent, trusting victims of an air crash are another.

Borman issued many of the orders involving Eastern's handling of those victims and their families, and in drawing a portrait of this man who was on the verge of becoming its president, it does not seem out of place to quote from a book written about Flight 401 by Rob and Sarah Elder; it was called *Crash* (Atheneum, 1977) and unlike so many books on air tragedies, in which authors seem determined to indict the airline involved, this one dug deep to reveal an airline's concern and sense of humane responsibility. They noted that when the Miami morgue was obviously understaffed to handle victim identification, Eastern paid for extra morgue attendants and sent its own staff officers to lend additional help. Continued the Elders:

Even while survivors still were being airlifted out of the Everglades, Eastern had sent executives to the various hospitals. At first, their only specific job was to give away money; they provided for the immediate incidental expenses of survivors and their families. . . . Immediately after the crash, Eastern representatives distributed seven thousand dollars in cash; later, a five-hundred-dollar check was given to each survivor, no questions asked. [A] company memorandum noted that "this $500 was a pure gratuity and not a release, a settlement of any claim, or a set-off against a final settlement."

Eastern seemed acutely aware of what the crash had cost the victims and their families. . . . "Reasonableness of anything is the main criterion," Craig Raupe, Eastern's vice president for consumer affairs, told employees who worked with victims and relatives. "I would like you to maintain this perspective—nothing is more valuable than life or health, and this has been taken away from many families.

The relatively small things we do for people now make a very lasting impression. While you should be alert to outright abuse, this is not the time for us to be technical or begrudging." There were some instances of outright generosity. A young Japanese women was injured in the crash; her husband was killed. When it became apparent that the widow had neither friends nor family in the United States, Eastern arranged for her mother and brother to be flown from Tokyo. An Eastern stewardess who spoke Japanese flew to Los Angeles and accompanied them from there to Miami. Later, the mother remained as a houseguest in the stewardess's home.

At the various hospitals, airline representatives relayed information, made telephone calls, shopped for clothing, and did other small chores. . . .

These chores, the Elders reported, including getting the president of a barber college down to a hospital so a survivor could have his beard trimmed—regular barbers had refused to make hospital calls. One Eastern official, Madison Kelly, personally shaved a survivor.

Borman himself remembers that he didn't leave the Everglades crash site until later the next morning. He went right to the office and changed clothes after taking a shower in Hall's office—the shower was one of Floyd's executive privileges that Borman was to inherit, although he personally considered the furnishings too plush and toned them down considerably after he became president.

What he had witnessed at the Everglades crash was not just tragedy, but his first glimpse of airline esprit de corps under the worst kind of pressure. He was to retain that impression and draw from it the confidence that Eastern's men and women could accomplish anything, given leadership and motivation.

"This airline has some great people," he told his wife when he finally got home.

He officially became president and chief operating officer May 27, 1975, Hall remaining as board chairman and chief executive officer.

Three weeks earlier, he had been in Hall's office talking to Floyd when the executive committee—Elkins, Woodward, and

Gilpatrick, who had been meeting in marathon sessions for days —came in and asked him to stand by in his own small office at 10 Rockefeller Plaza. Borman complied and a few minutes later the three directors returned to inform him he had just been elected president.

Borman said simply, "Thank you—I'll do my best." His first act was to call his wife and two sons. He was understandably that proud. They were among the few people who knew he got the job only after having come close to resigning.

Throughout dismal 1975 Eastern was so unstable that he was uncertain whether there was a future for him; it seemed to be a race between a definite offer from the board and the air-line's collapse. If the latter seems an exaggeration, it must be pointed out that for the fifteen years between 1960 and 1975, Eastern's accumulated net profit was a *minus* $114 million!

Toward the end of the year he heard that Hall was trying to get a highly regarded vice president away from another carrier and name him senior vice president. The man in question had such stature it seemed obvious to Borman that Hall had it in mind to eventually name him president. Borman charged into Hall's office and threatened to quit. It was only a short time later that the directors named him president and chief operating offi-cer. He had Hall's wholehearted blessing by then, although Floyd admits he entertained notions of staying in power at least for a while. His original twelve-year contract with EAL was about to expire and he actually had an appointment with the directors' compensation committee to discuss a new contract. Borman's election shelved this possibility and Floyd by that time was will-ing to relinquish the airline's destiny to a younger man.

"I think it was time for fresh blood," he says. "Time to bring in somebody who hadn't been around the track so god-damned many times he was dizzy. I realize now, as I look back on it, I really was one exhausted guy. I had serious health prob-lems. I was hospitalized for surgery about that time and the board heard I had cancer and would never leave the hospital. I don't know who started the rumor, but it was so widespread that one of Eastern's vice presidents—I won't tell you his name but it wasn't Frank—came up to New York and tried to sell some big headhunting firm on the idea of recommending him for the presidency because I was dying."

Hall did meet with the head of the compensation committee and was told that instead of writing a new contract, it would be better if Borman took over as president and that he stay on as chairman—for how long seems to be in dispute. Hall says the plan was that he should remain for two years, at which point he would have reached his sixty-fifth birthday and would retire. According to Floyd, in fact, Borman had made a promise to him much along the same lines—which Frank denies.

"How was I in a position to promise him anything?" he asks. "I met with the board's executive committee in New York and I laid down no conditions. We did have an understanding that Floyd eventually would fade out of the picture. Not that I had anything against him—he was loyal to me and he did want to stay on—but I believed the company was bigger than any individual and sometimes it's hard for people to understand that."

Whatever the case, Hall's tenure as chairman and chief executive officer fell far short of his intended two years. Just as Borman had feared, the division of authority so inherent in the appointment of one man as chief executive officer and the other as chief operating officer led to friction. Some executives were reporting directly to Hall and others to Borman, and it was the festering discord of Rickenbacker-versus-MacIntyre and Hall-versus-Higginbottom all over again. The directors became convinced that Eastern could no longer function with two heads, that if the airline was to be turned around, there had to be one boss, and one only.

As 1975 drew to a close, the airline still hadn't been turned around and the board made its move. On December 16, 1975, the board elected Frank Borman president and chief executive officer. Hall put up no fight—he was to say later that he went along with the decision because he didn't want the board to have to choose between them, and that if Borman had left in the wake of Lewis and Higginbottom, "we would have lost our credibility." Hall stayed on as board chairman for a year, retiring in December of 1976 when the directors added that post to Borman's titles.

Hall is much happier today, working with IATA, happily remarried, and no longer under the pressures of his turbulent tenure at Eastern. "You know, I consider myself one of the luckiest guys in the world because everything I've done in this industry has been exciting as hell. It was almost a shame to take money for it. I tried to get that spirit into Eastern—make people feel the excitement and get them to realize their job isn't just plodding. I'm proud of those years at Eastern. Hell, while I was there we got fifteen new routes that brought in $150 million a year in new revenue—Dwight Taylor was the man responsible. Absolutely superb in this area. As an administrator he wasn't worth a damn but on a route case, there was no one like him. Off the top of my hat, I can't think of anything I would have done differently, unless I had known then what I know now. In that case, I would have done things a hell of a lot differently."

The man who succeeded him was doing exactly that.

Armed with the authority he believed essential to the airline's very fate, Borman began moving—moving, it must be added, against a wall of defeatism and cynicism inevitable with a change in command that on the surface looked too much like all the previous changes in command. The men and women of Eastern expected the usual platitudes about economizing, teamwork, cooperation—"Let's all get to work and turn this company around, etc., etc." They figured that, as usual, they'd be doing all the economizing and sacrificing while the brass hats would continue drawing their fat, unsullied paychecks, submitting fat expense accounts, and riding around in expensive cars while proclaiming virtuously, "We all gotta get out there and work our tails off." And to most of them Borman was an unknown quantity—as a vice president he had kept a relatively low profile except in his own area of responsibility.

He was well aware that a lot of employees were referring to him as "Moonman," and it wasn't meant as a tribute to his astronaut's career. "What's Moonman gonna decide today? . . .

What's Moonman gonna do about this? . . . Is that another one of Moonman's bright ideas?"

No, they didn't know him very well. But he changed that in one hell of a hurry.

His earliest moves jolted Eastern to its roots, for he aimed the first economy axe in the direction of the executive echelons, whose ranks were thinned by dismissals, resignations, and early retirements over a period of a few months. Some of the dismissals he discussed first with Charlie Simons, by now his most trusted associate. Charlie had been caught in the middle of the Hall-Higginbottom impasse and hadn't been able to function effectively because he was never sure whose order was going to be the final one. Under Borman he finally knew where he stood, and Harper Woodward says of Simons: "He's a tremendous backup for Frank, a man who never reached his full potential until Borman took over because he kept getting caught in the crossfire between Floyd and Sam and half the time didn't know which side to be on."

The final decisions, however, were Borman's, and the firings were done on a face-to-face basis in his office. There was pleading, protesting, and in one case almost begging—Borman himself refers to corporate head-chopping as "the most difficult job in management."

In 1977 Borman hired the respected management consultant firm of R. Dixon Speas Associates to examine Eastern's maintenance and engineering personnel for possible reorganization. Speas's recommendations in this particular area convinced Borman that similar reforms could be applied elsewhere; the Speas study was extended to the airline's entire corporate structure—to discover where management was inefficient, and which jobs could be eliminated or consolidated.

By the end of 1977, well over two years after Borman took office, the relatively modest initial Speas report had mushroomed into a massive reshuffle. Hundreds of management jobs had been eliminated, many in middle management found themselves in positions involving sharp salary cuts, and three more vice presidents left the payroll. The final result showed nearly 800 fewer persons in management and the number of vice presidents had been shaved from the sixty-nine serving when Borman became president, down to thirty-eight—a smaller vice presidential corps than there was at Western, a carrier one fourth Eastern's size.

The Speas-generated reorganization plan took place when Eastern's profits were soaring. That in itself was significant—the old policy had been to let things slide so long as the airline was making money, but Borman didn't operate that way. He was always fine-tuning, watching, monitoring, going after waste and inefficiency no matter what the ledgers were showing. And he had to: As of the day he took over, Eastern's debts totaled more than a billion dollars.

It is conservatively estimated that the reorganization saved the airline nearly nine million dollars annually.

In some circles the mass shake-up gave Borman the reputation of being a cold-blooded computer with black ink for blood. Reportedly some of his fellow astronauts had thought him too tough and unfeeling. He is far from that, but both in the space program and at Eastern he was a man who had been given a job to do, goals to meet, and problems to overcome. In that respect he is single-minded, not cold-blooded.

Speas merely confirmed what he already suspected or knew: Eastern was woefully top-heavy in management. But although Borman already was convinced of this major weakness, he wanted the opinion of an unemotional, impartial outsider who understood the airline business, and Speas gave him the specific details he needed. The consultant's report included such items as these:

—In one department Eastern had sixty people doing the same job to which Delta had assigned twenty.

—In computer sciences Speas found that people had been brought in to initiate programs, but once the programs were well underway, they stayed there, in many cases creating work to justify their existence.

—Management had become so stratified that there were dozens of people between station personnel and the brass in Miami; decisions, information, and inquiries became lost in the clogged channels that separated the field from Building 16.

—There were scores of managers, directors, and regional vice-presidents, all forming a calcified, obstructive stratum that clogged the decision-making process; without clear guidance from Miami, a local manager would have to make decisions on his own and then accept all the blame if things went wrong.

This wasn't the way Borman operated. "I don't want very many people between me and the baggage handler," was his announced policy. Today, for example, a sales manager in Houston reports directly to a regional vice president who, in turn, reports directly to a senior vice president in Miami—which means the man in Houston is only one man removed from the top man in his department and only two men away from Borman.

Both Hall and Higginbottom had considered Borman impulsive. It may have been true when he first came into the airline business but the reorganization plan was carefully charted, plotted, and orchestrated with all the thorough advance planning of a space mission. He knew employees would be worried to the point of panic if word leaked out prematurely, and he made sure they got the word before rumors could spread and before the news media got in on the act. He utilized the company newspaper, *The Falcon,* to break the news to Eastern's 32,000 employees, composing a special column in which he explained why such drastic action was being taken. He stressed that nobody's job was secure just because the job had always been there or because it carried some sentimental attachment. To squelch any rumors of further cuts, he emphasized that no one under the rank of manager would be fired, although some employees would have to accept demotion to lower-paying positions. (He gave no such assurance to those of higher rank other than to promise them aid in finding other jobs.)

Through the public relations department, he made sure Miami newspapers and radio and television stations were briefed in advance under a pledge of secrecy until the *Falcon* made the first announcement; Borman knew that otherwise the news media might have gotten hysterical and that could have been dynamite in the employment-sensitive Miami area, where one third of Eastern's employees were based.

It must be noted that one thing was in his favor: He already had the airline solidly behind him. For remember, this second reorganization occurred after he had been running the airline for almost two years, although it had been in the works for almost that long. Because of what he had accomplished in those two years, they accepted his motives, believed his explanations, and supported his actions. Some hard feeling was inevitable—there is never an easy way to do what Borman did. He realized only too well that some of the people who got hurt had been made vulnerable through no fault of their own. Mostly by the nature of seniority, they had been moved into posts that were created or whose functions were no longer necessary; the blame belonged to the top officials who had let this situation develop. This was what Borman kept stressing—his responsibility not merely to the company and its stockholders, but to the majority of employees.

Borman had heard about or personally witnessed previous economy campaigns. At the first hint of executive dismissals, the wailing and the moaning started and management would cave in. When the dust settled, virtually no one had been let go. This had been true of Captain Eddie and every one of his successors, and Floyd Hall was no exception—Borman once remarked that Floyd was "a decent man who was honestly concerned about people, maybe too much so."

Economy moves involving nonmanagement employees invariably stirred resentment, especially in the Hall-Higginbottom regime when furloughs looked decidedly unfair against a backdrop of executive limousines, office showers, private jets, and all the other "rank hath its privileges" manifestations. Borman got away with his middle-management purge largely because he always had established himself as an unpretentious man with a surprisingly simple life-style. It was a bit difficult to gripe about executive trappings when the president, chief executive officer, and chairman of the board drove to work in a 1969 Chevrolet convertible his father had found for him in a Phoenix used-car lot; until Borman finally got around to having it repainted and installed a new top, it looked as if it had been through the Battle of the Bulge.

Nor did Borman ever let his fellow officers forget how the

other half worked. One of Eastern's traditions was the practice of having staff volunteers from Building 16 come out to Miami International right after New Year's and help with the holiday traffic crush—loading baggage, manning information desks, and directing the traffic flow in front of ticket counters. It was a job usually performed by such personnel as secretaries, office clerks, etc., but Borman thought the volunteer army should be expanded a bit. At a morning executive briefing—they are held daily starting at eight thirty sharp—Borman brought up the custom and added, "I expect you guys to go out there and help."

To the high-paid, well-tailored men in that room, it was the equivalent of telling ten colonels they had to help the enlisted men clean latrines. Borman beamed at their suddenly worried expressions, and turned to Marvin Amos, vice president of personnel. "Marv, I want you to coordinate all the volunteer schedules." Then he addressed Bob Christian, vice-president of public relations. "And Bob, I don't want to see any company photographer out there—this isn't a damned publicity stunt."

Christian went down to his own office and passed the word to Jim Ashlock. "Borman'll be there himself, working on the ticket counter," he informed Ashlock. "But don't tell the press—that's his orders."

Ashlock promised to keep the secret. The day before the event Don Bedwell of the Miami *Herald* phoned to inquire about the next day's activities.

"Anything unusual about tomorrow?" he wanted to know.

"Oh, you can say we're expecting a lot of volunteers."

"Anybody else—just the usual volunteers, like yourself?"

Truth wrestled with discipline. "There could be some officers," Ashlock said cautiously.

"How high?"

"Pretty high," Jim allowed.

"How high is high?"

Ashlock surrendered. "Well, about as high as you can get."

"That's all I wanted to know, Jim. Thanks."

The *Herald* ran a story the morning of the event and naturally TV cameras appeared—Borman wasn't happy but he decided not to make an issue out of it. His biggest worry was that not everyone expected to come had arrived yet. He had found the information counter well-manned, had gone outside to check the baggage area, and then had come running back to tell Ashlock, "They've got three no-shows out there—I'm gonna call Amos."

Amos was told to get more bodies out there, including himself. Marv sauntered in about ten A.M., looked around, and casually announced, "I'm going out to see Frank and I'll be back in ten minutes—I'm expecting a phone call."

At four thirty he was still outside loading bags. A conveyor belt was overloaded and Borman was among those piling luggage onto carts and pulling them into an elevator leading to the underground baggage room. Amos was working behind a loaded cart. He looked up as Ashlock approached, and mumbled, "Isn't the sonofabitch ever gonna quit?"

Borman finally did—at six P.M. He had worked straight through with no lunch break, and the only time he stopped was to sign autographs or politely refuse a tip.

The old-timers around Eastern invariably liken him to Rickenbacker, and Laurance Rockefeller thinks there is more truth than fiction in the comparison. "Frank is like the Captain in modern dress. The virtues are the same—guts, drive, energy, leadership. One big difference is that Eddie would take time out to relax, Frank won't—the word 'unremitting' describes him."

If he has EVR's virtues, however, he did not inherit the old man's faults. Borman is far more flexible, much more prone to delegate, and while just as demanding, not as unreasonable. Actually, he resembles Bob Six to a greater degree than he does Rickenbacker—more than one airline official has called him "a younger Six." The similarity is not a coincidence, for Borman is a great admirer of Six as well as a close friend. Of EVR, Borman says:

"I don't want to think I'm as mean or rough as he was. I admire the hell out of him—his drive, the determination he had to have to build this airline. People would die for him—I've read all about him. But he didn't change with the times. Six never got stale. He did change with the times—and that was the main difference between them. Six would say 'Okay you've analyzed the hell out of it, so now let's go do it.' That was one of our problems at Eastern—a lot of important decisions were based on blind acceptance of somebody's analysis."

Borman was never against scientific input, but he did believe it could be overdone. When Eastern picked up a route from Miami and Tampa to Mexico City, its competition was Pan American, which had been losing its corporate shirt in that market. Eastern won the route by promising to use L-1011's, but EAL analyists warned Borman it wouldn't work.

"There's not enough traffic," they told him. "We'll be killed."

Borman decided to go ahead anyway—a promise was a promise. The Miami–Mexico load factors to date have averaged well over eighty percent.

He has something else in common with Bob Six—he prowls around the executive offices and other EAL facilities like a restless bear, popping in unexpectedly to chat, question, or observe; "What's going on?" is the invariable opening line. He has Rickenbacker's natural charisma in that respect, but employees and officers alike know he is always probing for information.

He never thought he could turn Eastern around with one or two dramatic reforms, because the reasons the airline was about as airborne as a submarine were too myriad for a panacea. There were big decisions, but there also were small decisions—and a lot of small decisions can mount up.

He found, for example, that the average age of Eastern's ground equipment was twelve years. The policy had been never to buy a new tractor but to keep repairing the old one—even though the repairs amounted to three times what a new machine would have cost. Borman also did something about EAL's propensity always to go for the cheapest thing, a penny-wise and pound-foolish policy. He told one staff meeting, "I'd rather buy an engine that's too big, derate the thing, and have it run than buy a smaller engine which doesn't work."

He closed the books once and for all on the "Tale of Two

Cities," and Miami became the center of Eastern's world the minute he took over. This, too, caused some unhappiness, and one officer protested that "you can never get a good financial man to move from New York because he has to deal with all the financial institutions."

"Bull," Borman snapped. "How the hell can you run an organization when half of it's in one place and half in another? I know people in New York don't want to move, but you have to subordinate personal desires."

When he first came to Eastern, he brought along the diminutive, attractive, and efficient secretary who had been with him at NASA—Toni Zahn. Occasionally there is some question as to which one is the boss. She once asked Borman what his favorite TV program was.

"*Hogan's Heroes,*" he replied.

She shook her head. "You know something? You're a klutz."

It was the "klutz," however, who came up with one of the most daring, innovative, and exciting plans in the history of airline labor-management relations. It wasn't unveiled until 1977, but Borman began thinking about the concept early in his administration—as a matter of fact, not too soon after Eastern's lending institutions threw him a curve by refusing to give EAL a four-year extension on $75 million in short-term loans about to be called in. This happened only a few weeks following his election as president. Borman and Charlie Simons had gone to New York to make the presentation and thought they had prepared an excellent one. They had—in fact, they were warmly congratulated on its overall quality even though one banker was startled to see Borman at one point put his feet on the desk while informally discussing the airline's plans to reduce the debt structure. But after all the praise had finished gushing, the answer still was no.

Borman and Simons talked about the crushing failure all the way back to Miami. By the time they landed, they had agreed on the only step that might give Eastern some breathing room until they could convince the lenders there was a chance for a comeback.

The step was a voluntary wage freeze, which they both knew would be anathema to the unions. Borman insisted he could sell it to employees by telling them the truth: Without a freeze, the company was probably going under. But he added one vital incentive: the airline industry's first profit-sharing plan.

In a brief space of time he hit every city on the system—cajoling, pleading, arguing, demanding. He courted not only the rank and file but their leaders both on the local and national level, and in doing so he formed some unexpected friendships with opponents whose opinions and beliefs he came to respect. President John J. O'Donnell of ALPA, a former Eastern captain, was one of them, and Otto Schick, head of the ALPA Master Executive Council at Eastern, was another; Borman was so impressed with Schick that he talked him into becoming a management negotiator. Chuck Dyer was another MEC member whose open mind toward a wage freeze provided a lot of help.

The Transport Workers Union (TWU) represented the flight attendants, and the local TWU leader was Bernice "Bernie" Dolan; her skepticism and suspicion constituted a formidable roadblock until Borman won her over. He did the same with Ernie Mitchell, vice president of the TWU, and he also established good relationships with the national officers of the IAM, which represented the largest contingent of Eastern's unionized employees. The leaders on the local level, men like Jim Cates, John Peterpaul, and Steve Hrytzay, were tough but fair, and that was all Borman asked—or needed.

The unions' eventual acceptance of a wage freeze had the effect of keeping costs down while revenues were climbing, and the result was a $39.1 million net profit in 1976, up to then the highest in Eastern's history. Armed with that performance, Borman and Simons went back to the lenders and got their extension. (It must be noted that the initial extension refusal was what convinced the directors to turn complete control over to Borman; at the time Hall was still board chairman and chief executive officer.)

The unions' willingness to cooperate gave Borman the encouragement he needed to make an even more dramatic gesture—this one by management toward employees. With a profitable 1976 behind him, Borman disclosed his idea at an historic staff meeting. He called it the Variable Earnings Plan, or VEP. It was, in effect, another profit-sharing program, but it also provided for what might be termed deficit-sharing.

He explained to his colleagues, "Eastern always projects a profit but we seldom make what we'd said we'd make. It seems to me if I were a banker, holding our notes, I'd like to have some kind of backup which would assure me if the airline wasn't going to make it, the employees would subsidize it."

"The employees?" someone asked.

"Why not? Hell, forty-four cents of every dollar goes for salaries so that's a logical place to start. It's simple—if we make money, they'll share. If we don't, they'll share in that, too."

The details of VEP were worked at at subsequent staff meetings and Borman hit the evangelist trail again. Over and over again he explained how it would work. Starting in 1978 each employee would receive 96.5 percent of his or her base salary, the company retaining the balance as a guarantee that it would earn at least two cents on every sales dollar. If profits failed to reach that level, the VEP funds would be used to bring profits up to the two-cent level. But if profits were to go above two cents, employees would get one-third of all profits exceeding that level—up to a maximum of 3.5 percent of their base salaries. In other words, an employee would earn a minimum of 96.5 per cent of the base and a maximum of 103.5 per cent. The retroactive feature was added as a reward for participating in the 1976 wage freeze.

ALPA was the first union to go for VEP; the others took more persuading, and Borman adds that "the union leaders needed to be sold more than their members."

At one IAM meeting in Miami, Borman had just finished outlining VEP and asked for questions. A gnarled mechanic stood up.

"Yeah, I got a question. Why the hell should I trust a guy dumb enough to sit on top of a rocket built by the lowest bidder?"

Borman never got to answer the question because everyone was laughing so hard—himself included. It broke the tension and the IAM finally went along, the VEP going into effect at mid-year.

In 1978 Eastern netted a record $67.3 million. In February of 1979 each employee got back one dollar and thirty-five cents for every dollar they had "banked" with the airline during the previous year. That was their VEP dividend, and those who had selected profit-sharing in '76 (some had picked an alternate choice of stock warrants) realized even more return.

Borman's gamble had paid off; and that is exactly what he is—a gambler, willing to take calculated risks. He was to take another one; he pulled Eastern out of the industry's Mutual Aid Pact, convinced that employees who now had a financial stake in the company's welfare would think a long time before striking. As it turned out, deregulation of the airlines abolished Mutual Aid anyway but Borman's willingness to do it before he had to was another plus in his relations with the four unions, in 1978 representing some twenty-one thousand of the airline's thirty-seven thousand employees. It was his decision, after canvassing officers and discussing it at staff meetings.

What do the unions really think of him?

Steve Hrytzay, president of Eastern's IAM Local 702, once told a reporter, "I think he can walk on water—at least that's the impression he's trying to give us."

The IAM held out the longest against the wage freeze, including the profit-sharing plan—Hrytzay fought him for almost a year and the acceptance margin was 1,100 out of 8,000 votes. "I have to admire his tenacity," he said in an interview with Nancy Webb Hatton of the Miami *Herald*. "He said he would come a thousand times or a thousand and one times if he thought that one more time would do it. He's tenacious as hell, and he's an excellent strategist. He threw out just enough to older employees to sell them, and he put the fear of God into the younger employees, making them feel that things were so bad that if he didn't get his way, they'd be out on the streets looking for a job." (Hrytzay may not have wanted to admit it, but things *were* that bad.)

The union leader added, however, "Don't get me wrong—I

respect the man. I just wish he was on our side. We're adversaries in a particular situation. But the man himself? He's a very nice person. I wouldn't mind having him for a friend."

Comments Borman:

"I'll tell you honestly I'd rather not have unions. We could deal with our employees more fairly than we do now. Unions tend to protect the marginal and incompetent. I've tried to loosen them up through mutual respect—I don't know any other way to do it. Without Mutual Aid, I think we may even have more bargaining strength. This company would be badly damaged by a strike, and I think this would be a deterrent to any employee group thinking strike.

"Unions are under a tremendous strain. Their leadership has lost some of their power—there's not as much discipline and a great deal of fracturization. Rather than confront them, I'd rather try to educate them and treat them fairly. I don't mean you should let them run the company, but by the same token you should listen to their concerns. Unions are a fact of life."

Frank Borman is basically conservative, and his style of leadership is so overwhelming that many consider him a throwback to the Rickenbacker-Smith-Woolman-Trippe-Nyrop breed —those one-man airline giants who so totally dominated their carriers. So is Bob Six, for that matter, but the analogy is not really applicable to either Six or Borman. They are decisive, but not trigger-happy—they listen as well as command. Borman actually found a great reluctance among officers to voice their views when he first became Eastern's top man. There was a tendency to sit back and wait to see what the Colonel had to say first, just as so many executives in the Rickenbacker era used to sit back until they knew how the Captain felt. It took awhile for Borman to get across the idea that he welcomed complete openness and frankness.

He has a sharp sense of humor and a pithy vocabulary that comes out unfettered at the daily morning briefing. Even his sarcasm—and it can be razor sharp—is softened by a touch of humor. The briefing room is wired so Borman can talk to anyone on the system, and at one session he was getting a report on an L-1011 grounded in Seattle by a mechanical malfunction.

"Have you fixed it yet or are you gonna make a diner out of it?" he asked,

A DC-9 formerly owned by Allegheny was being modified to Eastern's Shuttle configuration and the work was behind schedule. Borman absorbed this bit of news at the briefing and grumbled, "What are they doing with the roots growing in the gear?"

He detests alibis and told one staff meeting, "What we need around here is more successes and fewer post mortems on failures." Yet as tough as he is, he has Rickenbacker's gift of displaying a not-too-well-hidden streak of thoughtfulness. He was in Washington one night, waiting to board a Miami flight, and bumped into an EAL stewardess named Raphelia Medlin, also waiting to board—it was the last one to Miami that night and she was on a space available pass.

"You look worried," Borman commented.

"I am, Colonel Borman. The flight looks full and I've got to work a trip out of Miami tomorrow."

"Stop worrying," he assured her. "If it's full, you can have my seat and I'll go back tomorrow."

His incisiveness sometimes gives a casual visitor the impression that he can be abrupt to the point of rudeness. Rude he is not, but Frank Borman does hate wasted motion and wasted words. Vice presidents who walk into his office armed with a thirty-minute presentation often are cut short in the first two minutes. "Sounds fine," Borman will say. "Let's go ahead and do it."

Waste. . . .

Whatever form it takes—verbosity, airliner seats that are too heavy, the spending of thousands on some piece of equipment before it has been tested thoroughly—waste is unacceptable to Borman.

Sample: Eastern has been trying out new, lighter seats, the weight reduction achieved by removing some of the back padding and changing the frame's contours without sacrificing comfort and leg room. Six samples were installed on a Shuttle plane to judge durability and passenger reaction. This was shortly after Borman had displayed them at a congressional hearing, at which he'd deliberately invited a few of the more rotund lawmakers to try them out. It made good copy and even better television exposure, and more than one rival airline official expressed admiration at its effectiveness.

"That's something else we're doing now," Borman explains. "Instead of going out and buying 80,000 yards of carpet material, we buy a couple of hundred yards and try it out on the Shuttle, where it gets the hardest wear. If they don't take it, we try something else. True elegance is simplicity. I want a carpet that looks nice, wears well, and can be kept clean—I don't care if it's not the fanciest thing in the world. And simplicity is what we're always seeking, from the seat to the whole airplane. I hate those seats with the tables buried in the armrests—they're too heavy and they're a plumber's nightmare."

It should come as no surprise that Borman doesn't share the average corporation executive's love of golf—he considers it too slow. His favorite recreational activity is a brisk hike, which also is the way he moves through a business day. Borman gets to his office no later than seven thirty A.M. and seldom leaves before six thirty P.M.

Eastern's flight attendants admire him and love Susan Borman. She is an attractive, unassuming woman, a native of Tucson, Arizona, who married Borman after he graduated from West Point. When Frank was with the space program and both their sons were attending the Point, she suffered a nervous breakdown that stemmed from sheer loneliness and worry. She loves Miami and regained her sense of security when they moved down there, far from the trauma of Apollo missions. She holds frequent luncheons for employee wives—not just the spouses of officers but of mechanics, skycaps, pilots, and office personnel, answering their questions about the airline and her husband. Those she can't answer she writes down on small cards and turns over to Borman.

Borman himself, now a trim fifty-one and looking ten years younger than his chronological age, was born in Gary, Indiana, and moved to Tucson, where he grew up. He learned to fly when he was only fifteen, soloing just before he was admitted to the

U.S. Military Academy, a dream he had had since boyhood. He figured he had no chance of winning an appointment and expected to enlist for eighteen months and then go to college under the GI Bill. But he got lucky—he was working in a department store with the son of a prominent judge who also happened to be an airplane buff. The judge would buy model airplane kits and Borman would build them for him. With that tenuous political backing he applied to West Point and was accepted.

He began his military aviation career as a fighter pilot after he graduated from the Academy and won his Air Force wings. Borman was on his way to Korea to fly combat missions but caught a cold, made the mistake of flying before it was cured, and perforated an eardrum. Grounded—they told him it was permanent—he served in the Philippines as a ground officer but kept taking treatments until he requalified for flight duty.

He was a good enough pilot to become an instructor (one of his assignments was checking out chief pilots of airlines that were just starting jet service) and from there went to California Institute of Technology, where he earned a master's degree in aeronautical engineering. His technical background resulted in an assignment dear to the heart of every West Pointer—teaching at the Academy (the subject was thermal dynamics), and both his sons grew up there. The boys—the older is Frederick and the younger Edwin—both wound up at West Point later, Fred turning down a football scholarship at Oklahoma so he could play guard for the Cadets; Edwin was a linebacker. Both sons were somewhat heftier than their father, who stands about five ten and weighs one hundred and sixty-eight pounds, which happens to be what he weighed as a fighter pilot.

Borman entered the space program in 1962 as an astronaut, serving as commander of the *Gemini* 7 mission in 1965 and three years later of *Apollo* 8. John "Shorty" Powers, the one-time "voice of Mercury Control" in the days of the early space flights, was a special admirer of Borman. He personally knew some forty astronauts and once commented, "There was always one guy who you knew was nine steps ahead of the others and that was Frank Borman."

As an astronaut he was not only skilled but outspoken. He once was informed that a NASA doctor had forced President Nixon to cancel a preflight dinner with the *Apollo 9* crew because he might contaminate them with germs. Borman called the cancellation "totally ridiculous"—a remark he not only said publicly but to which he added the comment that the doctor "should have kept his mouth shut." That didn't please the NASA public relations types, and they were even more displeased when Borman got hold of a script they were preparing for Nixon to read as Neil Armstrong was stepping foot on the moon. The dialogue included such questions as "What is the moon like? . . . is it hot up there . . . how far are you sinking in?" and a few other banal sentences. Borman sent Nixon a note suggesting that he throw the script away and just make a few brief, dignified remarks—which the President did. For all Borman's disillusionment with Watergate, however, he was decent enough to call the ailing ex-President at San Clemente and express concern over his health.

He is good copy to the news media, being articulate and blunt, but like so many in public life he can get annoyed at times at what he considers inaccurate reporting. Borman had some personal experience with this when he was on the *Gemini 7* mission; one of their assignments was to track the rocket that had put them into space, using an IR sensor, and in the tracking process they referred to the rocket as a "bogie." When they messaged, "Bogie at two o'clock," some writers immediately jumped to the conclusion that a UFO was chasing them, and to this day, books about UFOs still mention *Gemini 7* as proof we are being observed from outer space.

Borman called the twisted reports "garbage," which explains why he seethed when a book titled *The Ghost of Flight 401* by John Fuller (Berkeley, 1976) became a bestseller and eventually was made into a television movie. Fuller wrote what he claimed was a factual account of Eastern planes being haunted by the captain and flight engineer killed in the Everglades crash. Supposedly nonfiction, the book was so full of distortions, alleged quotes from flight attendants who were supposed to have

seen the ghosts, and accusations against EAL executives whom
Fuller said had tried to bully crews into keeping quiet, that Eastern seriously considered filing a libel suit. Borman ruled against
it, feeling that a lawsuit would merely publicize the book.

What Fuller started with was a rumor that Flight Engineer
Frank Repo's ghost actually had appeared on an Eastern
L-1011, one on which equipment salvaged from Flight 401 had
been installed. From there he went on to quote the various crews
who claimed to have seen not only Repo's ghost but the captain's
as well—Fuller didn't use their real names in order, he said, to
protect them from company reprisals. Let it be said right now,
based on what was learned about "the ghost of Flight 401" during the course of researching this history, that Fuller's story
should have been classified as fiction. Not one among the scores
of EAL officers and employees interviewed, including a half-
dozen flight attendants (one of whom was quoted in Fuller's
book under an assumed name), expressed any belief whatsoever
in the ghost story, and they resented what they felt was Fuller's
twisting or inventing quotes. "The one accurate quote in the
book," Borman comments, "was made by Jim Ashlock when he
called the whole story 'a bunch of crap.' "

Of Fuller's claim that Eastern tried to muzzle flight attendants who talked to him, even threatening to send them to the
company psychiatrist, PR chief Bob Christian says, "There were
no reprisals or threats—hell, we spent weeks trying to locate
anyone who claimed to have seen a ghost and couldn't find one
person."

There *was* a ghost rumor. Eastern's own efforts to track
down the validity of the wild yarns floating through the whole
industry finally revealed the source. An EAL L-1011 was being
ferried on two engines back to Miami from Mexico City. En
route it lost a second engine and the pilots made it down safely
on only one engine. At a party a few weeks later someone asked
one of the pilots what it was like trying to land an L-1011 on a
single engine.

"Scary," he replied. "For a minute I thought Frank Repo's
ghost was on the plane."

The whole ghost story stemmed from that offhand, half-joking remark and spread around the nation—it was even picked up and printed by the prestigious Flight Safety Foundation. The FSF account actually was written with tongue in cheek, but Fuller seized on it as proof that the story had to be true. There not only was no ghost, but nothing usable was ever salvaged from Flight 401's wreckage. From such flimsy evidence a best-selling "nonfiction" book was published; the movie was advertised by NBC as "based on an actual occurrence," and when Eastern protested, the network explained it was referring to the crash, not the ghost.

Anyway, Frank Borman was having enough headaches running the airline without paying too much attention to ghost stories. He found little time for his favorite exercise—hiking—and even less time for his favorite hobby, model airplanes. Occasionally he will write away for old copies of model airplane magazines—issues that cost twenty-five cents when new and are now priced at seven dollars a copy. Buying them is one of his few extravagances even though he never gets around to building the small planes anymore. There is one in his office, a model of the P-80 he flew in the Philippines, built by the son of Mort Ehrlich, senior vice president of planning. Occasionally Borman will sneak away to watch youngsters fly gas-powered models in some field or empty lot; it is a rather touching sight to see him out there—a man whose own fleet consists of more than 260 giant jets.

Including the most controversial airplane ever bought by this airline which has lived with controversy for more than a half century.

The A-300.

CHAPTER SIXTEEN

"WE'VE COME A LONG WAY BUT THERE'S STILL A LONG WAY TO GO"

Eastern's decision to buy a jetliner built in France was announced April 6, 1978.

But the gestation period for that momentous $778-million deal lasted thirteen months and involved some of the most unique bargaining techniques in airline history.

By the fall of 1976 Frank Borman and Charlie Simons, the latter now second-in-command with the title of vice chairman and executive vice president, had finished a study of Eastern's future equipment needs. Their input had come from virtually all departments—from men like Morton Ehrlich, senior vice-president of planning . . . Russ Ray, senior vice president of marketing . . . Tom Button, senior vice president of flight operations . . . Paul Johnstone, senior vice president, operations services . . . from scores of other officers, technicians, economists, route development specialists, and maintenance and flight service personnel.

What they had put into Borman's rather sparsely furnished office on the ninth floor of Building 16 formed a mosaic whose tiles consisted of airport-capacity outlook, traffic forecasts, estimates of future fuel costs and needs, maintenance costs on the rapidly aging portion of the current fleet, analysis of ability to handle additional debt burdens, possible new routes, status of competition planning.

The age of the fleet was a key tile, and Charlie Simons is an expert on aircraft geriatrics. He had taught Borman much about the economic penalties of obsolescence, that if an airline planned to use any transport more than twenty years, it was not only going to be technically obsolete but economically obsolete from the standpoint of both maintenance costs and competition. And the picture they were studying was dismaying.

Eastern at the time was operating forty-six Boeing 727-100s (this was the original model whose basic design dated back to 1958 and which began passenger service in 1964) and twenty-five 727-QCs, which were regular 727-100s equipped with large doors for fast conversion to all-cargo configuration— the "QC" stood for Quick Change. Those sixty-one airplanes constituted approximately a fourth of Eastern's fleet. Twenty-five of them would be twenty years old by 1984, another twenty by 1986, and the remainder by 1988. And this was just the outlook for the older 727s—by 1989 some of the stretched 727s, the 727-200 series, also would be two decades old along with a sizeable chunk of the DC-9 fleet.

Weighing this inevitable, not-too-far-over-the-horizon obsolescence against estimated traffic and route growth plus anticipated inflationary costs, it was obvious the airline was heading for equipment trouble. Nor could Borman afford to do much waiting—not even with the size of that debt burden, still well over $900 million at that stage. Rising fuel prices alone demanded more efficient aircraft—EAL's fuel costs had climbed from $112 million in 1973 to $375 million in 1977. Every airline president in the world knew that the airliner of the future, for the first time in aviation history, would be judged not by greater speed but by increased efficiency, with fuel economy equaling capacity in importance.

Typical of EAL's equipment problems was the 727-QC. Its all-cargo utilization ceased before Borman became president, but when it was being operated in that configuration it had a break-even load factor of 107 percent, which simply meant that even when carrying a full load of cargo, it not only couldn't break even but lost money. The reason was its excessive weight—the cargo conversion feature required a heavier airframe—and weight is a critical factor in airplane economics.

"What a hell of a difference it would have made if we had bought 200s instead," he remarked to Simons one day. It was an opinion he never was to change; Borman believes one of the biggest differences between Delta and Eastern is that the former went solely for the 727-200 when it finally decided to buy a number of Boeing three-holers; Eastern had picked the QC years earlier, when the 200 series was not available.

Borman would have liked to sell the entire QC fleet and as many 727-100s as possible, but he had no replacements available, especially for the routes the older Boeings were serving. It made little sense to replace them with 200's which, while far more efficient, weren't that much bigger—one 727-200, for example, couldn't do the work of two DC-9's or two 727-100's. And this was the crux of the decision he faced in that pivotal time of midsummer 1977: For Eastern's needs, there was no "off-the-shelf" U.S. transport plane available that matched the requisites. Eastern needed:

1. A payload roughly between the L-1011's capacity of 293 passengers and the 727-200's 137; the approximate target was an airplane with about 170 seats.

2. A "new technology" aircraft capable of achieving significant fuel savings and meeting all present and future noise reduction standards.

3. A medium-range airliner with New York–Miami non-stop capability, yet versatile enough to operate safely at such short-runway, high-density airports as La Guardia and National.

4. Delivery dates before 1980 so Eastern could start replacing aging, uneconomical equipment as quickly as possible.

5. A two-engine transport because both Borman and Simons were convinced that on short-to-medium distance routes, it was too expensive to operate three-engine aircraft.

Throughout the latter half of 1976 and early 1977, the three U.S. manufacturers made their pitch-pilgrimages to Miami, usually meeting with Simons alone but occasionally with Borman sitting in on their presentations.

McDonnell Douglas touted its DC-9 Super 80, typically another of its "rubber" airplanes with a DC-9 fuselage stretched to a length that was only fourteen feet shorter than the original DC-8. The Super 80, however, would have a new-technology wing for fuel economy and more powerful engines than the smaller DC-9 line. And because it was a DC-9 derivative, possessing the manufacturing advantage of considerable commonality, McDonnell-Douglas was promising early 1980 delivery.

Boeing had three designs on its Seattle drawing boards: the 757, a two-engine concept that combined the 727-200's fuselage (only longer) with a new type of wing airfoil said to be two years ahead of everyone else; the 767, also twin-engine, but a wide-body; and the 777—identical to the 767 except for three engines and greater range.

Lockheed was pushing a smaller version of the L-1011; like Douglas, it had gone the derivative route.

By January 1977, Simons and Borman had their doubts about all these designs; no single airplane met all five EAL requirements. The DC-9 Super 80 attracted some interest because it was a new-technology airplane with relatively early delivery assurances, but Simons was lukewarm.

"It's too damned small," he told Borman. "In the configuration we'd want it would have only 133 seats and that's fewer than what we already have in our 200's. As far as capacity goes, the Boeing 757 is exactly the size we're looking for."

Borman mused, "It's too far down the line, Charlie. Boeing hasn't even decided whether it'll build it."

Simons nodded. "Frank, we really ought to look at that A-300. What would you say to inviting Airbus Industrie in? It's already flying in Europe."

Borman wasn't quite sure. Airbus Industrie was French, and while he had absolutely no anti-French prejudices (he had once met General De Gaulle and got along extremely well with him), he knew that foreign-made transports had never won much popularity in the U.S. Britain's Viscount and BAC-111 failed to put much of a dent in the American air carrier market, and only United had bought the French-built Caravelle. But he finally consented to at least letting Airbus make its pitch.

The A-300's initial salesman was Roger Beteille, vice president and general manager of Airbus Industrie, who also happened to be one of the aircraft's designers. He made the first presentation almost entirely by himself and despite a considerable language barrier, he impressed Eastern officials sufficiently to warrant further meetings. Into the latter came George Warde, former president of American Airlines, a jovial, extremely effective horse trader who had joined Airbus as head of its North American sales operations.

The first day Warde showed up, Borman's opening remark was, "Why should we want to buy your airplane?"

Warde had done his homework. "Because if you don't, you're dead."

But it wasn't as simple as that. First, Eastern was short of capital and financing would play a large part in the negotiations regardless of how much Eastern liked the Airbus. Second, the A-300 was not quite what Simons had in mind—it carried almost 250 passengers, putting it close to the L-1011's capacity, and it was just too big. Simons kept pointing out that Eastern wanted a plane that could replace the 727-200 on this aircraft's current routes, enabling EAL in turn to substitute the 727-200 for its 727-100s.

Beteille said he understood, but suggested that if Eastern really needed a smaller plane than the A-300, Airbus was willing to adjust the price until traffic grew sufficiently to justify the bigger aircraft. Both Borman and Simons were intrigued—in effect, Airbus was proposing to charge Eastern an initial price reflecting a 170-seat airplane and if traffic grew as expected the airline would pay an additional amount later. Warde called it "operating support" and nothing like it had ever been proposed before.

Airbus Industrie's willingness to set this kind of precedent gave the Borman-Simons team another idea. Knowing that the French wanted very badly to crack the U.S. market, they asked if Airbus would be willing to let Eastern test four A-300s on EAL's routes for six months prior to any final contract. This would be another first and from the initial French reaction, Eastern might as well have suggested moving the Eiffel Tower to Miami Beach. Simons kept pressing.

"All we're proposing," he insisted, "is that we form a joint venture. We're naturally concerned about introducing a foreign-built airplane—remember that neither the Viscount, Caravelle, or BAC-111 were particularly successful operating in an American environment. If you think your product is that good, we'll be the ones to prove it. And it'll cost you a hell of a lot more to advertise the A-300 in the United States than it will to loan us four airplanes which will be four flying advertisements in themselves. Your part is to supply the aircraft for six months of testing over our route system. We'll supply the crew training and maintenance."

The French representatives looked dubious, but now it was Warde who was intrigued. He had the advantage of understanding U.S. carriers and their operating problems. He knew Eastern's financial handicaps. He was aware that there was always the chance of passenger prejudice against a foreign-made airliner. Between his pride and faith in the A-300 and his own U.S. airline background, he was the ideal go-between in the touchy negotiations; he was not afraid to voice agreement with Eastern's position, and simultaneously protect his own company's interests. Most important, he recognized that Eastern was skeptical and that the six-month test period was a logical way to overcome the doubts.

There were countless details to work out and major decisions yet to be made, but the tryout agreement reached in August 1977 was crucial. Eastern shipped a number of pilots and mechanics over to France for crew and maintenance training; test flights began in November and on December 13, 1977, Eastern started operating the four borrowed A-300s over high-density route segments. It didn't take the whole six months for Frank Borman to make up his mind.

From all sides came raves—pilots, mechanics, and passengers—a handful of passengers reacted negatively, the complaints coming from those who said it was unpatriotic for Eastern to be operating an airplane not built in the U.S. Borman was concerned about this from the start of Airbus negotiations—he already had evidence that it might be a public relations problem. Western Airlines had seriously considered the A-300 but backed away, partially because it had been clobbered by angry protests that the Los Angeles-based carrier was sinning against flag and country. Borman, figuring that ideological beliefs can be more volatile in southern California, also took comfort from the fact that the anti-Airbus letters coming into Eastern were a trickle compared to Western's flood. Yet he kept these decidedly minority views in mind, discussing their implications with Bob Christian, his PR vice president—for what he also feared was that they might presage criticism from Congress if EAL went ahead and actually bought the A-300.

What was all-important to Eastern, however, was the plane's performance under exposure to day-to-day system operations. After the first three months its grades in every category amounted to straight A's. The Airbus compiled the best reliability record of any plane in EAL's fleet, achieved impressive fuel savings (using thirty percent less than the Boeings and twenty percent less than the Lockheeds), and overall provided lower operating costs than even Borman and Simons had hoped. Its range was perfect for the vital New York–Miami nonstop market. One of the few complaints concerned the restrooms—they were placarded *"TOILET"* in accordance with European custom and had to be Americanized to *"LAVATORY."*

But while the number-one man at Eastern was convinced, others weren't. Borman's own planning department was nervous—they'd be for it one day and against it the next. Even Simons had jitters, worrying whether the Airbus might be too big, about reaction to a foreign airliner, and how the airline was going to pay for what would be a massive investment.

"Charlie is the best financial man in the industry," Borman remarks, "but he had dealt with adversity for so long that he really felt these things."

Despite Simons's natural misgivings, however, he was a soldier who followed his commanding officer and Frank Borman was convinced the A-300 should carry Eastern's colors—provided financing could be worked out. This was Simons's bailiwick and he responded. Negotiations with Airbus Industrie and George Warde resumed shortly after the initial three months of A-300 service. The first Eastern proposal was for a thirty-two airplane package, Airbus taking in ten L-1011's as a trade-in on twenty-two A-300's. Warde turned this down and Simons came back with an offer to sweeten the pot—take EAL preferred stock as partial payment. This, too, was turned down and now Simons was getting worried that the whole deal might fall through. On his desk every morning, and on Borman's too, was a glowing report on the A-300's performance the previous day; by now Simons was sharing Borman's enthusiasm for the plane. He got one break when he worked out a leasing arrangement with Cathay Pacific to lease two L-1011's, giving him a little more flexibility in his bargaining with Warde.

The bottom line was the $25-million price tag per Airbus—with the twenty-three Eastern figured it needed, this added up to a $778-million package including spare parts. The sum was beyond Eastern's resources because its lenders weren't ready to advance that much cash. But Simons worked out a complex financing plan which Borman still refers to as "magnificent."

From General Electric, eager to furnish the A-300's engines, he obtained $45 million in subordinated financing, and another $96 million worth of similar debentures from Airbus. Both these loans contained an unusual provision: The interest rates could fluctuate depending on the airline's profits—between 9 and 9.45 percent on the Airbus notes and between 8 and 10.5 percent on the GE debentures.

Airbus agreed to accept another $66 million in four-year senior notes carrying interest rates of slightly under eleven percent. And Airbus also arranged for $250 million worth of export credit financing through a group of European banks, at 8.25 percent interest. The final Airbus contribution was to credit Eastern with the total worth of the four A-300's it had been operating—almost $100 million.

The entire package accounted for more than $570 million in externally generated funding, leaving the airline with slightly over $200 million to raise internally over the fifteen-year period covering the terms of the agreement and the usable life of the aircraft. Simons was able to assure the airline's regular lenders that the sale of surplus L-1011's and the older Boeings would furnish most of this amount.

The contract for twenty-three planes included the four Eastern had been flying; these were converted from their trial-lease status to a long-term lease covering fourteen and a half years. The Airbus "operating support" for unused seats involved the manufacturer's promise to underwrite part of the operating costs of every A-300 for four years, using a fifty-seven-percent load factor as the base; for every percentage point above that figure, the subsidy diminished.

To Simons went the credit for masterminding one of the most complicated aircraft purchase plans in aviation history. To Borman went the credit for having the guts to stand behind him. They each knew when to retreat, when to compromise, when to insist and demand, and they each knew the importance of adding a fuel-efficient aircraft to the fleet in significant numbers—to an airline the size of Eastern, a one-cent-per-gallon hike in the cost of fuel means at least $100 million more in direct annual operating costs.

As expected, there were rumbles from a few congressmen about purchasing a non-American product. In speeches, news conferences, correspondence, and private meetings, Borman hammered away in defense of his decision. More than one third of the A-300's components are made in the U.S., he pointed out, and for that matter all U.S. airframe manufacturers use a high percentage of parts made abroad—there is no such thing as an "all-American" or "all-foreign" airliner. If there was an American-made transport as good as the A-300 and available for immediate delivery, he added, Eastern would have bought it.

After the A-300 contract was announced, Eastern's board happened to meet in Seattle and Harper Woodward found himself sitting next to retired Boeing board chairman Bill Allen, who was hosting a dinner for the EAL directors.

Allen half-jokingly asked, "Why don't you learn to buy American equipment, Harper?"

"Look, Bill," Woodward replied, "we're buying the Airbus because we got a good deal, because it's here today, because we're at a great competitive disadvantage and you won't have a plane for us until at least 1983."

Exactly five months from the day the A-300 contract was made public, Eastern disclosed it had signed with Boeing for twenty-one 757's and an option for twenty-four more. The specifications called for a 174-seat aircraft powered by Rolls-Royce RB-211-535 engines.

With the Boeing 757 order, a $560-million commitment, Borman virtually had completed Eastern's fleet-modernization program for the decade of the eighties. In less than one year he had bought some $1.42 billion dollars worth of new airplanes, but he also had taken out an insurance policy against such contingencies as rising fuel costs and sustained traffic growth. Boeing is promising that the 757 will be thirty-three percent more fuel-efficient than the 727-200, putting the new plane on a par with or even better than the A-300 in that vital respect. Eastern will finally have what it has lacked for so many years—a balanced fleet acquired in time to meet future needs.

For the time being the Lockheeds will serve the high-density long-haul routes, the A-300 will replace the 727-200 in medium-range markets, and the latter in turn will take over from the older Boeings. The 757, whose deliveries will not start until 1983, eventually will operate in short-haul markets now served primarily by the DC-9. Because the 757 is five years away, EAL has ordered eight additional 727-200's and has options for twenty-five A-310's, a slightly smaller version of the Airbus.

That Borman and his executive team, a skillful blending of youth with experience, could launch a rebuilding program of this scope comes close to the category of miracle. The primary ingredient of the reborn airline is confidence that flows in two directions—from Borman toward the people of Eastern and from them to him. He is one of the youngest airline presidents in the United States, yet in five short years he has become the most easily recognized and frequently quoted. He seems to personify what most Americans associate with dynamic leadership—a combination of competitive gambler and idealistic pragmatist, in precisely the right proportions, so that risk is always calculated and decisiveness is softened by humaneness.

It was no whim, no change-for-change's sake, that caused him to scrap Eastern's old, rather pretentious "Wings of Man" slogan in favor of "We Have to Win Our Wings Every Day." To Borman, the switch reflected the airline's altered image—that of a hard, lean, aggressive, no-nonsense air carrier dedicated to the basics of air travel: competent service, schedule reliability, and a friendly attitude all under the roof of safety.

His decision to appear on Eastern's television commercials drew some criticism—the gist being that he was doing it mostly for ego purposes. He does have ego—it goes with the leadership territory—and it is ego stemming from pride and confidence, not conceit. He agreed because he figured it would fit in with the image he was trying to project of the airline itself—Eastern was trying hard, and if it took the president of the company to get this across, so be it. He believed it personalized Eastern, that it brought passenger and airline together on a one-to-one footing.

He quickly became known as "one-take Borman." The men directing the commercials learned in a hurry that the Colonel didn't want to waste time reshooting. He would arrive at the studio, look over the script for not more than five minutes, and then tell the director, "Okay—let's get the darned thing over with." Invariably he was letter-perfect—his memory is outstanding—and he refuses to deliver a prepared speech. He talks from notes on small cards, to keep his remarks organized, but ninety-nine percent of a Borman speech is off-the-cuff.

While the TV commercials have brought him even more public recognition than he got as an astronaut, they also have been the source of a few problems. Viewers tend to identify with him to such an extent that most of the airline's complaints are addressed directly to him. A typical letter will start out:

"Dear Colonel Borman: Well, you didn't win your wings

today. I was on an Eastern flight and . . ." Or, "Your wings didn't flap today. . . ."

Jim Elkins, one of his closest friends, has been telling him to stop making commercials; he thinks there is such a thing as overexposure. Elkins says, "One night he met my wife and me at the Miami airport and he was absolutely swamped by a bunch of people who had just gotten off an Eastern flight that had been delayed a couple of hours. They kept shouting at him, 'You told us these things don't happen on Eastern.' I've seen something like this happen almost every time he walked around an airport. There's a good side, of course—he's the most easily recognized airline president in history."

Yet outwardly, anyway, Borman doesn't mind this personalization phenomenon, for the same reason Delta's C. E. Woolman refused to have an unlisted telephone. Borman won't go that far, but he is willing to exchange occasional inconvenience for the knowledge that the public no longer regards Eastern as a cold, impersonal corporation, nor its president as a remote, aloof monarch with a few thousand protective underlings standing between him and the customer.

But there are moments. . . .

Like this letter, which deserves to be quoted verbatim and in full:

Dear Col. Borman:

Your TV commercial allows the general public to view your kitchen in operation. The physical environment appears clean and organized. Undoubtedly it meets health standards.

However, when you finish explaining your clean and organized kitchen, you stand directly behind the apples, which are *not* covered, to continue your discussion.

May I remind you that as one talks (exhales), microorganisms are emitted into the air. Therefore, it is a poor health practice to have a general discussion over uncovered food.

Whether this poor practice is done only on the TV commercial or if it is permitted in your kitchen, I suggest it be terminated.

My family and I will be passengers on your airline this week to and from Miami. We (as well as others) should not be unnecessarily exposed to organisms that might be harmful.

The commercial in question was the one in which Borman finishes talking about Eastern's food service and as he walks through a Marriott kitchen he picks up an apple, tosses it in the air, and catches it. It was strictly ad lib—it wasn't in the script and the director was petrified for fear he'd miss the catch.

Originally it was Russell Ray who first approached Borman on commercial participation—in connection with Eastern's sponsorship of a televised golf tournament. Hall was still chairman then and when Ray suggested the idea to Borman, his reaction was decidedly cool.

"I'll do anything for this company but don't make me sell Tang," he told Ray.

"Tang?"

"That's the orange drink we used on space flights. Good stuff but if you're thinking of getting me up there and hawking wares, forget it."

Ray did forget it, but the subject was brought up again after Hall left and the golf sponsorship ended. Under Ray, Eastern's advertising staff had been cut from forty-four people to eleven, but the survivors included two sharp young men—Dave Kuntsler and Bill Dowse, now vice presidents. They were discussing future advertising campaigns when Dowse suddenly suggested, "Why don't we use Frank in TV commercials?"

Ray shook his head. "I've already talked to him about this but he doesn't want to be a pitchman."

"Look," Dowse said, "are we comfortable enough with our service so we can take it to the public?"

"Not overly confident yet but comfortable," Ray allowed cautiously.

"Then let's build a campaign around our service, and have Borman do the talking."

Kuntsler agreed. "He's good-looking, personable, believable, and he's no outsider," he pointed out.

They took the idea to Young and Rubicam president Ed

Ney, who didn't like it at first—he thought it might hurt Borman, particularly if Eastern's service turned sour.

"That would demolish Frank's credibility with the public and inside the airline as well," Ney argued. "It's too risky."

But Ray, Kuntsler, and Dowse weren't ready to abandon the idea entirely. They agreed with Ney on the risk being both external and internal. Yet they also were convinced that any new advertising campaign had to be aimed at both the public and Eastern's employees—if TV commercials were going to tell passengers the airline was trying harder, employees would get the same message. From this thinking evolved the campaign's concept: Emphasize Eastern's dedicated employees . . . make it soft-sell . . . admit faults but promise improvement. And, as far as all three men were concerned, this message had to be delivered not by a professional, glib-voiced announcer or some outside celebrity but by Borman himself.

This was the campaign motif they sold to Ney and the agency, and it was Young and Rubicam plus Dowse who came up with the "We Have to Earn Our Wings Every Day" theme. The target was the airline's bread-and-butter passengers—those who travel frequently. Eastern carried more than thirty-five million people in 1978, but only a half million constituted forty-five percent of the traffic. This is because on every airline, total traffic actually represents the number of tickets sold; it is the multitrip passenger who swells the count. Eastern, for example, actually flew only four million passengers in 1978 but a sufficient number of them traveled often enough to make the count reach the thirty-five-million mark.

The campaign worked. Surveys have shown that the new slogan is second only to United's "Friendly Skies" theme in quick recognition, and Borman's earnest credibility has resulted in a curious phenomenon: Most of the complaint letters, instead of beginning with the usual "I want to report a miserable experience . . ." open instead with "Dear Col. Borman, we thought you should know . . ."

The personal recognition factor is enormous. Ray once walked down the street with him in New York, looking for a location for a new city ticket office. "My God," Ray recalls, "people would turn around and stare at him—he's a conduit between people and the airline and in a sense he almost outshines the airline, which could be a danger."

Conversely, Borman knows he doesn't have to be the kind of leader who has to look back to see if anyone's following him. His is the team concept; if he's the fast halfback scoring the touchdowns and grabbing the headlines, his executives are the guys up front opening the holes—and Frank Borman is very conscious of that fact. Eastern is stronger in middle and top management talent today than it has been in years; the trust employees place in Borman he, in turn, hands down to his officers. By the very nature of his job and the strength of his personality, he is more visible than any of them but this doesn't dilute his own pride in and reliance on them.

He didn't form his present team overnight; it was forged over a long period, amid a great deal of shuffling and reshuffling until he was satisfied he had the right person in every key spot. The most significant fact about the team is that it was formed *within* Eastern; as of mid-1979 Borman had yet to recruit anyone from another airline. Each of the men who meet in the ninth-floor conference room of Building 16 for the daily executive staff briefing is "home grown"; all already were at Eastern when Borman assumed command, some in relatively minor positions.

Marv Amos, senior vice president of personnel and corporate administration, came to EAL in 1965 from Curtiss-Wright and previously had been with General Electric, RCA, and Goodyear as an industrial relations specialist.

William G. Bell, senior vice president of legal affairs, was with the Gambrell law firm before joining Eastern—a blunt man with a dry wit, he is regarded as the staff cynic.

Tom Button, senior vice president of flight operations, was picked for that post after several others had a shot at it. A TWA pilot before he came over to EAL, Button only nine years ago headed the ALPA negotiating committee and then switched to a management post as director of flight agreements and manpower training.

Mort Ehrlich, senior vice president of planning, is one of the industry's most respected economists; he became director of economic planning in 1968 and moved swiftly up the executive ladder.

John "Jack" Hurst's job as senior vice president of technical support embraces a huge area of responsibility and jurisdiction —it includes facilities, properties, computer sciences, communications, and parking. He was a classmate of Borman's at West Point (not his roommate, contrary to a widespread belief around Eastern) and is a retired colonel in the Corps of Engineers.

Russ Ray, senior vice president of marketing, *did* have a famous roommate—at Occidental College in California, he roomed with Jack Kemp, the pro quarterback who is now a U.S. congressman. Ray headed the sales team that launched the L-1011, and met Borman at the time when his job at Lockheed took him to Edwards Air Force Base; but it was Higginbottom who hired him as Eastern's vice president of consumer affairs, with Borman's endorsement.

Wayne A. Yeoman, senior vice president of finance, is another West Pointer and, like Borman, a native of Indiana who was raised in Arizona. A retired brigadier general, Yeoman was a fighter pilot who flew fifty-three missions in Korea.

Paul Johnstone, known to all as "Stoney," is senior vice president of operations services and has been with EAL fifteen years. A Notre Dame graduate, Johnstone formerly was with Douglas Aircraft and worked on the design of such transports as the DC-6, DC-7, DC-8, and DC-9; his initial post at Eastern was vice president of engineering.

And, of course, there is Charlie Simons, Borman's second-in-command, a veteran of forty years with the airline; he somehow managed to survive all the turmoil of those four hectic decades and emerge as a kind of elder statesman on whom his young leader relies heavily.

"I wouldn't trade that team for any other in the industry," Borman says feelingly.

And justifiably, for the turnaround in Eastern's image and financial health never could have been accomplished by one man, not even a Frank Borman.

A good example is EAL's handling of one of the industry's touchiest, most difficult problems: oversales. Eastern ranks extremely low in oversale percentages, and this is because of a unique system dreamed up by Dave Kuntsler, at the time vice president of reservations. Like all airlines, EAL had been plagued by the real parent of overbooking—"no-shows," which can reach as high as thirty percent on peak demand days. The standard weapon against no-shows was "planned capacity," a fancy name for deliberately overbooking a flight at levels determined by commuter load-factor analysis of given flights on given days in given traffic periods. The obvious weakness was that no computer could be perfect in its no-show forecast, and if the prediction was wrong there had to be a certain percentage of space promised to more passengers than the plane would hold.

It was Kuntsler who created what was at first called "leisure-class reservations"—for people who didn't absolutely have to leave on a particular flight. Such passengers were told, "We're overbooked, but because there probably will be no-shows, your chances of being boarded are good. If there's no coach seat available, we'll put you in first class at coach fares. And if there's no seat available, we'll put you on the next available flight and it won't cost you a cent."

The key was honesty to the public—incredibly, Ralph Nader originally attacked the plan as being anticonsumer. The "leisure class" label laid an egg and was changed to "conditional reservations," which became an instant success. So successful that in one year Eastern went from the industry's worst oversale record to the best and eventually won Nader's praise.

Roughly ninety-five percent of those holding conditional reservations are boarded on the flights for which they held this "probably" space. In effect Eastern is selling its no-show seats at a five-percent discount—averaging some fourteen million dollars in revenue from conditional sales, of which only five percent has to be refunded. Conditional sales begin when overbookings on a flight reach a point deemed to be a risk zone—on a 100-passenger airplane, for instance, agents would start accepting conditional reservations when 105 seats were sold.

The plan, first proposed in 1971, was one of the things

Borman didn't touch when he took over. In truth he has no desire to be a one-man airline; unlike the Rickenbackers and Trippes, he delegates authority and responsibility—up to a point. His main difficulty in that respect is his impulsiveness; it is hard for him *not* to get involved. Jim Elkins remembers traveling with him on one occasion from San Antonio to New York. Before takeoff their L-1011 developed a mechanical problem. Borman got off the plane and started working with the mechanic who was trying to fix the faulty part. When he returned, he insisted on briefing the passengers as to the exact reason for the delay.

He can be impatient as well as impulsive, a trait that showed even when he was an astronaut and bureaucratic rigidity infuriated him. On *Apollo* 8, getting his first glimpse of the entire earth from outer space, he called out to fellow astronaut Bill Anders, "Look at that sight—take a picture!"

"I can't," Anders said. "It's not on the schedule."

"Screw the schedule!" Borman snapped. "Gimme that camera."

But he learned to temper some of that impatience as he gained more confidence in the officers who form his team, and more knowledge of their problems. There is little margin for tolerance in Frank Borman, but at least he is willing to listen and learn. A poor meal on Eastern drives him up the wall, yet Gene Madill, director of EAL's dining service, has taught him why airline food is such a constant headache. Madill is a good example of Eastern's current management corps—experienced yet youthful enough not to be afraid of new ideas. He runs a department that spends well over $100 million a year, seventy percent of it going to Eastern's principal caterer, Marriott. Like Borman, he came into the airline business and achieved instant disillusionment with some of its aspects—mostly poor spending habits.

"I quickly learned that the airlines can't seem to do anything as cheaply as anyone else can," he says. "They're just one step below the government in that respect. I don't mean they're as lax—they're far better managed—but if something costs a dime, an airline will spend twelve cents without even questioning it."

This, of course, is the Gospel according to the Colonel and Madill has been known to go through the back door to Borman when he wants approval of something other officers have discouraged. Madill's chief aide is Wolfgang Diehl, a slim, precise German who came to EAL from Skychefs (an American subsidiary) and who started out as a kitchen helper in San Juan when he was nineteen. Someone asked him once, "What do they call you for short?"

"Wolfgang," he replied.

Now he's "Wolfy," and his job as manager of food-and-beverage service is to pick the menus and experiment with new ones. One of his biggest successes was a soup snack, and the story behind that provides an excellent look into airline food problems. In 1977 Diehl suggested soup as a coach snack and ran into immediate roadblocks. The soup itself was easy—he found a heavy stock but then came the question of the serving bowls. Ceramic was out—too costly and too breakable. Plastic bowls were sturdy enough but they couldn't withstand the heat of galley ovens, which reaches as high as 500 degrees; Madill even went to a restaurant show in Chicago and found there wasn't a plastic made that could take so much heat. He finally asked Monsanto for help and the chemical firm came up with a black nylon bowl that wouldn't melt under high heat; it could warm up soup to 180 degrees, and still could be taken out of the oven by a stewardess without burning her hand.

The soups included chicken gumbo, bacon, potato, chowder, and cheese—Diehl tried chili but never could get a recipe he liked. The last obstacle was Russ Ray, who voiced the opinion that he didn't want Eastern to become a soup airline. Madill circumvented this objection by taking the dispute to Borman, knowing Russ didn't have a chance: Borman likes simple food.

Which brings us to the touchiest part of any discussion on airline food:

Steaks.

On this matter, it is best to quote directly the views of Gene Madill:

"It's a shame steak has earned the image it has on the airlines, according to every survey the favorite entrée. Frankly, it's probably the poorest-served meal we offer. Sure, we buy U.S. choice tenderloins, like most good restaurants. The meat company packs the tenderloins and ships them frozen to the caterer. The caterer thaws, trims, then freezes them into loglike molds which can be cut by a machine to assure even portions. The steaks are then wrapped, packed, frozen again, and rethawed. The caterer puts on those grill marks so they look as if they've been cooked outdoors. Next they're chilled to thirty-eight degrees, carried out to the airplane in a chilled food box, and are finally cooked by the flight attendant in an oven which you can only pray has been calibrated properly. That poor piece of steak has been through so much, it doesn't stand a chance—if you get a good one, you're lucky. Its main appeal is that people know what they're getting; America isn't a gourmet country by a long shot. A steak is familiar, simple, and acceptable to practically everyone. That's why we provision sixty percent steak and forty percent of an alternate entrée—often there isn't enough of the latter, but most people don't gripe if you give 'em steak so it's safer that way."

The pitfalls are numerous. Eastern once tried seafood Newburgh but dropped it in a hurry when a few passengers complained they had broken their teeth on shell fragments. Dental dangers, incidentally, are why airlines avoid serving olives with pits—they invite lawsuits.

Madill, more than most of his industry counterparts, has to concentrate heavily on snacks; of Eastern's fifteen hundred daily departures, only two hundred are over two and a half hours' duration and almost four hundred are less than forty-five minutes. One popular coach snack consisted of the "three-bite delight"—three small sandwiches on a tiny tray (roast beef, turkey, and cheese) and Eastern serves six million trays a year. If a caterer decides to increase the price by a penny a tray, Madill has to advise Borman the food expenditures just went up by $60,000. This happened to the "three-bite delight," Borman said no way, and Diehl came up with a successful and far less expensive tray: an apple, two pieces of wrapped cheese, Fig Newtons, crackers, and peanuts.

Occasionally the dining service gets lucky. DC-9 ovens began to give off an unpleasant odor, traced to a poor sealing compound. The ovens were used only to retain heat and all of them were removed until the problem could be licked. Meanwhile, Madill had to figure out a temporary breakfast substitute and wound up putting on cold breakfasts for six weeks—fruit was served in a casserole dish, cold cereal in a salad bowl, and passengers loved it.

One of Borman's favorite food-service stories concerns the time he got a letter from comedian Soupy Sales, complaining that Eastern never had any steak sauce. Borman phoned Madill and asked why.

"Because it's too expensive," Gene informed him. "Anyway, nobody needs steak sauce—we butter our steaks to keep them moist."

"Makes sense," Borman acknowledged, "but maybe you'd better locate a box of the damned stuff and send it to him."

That should have ended the matter, except that a few weeks later Sales was a guest on the Merv Griffin show and told a story about a recent airline trip (not Eastern) when he asked a flight attendant if she had any steak sauce. The answer was no, so Sales opened his briefcase and took out the small box EAL had sent him. The passenger next to him asked if he could have a package, then a man across the aisle, and Sales ended up serving the entire first-class section.

"That's marvelous," Griffin laughed. "But where did you get all that sauce?"

"Oh, I just wrote Frank Borman—he runs Eastern—and he sent me a whole box."

Madill heard about the Griffin broadcast and braced for an avalanche of similar requests; at best, he figured he wouldn't be fired because it was Borman who had sent Sales the steak sauce in the first place. The strange thing was that despite the size of Griffin's audience, Eastern got exactly one letter asking for sauce —from the editor of a New York area newspaper. Suspecting that he was just panting to get turned down so he could write about the rejection, Madill sent him a box.

The average passenger who takes his airborne meal for

granted, figuring he has paid for it anyway as part of the price of his ticket, has no conception of what a carrier like Eastern has to shell out before a flight attendant puts a meal on the seat tray. Eastern pays a trucking charge for getting meals from the caterer's airport service center to the airplane, and also for unloading a flight at destination. The fees are set whether the truck goes a 100 yards or a mile—from $10 to the $190 a trip charged for an L-1011 provisioned in San Juan. The airline pays separately for all support items like soft drinks, orange juice, ice, wine, beer, coffee, and liquor—anything that isn't on the meal tray. Eastern pays a dishwashing fee ranging from ten cents a seat to fifty cents, and this applies even if the seat isn't occupied; there may have been only fifty passengers on a one-hundred-passenger airplane, but Eastern pays for all one hundred seats.

It costs Eastern about two dollars for the average coach meal and double that for a first-class dinner or lunch. Ironically, a snack tray may run more than a regular meal; EAL has one, a night coach flight between Atlanta and Los Angeles, which costs eight dollars per tray. But both Madill and Borman are convinced that Eastern and virtually every other airline are victims of rip-offs. Shortly after Madill joined the airline, he found that a caterer was charging Eastern fifteen cents to transport a six-ounce bottle of wine from its airport service center to the airplane. He called the caterer and raised hell.

"To produce that bottle of wine involves a $400 grapevine," he stormed. "The grapes had to be harvested, the wine had to be bottled and shipped all the way from California to Florida, and I can buy the bottle for twenty-six cents. I wish you'd tell me why the hell it costs fifteen cents to make it from your kitchen to our airplane!"

The caterer dropped the charge to ten cents, which Madill still regards as exorbitant. But even the nickel reduction was important, for when Eastern is buying a wedge of cheese for seven cents and some supplier offers the same wedge for 6.75 cents, it must be remembered that the airline buys $15 million worth of cheese wedges a year.

Eastern gives away or sells some twelve million liquor

miniatures a year, vodka being the biggest seller with scotch
second. The airline nets between $5 million and $6 million annually on liquor, a statistic which Borman cannot ignore even
though he is a strict teetotaler himself; he will fire any employee,
and that includes vice presidents, caught drinking during working hours whether on or off company premises.

If drinking on duty is a cardinal sin, it ranks only slightly
higher than carelessness in Borman's list of transgression priorities. Yet he is no stiff, unbending martinet who can see no humor
in anything vaguely resembling human frailty. There was one
memorable occasion when Mike Fenello had to tell a staff meeting that a pilot had brushed a 727 wingtip against the side of a
building the previous night. The reddest faces in the room belonged to Borman and the senior vice president of flight operations, Tom Button—the former because he was just plain angry
and the latter because to Button, an ex-line captain himself,
pilots could do no wrong.

"Last night," Fenello intoned dourly, "at thirteen oh three
hours, aircraft 514 damaged its right wingtip when it ran into
Building 21."

Before Borman could open his mouth, Bill Bell, senior vice-
president of legal and a man with a delightful dry wit, spoke
up.

"Tom," he asked innocently, "was the building parked in
the right place?"

And Borman led the laughter.

A remarkable man, this basically simple, excruciatingly
blunt, incredibly hardworking lover of anything that flies. He is
one of the lowest-paid airline chiefs in the U.S., drives a car that
resembles something a twenty-one-year-old mechanic would
take on a date, and commands loyalty not out of blind, sentimental affection but sheer respect that borders on awe.

Borman says, "I feel very, very beholden to the people of
this airline. I feel as if I'm working for them and I never want to
abrogate that trust. On the other hand I want to do what's required from the standpoint of firmness and toughness to make
sure I don't abrogate that trust. If we have to stand tight in what

we need in the way of productivity to offset a wage increase, I'm going to try to do it. I look at Sweden's political system with contempt. Everyone is a domestic rabbit kept in a cage, fed and watered. I'd rather be a jackrabbit, taking my chances but enjoying some freedom. The Swedes have driven everyone to a single level of mediocrity. I'd hate to see that happen either at Eastern or in this country."

His achievements at Eastern cannot be measured purely in terms of facts and figures, impressive though they may be. Annual reports, balance sheets, and ledgers cannot convey his greatest accomplishment—giving a sad-sack airline back its pride. It is not the "same old Eastern," even though it may trip, goof, or sin as any carrier will on occasion. What Borman created at Eastern was a state of mind and heart that wiped out all that was unpleasant about the past and all that seemed so terrifying in the future. In restoring internal pride, he forged external respect—not from just the public but from Eastern's competitors. To judge Frank Borman of Eastern with cool objectivity, one need only to talk to those who remember what it was like before he came on stage.

Like Dick Maurer of Delta. "I like Borman. When he first started the job, I felt he was riding around with a halo on his head. A little too much of that 'Colonel Borman' stuff, maybe. As time went by, I think he learned what the problems are and is making an effort to meet people on their own ground. Imitation is the sincerest form of flattery and he's said on many occasions there were certain things that Delta did that he wanted to copy. Not too fat a management group. Better utilization of equipment. Talking to Eastern people, I gather they have better morale than they have had in a long time. They enjoy working for Frank. We respect their competitive ability a lot more than we did a few years ago—he seems to have Eastern moving in the right direction."

Like Charlie Simons. "You're damned right he changed things. I remember when Hall was running the airline and everyone was insisting there were only two areas available for major cost reductions—maintenance and customer service. I kept telling Floyd there had to be a third and that was careful pruning of management. He'd say, 'I keep coming in here at seven or eight at night and see all these guys working overtime, so how in the hell can you tell me we've got too much staff?' 'Floyd,' I said, 'the next time you see one of these guys running around at eight o'clock at night, stop him and ask what he's doing. Sure, he'll tell you he's just being very dedicated, but then you ask yourself if you really need what he's doing.' And the manpower we used on esoteric things—like an advisory board looking into reentry of an airplane from space. The money we wasted pursuing every case before the CAB even when it didn't directly affect Eastern. If Hawaiian Airlines wanted to put a bigger airplane on an intra-island route, we'd have our lawyers preparing briefs on Eastern's attitude. The justification was that we might get involved later—so a fifty- or seventy-five-dollar-an-hour lawyer would spend weeks on it. I'm not saying the information wouldn't ever be useful, but the point was that we couldn't afford such information."

Like Frank Stulgaitis, "One incident sticks in my mind. Al Hirt, the trumpet player, was walking by an Eastern ticket counter in New Orleans. Everyone in New Orleans knew Al Hirt—he was an institution. But the people at our counter ignored him. He passed by Delta's counter and they practically mobbed him. Now New Orleans had a good station record at the time, but it was run by the book, with no personal touch. And that was basically one of the things wrong with Eastern. We could match anyone technically and operationally, but in human relationship—negative. We had adequate baggage handling, food service, and on-time performance but we just weren't warm and friendly. Delta does some unprofessional things that make other airlines quail, but they're so damned friendly that customers forgive their sins and keep coming back. And we're still paying for our old attitude. In L.A. when an Atlanta flight cancelled, we've had their passengers come over and tell us they really didn't want to ride Eastern but that Delta had sent them. We'd talk to 'em, give 'em great service, and we'd be told, 'Well, I'd still go back to Delta.' But slowly, it's changing. You can see it happening. Borman's making it happen."

Like Bob Christian, who only a few years ago used to be

Number Two in Delta's public relations. "You knew right from the start he was going to turn Eastern around, no matter what it took. We were driving somewhere in Florida one afternoon—he was going to make a speech that night. He was unusually quiet for a time, then he suddenly said, 'I guess I'd better tell you something. I'm gonna fire so-and-so tomorrow. He's getting too much money for doing nothing.' "

Like Jim Ashlock. "God, some of Hall's people were jealous of him. Afraid, too. I had been touring some of the small stations with Frank—we hit eight cities in less than three days and the guy was dynamite. When he got through talking to employees, they were ready to go out and stop a locomotive with their bare chests. Well, when I got back I wrote a story for the *Falcon* emphasizing his charisma. More than one vice president told me to stop playing him up so much. I was reporting directly to one of them—a senior vice president—who accused me of trying to elevate Borman into a higher position at Floyd's expense."

Like flight attendant Al Goodwin. "I've had passengers tell me, 'I wouldn't have flown Eastern five years ago.' "

Like flight attendant Ann Ruocco. "The spirit around this company under Borman is the best I've ever seen. You can see it even in the ship cleaners."

Like Gene Marfisi, director of FAA liaison. "It used to be an atmosphere of 'Don't hurt anybody.' We kept piling up deadwood and instead of getting rid of the bodies, we'd make a guy a vice president with an empty title and then we'd have to hire another vice president to do the job he had failed to do. You have to have the guts to chop off dead branches at the top of the tree as well as the bottom and Borman had those guts. He wasn't shy about asking any of us what the hell was wrong with this airline, either. He asked me and I told him, we should look at ourselves right in the face and say to ourselves, Hey, man, we're a cup-of-coffee–hand-you-your-bag–get-you-there-on-time airline. We're not a pheasant-under-glass airline. Borman believes this, too—that was the basis for his feud with Floyd—and so did Higginbottom. I'll tell you something else: Sam Higginbottom's biggest problem was Frank Borman, not Floyd Hall. He just couldn't comprehend that Frank had a better image than he did. A national hero, a very bright, intelligent person. If he had played on Frank's side, Sam would still be here as chairman. He was always on Frank's ass. He should have taken Frank under his wing and developed him, trained him. Instead he gave him impossible, unreasonable tasks and chewed him out when he couldn't handle them. Believe me, Borman learned the job the hard way. But it's all changed now. Those days when one vice president would join some fancy club and all the others thought they should, too—at Eastern's expense. When we were holding three-day sales meetings at plushy resorts and achieving absolutely nothing that couldn't have been done around a table at Building 16. And the free spending got contagious—it started at the top and seeped down through all management levels until everyone was turning in freewheeling expense accounts. And finally the rank and file would see all the limos and private jets, the parties and receptions, and the morale problem contaminated the whole company. Until Borman."

"... *until Borman*":

Who ordered the water feeding the Rickenbacker Fountain turned off because the electric pumps were wasting energy.

Whose office has simple shutters instead of expensive drapes.

Whose briefcase looks like it was purchased at an antique sale.

Who actually has been known to turn off the lights in any office he happens to find unoccupied during one of his prowling sessions.

He is a scrapper who won't take anyone's guff, and that includes government officials. There was, for example, the widely publicized Elizabeth Bailey incident—Bailey being a member of the Civil Aeronautics Board who boarded an Eastern flight at the last minute and then raised a fuss because there were no seats available in the nonsmoking section. When she refused to sit down even while the plane was taxiing toward its takeoff runway, there was an angry exchange between Bailey and a flight attendant. According to the accounts of other passengers, Bailey was abusive and arrogant and Borman, after assuring her the flight attendant would be disciplined, actually did nothing more than issue a mild reprimand—on other carriers, the flight attendant might have been fired.

When FAA Administrator Langhorne Bond, in the course of grounding the DC-10 last June, also grounded the A-300, Borman was on the phone to Washington two minutes after the grounding order was issued. What he told Bond is not known, but it is sufficient to say that the grounding order for the A-300 was in effect for less than three hours. Publicly, Borman's reaction was classic.

"Grounding our airplane because of what happened to the DC-10 was like recalling all Goodyear tires during Firestone's troubles," he told reporters.

Borman fought hard against deregulation—ironically, Eastern and Delta were the last holdouts—but when he realized it was inevitable, he quickly learned to live with it.

Under the impetus of deregulation, Eastern in 1978 started one new route after another. Atlanta–San Francisco. Miami–San Francisco. St. Louis–Salt Lake City. Ft. Myers–New York. Austin–Houston. Nonstop service between Atlanta and Detroit, Cleveland, Savannah, Charleston (South Carolina), and Columbia (South Carolina). The falcon spread its wings south over new routes to Haiti and three more cities in Mexico. In 1979 Eastern inaugurated service from Miami to Guatemala and the expansion isn't finished. Borman is aiming to make St. Louis a key traffic hub as Atlanta is now, for further expansion westward. He wants more routes out of Miami into Central America, which he describes as "the closest thing to a virgin market." Conversely, of course, deregulation brought fresh competition; in the Miami–San Juan market alone, an EAL monopoly, American, Delta, and National moved in.

His decision to seek a merger with National admittedly was strictly defensive at first—he just wanted to stop Pan Am from absorbing one of Eastern's toughest rivals. But Borman was never a defensive type; gradually he took the offensive and for the very good reason that what EAL would have to pay to acquire National was less than the value of National's modern fleet of DC-10's and 727-200's—plus the added incentive of gaining National's routes to Europe.

Eastern's explosive route development, a far cry from those long years of frustrating stagnation and disappointment, already has altered the airline's status as primarily a southern carrier, so heavily dependent on Atlanta. This does not mean Borman wants to abandon the "hub and spoke" concept that has been so successful for both Delta and EAL—a system by which traffic from smaller cities feeds into and connects with each carrier's long-haul flights out of the hub city.

The truth is that route case setbacks stopped being an Eastern problem from 1966 on. In the five-year period from 1966 through 1970, EAL picked up St. Louis to Seattle and Portland (adding Omaha to that segment later), Atlanta to Los Angeles, Dallas, Jamaica, and Mexico. The 1967 merger with Mackey Airlines, a small international carrier based in Miami, added a number of points in the Bahamas to the system. What almost wrecked Eastern was not lack of new route opportunities, but lack of effective management with consistent policies and programs.

This is not to say that before Borman, Eastern was being run by incompetents. Far from it; MacIntyre, Hall, Lewis, and Higginbottom were capable, intelligent men, and under different circumstances—perhaps with any airline other than Eastern— they might have written their own success stories. Certainly their pre-Eastern track records were excellent. It may well have been that they were the right men at the wrong time for America's most controversial airline, and conversely that Frank Borman was the right man at the right time. Laurance Rockefeller, who rejoined Eastern's board in 1977, replacing Hitesman, thinks just that.

"I am convinced," he says, "that Frank Borman was the only man in the United States who could have saved Eastern from disaster."

Strong words, but not farfetched. There was and is between the ex-fighter pilot and the airline a chemistry which merged

them both into a single entity—just as another ex-fighter pilot
had done almost a half century ago.

Inevitably, he will leave Eastern some day—Borman himself says he cannot see any man holding down a job like his for
more than fifteen years, although this would not preclude his
becoming board chairman. Rumors persist that he has political
ambitions, and there are even stronger rumors that others have
political ambitions for him. There has been more than one
printed report that Borman would make an excellent Republican
candidate—and he does have every attribute from personality to
intelligence, from integrity to a glittering record both as an
astronaut and a business leader. The only trouble with all this
speculation about his wanting to enter politics is that Frank
Borman says it's "absolutely untrue."

"My honest and sincere career objective—and this is Susan
Borman talking, not just Frank Borman—is to stay here, live
and die with this airline, making it number one in the industry.
We love Miami and we love the airline, and I can't foresee the
circumstances that would drive me away from it. I have absolutely no desire nor the arrogance to think that I could go out
and start pounding the streets for votes. I also don't think I have
the arrogance to think I can go on calling all the shots for the
rest of my life. I just want to stay here and give it my best shot
for as long as I'm here. We've come a long way but there's still a
long way to go."

Jim Elkins, who knows Borman as well as anyone, adds this
observation:

"I'd have to say honestly that purely from a patriotic standpoint, Frank would have political ambitions. From a purely
pragmatic standpoint, he has enough sense to know that it's a
here-today, gone-tomorrow world in politics, that he'd need a lot
more economic security for his family before he could take that
high road. I'd say if Frank was worth $3 million, he'd be in
politics tomorrow because first he's an idealist and second he'd
enjoy the competitiveness of it."

But he is not worth $3 million or anywhere near that kind
of financial independence. He is simply an airline president, one

of the ablest who ever headed an air carrier; he is "Borman of Eastern," and those three words imply a measure of achievement reached by few men in the most dynamic industry of all.

In terms of tenure, of chronological passage of time, he is thus far but a single chapter in the life of his airline, a single albeit important character in Eastern's turbulent history.

The same is true, of course, of Malcolm MacIntyre, who can still hold his head up with pride for having done his best.

The same is true of Lefty Lethridge, still the happy, peppery man who retired in 1975 and now plays tennis almost daily in Sarasota, Florida.

Of Sheppy, living in a handsome apartment for senior citizens in Stanford, Connecticut.

Of John Halliburton, happily retired on a ranch near San Antonio.

Of Brad Walker, who helps his son run a farm in Connecticut.

Of Frank Sharpe, as feisty and funny as he ever was, also retired in Florida.

Of Bob Winn, who lives near Disney World and occasionally sees Eastern's current director of Orlando operations, Ed Northcutt.

Of Floyd Hall, still active in IATA affairs and looking ten years younger than he did when he left Eastern.

Of Sam Higginbottom, Art Lewis, Dwight Taylor, Bill Costello, Tom Creighton, Todd Cole, Tom Armstrong, and all the other leading players in the Eastern drama who are either retired or have gone on to responsible positions elsewhere in American industry.

Of Johnny Ray, who comes stomping into Building 16 every Wednesday, chewing angrily on an unlit cigar and muttering about how lazy mechanics are today. He showed up once on Tuesday and had everyone checking the calendar.

They and so many others helped write the saga of Eastern, from the captain who started it on its flight to greatness, to the colonel who, in saving it from crashing, also put it on course for the future.

ACKNOWLEDGMENTS

Several people deserve special gratitude for their aid in the conception, gestation, and birth of this book. My thanks go to Bob Christian and Jim Ashlock of Eastern's public relations department in Miami, to June Farrell in Washington, whose patience and professionalism were always available, and to Walter J. "Mickey" Dane, whose early support of the project provided needed encouragement.

I doubt very much whether a complete history would have been possible without the input of former Eastern presidents Malcolm MacIntyre, Floyd Hall, Art Lewis, and Sam Higginbottom, who not only gave me hours of their valuable time but answered the tough questions with the same honesty and frankness as they did the easier ones.

Of the nearly seventy persons interviewed, no one furnished more interesting, colorful, and incisive information than Maurice "Lefty" Lethridge, to whom I am deeply indebted.

And I must say the same for EAL president Frank Borman, who subjected himself to the ordeal of six hours of taped interviews and whose suggested changes and revisions, after reading the manuscript, consisted of a single request to give more credit to his subordinates. It should be emphasized that this is in no way an "authorized" history; while Eastern was permitted to see the final manuscript, there was no censorship whatsoever and the only alterations involved accuracy.

A lion's share of appreciation belongs to the following who submitted to interviews, the majority lasting several hours each, and I list their names alphabetically:

Phyllis Ash
Gene Brown
Joe Burke
Tom Buttion
Todd Cole
Bill Costello
John de Rose
James Elkins
Mike Fenello
Dick Fisher
Ken Fletcher
Charles Froesch
Art Furchgott
Smythe Gambrell
Pat Gazda
Winnie Gilbert
John Gregg
Mark Hall
Najeeb Halaby

John Halliburton
Pat Kelly
Frank Kern
Dave Kuntsler
Sandy Logan
Gene Madill
Gene Marfisi
Dick Maurer
Dick Merrill
Chip North
Ed Northcutt
Wayne Parrish
Johnny Ray
Russell Ray
Jim Reinke
Vern Renaud
Carol Roberson
Maggie Robinson
Laurance Rockefeller

Ann Ruocco
Fritz Schwaemmle
Frank Sharpe
Margaret Shepherd
John Shields
Charlie Simons
Bob Six
C. R. Smith
Susan Smith
Frank Stulgaitis
Agnes Thompson
Brad Walker
George Warde
Jerry Wood
Harper Woodward
Bill Wooten
Ed Yarnell

Of great help in portraying Eastern's early days was an unpublished manuscript by Howard Weant.

My thanks, also, to the following who submitted anecdotes, pictures, and other material (some of which had to be omitted for reasons of space), or who helped in countless other ways:

Arthur L. Armstrong
Ed Barchard
Kelly Bohannon
Lee Bright

Maureen Gossett
Carl Gunther
Loretta Handley
S. M. Hooper

Ray Nau
June Pearlman
Joan Phillips
James Plinton, Jr.

R. J. Britton	J. P. Ingle	Fran Sisk
Bruce Byers	Gayle Jackson	Jim Tharpe
Jim Curtin	Dalton James	Linda Van Hook
Vicki Dokos	Jack King	Toni Zahn
Julie Gangler	Vance Murr	
Maureen Baal Gentile	Tom Myers	

To all the above, plus those whose names may inadvertently have been left out, I am beholden and can only hope that the final product does justice to the help they so willingly gave. I include in this my editor at Dial Press, Britt Bell, my wife Priscilla, and my friend Sue Lahmann, who contributed mightily by keeping two small fry off my back during working hours.

Robert J. Serling
Potomac, Maryland
June 1979

INDEX